CAMBRIDGE LIBRARY COLLECTION

Books of enduring scholarly value

Travel and Exploration

The history of travel writing dates back to the Bible, Caesar, the Vikings
and the Crusaders, and its many themes include war, trade, science and
recreation. Explorers from Columbus to Cook charted lands not previously
visited by Western travellers, and were followed by merchants, missionaries,
and colonists, who wrote accounts of their experiences. The development of
steam power in the nineteenth century provided opportunities for increasing
numbers of 'ordinary' people to travel further, more economically, and more
safely, and resulted in great enthusiasm for travel writing among the reading
public. Works included in this series range from first-hand descriptions of
previously unrecorded places, to literary accounts of the strange habits of
foreigners, to examples of the burgeoning numbers of guidebooks produced
to satisfy the needs of a new kind of traveller - the tourist.

The True History of the Conquest of New Spain

Bernal Díaz del Castillo (1492–1584) was a foot soldier in the army of
Mexico's conqueror Hernán Cortés, and participated in the campaigns
that led to the fall of the Aztec empire in 1521. This 1928 translation of his
journals derives from the 1904 edition by the Mexican historian Genaro
García – the first edition based on the original manuscript. Written as a
corrective to accounts that overemphasised Cortés's exploits, Díaz's epic
focuses on the experiences of the common soldier. The most complete
contemporary chronicle of the Mexican conquest, this important historical
document is also a captivating adventure narrative that combines factual
accuracy with many dramatic anecdotes. Volume 1, in which Díaz recounts
his first two expeditions to the Yucatán coast and the beginning of his service
in Cortés's army, contains chapters 1–81 and includes part of García's 1904
introduction to his edition.

Cambridge University Press has long been a pioneer in the reissuing of out-of-print titles from its own backlist, producing digital reprints of books that are still sought after by scholars and students but could not be reprinted economically using traditional technology. The Cambridge Library Collection extends this activity to a wider range of books which are still of importance to researchers and professionals, either for the source material they contain, or as landmarks in the history of their academic discipline.

Drawing from the world-renowned collections in the Cambridge University Library, and guided by the advice of experts in each subject area, Cambridge University Press is using state-of-the-art scanning machines in its own Printing House to capture the content of each book selected for inclusion. The files are processed to give a consistently clear, crisp image, and the books finished to the high quality standard for which the Press is recognised around the world. The latest print-on-demand technology ensures that the books will remain available indefinitely, and that orders for single or multiple copies can quickly be supplied.

The Cambridge Library Collection will bring back to life books of enduring scholarly value (including out-of-copyright works originally issued by other publishers) across a wide range of disciplines in the humanities and social sciences and in science and technology.

The True History of the Conquest of New Spain

VOLUME 1

BERNAL DÍAZ DEL CASTILLO
EDITED BY GENARO GARCÍA

CAMBRIDGE
UNIVERSITY PRESS

CAMBRIDGE UNIVERSITY PRESS

Cambridge, New York, Melbourne, Madrid, Cape Town, Singapore,
São Paolo, Delhi, Dubai, Tokyo

Published in the United States of America by Cambridge University Press, New York

www.cambridge.org
Information on this title: www.cambridge.org/9781108017053

© in this compilation Cambridge University Press 2010

This edition first published 1908
This digitally printed version 2010

ISBN 978-1-108-01705-3 Paperback

Additional resources for this publication at www.cambridge.org/9781108017053

WORKS ISSUED BY

The Hakluyt Society.

———o———

THE

CONQUEST OF NEW SPAIN.

SECOND SERIES.

No. XXIII.

ISSUED FOR 1908.

MEMBERS OF THE HAKLUYT SOCIETY, RESIDING ON THE CONTINENT, CAN PAY THEIR SUBSCRIPTIONS AND RECEIVE THEIR VOLUMES THROUGH

MESSRS. A. ASHER & CO.,

56, UNTER DEN LINDEN,

BERLIN.

Hernando Cortés

From an oil painting in the Hospital de Jesus Nazareno. City of Mexico

THE TRUE HISTORY

OF THE

CONQUEST OF NEW SPAIN

BY

BERNAL DÍAZ DEL CASTILLO,

ONE OF ITS CONQUERORS.

From the only exact copy made of the Original Manuscript.

EDITED AND PUBLISHED IN MEXICO,

BY

GENARO GARCÍA.

Translated into English, with Introduction and Notes,

BY

ALFRED PERCIVAL MAUDSLAY, M.A.,

HON. PROFESSOR OF ARCHÆOLOGY, NATIONAL MUSEUM, MEXICO.

LONDON:

PRINTED FOR THE HAKLUYT SOCIETY.

MDCCCCVIII.

LONDON :

PRINTED AT THE BEDFORD PRESS, 20 AND 21, BEDFORDBURY, W.C.

TO

FRANCIS C. A. SARG,

LATE HIS IMPERIAL GERMAN MAJESTY'S CONSUL

AT GUATEMALA,

TO MARK THIRTY-FIVE YEARS OF FRIENDSHIP

AND HIS UNTIRING HELP

IN THIS AND OTHER WORKS ON CENTRAL AMERICA

AND MEXICO.

COUNCIL

OF

THE HAKLUYT SOCIETY.

CONTENTS.

BOOK I.

THE DISCOVERY.
THE EXPEDITION UNDER FRANCISCO HERNÁNDEZ DE CÓRDOVA.

CHAPTER VI.

CHAPTER VII.

THE EXPEDITION UNDER JUAN DE GRIJALVA.

CHAPTER VIII.

CHAPTER IX.

CHAPTER X.

CHAPTER XI.

CHAPTER XII.

CHAPTER XIII.

BOOK II.

THE EXPEDITION UNDER HERNANDO CORTÉS.
THE VOYAGE.

CHAPTER XXI.

CHAPTER XXII.

CHAPTER XXIII.

CHAPTER XXIV.

CHAPTER XXV.

CHAPTER XXVI.

CHAPTER XXVII.

CHAPTER XXVIII.

CHAPTER XXIX.

CHAPTER XXX.

CHAPTER XXXI.

CHAPTER XXXII.

CHAPTER XXXIII.

CHAPTER XXXIV.

CHAPTER XXXV.

CHAPTER XXXVI.

CHAPTER XXXVII.

BOOK III.

THE MARCH INLAND.

CHAPTER XLVII.

CHAPTER XLVIII.

CHAPTER XLIX.

CHAPTER L.

CHAPTER LI.

CHAPTER LII.

CHAPTER LIII.

CHAPTER LIV.

CHAPTER LV.

CHAPTER LVI.

CHAPTER LVII.

CHAPTER LVIII.

CHAPTER LIX.

CHAPTER LX.

CHAPTER LXI.

BOOK IV.

THE WAR IN TLAXCALA.

2

CHAPTER LXXIX.

CHAPTER LXXX.

CHAPTER LXXXI.

LIST OF ILLUSTRATIONS.

2 *

NOTE —Nos. 2-10, and 12-16 have been reproduced for the Hakluyt Society by Mr. Donald Macbeth, of 66, Ludgate Hill, E.C.

EXTRACTS FROM THE INTRODUCTION

BY

SEÑOR DON GENARO GARCÍA.[1]

HE *True History of the Conquest of New Spain,* written by Bernal Díaz del Castillo, one of the Conquerors, was known and appreciated by historians and bibliographers before it was published. Antonio de Herrera[2] quotes it frequently, Friar Juan de Torquemada[3] also refers to it on several occasions, and

---

[1] The following extracts are translated direct from Señor Don Genaro García's Introduction. Any differences entertained with regard to the names of persons or places or the routes followed, will be explained in note attached to the translation of the text of Bernal Diaz's narrative.

[2] *Historia general de los hechos de los castellanos en las Islas i Tierra Firme del Mar Oceano.* Madrid, 1726-30, Decada 2ª passim. The first edition was published in 1601.

[3] *Los Veinte i un libros rituales y Monarchia Indiana.* Madrid, 1723, Tomo I passim. The first edition was published in 1615.

the Licentiate Antonio de Leon Pinelo[1] devotes some lines to it in his brief bibliography.

Although the original manuscript has always been kept in Guatemala, first by the Author, and afterwards by his descendants, and still later by the Municipality of the Capital, in whose archives it is preserved to-day, a copy of it was made in the sixteenth century and sent to Spain to King Philip II[2] and was there consulted by the Royal chroniclers. After its publication in Madrid by Friar Alonzo Remón of the Order of Mercy in the year 1632 the *True History* was universally accepted from that time onwards as the most complete and trustworthy of the chronicles of the Conquest of New Spain. A second edition followed almost immediately in the same city, some four years later a third, a fourth, and a fifth. It was translated into English by Maurice Keatinge in 1800 and John Ingram Lockhart in 1844; into German by Ph. J. von Rehfues in 1838 and Karl Ritter in 1848; into French by D. Jourdanet in 1876 and José María de Heredia in 1877,[3]

---

[1] *Epitome de la Biblioteca Oriental i Occidental, Nautica y Geografica.* Madrid, 1629. Page 75.

[2] So it was stated by Juan Rodriquez Cabrillo de Medrano in 1579. In the *Historia de Guatemala ó Recordacion Florida*, by D. Francisco Antonio de Fuentes y Guzmán. Madrid, 1882-83. Vol. i, page 398.—G. G.

[3] The French translations were—although an interval of one year lay between their publication —written simultaneously by the distinguished author of the *Influence de la pression de l'air sur la vie de l'homme,* and the excellent poet to whom France is indebted for the inimitable *Les Trophées.* This synchronism

and into Hungarian by Károly Brózik in 1878 and
Moses Gaal in 1899.

Several of these translations obtained the honours
of a second edition, as that of Keatinge in 1803, that
of Rehfues in 1843, and that of Jourdanet in 1877.

* * * *

It must be pointed out that no secret has ever
been made of Remón's extensive corruption of the
original text. Don Antonio de Leon Pinelo, in his
account of the *True History* in 1629, says, no doubt
without malice, that Friar Alonzo Remón kept in
readiness a "corrected" copy for publication. It
was no sooner printed than the author of the *Isagoge
Histórico Apologético*[1] found in it "many things
added which were not found in the original." More
explicitly and with a better judgment Don Francisco
Antonio de Fuentes y Guzmán, the great-great-
grandson of the author, and at that time the pos-
sessor of the manuscript, wrote at the end of the
same century that the book, published by the
reverend father Friar Alonzo Remón, differs considerably from the original, "for in some places
there is more and in others less than what my
great-grandfather the author wrote, for I find corruptions in chapters 164 and 171, and in the same
way in other parts in the course of the history, in
which not only is the credibility and fidelity of my

---

strongly indicates the extraordinary importance attributed to the
Historia Verdadera.—G. G.

[1] Published in Madrid, 1892.

Castillo clouded over, but many real heroes are defrauded of their just merit."

Fuentes y Guzmán states that this corruption (of the text) was not the least important of the motives that induced him to write his own work.[1] At the beginning of the following century Friar Francisco Vázquez proved that Friar Bartolomé de Olmedo was not in Guatemala at the time of its conquest, as is stated in the edition of Remón, and therefore he was not the first to spread the Christian faith through that province, unless, as he says, one should concede another miracle such as that of Saint Anthony of Padua, who managed to be in two different places at the same time.

Some years afterwards Don Andrés González Barcia, referring to the charge that Fuentes y Guzmán had launched against Remón, arbitrarily surmised that the differences that existed between the edition published by the latter and the original manuscript were matters of no importance, and simply inferred that it was "easy to believe that in copying the author should make some alterations, as ordinarily happens." This defence was not convincing, and on this account our great bibliographer in Mexico, Don Juan José de Eguiara y Eguren, delicately objected that P. Vázquez had declared even the first edition to be falsified, while in Spain the indefatigable chronicler Don Juan Bautista Muñoz endeavoured to procure a copy of the original

---

[1] *Historia de Guatemala ó Recordación Florida*, page 8.

manuscript with the object of ascertaining the
alterations due to Padre Remón.

Finally, if there could be any doubt remaining
about the bad faith of Remón, it was completely
dispelled by the Guatemalan historians Padre Domingo Juarros, Don José Milla, the Bishop Don
Francisco de Paula García Paláez, and Don Ramón
A. Salazar, who from personal inspection fully cor-
roborated what had been asserted by their predeces-
sors the author of the *Isagoge*, Fuentes y Guzmán,
and Vásquez.

As a matter of fact we can see at a glance in the
following notes (par. iv. and Appendix No. 2)[1] that
Fray Alonzo Remón in printing the *True History*
suppressed whole pages of the manuscript, inter-
polated others, garbled the facts, changed the
names of persons and places, increased or lessened
the numbers, modified the style and modernised
the orthography, moved thereto either by religious
fervour and false patriotism, or by personal sympathy and vile literary taste.   As all the later
editions, and all the translations without exception
were copied from the first edition published by

---

[1] This paragraph and appendix has not been translated.   As
we have now before us an accurate copy of the original text, the
reader would not be much interested in a discussion of the corruptions of the text by Padre Remón.   In most instances these
corruptions of the text were introduced for the purpose of mag-
nifying the importance of Padre Olmedo and the Friars of the
Order of Mercy, of which Order Padre Remón was himself a
member.   In the edition of Don Genaro García these matters are
fully investigated, and a complete bibliography is given.

Remón, it results that in reality we do not know the *True History*.

*   *   *   *

On the 20th October, 1895, Don Emilio León, the Envoy Extraordinary and Minister Plenipotentiary from the Republic of Guatemala accredited to Mexico, presented in the name of his Government to ours, "as a proof of friendship and especial regard," a photographic reproduction of the original manuscript. It was then, with some reason, believed that, at last, we should see the *True History* published ; but this could not be carried out, for accompanying the gift of the reproduction was a prohibition against its being copied and printed.

Five years later, when I wrote my book entitled "Caracter de la Conquista Española en America y en México," I was convinced that to perfect our Ancient history an exact edition of the *True History* was indispensable, and I desired to carry this work through.

Soon afterwards, in August, 1901, I wrote to the then President of Guatemala, Don Manuel Estrada Cabrera, telling him of my wish to print the precious manuscript.

This distinguished official had the kindness to reply on the first of the following month that on that very day he had decreed that "an exact and complete copy of the manuscript" should be made and sent to me for the purpose that I had stated. Señor Don Juan I. Argueta, Secretary of the Interior and Justice in that Republic, at once

began punctually to send me instalments of the
copy as soon as they were made, which copy I
corrected here, and perfected with all care and
accuracy by comparing it with the photographic
reproduction already referred to, which is preserved in our National Library.

*   *   *   *

The author says that, after making a fair copy
of his narrative, two licentiates of Guatemala
begged him to lend it to them, and that he
did so most willingly; but he warned them not
to correct it in any way, neither by addition nor
deletion, for all that he had written was true.

Assuredly with regard to truth the author would
find no fault with us, for we have taken care to
religiously respect the original text, without intro-
ducing the slightest variation, not even of the
artless orthography or punctuation.

Any change would have been dangerous, and
we might have fallen into the same error that we
attribute to Remón; everybody knows that by a
single comma one might reverse the meaning of a
statement.

We reproduce in notes placed at the foot of the
page all the erasures that can have any interest for
inquiring readers, and in like manner we have
transcribed all the various words blotted out,
which, besides exhibiting important variations, give
an idea of the method of composition employed by
the author.

Occasionally, when a full understanding of the

text necessitates it, or for the purpose of finishing off a clearly implied word or phrase, or of correcting some manifest numerical error, we have ventured to insert some word or number between brackets, so that it can be known at. once that it is not the author who is speaking, and the readers are left at liberty to admit or reject the slight interpolation; finally, we have allowed ourselves to indicate by dotted lines the gaps that are found in the original manuscript, which, happily, are very few in number, except on the first and last pages, which, in the course of time, have naturally suffered more than the others.

May our modest effort meet with the approbation of the intelligent and learned, for we long for it as much as we fear their censure.

BERNAL DIAZ DEL CASTILLO.

HIS LIFE.

*   *   *   *

Bernal Díaz del Castillo was born in the very noble, famous and celebrated town[1] of Medina del Campo in the year 1492 at the very time when Christopher Columbus was joining the two worlds.

Bernal tells us that at the time that he made up his mind to come to New Spain, about the year 1517, he was a youth "of about twenty-four years," a statement which corroborates the date of his birth.

His parents were Don Francisco Díaz del Castillo and Doña María Diez Rejón.

*   *   *   *

Bernal was not the only son, he tells us of his brother, probably older than himself, whom he wished to imitate.

*   *   *   *

Bernal himself writes that he was a gentleman,[2] and that his grandparents, his father and his brother were always servants of the Crown and of their Catholic Majesties Don Fernando and Doña Isabel, which Carlos V. confirms by calling them "our retainers and servants."

---

[1] "Muy noble é insigne y muy nombrada Villa." In old Spain towns and cities were formally granted such titles of honour.

[2] Hijodalgo.

If the family of Bernal had not enjoyed esteem and respect in Medina del Campo, the inhabitants would not have chosen Don Francisco as their *Regidor*.[1] On the other hand, his financial position must have been a very modest one, for the author most certainly came here to seek his fortune, and often complains of his poverty.

After all, the fact that in the *True History* he discloses a very scrupulous moral sense, a fair amount of learning, accurate philosophy, and a piety out of the common, permits us to infer that his family educated him with great care ; it would be exceptional for a man illiterate and untaught during his youth to acquire such qualities in his old age ; it is proven, on the other hand, that the author knew how to write when he reached New Spain. Nevertheless, we know nothing for certain about the childhood and youth of Bernal, our information begins in the year 1514.

The author was then twenty-two years old.

From some of his remarks one may judge that he was tall or of middle height, active, quick, well made and graceful ; his comrades called him "the elegant" (el galan).

*   *   *   *

Following the example of so many other Spanish youths, Bernal left his country in the year 1514 to emigrate to America in search of adventures and riches, resolved to be worthy of his ancestry. He

---

[1] Regidor = magistrate, prefect.

accompanied Pedro Arias de Avila, the Governor of Tierra Firme, as one of his soldiers.

When he reached Nombre de Dios he remained there three or four months, until an epidemic that broke out and certain disputes that arose between the Governor and his son-in-law, Vasco Nuñez de Balboa, obliged him to flee to Cuba, to his relation, Diego Velásquez, who was Governor of the Island.

During three years Bernal " did nothing worthy of record," and on that account he determined to set out on the discovery of unknown lands with the Captain Francisco Hernández de Córdova and one hundred and ten companions.

They sailed in three ships from the port of Ajaruco on the 8th February, 1517, and after enduring a passage occupying twenty-one days and one fierce gale, they arrived at Cape Catoche, where the natives gave them a hostile reception.

After touching at Lázaro they stopped at Chanpotón, where the natives killed forty-eight Spaniards, captured two of them, and wounded the rest, including the captain, who received ten arrow wounds, and the author, who received " three, and one of them in the left side which pierced my ribs, and was very dangerous."

The survivors returned by way of Florida to Cuba, disillusioned and in ill-health, suffering from burning thirst and barely escaping shipwreck, for the ships were leaking badly. When recounting these calamities the author exclaims—

" Oh! what a troublesome thing it is to go and

discover new lands and the risks we took it is hardly possible to exaggerate."

Nevertheless Bernal was not discouraged by experience; his poverty, which, of necessity, increased daily, impelled him to seek his fortune even at the risk of losing his life, and his youth made him naturally impatient; he did not care to wait for the Indians which Diego Velásquez had promised to give him as soon as there were some unemployed, and he at once enlisted in a second expedition, composed of four ships and two hundred soldiers, under the command of Juan de Grijalva, which weighed anchor in the port of Matanzas on the 8th April, 1518.

The author says that he went "as ensign," but it is doubtful

The expedition went by way of Cozumel and Chanpotón, whose intrepid inhabitants wounded Grijalva and broke two of his teeth, and killed seven soldiers, by the Boca de Términos, the Rio de Tabasco which they called the Rio de Grijalva, La Rambla, the Rios de Tonalá or de Santo Antón, de Coatzacoalcos, de Papaloapan or de Alvarado, and the Rio de Banderas, where they obtained by barter " more than sixteen thousand pesos in jewels and low grade gold." They sighted the Isla Blanca and the Isla Verde, and landed on the Isla de Sacrificios and the sand dunes of Ulúa; thence Alvarado, accompanied by certain soldiers, returned to Cuba in search of reinforcements, while Grijalva, with the rest of his followers, including the author, pushed ahead by Tuxtla,[1] Tuxpan and the Rio de Canoas, where the Spaniards were attacked by the natives to Cape Rojo; then Grijalva, yielding to the entreaties of his soldiers, agreed to return to Cuba.

Velásquez, fascinated beyond measure by the gold which Grijalva had obtained by barter, organised a third expedition consisting of "eleven ships great and small," and appointed Hernan Cortés to command it. Bernal again enlisted, as at this time he found himself much in debt. Cortés set out from the Port of Trinidad on the 18th February, 1519. The author had started eight days earlier in the company of Pedro de Alvarado. All met together again at the Island of Cozumel, where a review was held, which showed a muster of five hundred and eight soldiers, "not including ship-masters, pilots and seamen, who numbered one hundred, and sixteen horses and mares." Keeping on their course they passed close by Chanpotón without venturing to land; they stopped at Tabasco, where they fought with the natives, who gave the author "an arrow wound in the thigh but it was not a severe wound," and finally they arrived at Ulúa.

They went inland and marched to Cempoala and Quiahuiztlan, and in the neighbourhood of the latter they founded the Villa Rica de la Vera Cruz, and they determined to push on to México, whose

---

[1] This is an error. Tuxtla was passed before reaching the Isla de Sacrificios.

Prince, Motecuhzoma,[1] had been exciting their
cupidity by rich presents of gold and other objects
of value.

Before undertaking this march, the friends of
Cortés (one of whom was Bernal) advised him to
destroy the ships, lest any of the soldiers should
mutiny and wish to return to Cuba, and so that he
could make use of the ship-masters, pilots and seamen "who numbered nearly one hundred persons"
as we have already stated. When this had been
done, "without concealment and not as the chronicler
Gómara describes it," they started for Mexico in
the middle of August, probably on the sixteenth,
and passed without incident through Jalapa Xico-
chimalco, Ixhuacan, Texutla, Xocotla and Xalacingo, but on reaching the frontiers of Tlaxcala they
were stopped by the natives, who fought against
them for several days. There the author received
"two wounds, one on the head from a stone, and
the other an arrow wound in the thigh," from which
he was seriously ill in the Capital of Tlaxcala, after
Cortés had made peace and an alliance with the
inhabitants.

"On the 12th October" they continued their
march by Cholula, where they committed a shocking
massacre, Itzcalpan, Tlamanalco, and Itztapalatengo.
Here Cacamatzin the Lord of Tetzcoco met them in
royal state to welcome them in the name of Motecuhzoma, and they accompanied him along the

---

[1] Montezuma.

causeway of Itztapalapa, which crossed the lake in a straight line to Mexico, and from it could be seen on both sides innumerable " cities and towns," some in the water and others on dry land, all of them beautified by stately temples and palaces. This wonderful panorama, as picturesque as it was novel, made the deepest impression on Bernal and his companions, and he says, "we were amazed and said that it was like the enchantments they tell us of in the story of Amadis, on account of the great towers and cues[1] and buildings rising from the water, and all built of masonry. And some of our soldiers even asked whether the things that we saw were not all a dream."

When they reached the junction of the causeways of Itztapalapa and Coyohuacan they met many Caciques and Chieftains of importance coming in advance of Motecuhzoma, who received the Spaniards a little further on, almost at the gates of Mexico, with sumptuous pomp and extreme ceremony. Many times the Mexican sovereign had contemplated attacking the Spaniards, but weighed down by superstition and rendered powerless by a timid and vacillating character, he now conducted them into the great Tenochtitlan, only to deliver it up to them at once. The autocrat felt himself fatally conquered before beginning the struggle.

Thence step by step within a few days he suffered seven Spaniards, among whom was Bernal, to make

---

[1] Cue = temple. This is not a Nahua or Maya word but one picked up by the Spaniards in the Antilles.

him a prisoner in his own palace ; he allowed his
jailors to burn [to death] Quauhpopoca and other
native chieftains, whose crime consisted in having,
by his own orders, given battle to Juan de
Escalante and other Spanish soldiers ; he handed
over to Cortés Cacamatzin, Totoquihuatzin, Cuitláhuac and Cuauhtémoc, lords respectively of Tetzcoco,
Tlacopan, Itztapalapan and Tlatelolco, who wished
to set their sovereign at liberty, and finally, weeping
like a tender unhappy woman, he swore fealty to
the King of Spain.

With ease and in a short time Cortés was able to
collect an immense treasure which amounted to
"seven hundred thousand gold dollars," which he
found it necessary to divide among his soldiers ;
nevertheless, he made the division with such trickery
and cunning that there fell to the soldiers "a very
small share, only one hundred dollars each, and it
was so very little that many of the soldiers did not
want to take it, and Cortés was left with it all." If
the author did not complain of this as much as
some of his companions, for example, as Cárdenas,
who even "fell ill from brooding and grief," it was
owing to his having already received from Motecuhzoma some presents of "gold and cloths," as well
as of "a beautiful Indian girl . . . the daughter of
a chieftain," whom he ventured to beg of the
Sovereign through the good offices of the page
Orteguilla, a gift which he certainly thought that he
had gained by his respectful courtesy "for whenever I was on guard over him, or passed before

him, I doffed my helmet to him with the greatest respect."

The Spaniards began to enjoy the gold divided among them, abandoning themselves to a life of licentious pleasure, when in March 1520 Pánfilo de Narvaez arrived at Ulúa with sixteen ships,[1] fourteen hundred soldiers, ninety crossbowmen, seventy musketeers, and eighty horses.

Diego Velásquez had sent him to punish Cortés and his followers as traitors, because they had rebelled against him without reason. However, as Cortés was immensely rich, and there is no power greater than riches, he soon won over almost all the soldiers of Narvaez with ingots and jewels of gold, in such a way that when the fight took place at Cempoala, Narvaez was the only man who fought in earnest, until he was wounded and lost an eye. The author figures among his captors : " the first to lay hands on him was Pedro Sanchez Farfan, a good soldier, and I handed him (Narvaez) over to Sandoval."

After his victory Cortés returned with all speed to Mexico, where the inhabitants had risen in arms with the purpose of avenging the inhuman massacre carried out by Pedro de Alvarado in the precincts of the great Teocalli, which Alonzo de Avila pronounced to be disgraceful, saying that it would

---

[1] The author says that there were nineteen, but the Oidor Lucas Vásquez de Ayllon, who accompanied Narvaez, writes that there were sixteen. (Hernan Cortés, *Cartas y Relaciones*, Paris, 1866. Page 42.)—G. G.

for ever remain "an ill memory in New Spain."
Cortés now brought with him over thirteen
hundred soldiers, eighty crossbowmen and as many
musketeers, and ninety mounted men, without
counting his numerous native allies.

Although they all reached the great Tenochtitlan
" on the day of San Juan de Junio (St. John's Day)
in the year 1520" they could not make a stand
against the Mexicans, who, under the command of
Cuitláhuac and Cuauhtémoc, killed the greater
number of the invaders and forced the rest, wounded
and ruined, for they were unable to save the riches
they had collected, to flee to Tlaxcala. The
Tlaxcalans received them, lodged them and
attended to them with affection. When they were
somewhat recovered, the Spaniards began Vandal-
like forays through Tepeyácac, Cachula, Gua-
cachula, Tecamachalco, the town of the Guayabos,
Ozúcar, Xalacingo, Zacatami, and other places in
the neighbourhood, enslaving and branding with
a hot iron all the youths and women they met with ;
" they did not trouble about the old men : " the
inhuman mark was placed " on the face," and not
even the most beautiful young woman escaped it.

The author did not assist in all these forays
because " he was very ill from fever, and was
spitting blood."

Cortés then founded a second city, which he
named Segura de la Frontera.

After the Spaniards had been reinforced by
various expeditions that had come from Cuba, they

resolved to return to Mexico to recover their lost treasure, and they forthwith took the road to Tetzcoco.

They took with them many thousands of native allies.

When the headquarters had been established at Tetzcoco, Cortés opened hostilities by an assault on Itztapalapa, where he and his followers nearly lost their lives by drowning, for the Mexicans "burst open the canals of fresh and salt water and tore down a causeway : " the author was "very badly wounded by a lance thrust which they gave me in the throat near the windpipe, and I was in danger of dying from it, and retain the scar from it to this day."

Cortés did not think of a direct attack on Mexico, he understood that it could lead to no satisfactory result ; he proposed merely to invest the city and reduce it by starvation ; so as to accomplish this he had entrusted to the Tlaxcalans the construction of thirteen launches, which he anxiously awaited.

Meanwhile, he attacked the neighbouring towns with fire and sword. The author did not join in these earlier combats as he was still ill from his dangerous wound, but as soon as it healed, he again took up arms, and accompanied Cortés, who went to assist the natives of Chalco, and distinguished himself among the most intrepid soldiers.

On his side, Cuauhtémoc, who was now Lord

of Mexico, took measures for the defence of his country with unequalled courage ; he had obtained from his subjects a promise "that they would never make peace, but would either all die fighting or take our lives."

The strife was remarkably prolonged and bloody, and no quarter was given.

The siege began on the 21st May, 1521, and lasted eighty-five days. Not for one moment did the Mexicans show signs of discouragement, notwithstanding the scarcity of fresh water and provisions, the superiority of the arms of the Spaniards, and the immense number of their native allies ;[1] each day as it came was for them as the first day of the strife, so great was the determination and the strength with which they appeared on the field of battle, and, moreover, they never ceased fighting "from dawn to dusk."

When the greater number of them had already perished, the few who still remained stoically resisted thirst, hunger, weariness and pestilence in the defence of their country, and even then refused, with indomitable fortitude, the proposals of peace which Cortés repeatedly made to them. In this manner only did they die.

The army which was to attack the Mexicans by

---

[1] The author makes immoderate efforts to lessen the number of the allies, but Cortés informs us that there were "numberless people," "an infinite number," "which could not be counted," that those that accompanied him alone numbered "more than one hundred and fifty thousand men."—G. G.

land was divided from the beginning into three
sections.   It fell to the lot of the author to serve
in that of Tlacopan, commanded by Pedro de
Alvarado.   Many times Bernal was in danger of
losing his life, first of all when the siege had just
been commenced ;   a few days later when the
Mexicans succeeded in seizing him, "many Indians
had already laid hold of me, but I managed to get
my arm free, and our Lord Jesus Christ gave me
strength so that by some good sword thrusts that
I gave them, I saved myself, but I was badly
wounded in one arm ; " on another occasion they
succeeded in taking him prisoner, but "it pleased
God that I should escape from their power ; " and,
finally, at the end of June on the day that Cortés
suffered his terrible defeat, the author received "an
arrow wound and a sword thrust."

The siege ended on the 13th August, 1521, with
the capture of the north-east corner of the city,
where the few surviving Mexicans still offered a
heroic resistance.

As soon as Cortés was master of the Great
Tenochtitlan, he got together, for the second time,
a great quantity of gold, although it was not as
much as he had acquired before.   On the division
being made, again for the second time the Spaniards
were profoundly discontented, for they found that
after all their terrible hardships and their constant
danger of death, "there fell to the share of a
horseman eighty dollars, and to that of the crossbowmen, musketeers and shield bearers sixty or

fifty, I do not well remember which." The most annoying thing for the Spanish adventurers was "that some owed fifty or sixty dollars for cross-bows, and others fifty dollars for a sword, and similarly everything that we bought was equally dear, then too a surgeon named Master Juan, who dressed some severe wounds, charged an exorbitant price for his cures, as did also a sort of quack doctor named Murçia, who was an apothecary and barber and also undertook cures, and there were thirty other traps and trickeries for which we were in debt."

The author continued to contract debts in consequence, in spite of his sturdy fighting and his many and serious wounds.

Although his expectations had not been fulfilled, Bernal did not abandon the hope of mending his fortunes, which had brought him to Mexico, and he accompanied his friend Gonzalo de Sandoval to the conquest of Tuxtépec, a place which, according "to the tribute rolls of Montezuma," which the author had studied, abounded in gold. When he arrived there, Sandoval advised him to stay there, and offered him in allotment "the rich towns of Matlatan, Orizaba and Ozotequipa ; but Bernal refused, "for it seemed to me that unless I went with Sandoval and as his friend, that I should not be doing what was becoming to my rank."

He passed on to Coatzacoalcos, where the town of Espíritu Santo was established, and here Bernal settled,. for on the 20th September, 1522, Cortés gave him in allotment the towns of "Tlapa and Potonchan," which belonged to the province of Cimatan.   Neither one nor the other proved satisfactory to him, because the land was poor, or more probably because he found no gold there, the metal which represented the only acceptable form of riches to the author and his companions, who had migrated on that very account from the Valley of Mexico, because it produced "merely an abundance of maize and aloes."

The settlers at the town of Espíritu Santo chose him as their Magistrate, a clear proof of the esteem and consideration in which he was held.

After all, the new life that Bernal led did not free him from frequent turmoil ; he was continually obliged to sally forth and pacify the towns in the province, and this was not without risk, for on one occasion he was "struck by an arrow wound in the throat, and the great loss of blood, for at the time it was not possible either to bandage [the wound] or staunch the flow, greatly endangered my life."

During Lent in the year 1523 he set out with Captain Luis Marín to fight the natives of Chiapas, "the greatest warriors that I had seen in the whole of New Spain, although that includes Tlaxcalans, Mexicans, Zapotecs and Minxes."

The author now travelled on horseback—doubtless his towns were not in such poor land as he had imagined.

He had to suffer many hardships during this

expedition ; the people of Chiapas fought like
" rabid lions," and in Chamula they gave him "a
good blow with a lance which pierced my armour,
and had it not been made of thick cotton and well
quilted, they would have killed me, for good as it
was they thrust through it and out came a thick wad
of cotton, and they gave me a slight wound." In
spite of this he was one of the two first soldiers who
stormed and took the fortress of the natives.   As a
reward for his heroic conduct Luis Marín gave him
in allotment this town of Chamula, a place of great
importance.

On the return to Espíritu Santo he fought [a
duel] of swords with Godoy in a most noble cause,
and both were wounded.

Bernal did not enjoy his ease for long, for in
obedience to an order from Cortés, whom all the
Conquistadores greatly feared, he found himself
forced to follow Rodrigo Rangel to the conquest
of the Zapotecs ; it is fair to say that, although he
did so unwillingly, for he already felt wearied, and
Rangel did not inspire sympathy, he acquitted
himself with great efficiency throughout the expedition, for which he gained honourable praise.   It was
then[1] when the natives " had hung seven arrows on
him, which only failed to pierce on account of the
thickness of the cotton armour, and nevertheless I
emerged wounded in one leg ;" he would, however,

---

[1] This happened in a subsequent expedition under Rangel in
Tabasco.

not give way, but, in spite of all, he pursued the natives for a long distance until " they took refuge in some great quaking morasses which no man who entered them could get out of again except on all fours or with much assistance."

He returned to Espíritu Santo without having accomplished anything to his profit, and went on to Mexico, where he was present on the 18th or 19th June, 1524, at the magnificent reception given by Cortés to Fray Martín de Valencia and his twelve Franciscan companions, among them Fray Toribio de Benavente, whom the Indians named Motolinía, "which means in their language the poor Friar, for all that was given him for the sake of God he gave to the Indians, so that at times he went without food, and wore very ragged garments and walked barefoot, and he always preached to them, and the Indians loved him greatly for he was a saintly person."

The author returned to his town almost at once. He was there at the end of October in the same year when Cortés arrived on his way to the Hibueras,[1] whither he was going personally, resolved to punish Cristóbal de Olid, who had rebelled.

The conqueror was followed by a formidable army, and a numerous court of friars and clergy, doctors and surgeons, major domos, waiters, butlers, chamberlains, stewards, and keepers of his "great

---

[1] Honduras.

services of gold and silver," pages, orderlies, huntsmen, pipers, trumpeters and fifers, acrobats, conjurers, puppet players, equerries and muleteers, and "a great herd of pigs that they ate as they went along." Among the soldiers and attendants of Cortés there also marched, but not of their own will, Cuauhtémoc and other great native princes.

When Cortés arrived at Coatzacoalcos he ordered all the settlers to go with him to the Hibueras, and it was owing to this that the author had to accompany him : nobody would have then dared to disobey Cortés.

It was hard luck for Bernal, for as he says " At the time when we should have been resting from our great labours and endeavouring to secure some property and profit, he ordered us to go on a journey of over five hundred leagues, the greater part of it through hostile country, and all that we possessed we left behind and lost."

Bernal was not consoled by Cortés appointing him Captain on this occasion, nor by taking his own followers with him, who had been recruited from the towns of his *encomienda*.[1]

While the author marched upon Cimatán at the head of thirty Spaniards and three thousand natives, Cortés overran the towns of Tonalá and Ayagua-

---

[1] Encomienda = The Indian townships and land, with the Indians necessary for its cultivation, assigned or allotted to a Spaniard.

lulco, crossed a neighbouring estuary after throwing across it "a bridge which was nearly half a quarter of a league long, an astonishing feat, in the way they did it," and he went along the great river Mazapa to the towns of Iquinuapa where he rejoined the author.

Together, they soon passed through the towns of Copilco, Nacaxuxuyca, Zaguatan, Tepetitan and Itztapa. Going on in search of Hueyacalá, or " the great Acalá, for there was another town called Acalá the lesser," they penetrated into the forest [monte] and lost their way, and found themselves then compelled to clear a track with their swords through the thick undergrowth ; they suffered from hunger and four Spaniards and many of the natives died from it, for they fell down "as though in despair." In this extremity Bernal and Pero López saved the army, for they found the lost road which soon led them to Temastépec. The pipers, trum-peters and fifers no longer made music, for " they were used to luxury and did not understand hardship and they had sickened with the hunger ; only one of them had the spirit to play, and all of us soldiers refused to listen to him, and said that it sounded like the howling of foxes and coyotes and that it would be better to have maize to eat than music."

In Ciguatepécad the author and Gonzalo Mexía went on ahead by the order of Cortés to win over peacefully the inhabitants of Acalá, a mission which Bernal, on his part, accomplished satisfactorily, for he soon returned with a large quantity of provisions; but as the soldiers were starving they seized them all and fought one another for them.   In vain did the Steward cry out to them that they should leave something for Cortés, the soldiers answered petulantly "you and Cortés have had fine pigs to eat." When Cortés heard what had happened he put up with it, and asked the author in the mildest manner whether he had not left a little of the food hidden on the road, and ended by asking him most humbly for a share of it.   The author consented and generously invited him to partake of that which he had reserved for himself and the natives from the towns of his *encomiendas*.

The army entered the province of Acalá, and there at Izancánac Cortés ordered Cuauhtémoc and his cousin Tetepanquetzatl, the lord of Tlacopan, to be hanged, on suspicion of engaging in a conspiracy. The author tells us that he was very sorry for these great princes, and adds, "their death was very unjust and appeared an evil thing to all of us, who were on the march." This was at Shrovetide in 1525.

Cortés arrived at the land of the Mazatecas, and after passing through two towns, one situated on an island and another near a fresh-water lake, entered into Tayasal. A little further on Bernal began to feel very ill "from fever and from the power of the sun which had affected my head and all my body." In this condition, nevertheless, he was obliged to cross the toilsome range of the Pedernales, not so

very lofty, but whose stones "cut like knives." In
front of Tayca a river "which one could clearly
hear two leagues off" delayed the army for three
days, and Cortés threw a bridge across it similar to
the one constructed at Ayagualulco, bridges which
survived for many years, for the admiration of
travellers who were accustomed to say, "here are
Cortés' bridges as though they were speaking of the
Pillars of Hercules."

Again they felt the pangs of hunger, such as the
author had never before experienced; he suffered
anguish at this time "for I had nothing to eat or
to give to my people and I was ill with fever."
Cortés ordered him nevertheless to go out and
seek for food for the army, and the author, rising
superior to his serious infirmities, obeyed him.
Guided by his experience and sagacity, he was not
long in finding poultry, maize, beans and "other
vegetables," with which he promptly supplied all
the soldiers.

They went on to Tania, a town surrounded by
rivers and streams, from which they were unable
to get out, for once more they lost their way.
Cortés despatched several Spaniards to find it
again, but without result. It was necessary to
confide the task to the author, in spite of his illness,
for after God it was in him "that he had confidence
that he would bring help," and when he brought it,
for he succeeded in finding the road which they
were to follow, Cortés evinced profound gratitude,
and made him fair promises: "I pledge you," he

told him, "this, my beard, that I owe your honour a debt."

The conqueror arrived at last with his huge army at Ocoliztle, a town quite close to Naco, where he expected to fight with Cristóbal de Olid; it was not until then he learnt that he (Olid) had had his throat cut long before by Gil González de Avila and Francisco de las Casas. Nevertheless, before returning to Mexico, he wished to leave his rule established in that far off district, his boundless ambition making the vast territory of New Spain appear small to him. Thus he founded the town of La Natividad, "which is now called Puerto de Caballos," and obliged the natives who had been scared away to return and repopulate Naco.

While this was happening, news was received from Mexico that the Agent Gonzalo de Salazar, after spreading the report that Cortés and his soldiers had perished, seized their property and their Indians to divide them among his partizans; and he ordered the wives who had become widows to pray for the souls of their husbands and promptly proceed "to marry again, and he even sent to say so to Guaçacualco and other towns." It is certain that the wife of Alonzo Yáñez, an inhabitant of Mexico, respected the order, and hurriedly re-married.

Nevertheless, while all the soldiers were indignant and excited, as was only natural, and prepared themselves to return as fast as possible to New Spain to recover their wives, their Indians and their property, and even cursed Cortés and Salazar, "and our hearts throbbed with anger," Cortés, formerly energetic, prompt and venturesome to rashness, now weak, irresolute and timid, confined himself to weeping disconsolately, shutting himself up for long hours in his room, and permitting no one to see him : overmuch power had weakened his character. When at last he came out of his room, the soldiers unanimously addressed him and entreated him to embark at once in the three ships that were there and go to New Spain, and he answered us very affectionately : " Oh my children and companions, I see on one side that evil man, the Agent, has become very powerful, and I fear that when he knows that we are in the port, he will do some other shameless and daring things to us beyond what he has already done, or he will kill or drown me, or make me and all of you prisoners." The abundant riches which Cortés now possessed made him love life too much.

Selfishly abandoning the bulk of his army, he set out on the sea with a few followers. The author had begged him very urgently to take him in his company ; he had an abundant right to ask this and other much greater favours, but Cortés, ever deaf to gratitude, left him there to return by land.

So by land he went, once more suffering daily hardships, and having also to fight against the natives. He passed through Maniani and Cholulteca-Malalaca, the Chaparrastiques, Cuzcatlan or Cascacatan, whose inhabitants gave him an arrow wound, Petapa, Guatemala, Olnitépec, Soconusco, Tehuantépec, Oaxaca and Mexico. He entered the capital in the beginning of 1527, after a most laborious march extending over more than " two years and three months," during which he had served throughout " very well and loyally " without receiving " pay or any favour whatever." He returned poor, in debt, and with ragged clothes. Andrés de Tápia received him in his house, and Gonzalo de Sandoval sent him garments with which to clothe himself, " and gold and cacao to spend."

At this time Marcos de Aguilar was governing New Spain, and Bernal begged him to give him Indians in Mexico as those of Coatzacoalcos " were of no profit." Aguilar merely made him fine promises, alleging that he had not yet received power to apportion Indians.

During the same year Aguilar was succeeded by Alonzo de Estrada, first of all in company with Sandoval and afterwards alone, whose rule was very unfortunate for the author ; under it Baltazar Osorio and Diego de Mazariegos turned him out " by force " from his *encomiendas* of Micapy, Tlapa and Chamula, to the end that they might be incorporated in the new towns of Chiapas and Tabasco.

The author, finding it impossible " to carry on lawsuits with two towns," went to Estrada to obtain justice, and got from him, dated 3rd April, 1528, the *encomienda* " of the towns of Gualpitán and

Micapa, which are in the Cachulco range, and used to be subject to Cimatán, and of Popoloatán in the province of Citla." Nevertheless, the author was not satisfied owing to the fact that these towns were of little importance, and did not nearly compensate him for the loss of Tlapa, which contained "more than a thousand houses," and that of Chamula, which numbered "more than four hundred, and the farms more than two hundred."

At the end of this same year, 1528, Estrada was succeeded by the First *Audiencia*,[1] which wished to proceed at once to the perpetual assignment[2] of the Indians, and with this object ordered the cities and towns settled by Spaniards to appoint attorneys to come to the Capital. The arrangement could not have been more opportune nor more agreeable for Bernal, who could now believe with good reason that his labours and his poverty were soon going to cease. He set out in all haste for Espíritu Santo, and was successful in arranging that the settlers should entrust him with their authority, and he returned at once to Mexico. However, the much talked of division came to nothing, and the judges, far from favouring Bernal, imprisoned him twice on despicable pretexts, together with other old *Conquistadores*. He was obliged at last to return to Coatzacoalcos, persuaded that he would obtain no protection from the First Audiencia, and that he must resign himself to live there "in the midst of

---

[1] Audiencia = a Council of Government.
[2] The "Repartimiento."

d *

want," but maintaining "his high honour, and seeing to it that he lived uprightly and without indulging in any vice," and justly enjoying "a very good reputation."

When the First Audiencia retired in the month of January 1531, the honest members of the Second Audiencia assumed control, and, as they appreciated the merits of the author, they nominated him *Visitador General* of Coatzacoalcos and Tabasco, and they entrusted to him the delimitation of both those settlements, a duty which he carried out with prudence in company with the stipendiary Benito López. Encouraged by these distinctions, and trusting in the rectitude of the Second Audiencia, Bernal approached it [with a request] that he should be given some Indian towns in compensation for those "that had been taken from him by force," but the Judges told him that "unless the order came from his Majesty in Spain they were not able to give them."

In the year 1535 the first Viceroy, Don Antonio de Mendoza, arrived in Mexico, and Bernal approached him also with the same demand, and again met with a similar refusal.

However, if adversity and deception never ceased to lay in wait for and wound the author, he, on the other hand, never gave way to their blows, and always knew how to preserve his energy undiminished. It must certainly have been towards 1535 when, in spite of having already reached the age of forty-three years, and feeling "very weary and poor," he married Teresa Becerra, the eldest legitimate daughter of Captain Bartolomé Becerra, a *Conquistador* of Guatemala, and the first regular Mayor of that city.   By this marriage Bernal had several sons and daughters, the eldest being Francisco, who was born a year after the wedding.

Bernal had already born to him other children by a native woman, who was perhaps that beautiful girl he had begged from Montezuma through the good offices of the page Orteguilla.   Baltasar Dorantes de Carranza knew a "Diego Díaz de Castillo, a half-caste" and a natural son of Bernal, and Philip II mentions in a Royal Decree some brothers of this Diego.

The author proved to be an excellent father of a family, the greatest, in fact the chief, anxiety throughout his life, was not having the means with which to secure the future of his wife and children ; he constantly mentions this subject in all his letters, as well as in the *True History*.

As Bernal's difficulties necessarily increased with his growing family, and he knew by sad experience that he could hope for nothing from those governing New Spain, he resolved to go to Court to beg for justice from the Lords of the Royal Council.   Cortés and the Viceroy gave him letters of recommendation to them with which, and the authenticated record of his merits and services, he arrived in Spain about 1540.   Once there, he presented his petition in [proper] form.   The Lords of the Royal Council ordered it to be handed over to the Fiscal, the Licentiate Don Juan de Villalobos, who declared openly and frankly, for some reason of which we know nothing, that he would not allow him any-thing, because "he had not been a *Conquistador* such as he asserted."

The Fiscal doubly offended the author, because at the same time that he ignored his services given during so many years with painful toil and in frequent danger of death, he treated him publicly as an impostor, him who judged and proclaimed the truth to be "a thing blessed and holy."

This disillusion was without any doubt the most painful of all the author's sufferings. Fortunately the Lords of the Royal Council took no notice of the Fiscal's pleading in settling the matter, and issued a writ on the 15th April, 1541, advising that a Royal Decree should be given to the author addressed to the Viceroy of New Spain, to the end that "he should examine the quality and number of the towns which had been given to the said Bernal Díaz and which he held possessed and which were taken away from him to form the townships of Chiapas and Tabasco, and should give him in recompense for them other towns of the same kind and as good in the same province so that he might gain profit therefrom during his Majesty's pleasure."

The Decree was issued two months later, together with another to the same effect, which was addressed to Pedro de Alvarado, the Governor of Guatemala, which the author asked for with a view of obtaining the new towns in either of the two provinces, wherever they could most promptly be granted. Provided with these two Decrees he returned immediately to the New World. He obtained nothing in New Spain, but, when he went on to Guatemala, the Licentiate Alonzo Maldonado, who was Governor on the death of Alvarado, assigned him the towns of Zacatépec, Joanagacapa and Misten, which were clearly of " little worth," and promised him that as soon as there were others of greater importance he would give them to him and put him in charge of them. As the promise was never realised, Bernal never escaped from his life of poverty.

Without any incidents worth recording—at least so far as is known to us—time went on until 1550, in which year Bernal was summoned to Spain to assist at the Congress of Valladolid, in the character of " the oldest *Conquistador* of New Spain." He went there, joined in the Congress and voted for the perpetual assignment of the Indians, in spite of having heard the humanitarian and persuasive arguments alleged against it by the eminent Fray Bartolomé de las Casas and his worthy companions Fray Rodrigo de Labrada and Fray Tomás de San Martín ; his own poverty was a stronger argument.

Bernal utilised his short stay at Court to obtain a Royal Decree, dated the 1st December, 1550, ordering the Licentiate Alonzo López Zerrato, President of the Audiencia of Guatemala, to carry out the previous Decree recorded in 1541, and have it respected.

On the 1st September, 1551, the author exhibited his new Decree before the Licentiate López Zerrato, who unfortunately did not execute it, in spite of having that very day taken it in his hands, examined it and placed it above his head as was the custom, to show that he would obey it and carry it out.

We say that he did not carry it out, because a year later Bernal wrote to his Majesty that the said Licentiate cared only to give assignments "to his relations, servants and friends," without taking any notice of the *Conquistadores* who had won [the country] "by their sweat and blood;" on this account the author prays that his Majesty may be pleased to order him to be admitted "into his Royal house as one of his servants."

This petition shows that Bernal did not harbour any hope of improving his miserable lot. Here he nevertheless remained, for he did not succeed in being admitted into the number of his Majesty's servants.

Moreover, if it had not been possible for him to prosper during youth and middle life, it was still less so now that he was entering on old age, and we find, as was natural and even to be expected, that he writes to Fray Bartolomé de las Casas, on 20th February, 1558, that he was still "very straightened as he possessed so little property."[1]

---

[1] As the author then adds that he was "heavily burdened by children and grandchildren," and that he had a young wife, it is not hazardous to think that he had recently contracted a second marriage, etc.—G. G.

It must have been a great consolation to him that he continued to be esteemed and respected in Guatemala. He had not ceased to be a Magistrate, and this same year he was elected "arbitrator and executor," and he had been named the previous year to carry the banner on the feast of Santa Cecilia, an honour which was again conferred on him in 1560, on the occasion of the feast of Saint James the Apostle.[1] The affection and consideration which all the persons who knew him had for Bernal Díaz was owing to his "charming conversation" and noble sentiments, but principally to the fact that in spite of his poverty, he always managed to live "with great dignity."

Thus then, poor enough, although much loved and esteemed, fearing no one, he dedicated himself to the writing of his *True History* when he was over seventy years of age, convinced that in the history of the world there was no more daring deed than the conquest, nor more heroic men in existence than the *Conquistadores*, resigned to not having received the reward which was justly due to him, free from pessimism, rancour and regrets, with a perfectly tranquil conscience, with an exceptional memory and an intelligence uncommon in its full vigour. His work was now and then interrupted by visits to the towns assigned to him, sometimes accompanied by friends. Neither travel nor change of climate broke down his health ; he

[1] Garcia Peláez. *Memoria para la Historia del Antiguo Reyno de Guatemala.* Guatemala, 1851-52, vol. ii, page 227.—G. G.

himself tells us that even at that time he did not
use a bed, from habit acquired during the conquest,
nor was he able to sleep unless he walked "some
time in the open air, and this without any covering
on his head, neither cap nor kerchief, and, thanks
to God, it did me no harm." With all this, he
also tells us, not perhaps without exaggeration, that
by that time he had "lost his sight and hearing."
He had penned but little of the History when the
Chronicles composed by Paulo Giovio, Francisco
López de Gómara and Gonzalo de Illescas[1] came
into his hands. As soon as he began to read them,
"and observed from their good style the roughness
and lack of polish of my language," he gave up
writing his History. However, when the first
impression had faded, he returned to their perusal,
and was then able to decide that they spoke truth
neither in the beginning, nor the middle, nor the
end, and for this reason he definitely resolved to
continue his own work. Probably this did not
happen before 1566, for Bernal knew no Latin,
and could not, therefore, understand the Chronicle
of Giovio until Baeza published his translation in
Spanish.

However that may be, it is clear that in the year
1568 he made the fair copy of the *True History*.

We know nothing more of his life. We can

[1] The work of Giovio was published in Latin in 1550-52, and
translated into Spanish by Gaspar de Baeza in 1566 ; Gomara
printed his Chronicle in 1552-53, and Illescas published his in
1564. All three soon went through several editions.—G. G.

only add that the author died in Guatemala about 1581, poor as he had lived, leaving his numerous family no riches except "his true and wonderful story," which was, nevertheless, the chief title to glory for his descendants, for in it was enshrined his fair name of honourable *Conquistador* and genial Historian.

————

The original manuscript of the *True History* forms a large folio volume, containing 297 leaves in an old leather binding. Although it is generally in a fairly good condition, there are some leaves partly destroyed, principally those at the beginning and at the end.

All the writing, which covers both sides of the leaves, is in the handwriting of the author; on some pages it is well done and normal, on others careless and irregular. The author could not have preserved the same composure throughout the long time occupied in writing his work.

The principal subject of this work is the Conquest "of New Spain and its provinces and the Cape of Honduras and all that lies within these lands." Those who tax Bernal with vanity and conceit suppose that when he began the *True History* his only object was to tell about himself, an entirely gratuitous supposition, for the author frequently chronicles a series of years, without including one of his personal deeds. His work begins within the year 1514 and ends with that of 1568. He divides it into 214 chapters, perhaps

intending to finish it with Chapter CCXII, at
the end of which he placed his signature and
rubrica,[1] but he changed his intention, and wrote
two new chapters in the same year in which he had
written Chapter CCXII, namely, the year 1568.
He still intended to write another, or others, for
he declares at the end of Chapter CCXIV: "It
will be well in another chapter to speak of the
Archbishops and Bishops that there have been."
Surely Bernal did not finish his work, unless one
assumes the loss of the final pages, which is not
probable. The binder who bound up the manuscript understood little of the composition of
ancient writings, and attached to the last folio the
leaf which contained the signature of the author.

Bernal did not pretend to be a man of letters;
he confesses his slight knowledge of literature, and
on this account humbly begs the indulgence of his
readers: "May your honours pardon me in that I
cannot express it better." Nevertheless, his mode
of speech is still current to-day, and is interesting
and expressive, in spite of the immoderate use of
copulative conjunctions, of its almost complete want
of imagery, its words with variable spelling, either
obsolete or incorrect, its semi-arbitrary punctuation,
its erroneous concordances, its strange contractions
and its unusual abbreviations.

---

[1] *Rubrica*, the flourish which then and at the present time
forms part of a signature among Spaniards.

INTRODUCTION

TRANSLATOR.

OUR eye-witnesses of the discovery and conquest of Mexico have left written records :—

Hernando Cortés, who wrote five letters known as the *Cartas de Relacion* to the Emperor Charles V.

The First of these letters, despatched from Vera Cruz, has never been found, but its place is supplied by a letter written to the Emperor at the same time by the Municipality of Vera Cruz, dated 10th July, 1519.

The Second letter, from Segura de la Frontera (Tepeaca), is dated 30th October, 1520.

The Third letter was written from Coyoacan, and dated 15th May, 1522.

The Fourth letter was written from the city of Temixtitan (Mexico), and dated 15th October, 1524.

The Fifth letter, written from Temixtitan

(Mexico), dated 3rd September, 1526, deals with the march to Honduras.

The Anonymous Conqueror whose identity has never been ascertained.

The original of this document is lost, and its contents are preserved to us in an Italian translation. It deals only with the customs, arms, food, religion, buildings, etc., of the inhabitants of the city of Mexico, and adds nothing to our knowledge of events during the Conquest.

Andrés de Tápia, whose short but interesting account of the expedition under Cortés ends with the defeat of Narvaez.

This document was only brought to light during the last century.

Bernal Díaz del Castillo, whose stirring and picturesque narrative is given in the following pages.

To these may be added the *Itinerario de Grijalva*, an account written by the chaplain who accompanied Grijalva on his expedition when the coast of Mexico was first discovered; but this account ends with the return of the expedition to Cuba, and does not deal with the conquest of the country.

The original of this document has been lost, and it comes down to us in an Italian translation. If the title is correct, it must have been written by the priest Juan Diaz who accompanied the expedition. It seems to be written in a hostile spirit, and its statements should be received with caution.

Many writers followed during the next forty

years who had conversed with actors in the events, and some of whom had heard the story from the mouths of the conquered Indians, and much additional information was thus added to the record ; but for a vivid impression of this daring plunge into the unknown, and the triumphant struggle of an isolated handful of Spaniards against a powerful and warlike race, we must rely on the accounts given by those two great soldiers and adventurers, leader and follower, Hernando Cortés and Bernal Díaz del Castillo.

The scene of the principal part of Bernal Díaz's narrative lies within the southern half of the present republic of Mexico, Western Central America and the peninsula of Yucatan, a land wholly within the tropics, which, however, owing to its physical conformation, furnishes almost every variety of climate.

A great range of volcanic mountains runs almost continuously through Mexico and the greater part of Central America, near the Pacific Coast and parallel to it. A second range of mountains, not so continuous and distinct, runs almost parallel to the Atlantic coast. The whole of the interior of the country between these two ranges may be said to be mountainous but intersected by many high-lying plains from 4000 to 8000 feet above sea level, which form one of the most characteristic features of the country. These plains are sometimes seamed with narrow *barrancas*[1] hundreds of feet in depth,

---

[1] *Canyons,* ravines.

often with precipitous sides, caused by the washing
away of the thick covering of light volcanic ash
down to the bed rock.   In common speech the
land is divided into the *tierra caliente*, the *tierra
templada*, and the *tierra fria*, the hot, temperate and
cold lands.   As the slope of the mountains is rather
more gradual towards the Atlantic than towards the
Pacific, the *tierra caliente* is more extensive in the
former direction.   Three volcanic peaks, Orizaba,
Popocatépetl and Ixtacíhuatl, almost in the middle
of Southern Mexico, rise above the line of perpetual snow and reach a height of about 17,000
feet, and several of the somewhat lower peaks are
snow-capped during some months of the year.   None
of the rivers of Mexico west of the Isthmus of
Tehuantépec are navigable in the sense of being
highways of commercial importance.   Passing to
the east of the Isthmus of Tehuantépec the country
of Chiapas and Guatemala does not differ materially
in its general characteristics from that already described, with the exception that the rivers are
relatively of greater importance, and the waters
of the Usumacinta and Grijalva form innumerable
lagoons and swamps before entering the Gulf of
Mexico.

North and west of the Usumacinta and its tribu-
taries, the land, with the exception of the Cockscomb
range in British Honduras, is all low, and the
peninsula of Yucatan appears to be little more
than a coral reef slightly raised above sea level.
There are no rivers, for the rain sinks easily

through the porous limestone rock, and the natives
have often to seek their drinking water 100 feet
or more below the surface in the great *cenotes*
(*tznótes*) or limestone caverns.

The sea round the north and west coast of the
peninsula is very shallow, the 100 fathom line
being in some parts as much as ninety miles distant
from the shore.

The wet season in Mexico and Central America
may (subject to local variations) be said to extend
from June to October, but it lasts somewhat longer
on the Atlantic than on the Pacific slope.   During
these months the rainfall is often very heavy, the
States of Tabasco and Vera Cruz probably receiving
the larger amount.

During the winter months occasional strong cold
gales sweep the Gulf of Mexico from the North,
the dreaded *Norte* so often mentioned in Bernal
Díaz's narrative.   This wind causes some dis-
comfort even on the high plateau of the *tierra
templada*, which, notwithstanding this drawback,
may safely be said to possess one of the most
perfect climates in the world.

The first question always asked regarding the
Conquest is, "Who were the Mexicans, and how
did they get to Mexico?" and to these questions
no certain answer can be given.   All that can be
said is that the whole American race, although
it may have originated from more than one stock,
reached America in a very early stage of human
development, and that the Nahua tribes to which

Mexicans belong came from the north-west coast, which is generally assumed to have been the earliest home of the American race. Whether the people came from Asia at a time when the Northern continents were continuous is a question not easily settled, but if such were the case, the migration must have taken place before the cultivation of cereal crops or the smelting of iron ore was known to the Northern Asiatics, for no iron implements were found in America, and no cereal was found there that was known in the East, the only cereal cultivated in America being the Indian corn or maize, and this is clearly of indigenous origin.

It is, therefore, not necessary to consider further such a very distant connection, if such existed, between the extreme east and west.

There is, of course, the possibility of isolated drifts from Asia to America; several instances of Polynesians having drifted in their canoes almost incredible distances in the Pacific are on record, and derelict junks have been known to reach the coast of America; but the survivors of such drifts, although they may have introduced a new game or some slight modification of an existing art, are not likely to have affected very materially the development of American culture.

The waves of migration from north to south, due probably to pressure of population or search for supplies of food, must necessarily have been intermittent and irregular, and must have been broken up by numerous cross currents due to natural obstacles. It seems natural to speak of a wave of migration, and to treat it as though it followed the laws governing a flow of water ; but to make the simile more complete we must imagine not a flow of water, but of a fluid liable to marked chemical change due to its surroundings, which here may slowly crystallise into a stable form, and there may boil over with noticeable energy, re-dissolving adjacent crystals and mixing again with a neighbouring stream. There is no reason to suppose that this process had not been going on in America as long as it had in other parts of the world, but there we are often helped to understand the process by written or carved records, which go back for hundreds and even thousands of years, whereas in America written records are almost non-existent, and carved records are confined to a small area, and both are almost undecipherable.

In Mexico and Central America accepted tradition appears to begin with the arrival of the Toltecs, a branch of the Nahua race, and history with that of the later Nahua tribes, but as to who the people were whom the Toltecs found in possession of the country, tradition is silent.

The commonly accepted story is that the Toltecs, whose capital was at Tula, were a people of considerable civilisation, who, after imparting something of their culture to ruder Nahua hordes that followed them from the North, themselves migrated

e

to Guatemala and Yucatan, where they built the great temples and carved the monuments which have been so often described by modern travellers. I am not, however, myself able to accept this explanation of the facts known to us. The monuments and architectural remains of Guatemala and Yucatan are undoubtedly the work of the Mayas, who, although nearly related to the Nahuas, are admitted to be a distinct race, speaking a different language; and I am inclined to believe that the Maya race formerly inhabited a considerable portion of Central and Southern Mexico, and it is to it that we must give credit for Tula, Cholula and, possibly, Teotehuacan, all lying within Central Mexico, as well as for the highest culture ever attained by natives on the continent of North America.

Driven from their Mexican homes by the pressure of Nahua immigrants, they doubtless took refuge in the high lands of Chiapas and Guatemala, and along the banks of the Rivers Usumacinta and Motagua, and pressed on as far as the present frontier of Guatemala and Honduras; but it must be admitted that, so far, no account of this migration and settlement is known to us.

Once settled in Central America, the Mayas would have held a strong defensive position against Nahua invaders, for they were protected on the Gulf side by the intricate swamps and waterways which Cortés found so much difficulty in crossing on his march to Honduras, and on the land side by the mountain ranges which rise abruptly to the east of the Isthmus of Tehuantépec. The passes through the great volcanic barrier which runs parallel to the Pacific Coast could have been easily defended, while a road was left open along the lowlands between the mountains and the sea, of which the Nahua hordes apparently availed themselves, for Nahua names and dialects are found as far east as Nicaragua.

Judging from the architectural remains and the sculptured stones, it may be safely assumed that it was in Central America that the Mayas reached the highest point of their culture, and that they there developed their peculiar script. No Maya hieroglyphic inscriptions have yet been found in Central Mexico, and it is only within the last few years that attention has been called to what appears to be a somewhat crude form of Maya script unearthed as far west as Monte Alban in the State of Oaxaca.

I am further inclined to believe, that after some centuries of peaceful development had elapsed, the Maya defence failed, and that the people were again driven from their homes by invaders from the North west, and leaving Chiapas and Guatemala, took refuge in Yucatan, where they founded Chichén-Itzá, Uxmal and the numerous towns whose ruins may still be seen throughout the northern part of the peninsula. It is worthy of note that weapons of war are almost entirely absent from the Central American sculptures, and at Copan one of the most important sculptured figures is that of a woman, whereas in Yucatan every man is depictured as a warrior with arms in his hands, and the only representation of a woman known to me is in a mural painting at Chichén-Itzá, where the women stand among the houses of a beleagured town, apparently bewailing their fate, while the battle rages outside.

At the time of the Spanish conquest the highlands of Guatemala were held by tribes of the Maya Quiché race, who were probably descendants of the Mayas and their Nahua conquerors, and were of an entirely lower standard of culture than the pure Mayas.

Yucatan was still Maya, but the influence of its powerful Nahua neighbours was strongly felt, and civil wars had caused the destruction and abandonment of most of the old towns.

There is yet one Maya area which has so far not been mentioned, the land of the Huastecs around the mouth of the Rio Panuco (the river dividing the modern States of Vera Cruz and Tamaulipas). It seems probable that the Huastecs, and possibly also their neighbours the Totonacs, were the remnant of the Maya race left behind when the main body was driven to the south-east. If they were a Maya colony from the south, as has sometimes been asserted, they would certainly have brought with them the Maya script, but no Maya hieroglyphs have, so far as I know, ever been found in the Huastec country. If, however, they were a remnant left behind when the Mayas migrated to the south-east, we should not expect to find the

Maya script in their country, for if my assumption is correct, at the time of the migration that script had not yet been developed. It should be noted that Tula, the reputed capital of the Toltecs, stands on the head waters of the Rio Panuco, and it may be that if such people existed, on occupying Tula they acquired something of the Maya culture, and thus gained their reputation of great builders and the teachers of the later Nahua immigrants.

The exact reason for the disappearance of the earlier races who inhabited Mexico, and of the abandonment of the Central American cities, may never be known, but religious differences cannot be left out of the question, and one way of regarding the change is as the triumph of the ruthless and sanguinary War God Huitzilopochtli over the mild and civilising cult of Quetzalcoatl or Kukulcan. Were I asked to give definitely all my reasons in support of the foregoing statements, which differ very considerably from those made by such a recent authority as Mr. Payne in his history of the American people, I must own that I should be at a loss how to do so.   However, I think it will be admitted by all students of the subject that we are a very long way indeed from having collected and sifted all the evidence procurable, and until the architecture, sculpture and other remains of the very numerous ruined towns which may be found throughout the country are more carefully studied and classified, and until the inscriptions have been deciphered, we must put up with such working hypotheses as may best enable us to group such information as has already been obtained.

In my own case, a somewhat intimate acquaintance with the sculptures and ruined buildings both in Central America and Mexico has left impressions on my mind as to their relation to one another which it is not always easy to express in definite terms. In another place[1] I have given my reasons for believing that the ruined towns of Central America, and probably the majority of those of Yucatan, had been abandoned by their inhabitants long before the Spanish conquest, and consequently the Spaniards are not responsible for the amount of damage that is sometimes attributed to them.

In the story of Bernal Díaz, we shall meet with the Mayas in the early pages describing the discovery of Yucatan and the passage of the three expeditions along the coast of the peninsula, and then again we shall come in touch with them after the conquest of Mexico on Cortés' journey across the base of the peninsula to Honduras.

No attempt was made to subdue the Mayas until 1527, six years after the fall of Mexico, and such redoubtable warriors did they prove themselves to be that, although Francisco de Montejo landed his forces and marched right across the northern part of the peninsula, he was eventually obliged to retreat, and by 1535 every Spaniard was driven out of the country. It was not until 1547

---

[1] *A Glimpse at Guatemala.* John Murray, London, 1899.

that the Spaniards brought the Mayas into subjection.

To turn now to the time of the Spanish conquest
we find Mexico peopled by a number of different
tribes more or less nearly alike in habits and
customs, and not differing greatly from each other
in race, but speaking different languages and
dialects. Some of these peoples or tribes, such
as the Zapotecs and Mixtecs of Oaxaca and the
Tarascos of Michoacan, extended over a considerable extent of country ; they were not however
homogeneous nations acting under the direction
of one chief or of a governing council. The
township or *pueblo* appears to have been the unit
of society, and the *pueblos* of the same race and
speech acted together when compelled by necessity
to do so, as it will be seen that the Tlaxcalans acted
together owing to the continued hostility of the
Mexicans. The main factor in the situation at the
time when the Spaniards landed was the dominance
of the *Pueblo* of Tenochtitlan or Mexico.

The Mexicans or Astecs were a people of Nahua
race who, after many years of wandering on their
way from the North, finally settled in the high
plain, or valley, which still retains their name.
For some years they appear to have been almost
enslaved by other tribes of the Nahua race, who
had already settled in the valley, and it was not
until the fourteenth century that they established
their home on the two small muddy islands of
Tlatelulco and Tenochtitlan in the Great Lake,

By their own warlike prowess and diplomatic alliances with neighbouring towns they gradually increased in power until they gained the hegemony of the tribes and peoples of the valley, and then carried their warlike enterprises into distant parts of the country, even as far as Tabasco and Guatemala. In fact, they became the head of a military and predatory empire, dependent for their food, as well as their wealth, on tribute drawn from subject tribes and races. They were not a civilising power, and as long as the tribute was paid, they did not appear to concern themselves with the improvement of the local government of their dependencies. The education of the sons and daughters of the upper classes was carefully attended to under the direction of the priesthood, but, as was only natural in a society so constituted, soldierly qualities were those most valued in the men, and the highest reward went to those who showed the greatest personal bravery in battle.

As the field of tribute extended, and wealth accumulated, the office of the principal *Cacique*[1] of Mexico, who was also the natural leader of their armies, rose in importance and dignity; and we learn from the narrative that Montezuma, who was the ninth in succession of the great *Caciques* of Mexico, was treated by his people with more than royal ceremonial.

---

[1] *Cacique* is the term usually employed by the Spaniards as equivalent to chief or king. It is not a Mexican but a Cuban word.

The arms and armour of all the Indian tribes appear to have been nearly alike, and they are often described by the conquerors, and are shown in the native picture writings that have come down to us. They are the

Macana or *Maquahuitl*, called by the Spaniards a sword, a flat blade of wood three to four feet long, and three inches broad, with a groove along either edge, into which sharp-edged pieces of flint or obsidian were inserted, and firmly fixed with some adhesive compound.

Bows and stone-tipped *arrows*.

Slings.

Long Spears with heads of stone or copper.

Javelins made of wood with points hardened in the fire (*varas tostadas*). These javelins, which were much dreaded by the Spaniards, were hurled from an *Atlatl* or throwing stick (*tiradera*).

It is worth noting that no bows or arrows are shown on any of the Maya sculptures, but in the stone carvings in Yucatan (on which weapons are always prominent) all the men are represented as armed with short spears or javelins and an *Atlatl.*

It may be that bows and arrows were unknown to the Mayas until they were introduced by the Nahua races.[1]

---

[1] I cannot call to mind any Mexican or Central American sculpture showing bows and arrows. Such representations appear to be confined to the *lienzos* (painted cloths) and picture writings, but I am not now able to verify this statement.

The defensive armour consisted of padded and quilted cotton worn on the arms or body—a protection which the Spaniards themselves hastened to adopt—and shields, usually round shields made of wicker and covered with hide or other material, and often beautifully decorated.   Sometimes they were oblong in shape, and large enough to cover the whole body ; these latter could be folded up when not in use.   Head-dresses or helmets, usually in the form of grotesque animals' heads, were used by the Chieftains, and feathers were freely used in decoration, both in the form of beautiful feather patterns worked into cotton fabrics or as *penachos*, lofty head-dresses of feathers supported on a light wood or reed framework.

A Mexican army in battle array must have been both a beautiful and imposing spectacle, a blaze of colour and barbaric splendour.

This is not the place to discuss fully the moral aspects of the Conquest, but in considering the conduct of the *Conquistadores* and their leader we must always keep in mind the traditions that influenced them and the laxity of the moral code of the time in which they lived.   Some of the Spaniards had served in Italy under Gonsalvo de Córdova, *el gran Capitan*, and may have seen Cæsar Borgia himself—what can we expect from such associations ?   All of them were adventurers seeking for wealth ; some, no doubt, were freebooting vagabonds who would have been a pest in any community.   The wonder of it all is that

Cortés, with no authority from the Crown and only
a few ardent partizans to support him, could have
kept the control of such a company for so long.
He dared to cheat these men out of part of their
hard-earned spoil that he might have gold with
which to bribe the leaders of the force which he
must always have known would be sent in pursuit
of him.   When the city fell he allowed Guatémoc
to be tortured to force him to disclose the supposed
secret of where his treasure was hidden—could
even his authority have prevented it?   It would
have been a splendid act of heroism had he made
the attempt ; but we must think of the disappointed
men around him, with the terrible strain of the
siege suddenly relaxed, and all their hopes of riches
dissipated.   Then there is the greatest blot of all
on Cortés' career, the execution of Guatémoc
during the march to Honduras ; no one can help
feeling that it was wrong, but there is nothing
to show that the reason advanced by Cortés was
not a good one.   It was only too probable that the
Mexicans, longing to return to their homes, were
plotting against the Spaniards to effect it.   Had
such a plot been successful the Spaniards were
inevitably lost.   That Cortés was not in a state of
mind propitious to the careful weighing of evidence
may at once be admitted ; a long, dangerous and
toilsome march through a tropical forest is not
conducive to unruffled temper.   However, the
execution of Guatémoc, if it was an error, may
have been more distinctly an error than a crime.

From our point of view the Spaniards were cruel and ruthless enough; an army of unbaptized Indians was no more to them than a herd of swine, but their callous cruelty can be no more surprising to us than their childlike belief in the miraculous power of the images and crosses which they substituted for the native idols, or their firm belief in the teaching of their Church, which did not admit that an Indian had the rights of a human being until he was baptized.

Neither in the sixteenth nor the twentieth century would troops that have seen their companions-in-arms captured and led to execution to grace the festival of a heathen god, and afford material for a cannibal feast, be likely to treat their enemies with much consideration, but the fate of the vanquished Mexicans was humane to what it would have been had the victors been Tlaxcalans or other tribes of their own race and religion.

These concluding remarks are not made with the intention of whitewashing the character of the *Conquistadores*, their faults are sufficiently evident, but to impress on the reader the necessity of taking all the factors of the case into consideration when forming a judgment.

The bravery of the Indians was magnificent, and their courage and endurance during the last days of the siege of Mexico is unrivalled, but Bernal Díaz's narrative is written from the Spanish point of view, and it is on the conduct of the Spaniards alone that I feel the need of making any comment.

The character of Bernal Díaz himself shows clearly enough in his story ; it is that of a lovable old soldier such as novelists have delighted to portray in Napoleon's "Old Guard," simple, enduring, splendidly courageous and unaffectedly vain.

Censure without stint has been heaped on Cortés and his followers for their treatment of the Indians, but no one has ever ventured to question the spirit and resource of that great leader nor the daring courage and endurance shown both by him and his followers.

I gladly take this opportunity of thanking Don Genaro García for permission to make the Translation from his Edition of the *True History* and for his unfailing courtesy and encouragement during the progress of the work, and of thanking Don José Romero of the Mexican Foreign Office for the loan of books of reference from his valuable collection and for other acts of kindness.

NOTE ON SPELLING, Etc.

GREAT difficulty has arisen over the spelling of the Indian names of persons and places. In the original text a native name has often several variants, and each one of these may differ from the more generally-accepted form.

In the Translation a purely arbitrary course has been adopted, but it is one which will probably prove more acceptable to the general reader. Such words as Montezuma (Motecuhzoma) and Huichilobos (Huitzilopochtli) are spelt as Bernal Díaz usually spells them ; others, such as Guaçacalco, which occurs in the text in at least three different forms, has in the Translation always been given in the more generally-accepted form of Coatzacoalcos.

At the end of each volume a list of names is printed, arranged alphabetically, showing the variants in the original text, the usually-accepted forms, the spelling of place-names generally found in modern maps, and when possible the form now used by modern Maya and Nahuatl scholars.

Spanish names are always printed in the Translation in the generally-accepted forms : thus Xpvl de Oli of the text is printed as Cristóbal de Olid. The names of certain Spanish offices, such as Alguacil, Regidor, are retained in the Translation, as well as the " Fraile (or Padre) de la Merced " for the " Friar of the Order of Mercy," but all foreign words used in the Translation are printed in italics when they first occur, and are referred to in foot-notes, and a Glossary is given at the end of each volume.

Square brackets [ ] enclose words inserted by the translator.

Notes to the Mexican Edition of 1904, edited by Sʳ Don Genaro García, are marked " G. G."

The 214 Chapters have been divided into Books with sub-headings by the Translator for convenience of reference. No such division or sub-headings exist in the original Manuscript or in Sʳ García's Mexican Edition.

ITINERARY.

THE EXPEDITION UNDER FRANCISCO HERNÁNDEZ DE CÓRDOVA.

	Santiago de Cuba.
8th Feb., 1517 .	Axaruco (Jaruco).
	Gran Cairo, Yucatan (near Cape Catoche).
Sunday, day of San Lázaro.	Campeche (San Lázaro).
	Chanpotón (or Potonchan).
(Return Voyage) .	Estero de los Lagartos.
	Florida.
	Los Martires—The Shoals of the Martyrs.
	Puerto de Carenas (the modern Havana).

THE EXPEDITION UNDER JUAN DE GRIJALVA.

	Santiago de Cuba.	
8th April, 1518 .	Matanzas . . .	18 April, 1518.
	Puerto de Carenas (Havana)	22 April, 1518.
	Cape San Anton . .	1 May.
The day of Santa Cruz, 3rd May.	Cozumel (Santa Cruz) .	3-11 May.
	Bahia de la Ascencion .	13-16 May.
	Chanpotón . . .	25-28 May.
	Boca de Términos (Puerto Deseado or P. Real).	31 May to 5 June.
	Rio de Grijalva (Tabasco) .	7-11 June.
	Sighted Ayagualulco (La Rambla).	
	Sighted Rio de Tonalá (San Anton).	
	Sighted Rio de Coatzacoalcos.	
	Sighted Sierra de San Martin.	
	Rio de Papaloapan (Rio de Alvarado) and Tlacotlalpan.	
	Rio de Banderas (Rio Jamapa)	
	Sighted Isla Blanca and Isla Verde.	
	Isla de Sacrificios . .	17 June.

St. John's day, 24th June.	San Juan de Ulua . .	18-24 June.
	Sighted the Sierra de Tuxpan.	
	Rio de Canoas (R. Tanguijo) (Cape Rojo).	28 June.
Return Voyage .	Sighted Rio de Coatzacoalcos	9 July.
	Rio de Tonalá (San Anton) .	12-20 July.
	Puerto de Términos . .	17-22 August.
	Puerto Deseado . .	1 September.
	Small island near Chanpotón	3 September.
	Campeche . . .	5-8 September.
	Bajos de Sisal (?) . .	11-12 September.
	Rio de Lagartos . .	14-15 September.
	Conil near Cape Catoche .	21 September.
	Sighted Cuba . . .	29 September.
	Puerto de Carenas (Havana)	30 September.
	Jaruco	4 October.
	Santiago de Cuba . .	15 November.[1]

EXPEDITION UNDER HERNANDO CORTÉS.

	Santiago de Cuba . . .	18th Nov., 1518.
	Sailed from Trinidad . .	January, 1519.
10th Feb., 1519	Sailed from (San Cristóbal ?) de Havana on the South Coast near Batabano.	10th Feb., 1519.
	Sailed from Cape San Anton .	11th Feb., 1519.
	Sailed from Cozumel . .	5th March.
	Sailed from Punta de las Mujeres	6th March.
	Returned to Cozumel.	
4th March .	Sailed from Cozumel . .	13th March.
	Boca de Términos.	
12th March[2] .	Arrived at Rio de Grijalva or Tabasco.	22nd March.
25th March, Lady Day.	Battle of Cintla . . .	25th March.
Palm Sunday .	Sailed from Santa Maria de la Victoria.	18th April.
Holy Thursday	Arrived at San Juan de Ulua .	21st April, Holy Thursday.

In the above Itineraries the dates given by Bernal Díaz, which are few in number, are placed on the left.

---

[1] See Padre Agustin Rivera, *Anales Mexicanos*, vol. i, p. 47.

[2] This is clearly an error.

Orozco y Berra (*Hist. Antigua*, vol. iv) has compiled an account of the voyage, with dates, from many sources, including "The Itinerario," Oviedo, Las Casas, Herrera, Gomara, etc.   These dates will be found on the right-hand column.

Places not mentioned by Bernal Díaz as stopping-places of the expedition are printed in italics.

The True History

of the

Conquest of New Spain,

BY

BERNAL DÍAZ DEL CASTILLO,

ONE OF ITS CONQUERORS.

From the only exact copy made of the Original Manuscript.

EDITED, AND PUBLISHED IN MEXICO,

BY

GENARO GARCÍA.

TRANSLATED INTO ENGLISH, WITH INTRODUCTION AND NOTES,

BY

ALFRED PERCIVAL MAUDSLAY, M.A.,

HON. PROFESSOR OF ARCHÆOLOGY, NATIONAL MUSEUM,
MEXICO.

VOL. I.

CHS. I—LXXXI.

[PREFACE.]

I HAVE observed that the most celebrated chroniclers before they begin to write their histories, first set forth a prologue and preface with the argument expressed in lofty rhetoric in order to give lustre and repute to their statements, so that the studious readers who peruse them may partake of their melody and flavour. But I, being no Latin scholar, dare not venture on such a preamble or prologue, for in order properly to extol the adventures which we met with and the heroic deeds we accomplished during the Conquest of New Spain and its provinces in the company of that valiant and doughty Captain, Don Hernando Cortés (who later on, on account of his heroic deeds, was made Marqués del Valle[1]) there would be needed an eloquence and rhetoric far beyond my powers. That which I have myself seen and the fighting I have gone through, with the help of God I will describe, quite simply, as a fair eye witness without twisting events one way or another. I am now an old man, over eighty-four years of age, and I have lost my sight and hearing, and, as luck would have it, I have gained nothing of value to leave to my children and descendants, but this my true

[1] Created Marqués del Valle de Guajaca (Oaxaca) by the Emperor Charles V. The *Cedula* is dated Barcelona, 6th July, 1529.

story, and they will presently find out what a wonderful story it is.

I will do no more now than give evidence of my nationality and birthplace, and note the year in which I set out from Castille and the names of the captains in whose company I went as a soldier, and state where I am now settled and have my home.

BOOK I.—THE DISCOVERY.

THE EXPEDITION UNDER FRANCISCO HERNÁNDEZ DE CÓRDOVA

CHAPTER I.

The beginning of the story.

 BERNAL DÍAZ DEL CASTILLO, citizen and Regidor of the most loyal city of Santiago de Guatemala, one of the first discoverers and conquerors of New Spain and its provinces, and the Cape of Honduras and all that lies within that land, a Native of the very noble and distinguished town of Medina del Campo, and the son of its former *Regidor*, Francisco Díaz del Castillo, who was also called "The graceful," (may his soul rest in glory), speak about that which concerns myself and all the true conquerors my companions who served His Majesty by discovering, conquering, pacifying and settling most of the provinces of New Spain, and that it is one of the best countries yet discovered in the New World, we found out by our own efforts without His Majesty knowing anything about it.

I also speak here in reply to all that has been said and written by persons who themselves knowing nothing, have received no true account from others of what really took place, but who nevertheless now put forward any statements that happen to suit their fancy. As there is no account of our many and remarkable services such as their merits deserve * * * * * * * these indifferent story-tellers are now unwilling that we should receive the recompense and * * * * * which His Majesty has ordered his Governors and Viceroys to afford us.

Apart from these reasons such deeds as those I am going on to describe, cannot be forgotten, and the truth about them will be proved afresh, but, as in the books which have been written on the subject the truth has so often been perverted, [I write this history] so that when tales are told of daring deeds our fame shall not suffer, and that on account of such brilliant adventures our names may be placed among the most famous, for we have run the risk of death and wounds, and have suffered a thousand other miseries, venturing our lives in discovering lands about which nothing whatever was known, battling by day and by night with a host of doughty warriors, at so great a distance from Castille that no aid or assistance could reach us, save the only true help, namely the loving kindness of our Lord God whom it has pleased that we should conquer New Spain and the far-famed city of Tenochtitlan,[1] Mexico, for so it is called, and many other cities and provinces which are too numerous for me to name. As soon as we had the country pacified and settled by Spaniards, we thought it to be our duty as good and loyal subjects of His Majesty, with much respect for our King and natural Lord, to hand the country over to him. With that

---

[1] Tenuztitlan in the original.

intent we sent our Ambassadors to Castille and thence to Flanders where his Majesty at that time held his Court. I shall also tell about all the good results that came of it, and about the large number of souls which have been saved, and are daily being saved, by conversion to the faith, all of which souls were formerly lost in Hell. In addition to this holy work, attention will be called to the great treasure which we sent as a present to his Majesty, and that which has been sent and is being sent daily and is in the form of the Royal Fifths,[1] as well as in the large amounts carried off by many persons of all classes. I shall tell in this story who was the first discoverer of the province of Yucatan, and how we went to the discovery of New Spain and who were the Captains and soldiers who conquered and settled it and many other things which happened during the conquest, which are worth knowing and should not be forgotten; all this I shall relate as briefly as possible, and above all with the assured truth of an eye witness.

[2]If I were to remember and recount one by one the heroic [deeds] which we, one and all of us valiant captains and brave [soldiers] accomplished, from the beginning to the end of the conquest, reciting each deed as it deserved, it would, indeed, be a great [undertaking,] and would need a very famous historian [to carry it out] with greater eloquence and style than my poor words [can compass.] As later on *   *   *   * when I was present and saw and understood, and I will call to mind *   *   *   * that repeats *   *   *   * imposed as a duty—and delicate style and I *   *   *   * I will write it with God's

---

[1] The tax on all bullion and other treasure paid to the Crown.

[2] In the following passages many of the words of the Manuscript are rubbed and worn out. When the meaning is obvious the missing words are supplied in brackets in the translation. When the meaning is not clear the spaces are marked with asterisks.

help with honest truth * * * * of the wise
elders who say that a good style * * * * is
to tell the truth and * * * * [not] to exaggerate
and flatter * * * * others, especially in a nar-'
rative like this * * * * would die of it, and
because I am no latin scholar and do not understand
the art * * * * I will not treat of it, for I say I
understand [only] the battles and pacifications where I
was myself present, for I was one of the first [to set out]
from Cuba in the company of a Captain named Francisco
[Hernández de Córdova] and we were accompanied on
that voyage by one hundred and ten soldiers, we explored
* * * * they stopped (?) at the first place at
which one landed which is called Cape [Catoche and at] a
town further on called Chanpoton more than half of us
[were killed and] the Captain received ten arrow wounds
and all the rest of us soldiers got two [arrow wounds and
the Indians] a[ttack]ing us with such skill we were obliged,
with the greatest difficulty to return to the Island [of
Cuba whence] we had set out with the fleet, and the
captain died almost as soon as we landed, and of the
one hundred and ten soldiers who set out with us, fifty-
seven were left behind, dead.

After this first warlike expedition, I set out a second
time from this same Island of Cuba under another captain,
named Juan de Grijalva, and we again had great warlike
encounters with these same Indians of the *Pueblo* of
Chanpoton, and in this second battle many of our soldiers
were killed. From that Pueblo we went on along the
coast, exploring, until we arrived at New Spain and then
kept on our way until we reached the province of Panuco.
Then a second time we had to turn back to the Island
of Cuba, baffled and exhausted both from hunger and
thirst, and from other reasons which I will set forth in the
chapter which treats of this expedition.

To go back to my story ; I set out for the third time with the daring and valiant captain Don Hernando Cortés, who later on was made Marqués del Valle and received other titles of honour. I repeat that no other captain or soldier went to New Spain three times in succession on one expedition after another as I did, so that I am the earliest discoverer and conqueror who has ever lived or is now living in New Spain. Although many soldiers went twice on voyages of discovery, the first time with Juan de Grijalva whom I have already mentioned, and the second time with the gallant captain Cortés, yet they never went three times in succession. If they went the first time with Francisco Hernández de Córdova, they did not go the second time with Grijalva, nor the third time with the valiant Cortés. God has been pleased to preserve me through many risks of death, both during this laborious discovery, and in the very bloody Mexican wars (and I give God many thanks for it), in order that I may tell and declare the events that happened in those wars, so that studious readers may give them attention and thought.

I was twenty-four years old when Diego Velásquez, the Governor of the Island of Cuba, who was my kinsman, promised to give me some Indians as soon as there were any available, but I did not care to be kept waiting until this should happen. I always had a zeal for soldiering, as it is becoming that a man should have, both in order to serve God and the king and to endeavour to gain renown, and as being such a life that honourable men should seek, and I gradually put from my mind the death of my companions who were killed in those times and the wounds that I myself received, and the fatigue and hardship I endured and which all must endure who set out to discover new lands, and, being as we were, but a small company, dare to enter into great towns swarming with hostile warriors. I myself was always at the front and never descended to the many vices prevalent in the island of Cuba, as will be clearly seen in the course of this story.

In the year fifteen hundred and fourteen, I came from Castille and began my career as a soldier on Tierra-firme,[1] then went on to the discovery of Yucatan and New Spain, and as my forefathers, my father and my brother had always been servants of the crown and of the Catholic kings of glorious memory Don Fernando and Doña Ysabel, I wished to be something like them.

In the year 1514, as I have already said, there came out as Governor of Tierra-firme, a gentleman named Pedrárias Dávila.[2] I agreed to go with him to his Government and the country conquered by him. So as to shorten the story, I will not relate what happened on the voyage, more than to say sometimes with good weather and other times with bad weather, we arrived at Nombre de Dios, for so it was named.

Some three or four months after the settlement was formed, there came a pestilence from which many soldiers died, and in addition to this, all the rest of us fell ill and suffered from bad ulcers on the legs. Then disputes arose between the Governor and a nobleman named Vasco Nuñez de Balboa, the captain, who had conquered that province, to whom Pedrárias Dávila had given his daughter (Doña somebody Arias de Peñalosa) in marriage. But it seems that after marriage, he grew suspicious of his son-in-law, believing that he would rise in rebellion and lead a body of soldiers towards the South Sea, so he gave orders that Balboa should have his throat cut and certain of the soldiers should be punished.

As we were witnesses of what I have related, and of other revolts among the captains, and as the news reached

---

[1] Tierra-firme = the Spanish Main.

[2] Pedro Arias de Ávila.

us that the Island of Cuba had lately been conquered and
settled, and that a gentleman named Diego Velásquez, a
native of Cuellar, who has already been mentioned by me,
had been made Governor of the Island, some of us gentlemen and persons of quality, who had come out with
Pedrárias Dávila, made up our minds to ask him to give
us permission to go to Cuba, and he willingly did so, as he
had no need of all the soldiers he had brought with him
from Castille, as there was no one left to conquer.   Indeed
the country under his rule is small and thinly peopled,
and his son-in-law Vasco Nuñez de Balboa had already
conquered it and ensured peace.

As soon as leave was granted we embarked in a good
ship and with fair weather reached the Island of Cuba.
On landing we went at once to pay our respects to the
Governor, who was pleased at our coming, and promised
to give us Indians as soon as there were any to spare.

When three years had gone by, counting both the time
we were in Tierra-firme and that which we had passed in
the Island of Cuba, and it became evident that we were
merely wasting our time, one hundred and ten of us got
together, most of us comrades who had come from Tierra-
firme, and the other Spaniards of Cuba who had had no
Indians assigned to them, and we made an agreement with
a gentleman named Francisco Hernández de Córdova,[1]
whose name I have already mentioned, a rich man who
owned an Indian Pueblo in the Island, that he should be
our leader, for he was well fitted for the post, and that we
should try our fortune in seeking and exploring new lands
where we might find employment.

With this object in view, we purchased three ships, two

---

[1] The three partners in this expedition were Francisco Hernández
de Córdova, Lope Ochoa de Caicedo and Cristóval Morante. (See
letter from the Municipality of Vera Cruz, dated 10th July, 1519.
Usually known as Cortés' first letter.)

of them of good capacity, and the third, a bark, bought on
credit from the Governor, Diego Velásquez, on the condition that all of us soldiers should go in the three vessels
to some islands lying between Cuba and Honduras, which
are now called the Islands of the Guanajes,[1] and make war
on the natives and load the vessels with Indians, as slaves,
with which to pay him for his bark.   However, as we
soldiers knew that what Diego Velásquez asked of us was
not just, we answered that it was neither in accordance
with the law of God nor of the king, that we should make
free men slaves.   When he saw that we had made up
our minds, he said that our plan to go and discover new
countries was better than his, and he helped us in providing
food for our voyage.   Certain inquisitive gentlemen have
asked me why I have written down these words which
Diego Velásquez uttered about selling us the ship, and
they say they have an ugly look and should not have been
inserted in this history.   I reply that I write them here
because it is desirable on account of the law suits which
Diego Velásquez and the Bishop of Burgos and Archbishop of Rosano, whose name is Juan Rodríguez de
Fonseca, brought against us.

To return to my story, we now found ourselves with
three ships stored with Cassava[2] bread, which is made
from a root, and we bought some pigs which cost three
dollars apiece, for in those days there were neither sheep
nor cattle in the Island of Cuba, for it was only beginning
to be settled, and we added a supply of oil, and bought
beads and other things of small value to be used for
barter.   We then sought out three pilots, of whom the
chief, who took charge of the fleet, was called Anton de
Alaminos a native of Palos, the second came from Triana

---

[1] Roatan, Bonacca, etc.   Islands near the coast of Honduras.
[2] Cassava bread.   Made from the root of Manihoc utilissima.

and was named Camacho, and the third was Juan Alvarez " el Manquillo "[1] from Huelva. We also engaged the necessary number of sailors and procured the best supply that we could afford of ropes, cordage, cables, and anchors, and casks for water and other things needed for the voyage, and thⁱs all to our own cost and regret.

When all the soldiers were mustered, we set out for a port which in the Indian language is called Axaruco,[2] on the North coast, eight leagues from a town named San Cristóbal, which was then inhabited and which two years later was moved to the present site of Havana. In order that our voyage should proceed on right principles we wished to take with us a priest named Alonso González who was then living in the said town of San Cristóbal, and he agreed to come with us. We also chose for the office of *Veedor*,[3] (in his Majesty's name), a soldier named Bernaldino Yñiguez, a native of Santo Domingo de la Calzada, so that if God willed that we should come on rich lands, or people who possessed gold or silver or pearls or any other kind of treasure, there should be a responsible person to guard the Royal Fifth.

After all was arranged and we had heard Mass, we commended ourselves to God our Lord, and to Our Lady, the sainted Virgin Mary, His blessed Mother, and set out on our voyage in the way I will now relate.

---

[1] El Manquillo = the little maimed or one-handed man.

[2] Jaruco is shown on modern maps about twelve miles to the east of the present city of Havana.
The name of Havana at this time appears to have applied to the district.
San Cristóbal was on the south coast of the Island, which is here about eight leagues across from sea to sea.

[3] Veedor (obsolete) = overseer, caterer, official in charge of the stores.

CHAPTER II.

How we discovered the Province of Yucatan.

ON the eighth day of the month of February in the year
fifteen hundred and seventeen, we left the Havana from
the port of Axaruco, which is on the North coast, and in
twelve days we doubled Cape San Antonio, which is also
called in the Island of Cuba the land of the Guanaha-
taveyes, who are Indians like savages. When we had
passed this Cape we were in the open sea and trusting
to luck we steered towards the setting sun, knowing
nothing of the depth of water, nor of the currents, nor of
the winds which usually prevail in that latitude, so we ran
great risk of our lives, then a storm struck us which lasted
two days and two nights, and raged with such strength
that we were nearly lost.   When the weather moderated,
we kept on our course, and twenty-one days after leaving
port, we sighted land, at which we rejoiced greatly and
gave thanks to God.   This land had never been discovered
before and no report of it had reached us.   From the
ships we could see a large town standing back about two
leagues from the coast, and as we had never seen such a
large town in the Island of Cuba nor in Hispaniola, we
named it the Great Cairo.

We arranged that the two vessels which drew the least
water should go in as near as possible to the Coast, to
examine the land and see if there was an anchorage near
the shore.   On the morning of the 4th March, we saw ten
large canoes, called *piraguas*, full of Indians from the
town, approaching us with oars and sails.   The canoes
were large ones made like hollow troughs cleverly cut out
from huge single logs, and many of them would hold forty
Indians.

To go back to my story ; the Indians in the ten canoes

came close to our ships, and we made signs of peace to them, beckoning with our hands and waving our cloaks to induce them to come and speak to us, although at that time we had no interpreters who could speak the languages of Yucatan and Mexico. They approached quite fearlessly and more than thirty of them came on board the flagship, and we gave them each a present of a string of green beads, and they passed some time examining the ships. The chief man among them, who was a *Cacique*, made signs to us that they wished to embark in their canoes and return to their town, and that they would come back again another day with more canoes in which we could go ashore.

These Indians were clothed in cotton shirts made like jackets, and covered their persons with a narrow cloth which they call *masteles*, and they seemed to us a people superior to the Cubans, for the Cuban Indians go about naked, only the women wearing a cloth reaching to the thighs, which cloths they call *naguas*.[1]

To return to my story; the next morning the same *Cacique* returned to the ships and brought twelve large canoes, which I have already said are called *piraguas*, with Indian rowers, and with a cheerful face and every appearance of friendliness, made signs that we should go to his town, where they would feed us and supply all our needs, and that in those canoes of his we could land.

He kept on saying in his language, " *cones catoche*", " *cones catoche*", which means " come to my houses", and for that reason we called the land Cape Catoche, and it is still so named on the charts.

When our captain and the soldiers saw the friendly

---

[1] Why the author should have written " que llaman naguas " is not clear. Enaguas or naguas is the Spanish, not the Cuban, word for the skirt, petticoat or upper skirt of a woman's dress.

overtures the chief was making to us, we agreed to lower the boats from our ships, and in the vessel of least draught, and in the twelve canoes, to go ashore all together, and because we saw that the shore was crowded with Indians from the town, we arranged to land all of us at the same moment.   When the Cacique saw us all on shore, but showing no intention of going to his town, he again made signs to our captain that we should go with him to his houses, and he showed such evidence of peace and good-will, that our captain asked our advice whether we should go on or no, and most of the soldiers were of opinion that with the precaution of taking all our arms with us we should go on, and we took with us fifteen crossbows and ten muskets, so with the Cacique as our guide, we began our march along the road, accompanied by many Indians.

We moved on in this way until we approached some brush-covered hillocks, when the Cacique began to shout and call out to some squadrons of warriors who were lying in ambush ready to fall upon us and kill us.   On hearing the Cacique's shouts, the warriors attacked us in great haste and fury, and began to shoot with such skill that the first flight of arrows wounded fifteen soldiers.

These warriors wore armour made of cotton reaching to the knees and carried lances and shields, bows and arrows, slings and many stones.

After the flight of arrows, the warriors, with their feathered crests waving, attacked us hand to hand, and hurling their lances with all their might they did us much damage.   However, thank God, we soon put them to flight when they felt the sharp edge of our swords, and the effect of our guns and crossbows, and fifteen of them fell dead.

A short distance ahead of the place where they attacked us, was a small *plaza* with three houses built of masonry, which served as *Cues*[1] and oratories.[2]　These houses contained many pottery Idols, some with the faces of demons and others with women's faces, and there were others of evil figures of Indians who appeared to be committing sodomy one with another.

Within the houses were some small wooden chests, and in them were some other Idols, and some little discs made partly of gold but more than half of copper, and some necklaces and three diadems, and other small objects in the form of fish and others like the ducks of the country, all made of inferior gold.

When we had seen the gold and the houses of masonry, we felt well content at having discovered such a country, for at that time Peru was unknown, indeed, it was not discovered until twenty years later.

While we were fighting with the Indians, the priest González had accompanied us, and he took charge of the chests and the gold, and the Idols, and carried them to the ship.　In these skirmishes we took two Indians prisoners, and later on, when they were baptized, one was named Julian and the other Melchior, both of them were cross-eyed.　When the fight was over we returned to our ships, and went on exploring along the coast towards the setting sun, we set sail as soon as the wounded were cared for, and what else happened I will tell later on.

---

[1] *Cue* is the name commonly applied to the Indian shrines or temples, usually small buildings raised on pyramidal foundations.　It is not a Maya or Mexican word, but one picked up by the Spaniards in the Antilles.

[2] It should be noted that, although the Spaniards had now been in America for twenty-four years and had explored the Islands and the coast of the mainland from the mouth of the Orinoco to the Bay of Honduras, and part of the coast of Florida, this was the first time they had seen houses and temples built of stone ; and with the exception of the crew of a canoe which Columbus met during his fourth voyage near the Islands of the Guanajes off the coast of Honduras, this was the first meeting of the Spaniards with any of the more civilised races of America.

CHAPTER III.

How we coasted along towards the west, discovering capes and
deep water, roadsteads and reefs.

BELIEVING this land to be an Island, as the Pilot, Anton
de Alaminos, had assured us that it was, we travelled with
the greatest caution, sailing only by day and anchoring by
night.   After voyaging in this manner for fifteen days, we
descried from the ship, what appeared to be a large town
near to a great bay or creek, and we thought that there
might be a river or stream there, where we could provide ourselves with water of which we had great need,.
because the casks and other vessels which we had brought
with us, were not watertight.   It was because our fleet was
manned by poor men who had not money enough to
purchase good casks and cables, that the water ran short.
We had to land near the town, and as it was Sunday, the
day of San Lazaro, we gave the town that name, and so it
is marked on the charts, but its proper Indian name is
Campeche.

In order that we could all of us land at the same time,
we agreed to approach the shore in the smallest of the
vessels, and in the three boats, with all our arms ready, so
as not to be caught as we had been at Cape Catoche.

In these roadsteads and bays, the water shallows very
considerably at low tide, so that we had to leave our ships
anchored more than a league from the shore.

We went ashore near the town where there was a pool
of good water, used by the people of the place for drinking
water, for as far as we had seen there were no rivers in this
country.   We landed the casks, intending to fill them with
water, and return to our ships.   When the casks were full,
and we were ready to embark, a company of about fifty
Indians, clad in good cotton mantles, came out in a peace-

ful manner from the town. From their appearance we
believed them to be Caciques, and they asked us by signs
what it was we were looking for, and we gave them to
understand that we had come for water, and wished to
return at once to our ships. They then made signs with
their hands to find out whether we came from the direction
of the sunrise, repeating the word " Castilan " " Castilan "
and we did not understand what they meant by Castilan.
They then asked us by signs to go with them to their
town, and we took council together as to what we should
do, and decided to go with them, keeping well on the alert
and in good formation.

They led us to some large houses very well built of
masonry, which were the Temples of their Idols, and on
the walls were figured the bodies of many great serpents
and snakes and other pictures of evil-looking Idols. These
walls surrounded a sort of Altar covered with clotted
blood. On the other side of the Idols were symbols like
crosses, and all were coloured. At all this we stood
wondering, as they were things never seen or heard of
before.

It seemed as though certain Indians had just offered
sacrifices to their Idols so as to ensure victory over us.
However, many Indian women moved about us, laughing,
and with every appearance of good will, but the Indians
gathered in such numbers that we began to fear that
there might be some trap set for us as at Catoche. While
this was happening, many other Indians approached us,
wearing very ragged mantles and carrying dry reeds,
which they deposited upon the plain, and behind them
came two squadrons of Indian archers in cotton armour,
carrying lances and shields, slings and stones, and each
captain drew up his squadron at a short distance from
where we stood. At that moment, there sallied from
another house, which was an oratory of their Idols, ten

Indians clad in long white cotton cloaks, reaching to their feet, and with their long hair reeking with blood, and so matted together, that it could never be parted or even combed out again, unless it were cut. These were the priests of the Idols, who in New Spain are commonly called *papas* and such I shall call them hereafter. These priests brought us incense of a sort of resin which they call *copal*, and with pottery braziers full of live coals, they began to fumigate us, and by signs they made us understand that we should quit their land before the firewood which they had piled up there should burn out, otherwise they would attack us and kill us. After ordering fire to be put to the reeds, the priests withdrew without further speech. Then the warriors who were drawn up in battle array began to whistle and sound their trumpets and drums. When we perceived their menacing appearance and saw great squadrons of Indians bearing down on us we remembered that we had not yet recovered from the wounds received at Cape Catoche, and had been obliged to throw overboard the bodies of two soldiers who had died, and fear fell on us, so we determined to retreat to the coast in good order, and began to march along the shore towards a large rock which rose out of the sea, while the boats and the small bark laden with the water casks coasted along close in shore. We had not dared to embark near the town where we had landed, on account of the great press of Indians, for we felt sure they would attack us as we tried to get in the boats. As soon as we had embarked and got the casks on board the ships, we sailed on for six days and nights in good weather, then we were struck by a *norther* which is a foul wind on that coast and it lasted four days and nights, and so strong was the storm that it nearly drove us ashore, so that we had to drop anchor, but we broke two cables, and one ship began to drag her anchor. Ah! the danger was terrible, for if

our last cable had given way we should have been driven
ashore to destruction, but thank God we were able to ease
the strain on the cable by lashing it with pieces of rope
and hawsers, and at last the weather moderated.   Then
we kept on our course along the coast, going ashore
whenever we were able to do so to get water, for, as I have
already said, the casks we carried were not only leaky, but
were gaping open, and we could not depend upon them,
and we hoped that by keeping near the coast we should be
able to find water, whenever we landed, either in pools or
by digging for it.

As we were sailing along on our course, we came in
sight of a town, and about a league on the near side of it,
there was a bay which looked as though it had a river or
stream running into it ; so we determined to anchor.   On
this coast the tide runs out so far that there is danger of
the ships being stranded, so for fear of this we dropped
anchor at the distance of a league from the shore, and we
landed in that bay from the vessel of least draught and
from the boats, carrying all our casks along with us to fill
them with water.   We landed soon after mid-day, well
armed with crossbows and guns.   This landing place was
about a league from the town, near to some pools of
water, and maize plantations, and a few small houses
built of masonry.   The town is called Potonchan.[1]

---

[1] This town is called both Potonchan and Chanpoton by Bernal
Díaz, and Chanpoton in the " Itinirario" and in the Letter from the
Municipality of Vera Cruz to Chas. V.   In modern maps it is called
Champoton.   There is a further difficulty about the name of this
town, because the town at the mouth of the Rio de Grijalva (Sta.
Maria de la Victoria) was also called Potonchon or Potonchan.   In
the "Relacion de la Villa de Santa Maria de la Victoria" (1579), printed
in the Documentos Ineditos, Relaciones de Yucatan (Madrid, 1898)
we find : "This province is called the province of Tabasco, because
the Lord of this town was called Tabasco, and the name of the town
is Potonchan, which in Spanish means the Chontal tongue, almost as
though we should say the barbarous tongue, for Chontal in the Mexican
language is the same as barbarous, and so this town is called Potonchan, as that is the language generally used in this province ; and as

We filled our casks with water, but we could not carry them away on account of the great number of warriors who fell on us. I will stop now and tell later on about the attack they made on us.

CHAPTER IV.

Concerning the attack made on us as we stood among the farms and maize fields already mentioned.

As we were filling our casks with water there came along the coast towards us from the town of Potonchan[1] (as it is called) many squadrons of Indians clad in cotton armour reaching to the knees, and armed with bows and arrows, lances and shields, and swords like two handed broad swords, and slings and stones and carrying the feathered crests which they are accustomed to wear. Their faces were painted black and white, and ruddled and they came in silence straight towards us, as though they came in peace, and by signs they asked whether we came from where the sun rose, and we replied that we did come from the direction of the sunrise. We were at our wits end considering the matter and wondering what the words were which the Indians called out to us for they were the same as those used by the people of Lázaro, but we never made out what it was that they said.

---

the Lord of this town was called Tabasco the province is called Tabasco."

Santa Maria de la Victoria appears to have lost both its original native and its Spanish name, and soon became known as the town of Tabasco, and is so marked on the map of Melchor de Santa Cruz (1579); not long afterwards the town itself disappeared.

Chanpoton has retained its name, and when Bernal Díaz mentions Chanpoton or Potonchan he invariably intends to indicate the site of the modern Champoton, between Campeche and the Laguna de Términos, the "Costa de Mala Pelea" of the expedition under Francisco Hernández de Córdova.

[1] Here written Pontuchan in the original text = Chanpoton.

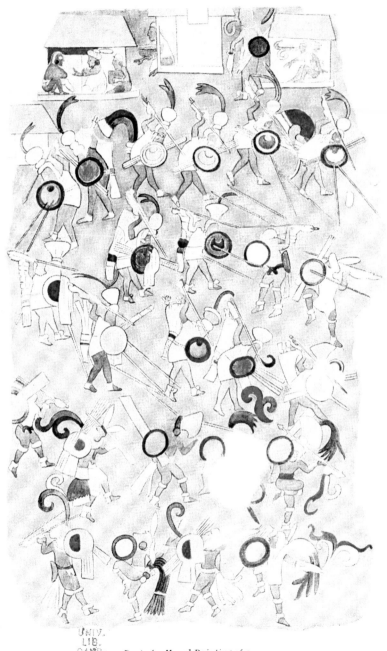

Part of a Mural Painting of a
BATTLE FROM THE BALL COURT TEMPLE CHICHÉN ITZÁ, YUCATAN.
After a drawing by Miss Adela Breton.
Reproduced and printed for the Hakluyt Society by Donald Macbeth. 1908.

Plate 2.　　　　　　　　　　　　　　　　　　　　*To face page 22.*

All this happened about the time of the Ave Maria, and the Indians then went off to some villages in the neighbourhood, and we posted watchmen and sentinels for security, for we did not like such a large gathering of Indians.

While we were keeping watch during the night we heard a great squadron of Indian warriors approaching from the town and from the farms, and we knew well that their assembly boded us no good, and we took council together as to what should be done. Some of the soldiers were of opinion that we should embark without delay; however as always happens in such cases, some said one thing and some said another, but the Indians being in such numbers it seemed to most of my companions that if we made any attempt to embark they would be sure to attack us, and we should run great risk of losing our lives. Some others were of opinion that we should fall upon the Indians that very night, for, as the proverb says "who attacks conquers". On the other hand we could see that there were about two hundred Indians to every one of us. While we were still taking council the dawn broke, and we said one to the other "let us strengthen our hearts for the fight, and after commending ourselves to God let us do our best to save our lives."

As soon as it was daylight we could see, coming along the coast, many more Indian warriors with their banners raised, and with feathered crests and drums, and they joined those warriors who had assembled the night before. When their squadrons were formed up they surrounded us on all sides and poured in such showers of arrows and darts, and stones thrown from their slings that over eighty of us soldiers were wounded, and they attacked us hand to hand, some with lances and the others shooting arrows, and others with two-handed

knife edged swords,[1] and they brought us to a bad pass.
We gave them a good return of thrusts and cuts and the
guns and crossbows never ceased their work, some being
loaded while the others were fired. At last feeling the
effects of our sword play they drew back a little, but
it was not far, and only enabled them to shoot their
stones and darts at us with greater safety to themselves.

While the battle was raging the Indians called to one
another in their language " *al Calachuni, Calachuni* " which
means " let us attack the Captain and kill him," and ten
times they wounded him with their arrows ; and me they
struck thrice, one arrow wounding me dangerously in the
left side, piercing through the ribs. All the other soldiers
were wounded by spear thrusts and two of them were
carried off alive, one named Alonzo Boto, and the other
an old Portuguese man.

Our captain then saw that our good fighting availed us
nothing ; other squadrons of warriors were approaching
us fresh from the town, bringing food and drink with them
and a large supply of arrows. All our soldiers were
wounded with two or three arrow wounds, three of them
had their throats pierced by lance thrusts, our captain was
bleeding from many wounds and already fifty of the
soldiers were lying dead.

Feeling that our strength was exhausted we determined
with stout hearts to break through the battalions surrounding us and seek shelter in the boats which awaited
us near the shore, and proved to be a great assistance to
us ; so we formed in close array and broke through the
enemy.

Ah ! then to hear the yells, hisses and cries, as the

---

[1] *Macana* or *Macuahuitl*, a wooden sword edged with sharp flint
or obsidian.

enemy showered arrows on us and hurled lances with all their might, wounding us sorely.

Then another danger befell us ; as we all sought shelter in the boats at the same time and there were so many of us they began to sink, so in the best way we could manage hanging on to the waterlogged boats and half swimming, we reached the vessel of lightest draught which came in all haste to our assistance.

Many of us were wounded while we embarked, especially those who were sitting in the stern of the boats, for the Indians shot at them as targets, and even waded into the sea with their lances and attacked us with all their strength. Thank God ! by a great effort we escaped with our lives from the clutches of those people.

When we got on board the ships we found that over fifty of our soldiers were missing, among them two who had been carried off alive. Within a few days we had to cast into the sea five others who died of their wounds and of the great thirst which we suffered. The whole of the fighting occupied only one hour.

The place is called Potonchan,[1] but the pilots and sailors have marked it on the chart as the "Costa de Mala Pelea" (the coast of the disastrous battle). When we were safely out of that affray we gave hearty thanks to God.

As the wounds of the soldiers were being dressed, some of them complained of the pain they felt, for they began to be chilled and the salt water caused considerable swelling, and some of them began to curse the pilot Anton de Alaminos and his voyage and discovery of the Island, for he always maintained that it was an Island and not the main land.

Here I must leave off and I will tell what happened to us later on.

---

[1] Chanpoton.

CHAPTER V

How we agreed to return to the Island of Cuba and of the great hardships we endured before arriving at the Port of Havana.

As soon as we got on board ship again, in the way I have related, we gave thanks to God, and after we had attended to the wounded (and there was not a man among us who had not two, three or four wounds, and the Captain was wounded in ten places and only one soldier escaped without hurt) we decided to return to Cuba.

As almost all the sailors also were wounded we were shorthanded for tending the sails, so we abandoned the smallest vessel and set fire to her after removing the sails, cables and anchors, and we divided the sailors who were unwounded between the two larger vessels. However, our greatest trouble arose from the want of fresh water, for owing to the attack made on us at Chanpoton, and the haste with which we had to take to the boats, we could not carry away with us the casks and barrels which we had filled with water, and they were all left behind.

So great was our thirst that our mouths and tongues were cracked with the dryness, and there was nothing to give us relief. Oh! what hardships one endures, when discovering new lands, in the way we set out to do it; no one can appreciate the excessive hardships who has not passed through them as we did.

We kept our course close to the land in hope of finding some stream or bay where we could get fresh water, and at the end of three days we found a bay where there appeared to be a river or creek which we thought might hold fresh water. Fifteen of the sailors who had remained on board and were unwounded and three soldiers who were out of danger from their wounds went ashore, and

they took hoes with them, and some barrels to fill with
water; but the water of the creek was salt, so they dug
holes on the beach, but there also the water was as salt
and bitter as that in the creek.   However, bad as the
water was, they filled the casks with it and brought it
on board, but no one could drink such water and it did
harm to the mouths and bodies of the few soldiers who
attempted to drink it.

There were so many large alligators in that creek that
it has always been known as the *estero de los Lagartos* and
so it is marked on the charts.

While the boats went ashore for water there arose such
a violent gale from the North East that the ships began to
drag their anchors and drift towards the shore, for on that
coast contrary winds prevail from the North or North East.
When the sailors who had gone on shore saw what the
weather was like they returned with the boats in hot
haste and arrived in time to put out other anchors and
cables, so that the ships rode in safety for two days and
nights.   Then we got up anchor and set sail continuing
our voyage back to the island of Cuba.

The pilot Alaminos then took council with the other two
pilots, and it was settled that from the place we then were
we should cross over to Florida, for he judged from his
charts and observations that it was about seventy leagues
distant, and that having arrived in Florida they said that
it would be an easier voyage and shorter course to reach
Havana than the course by which we had come.

We did as the pilot advised, for it seems that he had
accompanied Juan Ponce de Leon on his voyage of
discovery to Florida fourteen or fifteen years earlier,[1]
when in that same land Juan Ponce was defeated and

---

[1] Juan Ponce de Leon discovered Florida on Easter Sunday
(Pascua Florida), 27th March, 1513.

killed.   After four days' sail we came in sight of the land of Florida, and what happened to us there I will tell next.

CHAPTER VI.

How twenty of us soldiers went ashore in the Bay of Florida, in
company with the Pilot Alaminos, to look for water, and the
attack that the natives of the land made on us, and what else
happened before we returned to Havana.

WHEN we reached Florida it was arranged that twenty of the soldiers, those whose wounds were best healed, should go ashore. I went with them, and also the Pilot, Anton de Alaminos, and we carried with us such vessels as we still possessed, and hoes, and our crossbows and guns. As the Captain was very badly wounded, and much weakened by the great thirst he had endured, he prayed us on no account to fail in bringing back fresh water as he was parching and dying of thirst, for, as I have already said, the water we had on board was salt and not fit to drink.

We landed near a creek which opened towards the sea, and the Pilot Alaminos carefully examined the coast and said that he had been at this very spot when he came on a voyage of discovery with Juan Ponce de Leon and that the Indians of the country had attacked them and had killed many soldiers, and that it behoved us to keep a very sharp look out. We at once posted two soldiers as sentinels while we dug deep holes on a broad beach where we thought we should find fresh water, for at that hour the tide had ebbed. It pleased God that we should come on very good water, and so overjoyed were we that what with satiating our thirst, and washing out cloths with which to bind up wounds, we must have stayed there an hour. When, at last, very well satisfied, we wished to go on board with the water, we saw one of the soldiers whom we had placed on guard coming towards us crying out, "to arms, to arms! many Indian warriors are coming on foot and others down the creek in canoes." The soldier who came shouting, and the Indians reached us nearly at the same time.

These Indians carried very long bows and good arrows and lances, and some weapons like swords, and they were clad in deerskins and were very big men. They came straight on and let fly their arrows and at once wounded six of us, and to me they dealt a slight arrow wound. However, we fell on them with such rapidity of cut and thrust of sword and so plied the crossbows and guns that they left us to ourselves and set off to the sea and the creek to help their companions who had come in the canoes and were fighting hand to hand with the sailors, whose boat was already captured and was being towed by the canoes up the creek, four of the sailors being wounded, and the Pilot Alaminos badly hurt in the throat. Then we fell upon them, with the water above our waists, and at the point of the sword, we made them abandon the boat. Twenty of the Indians lay dead on the shore or in the water, and three who were slightly wounded we took prisoners, but they died on board ship.

As soon as the skirmish was over we asked the soldier who had been placed on guard what had become of his companion Berrio (for so he was named). He replied that he had seen him go off with an axe in his hand to cut down a small palm tree, and that he went towards the creek, whence the Indian warriors had approached us, that he then heard cries in Spanish, and on that account he had hurried towards us to give us warning, and it was then that his companion must have been killed.

The soldier who had disappeared was the only man who had escaped unwounded from the fight at Potonchan[1] and it was his fate to come on here to die. We at once set to work to search for our soldier along the trail made by the Indians who had attacked us. We found a palm tree partly cut through, and near by the ground was much trampled by footsteps more than in other parts, and as there was no trace of blood we took it for certain that they had carried him off alive. We searched and shouted all round about for more than an hour, but finding no trace of him we got into the boats and carried the fresh water to the ship, at which the soldiers were as overjoyed as though we had given them their lives. One soldier jumped from the ship into the boat, so great was his thirst, and clasping a jar of water to his chest drank so much water that he swelled up and died within two days.

As soon as we had got the water on board and had hauled up the boats, we set sail for Havana, and during the next day and night the weather was fair and we were near some Islands called *Los Martires* among the shoals called the shoals of the Martyrs. Our deepest soundings gave four fathoms, and the flagship struck the ground when going between the Islands and made water fast, and with all of us soldiers working at the pumps we were not able to check it, and we were in fear of foundering.

We had some Levantine sailors on board with us, and we called to them, "Comrades, come and help to work the pump, for you can see that we are all badly wounded and weary from working day and night." And the Levantines answered, "Do it yourselves, for we do not get any pay as you do, but only hunger and thirst, toil and wounds." So then we made them help us with the work.

---

[1] Chanpoton.

Ill and wounded as we were we managed to trim the sails and work the pump until our Lord carried us into the Port of Carenas,[1] where now stands the city of Havana, but it used to be called *Puerto de Carenas*, and when we got to land we gave thanks to God.

I must remember to say that when we got to Havana, a Portuguese diver who happened to be in that port soon got the water out of the flagship.

We wrote in great haste to the Governor of the Island, Diego Velásquez, telling him that we had discovered thickly - peopled countries, with masonry houses, and people who covered their persons and went about clothed in cotton garments, and who possessed gold and who cultivated maize fields, and other matters which I have forgotten.

From Havana our Captain Francisco Hernández went by land to the town of Santispíritus, for so it is called, of which he was a citizen, and where he had his Indians ; but he was so badly wounded that he died within ten days.

Three soldiers died of their wounds in Havana, and all the rest of us dispersed and went some to one and some to other parts of the Island.   The ships went on to Santiago where the Governor was living, and the two Indians whom we captured at Cape Catoche, whom we named Melchorejo and Julianillo were sent on shore, as were also the little chest with the diadems and the ducks and little fish and other articles of gold and the many idols.   These showed such skilful workmanship that the fame of them travelled throughout the Islands including Santo Domingo and Jamaica and even reached Spain.   It was said that better lands had never been discovered in the world ; and when the pottery idols with so many different

---

[1] The Havana of to-day.

shapes were seen, it was said that they belonged to the
Gentiles, and others said that they were the work of the
Jews whom Titus and Vespasian had turned out of Jeru-
salem and sent to sea in certain ships which had carried
them to this land which as Peru was as yet undiscovered
(indeed it was not discovered for another twenty years)
was held in high estimation.

There was another matter about which Diego Velásquez
questioned these Indians, whether there were gold mines
in their country, and to all his questions they answered by
signs " Yes." They were shown gold dust, and they said
that there was much of it in their land, and they did not
speak the truth, for it is clear that neither at Cape Catoche
nor in all Yucatan are there any mines either of gold or of
silver. These Indians were also shown the mounds of
earth in which the plants are set, from the roots of which
Cassava bread is made. This plant is called *Yuca* in the
Island of Cuba and the Indians said that it grew in their
country, and they said *Tlati* for so they call the ground in
which the roots are planted ; and, because *Yuca* and *Tlati*
would make *Yucatan* the Spaniards who had joined in the
conversation between Diego Velásquez and the Indians,
said, " Señor, these Indians say that their country is
called *Yucutlan*"; so it kept that name, but in their own
language they do not call it by that name.

I must leave this subject and say that all of us soldiers
who went on that voyage of discovery spent the little we
possessed on it and we returned to Cuba wounded and in
debt. So each soldier went his own way, and soon afterwards our captain died, and we were a long time recovering
from our wounds, and according to our count, fifty-seven
soldiers died, and this was all the profit we gained by that
expedition and discovery. But Diego Velásquez wrote
to the Lords Councillors who were at that time managing
the Royal Council of the Indies, to say that he had made

the discovery, and had expended on the expedition a great number of gold dollars, and so it was stated and published by Don Juan Rodríguez de Fonseca, Bishop of Burgos and Archbishop of Rosano (for thus he was called) who was President of the Council of the Indies, and he wrote to that effect to His Majesty in Flanders, giving much credit in his letters to Diego Velásquez, and he made no mention of us who made the discovery. Now I must stop, and I will tell later about the hardships which befel me and three other soldiers.

CHAPTER VII.

About the hardships I endured on the way to a town called Trinidad.

I HAVE already said that some of us soldiers who had not yet recovered from our wounds remained in Havana, and when we had got better three of us soldiers wished to go to the town of Trinidad, and we arranged to go with a certain Pedro de Ávila, a resident in Havana who was going to make the voyage in a canoe along the southern coast.[1]   The canoe was laden with cotton shirts which Pedro de Ávila intended to sell at the town of Trinidad.

I have already said that the canoes are made like hollow troughs, and in these countries they are used for paddling along the coasts.

The arrangement we made with Avila was that we should give him ten gold dollars to take us in his canoe. So we set out along the coast, sometimes rowing and sometimes sailing, and after eleven days travelling, when near a village of friendly Indians, called Canarreo, which

---

[1] Bernal Díaz crossed overland to San Cristóval de Havana—the Havana of that time—situated on the south coast (on the river Onicaxinal, see *Orozco y Berra*, vol. iv., p. 71), and thence took canoe to Trinidad.

was the boundary of the township of Trinidad, there arose
such a heavy gale in the night that the canoe could not
make headway against the sea although we were all of
us rowing, as well as Pedro de Ávila and some Indians
from Havana, very good rowers whom we had hired to
come with us; we were cast upon some rocks (*Seborucos*),
which thereabouts are very large, and in so doing the canoe
went to pieces and Ávila lost his property. We all got
ashore disabled and naked to the skin, for so as to swim
more freely in our efforts to keep the canoe from breaking
up we had thought it best to take off all our clothes.

Having escaped from that mishap we found that there
was no trail along the coast to the town of Trinidad,
nothing but rough ground and *Seborucos* as they call
them, stones that pierce the soles of one's feet; moreover
the waves continually broke over us, and we had nothing
whatever to eat. To shorten the list of hardships I will
leave out all one might say about the bleeding from our
feet and other parts of our bodies.

It pleased God that after great toil we came out on a
sandy beach, and after travelling along it for two days we
arrived at an Indian village named Yaguarama, which at
that time belonged to Padre Fray Bartolomé de las Casas
who was the parish priest, whom I afterwards knew as a
doctor and a Dominican friar, and who afterwards became
Bishop of Chiapas,—and at that village they gave us food.

Next day we went on to a village called Chipiana which
belonged to Alonzo de Ávila, and a certain Sandoval,
(not the Captain Sandoval of New Spain, but another, a
native of Tudela de Duero) and from there we went to
Trinidad.

A friend and countryman of mine named Antonio de
Medina supplied me with some clothes, such as are
worn in the Island. From Trinidad with my poverty
and hardships I went to Santiago de Cuba where lived

the Governor, who received me with a good grace ; he was already making haste to send off another fleet.

When I went to pay my respects to him, for we were kinsmen, he joked with me, and going from one subject to another, asked me if I was well enough to return to Yucatan, and I, laughing, asked him who had given the name Yucatan for in that country it was not so called, and he replied, " the Indians you brought back with you call it so," so I told him " you had better call it the land where half the soldiers who went there were killed and all those who escaped death were wounded." He answered, " I know that you suffered many hardships, that always happens to those who set out to discover new lands and gain honour, and His Majesty will reward you, and I will write to him about it, and now my son, go again in the fleet I am getting ready and I will tell the Captain Juan de Grijalva to treat you with honour." I will stop here and relate what happened later.

Here ends the discovery made by Francisco Hernández whom Bernal Díaz del Castillo accompanied ;—Let us relate what Diego Velásquez was proposing to do.

THE EXPEDITION UNDER JUAN DE GRIJALVA.

CHAPTER VIII.

How Diego Velásquez, Governor of the Island of Cuba, ordered another fleet to be sent to the lands which we had discovered and a kinsman of his, a nobleman named Juan de Grijalva, went as Captain General, besides three other Captains, whose names I will give later on.

In the year 1518 the Governor of Cuba hearing the good account of the land which we had discovered, which is called Yucatan, decided to send out another fleet, and made search for four vessels to compose it. Two of these vessels were two of the three which had accompanied Francisco Hernández, the other two were vessels which Diego Velásquez bought with his own money.

At the time the fleet was being fitted out, there were present in Santiago de Cuba, where Velásquez resided Juan de Grijalva, Alonzo de Ávila, Francisco de Montejo, and Pedro de Alvarado, who had come to see the Governor on business, for all of them held *encomiendas* of Indians in the Island. As they were men of distinction, it was agreed that Juan de Grijalva who was a kinsman of Diego Velásquez, should go as Captain General, that Alonzo de Ávila, Pedro de Alvarado, and Francisco de Montejo should each have command of a ship. Each of these Captains contributed the provisions and stores of Cassava bread and salt pork, and Diego Velásquez provided the four ships, crossbows and guns, some beads and other articles of small value for barter,

Facsimile (reduced) of Title-page of

HERRERA, DECADE II.

Showing portraits of DIEGO VELASQUEZ, & JUAN DE GRIJALVA.

From Mr. Grenville's copy in the British Museum.

Reproduced and printed for the Hakluyt Society by Donald Macbeth, 1908.

To face page 36.

and a small supply of beans. Then Diego Velásquez ordered that I should go with these Captains as ensign.

As the report had spread that the lands were very rich and that there were masonry houses there, and the Indian Julianillo whom we had brought from Cape Catoche had said that there was gold, the soldiers and settlers who possessed no Indians in Cuba were greedily eager to go to the new land, so that 240 companions were soon got together.

Then every one of us, out of his own funds, added what he could of stores and arms and other suitable things ; and I set out again on this voyage as ensign, as I have already stated.

As far as I can make out the instructions given by the Governor were that we should obtain by barter all the gold and silver that could be procured, and that if it appeared to be advisable to form a settlement, and if we could venture to do so, that a settlement should be made, but if not that then we should return to Cuba.

There came with us, as Veedor of the fleet, a man named Peñalosa, a native of Segovia, and we took with us a priest named Juan Diaz, a native of Seville, and the same two pilots who were with us on the former voyage, namely, Anton de Alaminos of Palos, Camacho of Triana, besides Juan Álvarez el Manquillo, from Huelva, and there was also another pilot who called himself Sopuesta, who came from Moguer.

Before I go any further, as I shall have to speak many times of these *hidalgos* who were our Captains, and it seems to me discourteous merely to give their names, let it be known that later on they all become persons of title ; Pedro de Alvarado became Adelantado[1] and Governor of Guatemala and a Commander of the Order of Santiago,

---

[1] Adelantado = Governor-in-chief.

Montejo, Adelantado of Yucatan and Governor of Honduras, but Alonzo de Ávila did not have the same luck as the others for he was captured by the French, as I will relate later on in the chapter which treats of the subject. I shall speak of these gentlemen simply by their own names, until such time as His Majesty conferred on them the dignities I have mentioned.

To return to my story; we set out in the four ships along the north coast to a port called Matanzas, near to the old Havana,[1] (for at that time Havana was not in its present position), and in that port most of the settlers of Havana had their farms whence the ships obtained all the supplies they needed of Cassava and pork, for, as I have already said, there were as yet neither sheep nor cattle in Cuba, for the Island was but lately conquered. Here we were joined by the Captains and soldiers who were going to make the voyage.

Before going on, although it does not concern the story, I wish to say why this port was called Matanzas. I call it to mind because I have been asked the question by a historian in Spain who records matters that have happened, and this is the reason why the name was given it. Before the Island of Cuba was conquered a ship with more than thirty Spanish men and two women on board was driven ashore on the coast near the river and port now called Matanzas. Many Indians from Havana and the neighbouring towns came out with the intention of killing the Spaniards, but as the Indians did not dare to attack them on land, they offered, with fair words and flattery, to ferry the Spaniards in canoes across the river, which is very large and rapid, and to take them to their houses and give them food.

When the middle of the river was reached, the Indians

---

[1] Axaruco.

upset the canoes and killed all the Spaniards except three men and one woman who was beautiful and was carried off by one of the caciques concerned in the plot, and the three Spanish men were divided among the other caciques. This is the reason why the place is called Matanzas.[1]

I knew the woman, and after the conquest of Cuba she was taken from the Cacique in whose power she had been, and I saw her married to a settler named Pedro Sánchez Farfan in the town of Trinidad. I also knew the three Spaniards, one was named Gonzalo Mejía, an old man from Jerez, another was Juan Santistéban, a youth from Madrigal, and the other was called Cascorro[2] a seaman, a native of Moguer.

I have delayed too long in telling this old tale, and it will be said that in spinning old yarns I am forgetting my narrative, so let us get back to it :—

As soon as all of us soldiers had got together and the pilots had received their instructions and the lantern signals had been arranged, after hearing mass, we set out on the 8th April, 1518.

In ten days we doubled the point of Guaniguanico which is also called San Anton and after eight days sailing we sighted the Island of Cozumel,[3] which was then first discovered, for with the current that was running we made much more lee-way than when we came with Francisco Hernández de Córdova, and we went along the south side of the Island and sighted a town with a

---

[1] *I.e.*, the place of killing.

[2] The Alonzo Remón Edition adds : " The cacique with whom he stayed married him to his daughter, and he had his ears and nose pierced like an Indian."

[3] This would imply that land was first sighted on the 26th April. The *Itinerario* says that the fleet left Cuba on the 1st May, and that land was sighted on the 3rd May, and as it was the day of Santa Cruz they gave the land that name.

few houses, near which was a good anchorage free from reefs.

We went on shore with the Captain and a large company of soldiers, and the natives of the town had taken to flight as soon as they saw the ships coming under sail, for they had never seen such a thing before.

We soldiers who landed found two old men, who could not walk far, hidden in the maize fields and we brought them to the Captain. With the help of the two Indians Julianillo and Melchorejo whom Francisco Hernández brought away, who thoroughly understood that language (for there is not more than four leagues of sea between their land and the Island of Cozumel, and the language is the same) the captain spoke kindly to these old men and gave them some beads and sent them off to summon the cacique of the town, and they went off and never came back again.

While we were waiting, a good-looking Indian woman appeared and began to speak in the language of the Island of Jamaica, and she told us that all the men and women of the town had fled to the woods for fear of us. As I and many of our soldiers knew the language she spoke very well, for it is the same as that spoken in Cuba, we were very much astonished, and asked the woman how she happened to be there ; she replied that two years earlier she had started from Jamaica with ten Indians in a large canoe intending to go and fish near some small islands, and that the currents had carried them over to this land where they had been driven ashore, and that her husband and all the Jamaica Indians had been killed and sacrificed to the Idols. When the Captain heard this it seemed to him that this woman would serve very well as a messenger, so he sent her to summon the people and caciques of the town, and he gave her two days in which to go and return. We were afraid that the

Indians Melchorejo and Julianillo if once they got away from us would go off to their own country which was near by, and on that account we could not trust them as messengers.

To return to the Indian woman from Jamaica, the answer she brought was that notwithstanding her efforts she could not persuade a single Indian to approach us.

We called the town Santa Cruz because it was the day of Santa Cruz when we first entered it; we found there very good hives of honey and many sweet potatoes, and herds of the pigs of the country which have the navel[1] above the spine.

There are three townships on the Island, the one where we landed being the largest and the other two smaller, and each one stood at one end of the island, these I saw and visited when I returned the third time with Cortez.

The Island is about two leagues[2] in circumference.

I must go on to say that as the Captain Juan de Grijalva saw that it would be merely losing time to wait there any longer, he ordered us to go on board ship, and the Indian woman went with us, and we continued our voyage.[3]

---

[1] A scent gland.

[2] This must be a misprint for "twenty leagues," for the island is at least fifty-five miles in circumference.

[3] From the accounts given in the *Itinerario de Grijalva* and in the letter written to Charles V by the Municipality of Vera Cruz (10th July, 1519) it seems clear that on leaving Cozumel, Grijalva sailed for about fifty miles southwards along the east coast of Yucatan until he reached the Bay of Ascension, which he named, and then turned north again and rounded Cape Catoche. In this passage the author of the *Itinerario* says, "Arrived at the coast we saw three large towns separated about two miles one from the other, and we saw in them many stone houses and very high towers, and many houses of thatch."
Possibly this town was what is now known as the Ruins of Tulum.

CHAPTER IX.

How we followed the same course that we had taken with Francisco
Hernández de Córdova ; how we landed at Chanpoton and how
an attack was made on us, and what else happened.

As soon as we were all on board we kept on the old course,
the same that was followed by Francisco Hernández de
Córdova, and in eight days we reached the neighbourhood
of the town of Chanpoton which was the place where the
Indians of that province had defeated us, as I have already
related in a former chapter. As the tide runs out very
far in the bay, we anchored our ships a league from the
shore and then making use of all the boats we disembarked
half the soldiers close to the houses of the town.

The Indians of the town and others from the neighbourhood at once assembled, as they had done on the other
occasion when they killed over fifty-six of our soldiers
and wounded all the rest, as I have already related, and
for that reason they were now very proud and haughty,
and they were well armed in their own manner with
bows, arrows, and lances, some of them as long as our
lances and some of them shorter, and shields and *macanas*
and two-handed swords and slings and stones, and they
wore cotton armour and carried trumpets and drums, and
many of them had their faces painted black and others red
and white. They were drawn up in array and awaited us
on the shore, ready to fall on us as we landed. As we had
already gained experience from our former expedition, we
had brought with us in the boat some falconets and were
well supplied with crossbows and guns.

As we approached the shore they began to shoot arrows
and hurl lances at us with all their might, and although we
did them much damage with our falconets, such a hail
storm of arrows fell on us before we could land that half of
us were wounded. As soon as all the soldiers got on shore

we checked their ardour with our good sword play and with our crossbows, and although they still shot at us as at targets, we all wore cotton armour, yet they kept up the fight against us for a good while until we drove them back into some swamps near to the town.   In this fight seven soldiers were killed, among them Juan de Quiteria, a man of importance, and our Captain Juan de Grijalva received three arrow wounds, and had two of his teeth broken, and more than sixty of us were wounded.[1]

When we saw that all the enemy had taken to flight we entered the town and attended to the wounded and buried the dead.   We could not find a single person in the town, nor could we find those who had retreated into the swamp for they had all disappeared.   In that skirmish we captured three Indians one of whom was a chief, and the Captain sent them off to summon the cacique of the town, giving them clearly to understand through the interpreters Julianillo and Melchorejo that they were pardoned for what they had done, and he gave them some green beads to hand to the cacique as a sign of peace, and they went off and never returned again.   So we believed that the Indians, Julianillo and Melchorejo had not repeated to the prisoners what they had been told to say to them but had said something quite different.

At that town we stayed for three days.

I remember that this fight took place in some fields where there were many locusts, and while we were fighting they jumped up and came flying in our faces, and as the Indian archers were pouring a hail storm of arrows on us we sometimes mistook the arrows for locusts and did not shield ourselves from them and so got wounded ; at other times we thought that they were arrows coming towards

---

[1] The author of the *Itinerario* and the Letter from the Municipality of Vera Cruz to Charles V make this fight take place at Campeche and say one Spaniard was killed.

us, when they were only flying locusts and it greatly hampered our fighting. I must leave this and go on to tell how we embarked and kept on our course.

CHAPTER X.

How we went on our way and entered a large and broad river to which we then gave the name of the Boca de Términos.

KEEPING on our course we reached what seemed to be the mouth of a very rapid river, very broad and open, but it was not a river as we at first thought it to be, but it was a very good harbour.

Because there was land on both sides of us and the water was so wide that it looked like a strait, the pilot Alamínos said that here the Island ended and the mainland began, and that was the reason why we called it the Boca de Términos,[1] and so it is named on the charts.

The Captain Juan de Grijalva went ashore with all the other Captains already mentioned and many soldiers. We spent three days taking soundings at the mouth of the strait and exploring up and down the bay until we came to the end of it, and found out that there was no island, but that we were in a bay which formed a very good harbour. On shore we found some houses built of masonry, used as oratories of their Idols, and many Idols of pottery, wood and stone, which were the images of their gods, and some of them were figures of women

---

[1] It is not quite clear by which opening the vessels entered the Laguna de Términos. Orozco y Berra (*Hist. Antigua*, vol. iv, page 31) says at the Puerto Escondido—it seems more likely to have been at the Puerto Real. Had they entered by the west entrance or Puerto Principal they must have attracted the attention of the people of Xicolango, then a considerable town and a Mexican outpost. (See *Relacion de Melchor de Alfaro Santa Cruz* in *Coleccion de Documentos Ineditos, Relaciones de Yucatan*, vol. ii. Madrid, 1898).

and others figures of serpents and there were many deer's antlers.

We thought there must be a town close by, and as it was such a safe port we considered that it would be a good place for a settlement, but we found out that it was altogether uninhabited, and that the oratories were merely those belonging to traders and hunters who put into the port when passing in their canoes and made sacrifices there. We had much deer and rabbit hunting and with the help of a lurcher we killed ten deer and many rabbits. At last when we had finished our soundings and explorations we made ready to go on board ship, but the lurcher got left behind. The sailors call this place the Puerto de Términos.

As soon as we were all on board we kept our course close along the shore until we arrived at a river which they call the Rio de Tabasco, which we named Rio de Grijalva.

CHAPTER XI.

How we arrived at the Rio de Tabasco which we named the River Grijalva, and what happened to us there.

MAKING our way along the coast towards the west, by day, but not daring to sail during the night for fear of shoals and reefs, at the end of three days we came in sight of the mouth of a very broad river, and we went near in shore with the ships, as it looked like a good port. As we came nearer in we saw the water breaking over the bar at the mouth of the river, so we got out boats, and by sounding we found out that the two larger vessels could not enter the river, so it was agreed that they should anchor outside in the sea, and that all the soldiers should go up the river in the other two vessels which drew less water and in the boats.

This we did because we saw many Indians in canoes along the banks of the river armed with bows and arrows and other weapons, after the manner of the people of Chanpoton, and we knew that there must be a large town in the neighbourhood.

As we had coasted along we had already seen nets set in the sea for catching fish, and had gone in the boat which was towed astern of the flagship and had taken fish out of two of them.

This river was called the Rio de Tabasco because the chief of the town called himself Tabasco, and as we discovered it on this voyage and Juan de Grijalva was its discoverer, we named it the Rio de Grijalva and so it is marked on the charts.

To go back to my story, when we arrived within half a league of the town we could hear the sound of chopping wood for the Indians were making barriers and stockades and getting ready to give us battle. When we were aware of this, so as to make certain, we disembarked half a league from the town on a point of land where some palm trees were growing. When the Indians saw us there a fleet of fifty canoes approached us full of warriors clad in cotton armour and carrying bows and arrows, lances and shields, drums and plumes of feathers. Many other canoes full of warriors were lying in the creeks, and they kept a little way off as though they did not dare to approach as did the first fleet. When we perceived their intentions we were on the point of firing at them with guns and crossbows, but it pleased God that we agreed to call out to them, and through Julianillo and Melchorejo, who spoke their language very well, we told them that they need have no fear, that we wished to talk to them, for we had things to tell them which when they understood them they would be glad that we had come to their country and their homes.

Moreover, we wished to give them some of the things we had brought with us. As they understood what was said to them, four of the canoes came near with about thirty Indians in them, and we showed them strings of green beads and small mirrors and blue cut glass beads,[1] and as soon as they saw them they assumed a more friendly manner, for they thought that they were *chal-chihuites*[2] which they value greatly.

Then through Julianillo and Melchorejo as interpreters, the Captain told them that we came from a distant country and were the vassals of a great Emperor named Don Carlos, who had many great lords and chiefs as his vassals, and that they ought to acknowledge him as their lord, and it would be to their advantage to do so, and that in return for the beads they might bring us some food and poultry.

Two of the Indians answered us, one of them was a chief and the other was a Papa, that is, a sort of priest who has care of their Idols, for as I have said before, in New Spain they are called Papas. They replied that they would bring the food which we asked for, and would barter their things for ours; but as for the rest, they already had a chief, that we were only just now arrived and knew nothing about them, and yet we wanted to give them a chief. Let us beware not to make war on them as we had done at Potonchan,[3] for they had more than three *jiquipiles* of warriors from all the provinces around in readiness (every *jiquipil* numbers eight thousand men) and they said that they were well aware that only a few days earlier we had killed and wounded more than two hundred men at Potonchan[3] but that they were not

---

[1] Literally, blue diamonds.

[2] Chalchihuitli is Jadeite, which was treasured as a precious stone by the Indians.

[3] Chanpoton.

weaklings such as those, and for this reason they had come to talk to us and find out what we wanted, and that whatever we should tell them they would go and report to the chiefs of many towns who had assembled to decide on peace or war.

Then our Captain embraced the Indians as a sign of peace, and gave them some strings of beads and told them to go and bring back an answer as soon as possible, but he said that although we did not wish to anger them, that if they did not return we should have to force our way into their town.

These messengers whom we sent spoke to the Caciques and Papas, who also have a voice in their affairs, and they decided that it was better to keep the peace and supply us with food, and that between them and the neighbouring towns they would soon seek a present of gold to give us and secure our friendship, so that what had happened to the people of Potonchan[1] would not happen to them.

From what I saw and learnt afterwards, it is the custom in these provinces, and in other countries in New Spain to give presents when making peace, and this will be clearly seen later on.

The following day more than thirty Indians with their chief came to the promontory under the palm trees where we were camped and brought roasted fish and fowls, and zapote fruit and maize bread, and brasiers with live coals and incense, and they fumigated us all. Then they spread on the ground some mats, which here they call *petates*, and over them a cloth, and they presented some golden jewels, some were diadems, and others were in the shape of ducks, like those in Castille, and other jewels like lizards and three necklaces of hollow beads, and other articles of gold but not of much value, for they were not

---

[1] Çhanpoton,

worth more than two hundred dollars. They also brought some cloaks and skirts, such as they wear, and said that we must accept these things in good part as they had no more gold to give us, but that further on, in the direction of the sunset, there was plenty of gold, and they said " Colua, Colua, Méjico, Méjico," but we did not know what this Colua or Méjico could be. Although the present that they brought us was not worth much, we were satisfied, because we thus knew for certain that they possessed gold. As soon as they had given their present they said that we should at once set out on our way and the Captain, Juan de Grijalva, thanked them for their gift and gave them a present of beads. It was decided that we should go on board at once, for the two ships were in much danger should a northerly gale blow for it would put them on a lee shore, and moreover we wanted to get nearer to where we were told there was gold.

CHAPTER XII.

How we followed along the coast towards the setting sun, and arrived at a river called the Rio de Banderas, and what happened there.

WE returned on board and set our course along the coast and in two days came in sight of a town called Ayagualulco, and many of the Indians from that town marched along the shore with shields made of the shells of turtle, which sparkled as the sun shone on them, and some of our soldiers contended that they were made of low grade gold.

The Indians who carried them as they marched along the sandy beach, knowing that they were at a safe distance,

E

cut capers, as though mocking at the ships. We gave the town the name of La Rambla, and it is thus marked on the charts.

Coasting along we came in sight of a bay into which flows the river Tonalá, which we entered on our return journey and named the Rio de San Antonio, and so it is marked on the charts.

As we sailed along we noted the position of the great river Coatzacoalcos, and we wished to enter the bay [not merely] to see what it was like, but because the weather was unfavourable. Soon we came in sight of the great snow mountains, which have snow on them all the year round, and we saw other mountains, nearer to the sea, which we called the range of San Martin, and we gave it that name because the first man to see them was a soldier from Havana who had come with us named San Martin.

As we followed along the coast, the Captain Pedro de Alvarado, went ahead with his ship and entered a river which the Indians call Papaloapan, and which we then called the Rio de Alvarado because Alvarado was the first to enter it. There, some Indian fishermen, natives of a town called Tlacotalpa gave him some fish. We waited at the mouth of the river with the other three ships until Alvarado came out, and the General was very angry with him for going up the river without his permission, and ordered him never to go ahead of the other ships again, lest an accident should happen when we could not give him help.

We kept on our course, all four ships together until we arrived at the mouth of another river, which we called the Rio de Banderas,[1] because we there came on a great number of Indians with long lances, and on every

---

[1] Rio de Banderas is the Rio Jamapa of the modern maps.

lance a great cloth banner which they waved as they beckoned to us. And what happened I will tell in the next chapter.

CHAPTER XIII.

How we arrived at the Rio de Banderas and what happened there.

SOME studious readers in Spain and other people who have been to New Spain, may have heard that Mexico was a very great city built in the water like Venice, and that it was governed by a great prince who was King over many provinces and ruled over all the lands of New Spain, a territory which is more than twice as large as Castille, and that this Prince was called Montezuma, and that as he was so powerful he wished to extend his rule beyond what was possible. He had received news of our arrival when we came first, with Francisco Hernández de Córdova, and of what had happened at the battle of Catoche and at Chanpoton, and also what had happened at the battle at this same Chanpoton during this voyage, and he knew that we soldiers being few in number had defeated the warriors of that town and their very numerous allies, and he knew as well that we had entered the Rio Tabasco and what had taken place between us and the caciques of that town, moreover he understood that our object was to seek for gold, in exchange for the things we had brought with us. All this news had been brought to him painted on a cloth made of *hennequen*[1] which is like linen, and as he knew that we were coasting along towards his provinces he sent orders to his governors that if we should arrive in their

---

[1] Hennequen, or Sisal hemp, is a species of Aloe (Agave Ixtli) now largely used for cordage.

neighbourhood with our ships that they should barter
gold for our beads, especially the green beads, which are
something like their *chalchihuites*, which they value as
highly as emeralds ; he also ordered them to find out
more about our persons and our plans.

It is a fact, as we now know, that their Indian ancestors
had foretold that men with beards would come from the
direction of the sunrise and would rule over them.   Whatever the reason may have been many Indians sent by the
Great Montezuma were watching for us at the river I have
mentioned with long poles, and on every pole a banner of
white cotton cloth, which they waved and called to us, as
though making signals of peace, to come to them.

When from the ships we saw such an unusual sight we
were fairly astonished, and the general and most of the
Captains were agreed that to find out what it meant we
should lower two of the boats, and that all those who
carried guns or crossbows and twenty of the most daring
and active soldiers should go in them, and that Francisco
de Montejo should accompany us, and that if we should
discover that the men who were waving the banners were
warriors that we should at once bring news of it and of
anything else that we could find out.

Thank God at that time we had fine weather which is
rare enough on this coast.   When we got on shore we
found three Caciques, one of them the governor appointed
by Montezuma, who had many of the Indians of his household with him.   They brought many of the fowls of the
country and maize bread such as they always eat, and
fruits such as pineapples and zapotes, which in other
parts are called mameies, and they were seated under the
shade of the trees, and had spread mats on the ground,
and they invited us to be seated, all by signs, for
Julianillo the man from Cape Catoche, did not understand their language which is Mexican.   Then they

brought pottery braziers with live coals, and fumigated us with a sort of resin.

As soon as the Captain Montejo had reported all that had taken place to the general, he [the captain general] determined to anchor his ships and go ashore with all his captains and soldiers.   When the Caciques and governors saw him on land and knew that he was the Captain General of us all, according to their custom, they paid him the greatest respect.   In return he treated them in a most caressing manner and ordered them to be given blue and green glass beads and by signs he made them understand that they should bring gold to barter with us. Then the Governor sent orders to all the neighbouring towns to bring jewels to exchange with us, and during the six days that we remained there they brought more than sixteen thousand dollars worth of jewelry of low grade gold, worked into various forms.

This must be the gold which the historians Gómara, Yllescas and Jovio say was given by the natives of Tabasco, and they have written it down as though it were true, although it is well known to eye witnesses that there is no gold in the Province of the Rio de Grijalva or anywhere near it and very few jewels.

When the General saw that the Indians were not bringing any more gold to barter, and as we had already been there six days and the ships ran risk of danger from the North and North East wind, he thought it was time to embark.

So we took [formal] possession of the land in the name of His Majesty, and as soon as this had been done the General spoke to the Indians and told them that we wished to return to our ships and he gave them presents of some shirts from Spain.   We took one of the Indians from this place on board ship with us, and after he had learnt our language he became a Christian and was named

Francisco, and later on I met him living with his Indian wife.

As we sailed on along the coast we sighted an Island[1] of white sand which the sea washed over, it appeared to be about three leagues distant from the land, and we called it the Isla Blanca and it is marked thus on the charts. Not far from the Isla Blanca we observed another Island with many green trees on it, lying about four leagues from the coast and we gave it the name of Isla Verde and going on further we saw an Island somewhat larger than the others about a league and a half off the shore, and in front of it there was a good roadstead where the General gave orders for the ships to come to anchor.

As soon as the boats were launched the Captain Juan de Grijalva and many of us soldiers went off to visit the Island for we saw smoke rising from it, and we found two masonry houses very well built, each house with steps leading up to some altars, and on these altars were idols with evil looking bodies, which were the gods of the Indians and that very night five Indians had been sacrificed before them ; their chests had been cut open, and the arms and thighs had been cut off and the walls were covered with blood.

At all this we stood greatly amazed, and gave the Island the name of the Isla de Sacrificios and it is so marked on the charts.

We all of us went ashore opposite that Island, and on the broad sandy beach we put up huts and shelters made with branches of trees and sails taken from the ships.

Now many Indians had come down to the coast bringing gold made into small articles which they wished to barter as they had done at the Rio de Banderas, and, as we

---

[1] Bernal Díaz is not quite correct about the comparative size of the Islands. The accompanying chart shows their size and position.

afterwards found out the great Montezuma had ordered them to do so. These Indians who brought the gold were very timid and the gold was small in quantity, for this reason the Captain Juan de Grijalva ordered the anchors to be raised and sail set, and we went on to anchor opposite another Island, about half a league from land, and it is at this Island that the port of Vera Cruz is now established.

CHAPTER XIV.

How we arrived at the Island now called San Juan de Ulúa, and the reason why that name was given to it, and what happened to us there.

WE landed on a sandy beach, and so as to escape the swarms of mosquitos we built huts on the tops of the highest sand dunes, which are very extensive in these parts.

From our boats we made careful soundings of the harbour and found that there was a good bottom and that under the shelter of the Island our ships would be safe from the Northerly gales.

As soon as this was done the General and thirty of us soldiers, well armed, went in two boats to the Island and we found there a temple where there was a very large and ugly idol which was called Tescatepuca[1] and in charge of it were four Indians with very large black cloaks and hoods, such as the Dominicans or canons wear, or very much like them, and these were the priests of the idols, and they are commonly called Papas in New Spain, as I have said before.

They had this day sacrificed two boys and cut open

---

[1] Tetzcatlipoca.

their chests, and offered the blood and hearts to that cursed Idol. The priests came towards us to fumigate us with the incense with which they had fumigated their Tescatepuca, for when we approached them they were burning something which had the scent of incense, but we would not allow them to fumigate us, for we all felt much pity at seeing those two boys who had just been killed and at beholding such great cruelty. The General asked the Indian Francisco, already mentioned by me, whom we had brought from the Rio de Banderas, and who seemed to be fairly intelligent what they had done this for, and Francisco by means of signs (we had no interpreter, for as I have already said, Julianillo and Melchorejo did not understand the Mexican language) replied that the people of Culúa had ordered the sacrifice to be made. As he was halting in his speech he said Ulúa, Ulúa, and as our Captain who was present was named Juan, and it was the day of San Juan in June, we called the Island San Juan de Ulúa. This port is now very well known, and great shelter walls have been erected so as to protect the ships from the North wind, and it is here that all the merchandise from Castille for Mexico and New Spain is landed.

To go back to my story, while we were encamped on the sand hills, Indians from the towns round about came to barter gold and jewels in exchange for our goods, but they brought so few things and those of such poor value that we took no count of it.

We stayed there for seven days, but we could not endure the mosquitos, and seeing that we were wasting time, and as we now knew for certain that these lands were not Islands but the Mainland, and that it contained large towns and multitudes of Indians, and seeing that our cassava bread was very mouldy and dirty with weevils and was going sour, and that the soldiers of our company were not numerous enough to form a settlement, all the more so as thirteen soldiers had died of their wounds, and four others were still suffering, so taking all I have said into consideration it was agreed that we should send to inform the Governor Diego Velásquez of our condition, so that he could send us help.

Juan de Grijalva had the greatest desire to form a settlement even with the few soldiers he had with him, and always showed the courage of a very valiant and energetic Captain, and was not such a man as the historian Gómara describes.

It was therefore decided that the Captain Pedro de Alvarado should go in a very good ship called the *San Sebastian* to carry the message. This was agreed to for two reasons, one was that Juan de Grijalva and the other captains were not on good terms with Alvarado on account of his entry into the Rio Papaloapan (which we then named the Rio Alvarado) the other reason was that Alvarado had come on this voyage unwillingly, as he was far from well.

It was also arranged that the sick men and all the gold and the cloth which had been gained by barter should be sent back in the *San Sebastian*. The Captains wrote to Diego Velásquez, each one what he thought fit, and then the ship set sail and made for the Island of Cuba, and there I will leave them for the present, both Pedro de Alvarado and his voyage, and will tell how Diego Velásquez had sent in search of us.

CHAPTER XV.

How Diego Velásquez, the Governor of Cuba, sent a ship in search
of us, and what else happened.

No sooner had we sailed from the Island of Cuba on
our voyage with Captain Juan de Grijalva, than Diego
Velásquez began to be anxious lest some calamity had
befallen us, and he was always longing for news of us, so
he sent a small ship with some soldiers in search of us,
under the command of Cristóval de Olid, a person of
consideration and very energetic (who was afterwards
Maestro de Campo[1] in the expedition under Cortés).
Diego Velásquez ordered him to follow the track
of Francisco Hernández de Córdova until he should
overtake us.

It appears that Cristóval de Olid, when he went in
search of us, was struck by a heavy gale while anchored
near the coast of Yucatan, and the pilot whom they had
on board, so as to save the vessel from foundering at
anchor, ordered the cables to be cut, so they lost their
anchors and returned to Santiago de Cuba.

Diego Velásquez was at the port and heard that they
brought no news of us, and if he was anxious before, he
was doubly so now. However, about this time the Captain,
Pedro de Alvarado, arrived with the gold, and the cloth,
and the sick men, and with the whole story of what we
had discovered ; and when the Governor beheld the gold
jewelry that the Captain Pedro de Alvarado had brought
with him, he greatly overestimated its value.

There were present with Diego Velásquez many inhabitants from the city and from other parts of the
Island, who had come on business, and when the king's

---

[1] Quartermaster.

HISTORIA GENE
RAL DE LOS HECHO
DE LOS CASTELLANOS
EN LAS. ISLAS I TIERRA
FIRME DEL MAR OCEANO
ESCRITA POR ANTONIO DE
HERRERA CORONISTA
MAIOR DE SV M.D DE LAS
INDIAS Y SV CORONISTA
DE CASTILLA.

DE CADA TERZERA
Al Rey, Nu.tro. Senor

En Madrid en la emplen.ta Real. 1601.

Legran Ciudad de Mexico en la laguna

Aqui fue preso el Rey Quautimoc

El Rey de Mechoacan vifita a cortes

El ex. cast. camina a las ybueras

Mexico se Redifica

Descubre Magallanes el estrecho

Magallanes pasa a la mar del Sur

Muere magallanes peleando con los yndios

la nao bitoria. llega a Seuilla Rodeado el mundo

Disputase en la particion del mundo

Facsimile (reduced) of Title-page of
HERRERA, DECADE III.
Showing portraits of CORTES, CRISTOVAL DE OLID, GONZALO DE SANDOVAL,
the capture of GUATEMOC, etc.

Reproduced and printed for the Hakluyt Society by Donald Macbeth, 1908.

To face page 58.

Plate 4.

officers took the Royal Fifth, which belongs to His Majesty, they were astonished at our having discovered such rich lands, (for Peru was not discovered until twenty years later).

Pedro de Alvarado knew very well how to tell his story, and they say that Diego Velásquez could do nothing but embrace him, and order great rejoicings and sports for eight days. Report had been rife enough before about these rich lands, and with the arrival of the gold it rose to exaggeration throughout the Islands and in Castille, as I shall tell later on ; but I must leave Diego Velásquez keeping holiday, and return to our ships which were at San Juan de Ulúa, and I shall go on to relate how we agreed to proceed with our exploration of the coast.

CHAPTER XVI.

How we went on exploring the coast as far as the Province of Panuco, and what else happened before our return to Cuba.

AFTER the Captain, Pedro de Alvarado had left us to go to the Island of Cuba, (as I have already related) it was decided by the General, Captains, and soldiers, and approved of by the Pilots, that we should keep in close to the shore and discover all that we were able on the coast. Keeping on our course we came in sight of the Sierra de Tuztla,[1] and further on, two days later, we saw some other higher ranges which are now called the Sierra de Tuzpa, after a town of that name near by. As we coasted along, we saw many towns apparently two or

---

[1] This is an error ; the Sierra de Tuxtla lies between the Sierra San Martin and the mouth of the Papaloapan River, and had been passed before arriving at San Juan de Ulúa. It is Tuxpan (about lat. 20 deg. N.) that was now sighted.

three leagues inland and these would belong to the province of Panuco.   Continuing our course, we came to a great and rapid river which we called the Rio de Canoas[1] and dropped anchor at the mouth of it.

When all three ships were anchored and we were a little off our guard, twenty large canoes filled with Indian warriors, armed with bows, arrows, and lances, came down the river and made straight for the smallest ship which lay nearest the shore, and was commanded by Francisco de Montejo.   The Indians shot a flight of arrows which wounded five soldiers, and they made fast to the ship with ropes intending to carry her off, and even cut one of her cables with their copper axes.   However, the captain and soldiers fought well, and upset three of the canoes, and we hastened to their assistance in our boats, with guns and crossbows, and we wounded more than a third of the Indians, so they returned from their unlucky expedition whence they had come.   Then we got up anchor and set sail and followed along the coast until we came to a great Cape[2] which was most difficult to double, for the currents were so strong we could make no headway.

Then the Pilot, Alaminos, said to the General, that it was no use trying to go further in that direction, and gave many reasons for his opinion.   So counsel was taken as to what had best be done, and it was settled that we should return to Cuba.   One reason for this was that the rains[3] had already begun, and we were short of provisions, and one ship was leaking badly.   However, the Captains were not of one mind, for Juan de Grijalva said that he wanted

---

[1] Orozco y Berra says, in a note (page 55), that this Rio de Canoas is the Rio Tanhuijo, 21 deg. 15 mins. 48 secs. N. lat.

[2] Punta Majahua or Cabo Rojo.

[3] *Invierno* (winter) is the word in the text ; it must here mean the rainy season.

to form a settlement, and Alonzo de Ávila, and Francisco
de Montejo objected, saying that they would not be able
to hold out against the great number of warriors which the
country contained, moreover, all of us soldiers were
thoroughly tired of seafaring.

So we turned round and set all sail before the wind,
and aided by the currents, in a few days we reached the
mouth of the great Rio de Coatzacoalcos, but we could
not enter it on account of unfavourable weather, and going
close in shore we entered the Rio de Tonalá, to which we
gave the name of San Anton. There we careened one of
the ships which was making water fast, for on entering the
river she had struck on the bar where the water is very
shallow.

While we were repairing the ship many Indians came
in a most friendly manner from the town of Tonalá, which
is about a league distant, and brought maize bread, and
fish and fruit, and gave them to us with great good will.
The captain showed them much attention and ordered
them to be given white and green beads, and made signs
to them that they should bring gold for barter and we
would give them our goods in exchange ; so they brought
jewels of low grade gold, and we gave them beads in
return. People came also from Coatzacoalcos and the
other towns in the neighbourhood and brought jewelry,
but this did not amount to anything.

Besides these things for barter, the Indians of that
province usually brought with them highly polished
copper axes with painted wooden handles, as though
for show or as a matter of elegance, and we thought
that they were made of inferior gold, and began to barter
for them, and in three days we had obtained more than
six hundred, and we were very well contented thinking
that they were made of debased gold, and the Indians
were even more contented with their beads, but it was no

good to either party, for the axes were made of copper, and the beads were valueless. One sailor had bought seven axes, and was very well pleased with them.[1]

I also remember that a soldier named Bartolomé Pardo, went to one of the Idol Houses which stood on a hill, (which as I have already said are called Cues, which means houses of the Gods) and in that house he found many Idols, and copal, which is a resin used as incense, and stone knives used for sacrifices and circumcision, and in a wooden chest he found many articles of gold, such as diadems and necklaces, and two Idols and some hollow beads. The soldier took the gold for himself and the other Idols and offerings he brought to the captain. However, someone had seen what was done, and reported it to Grijalva, and he wanted to take the gold from the soldier, but we begged that it might be left to him, as he was a respectable man, so after the Royal Fifth had been taken for His Majesty, the rest was given back to the poor soldier, and it was worth about one hundred and fifty dollars.[2]

---

[1] The Alonzo Remón Edition says that he bought them secretly, "and it seems that another sailor told this to the captain, and he ordered them to be given up, but as we all pleaded for him, thinking that the axes were gold, the captain gave them back again."

[2] In the original MSS. the following passage is blotted out :—

I sowed the seeds of some oranges near to another Idol house, and it happened thus :—There were so many mosquitos near the river that ten of us soldiers went up to sleep in a lofty Idol house, and close by that house I sowed the seeds which I had brought from Cuba, for there was a rumour that we were coming back to settle, they came up very well, for it seems that the Papas, when they saw that they were plants differing from those they knew, protected them and watered them and kept them free from weeds ; and all the oranges in that province are the descendants of these plants. I know well that it will be said that these old tales have nothing to do with my history, so I must leave off telling them.—G. G.

The Alonzo Remón Edition adds :—And I have called this to mind because these were the first oranges planted in New Spain. After the fall of Mexico, when the towns subject to Coatzacoalcos had been pacified, this was looked on as the best province, being the best situated in all New Spain, both on account of the mines it possessed

Facsimile (reduced) of Title-page of
HERRERA'S "DESCRIPCION," 1601.
Showing Mexican Gods, Temples, etc.

Reproduced and printed for the Hakluyt Society by Donald Macbeth, 1908.

Plate 5.

To face p. 62.

We left the Indians of those provinces well contented, and going on board ship again, we went on our way towards Cuba,[1] and in forty-five days, sometimes with fair weather and at other times with bad weather, we arrived at Santiago de Cuba where Diego Velásquez was residing, and he gave us a very good reception.

When the Governor saw the gold that we brought, which was worth four thousand dollars, and with that which had already been brought by Pedro de Alvarado, amounted in all to twenty thousand dollars, (and some say that it was more) he was well contented. Then the officers of the King took the Royal Fifth, but when the six hundred axes which we thought were low grade gold were brought out, they were all rusty like copper which they proved to be, and there was a good laugh at us, and they made great fun of our trading.

The Governor was very pleased at all this, but he did not seem to be on good terms with his kinsman Grijalva, and he had no cause for it, merely that Francisco de Montejo and Pedro de Alvarado were not on good terms with Grijalva, and Alonzo de Ávila added to the trouble. As soon as these squabbles were over there began to be talk of sending another fleet, and gossip as to who would be chosen as captain, but I will leave this for the present and will tell how Diego Velásquez sent to Spain to petition His Majesty to give him a commission to trade and to conquer, settle and apportion, the lands which had been discovered.

---

as well as for its good harbour, for it was a land both rich in gold, and in pasture for cattle. For this reason it was settled by the principal *Conquistadores* of Mexico, of whom I was one. So I went to look for my orange trees and transplanted them and they turned out very well.

[1] The author of the *Itinerario* says that they touched at Campeche and secured enough maize, water and firewood to supply them for the remainder of the voyage.

BOOK II.

THE EXPEDITION
UNDER HERNANDO CORTÉS.
THE VOYAGE.

CHAPTER XVII.

How Diego Velásquez sent to Spain to petition His Majesty to grant him a commission, to trade with, and conquer the country, and to settle and apportion the land as soon as peace was established.

LTHOUGH it may seem to the reader that in relating what I now call to mind, I am wandering far away from my story, nevertheless it seems to me proper that, before I begin to tell about the valiant and energetic Captain Cortés, certain things should be mentioned, both for reasons which will be apparent later on, and because when two or three events happen at the same time, one cannot relate them together, but only that one which falls into its place in the story.

The fact is that when the captain, Pedro de Alvarado arrived at Santiago de Cuba with the gold from the lands which we had discovered, as I have already related, Diego Velásquez was in fear lest, before he could make his report to His Majesty, some court favourite should rob him of his reward, and ask it from His Majesty for himself. For this reason he sent to Spain his chaplain, named Benito Martínez, a man well skilled in business, with the evidence and letters for Don Juan Rodríguez de Fonseca, Bishop of Burgos, and Archbishop of Rosano, for such are his titles, and to the Licentiate, Luis Zapata, and to the Secretary, Lope de Conchillos, who at that time looked after the Affairs of the Indies. Diego Velásquez was the very humble servant of them all, especially of the Bishop, and he gave them Indian townships in the Island of Cuba, so that their inhabitants might extract gold from the mines for them, and for this reason they were ready to do much for Diego Velásquez.

At this time His Majesty was away in Flanders. Velásquez also sent to these gentlemen, just now mentioned by me, some of the jewels of gold which we had obtained by barter. Now everything that was done by the Royal Council of the Indies was done by the orders of these gentlemen, and that which Diego Velásquez wished to have arranged was, that he should be given authority to trade with, conquer and settle all this land which he had recently discovered, and any that he might thereafter discover. He said in his reports and letters that he had spent many thousands of gold dollars in the discovery. So the Chaplain, Benito Martínez, went to Spain and succeeded in obtaining all that he asked for, and even more, for he brought back a decree appointing Diego Velásquez, Adelantado of the Island of Cuba. Although what I have here stated was already settled, the despatches did not arrive before the valiant Cortés had already sailed with a fresh fleet. I must leave this matter here, both the despatches of which Benito Martínez was the bearer, and the fleet of the captain Cortés, and state that while writing this story I have seen the chronicles written by the historian, Francisco

F

Lopes de Gómara, and those of the Doctor Yllescas and of Jovio, in which they treat of the conquest of New Spain. I feel bound to declare that, wherever it appears to contradict the others, my story represents events clearly and truly, and runs very differently from what the historians I have named have written.

CHAPTER XVIII.

Concerning some errors and other things written by the Historians Gómara and Yllescas about affairs in New Spain.

WHILE I was writing this story, I saw by chance, what had been written by Gómara, Yllescas and Jovio, about the conquest of Mexico and New Spain, and when I had read their accounts and saw and appreciated their polished style, and thought how rudely and lamely my story was told, I stopped writing it, seeing that such good histories already existed. Being in this perplexed state of mind, I began to look into the arguments and discourses which are told in these books, and I saw that from beginning to end they did not tell correctly what took place in New Spain. When they begin to write about the great cities, and the great number of the inhabitants, they are as ready to write eighty thousand as eight thousand. Then about the great slaughter which they say we committed :—As we were only four hundred and fifty soldiers who marched to that war, we had enough to do to defend ourselves from being killed or defeated and carried off ; and even had the Indians been craven cowards, we could not have committed all the slaughter attributed to us, more particularly as the Indians were very bold warriors who had cotton armour which shielded their bodies, and were armed with bows, arrows, shields, long lances, and two-handled stone-edged swords, which cut better than our swords did,

Nevertheless, the historians say that we made as great a slaughter and committed as great cruelties as did Alaric, that bravest of kings, and the haughty warrior Attila, on the battlefields of Catalonia. To go back to my story, they say that we destroyed and burnt many cities and temples, that is their *Cues,* and in saying this, they seem to think that they are giving pleasure to those who read their histories, and they do not understand when they write, that the conquerors themselves, and the inquisitive readers, who know what really took place, could tell them clearly that if they write other histories in the way they have written that of New Spain, such history will be worthless. The amusing part of it is, that they exalt some captains, and belittle others, and they speak of some, who were not even present at the conquest, as though they were there, and they make many other statements of equal value, but there are so many matters about which they are ignorant, that I cannot note them all. But there is one thing that they say worse than all and that is that Cortés sent secret orders to scuttle the ships, on the contrary, it was on the distinct advice of most of the other soldiers and my own, that he sent to have the ships sunk without any conceal-ment whatever, and it was done so that the sailors who were in them might help to keep watch and make war. Indeed, in all they write, they speak with prejudice, so why should I go on dipping my pen to mention each item separately, it is merely wasting ink and paper, moreover I should say it badly, for I have got no style.

Let us leave this discussion and get back to my theme. After having carefully examined all that I have said as to the nonsense that has been written about the affairs of New Spain, I continued writing my own story, for it is the truest politeness and the most courteous style to tell the truth in what one writes, and knowing this, I made up my mind to carry out my plan, with such embellishments and discourses as will be seen further on, so that the conquest of New Spain may be brought to light and may be clearly seen in the way it ought to be seen.

I wish to return to my story pen in hand as a good pilot carries his lead in hand at sea, looking out for shoals ahead, when he knows that they will be met with, so will I do in speaking of the errors of the historians, but I shall not mention them all, for if one had to follow them item by item, the trouble of discarding the rubbish would be greater than that of gathering in the harvest.

I say that upon this story of mine the historians may build up and give as much praise as pleases them to the valiant captain Cortés and to the sturdy Conquistadores. It was a great enterprise that was accomplished by our hands, and what historians may write about it, we, who were eye witnesses will certify when it is true, as we now certify to the errors, and as so much daring and zeal has been shown in writing falsely and with prejudice, we appreciate how holy and blessed is the truth, and that all that is said against it is cursed.

Moreover it appears that Gómara[1] was inspired to write with such laudation of Cortés, for we look upon it as certain that his palms were greased, for he dedicated his history to the present Marquis, the son of Cortés, insisting on his right so to dedicate and recommend it before our lord the King, and the members of the Royal Council of the Indies ought to have had the mistakes erased that are written down in his books.

---

[1] Alonzo Remón Edition adds :—" Not only did Gómara write down so many mistakes and things that are not true, but he misled many writers and historians who since his time have written about the affairs of New Spain, such as the Doctor Yllescas and Pablo Jovio who copy his very words."

CHAPTER XIX.

How we came again with another fleet to the newly discovered lands
    with the valiant and energetic Don Hernando Cortés (who was
    afterwards Marqués del Valle) as captain of the fleet, and the
    attempts that were made to prevent his going in command.

AFTER the return of the Captain Juan de Grijalva to
Cuba, when the Governor Diego Velásquez understood
how rich were these newly discovered lands, he ordered
another fleet, much larger than the former one to be sent
off, and he had already collected in the Port of Santiago,
where he resided, ten ships, four of them were those in
which we had returned with Juan de Grijalva, which had
at once been careened, and the other six had been got
together from other ports in the Island. He had them
furnished with provisions, consisting of Cassava bread and
salt pork, for at that time there were neither sheep nor
cattle in the Island of Cuba, as it had been only recently
settled. These provisions were only to last until we
arrived at Havana, for it was at that port that we were
to take in our stores, as was afterwards done.

I must cease talking of this and tell about the disputes
which arose over the choice of a captain for the expedition.
There were many debates and much opposition, for some
gentleman said that Vasco Porcallo, a near relation of the
Conde de Feria, should be captain, but Diego Velásquez
feared that he would rise against him with the fleet, for
he was very daring ; others said that Agustin Bermudez
or Antonio Velásquez Borrejo, or Bernadino Velásquez,
kinsman of Diego Velásquez should go in command.

Most of us soldiers who were there said that we should
prefer to go again under Juan de Grijalva, for he was
a good captain, and there was no fault to be found either
with his person or his capacity for command.

While things were going on in the way I have related,

two great favourites of Diego Velásquez named Andrés
de Duero, the Governor's Secretary, and Amador de Lares,
His Majesty's accountant, secretly formed a partnership
with a gentleman named Hernando Cortés, a native of
Medellin, who held a grant of Indians in the Island. A
short while before, Cortés had married a lady named
Catalina Juarez la Marcayda ; this lady was sister of a
certain Juan Juarez who after the conquest of New Spain
was a settler at Mexico. As far as I know, and from what
others say, it was a love match. On this matter of the
marriage other persons who saw it have had much to say,
and for that reason I will not touch any more on this
delicate subject.

I will go on to tell about this partnership, it came about
in this manner :—These two great favourites of Velásquez
agreed that they would get him to appoint Cortés Captain
General of the whole fleet, and that they would divide
between the three of them, the spoil of gold, silver and
jewels which might fall to Cortés' share. For secretly
Diego Velásquez was sending to trade and not to form
a settlement, as was apparent afterwards from the instructions given about it, although it was announced and
published that the expedition was for the purpose of
founding a settlement.

When this arrangement had been made, Duero and the
accountant went to work in such a way with Diego
Velásquez, and addressed such honied words to him,
praising Cortés highly, as the very man for the position
of Captain, as in addition to being energetic he knew how
to command and ensure respect, and as one who would be
faithful in everything entrusted to him, both in regard to
the fleet and in everything else, (pointing out too, that
he was his godson, for Velásquez was his sponsor when
Cortés married Doña Catalina Juarez), that they persuaded
him to choose Cortés as Captain General.

Andrés de Duero, the Governor's Secretary, drew up the documents in very good ink[1] as the proverb says, in the way Cortés wished with very ample powers.

When the appointment was made public, some persons were pleased and others annoyed.

One Sunday when Diego Velásquez went to Mass,—and as he was Governor he was accompanied by the most distinguished persons in the town,—he placed Hernando Cortés on his right hand so as to pay him honour. A buffoon, called the mad Cervantes, ran in front of Diego Velásquez, making grimaces and cracking jokes and he cried out—

> "The parade of my friend Diego, Diego,
> " Who then is this captain of your choice?
> " He comes from Medellin in Estramadura
> "A very valiant captain indeed
> " Have a care lest he run off with the fleet
> " For all judge him a man to take care of his own."

And he cried out other nonsense, all of it somewhat malicious. And as he would go on shouting in this way, Andrés de Duero who was walking near Diego Velasquez, gave the buffoon a cuff and said "Silence thou crazy drunkard, and don't be such a rogue, for we are well aware that these malicious sayings, passed off as wit, are not made up by thee," and still the madman ran on, notwithstanding the cuffs, saying, " Viva, Viva, the parade of my friend Diego and his daring Captain Cortés, I swear friend Diego that so as not to see thee weeping over the bad bargain thou hast made this day, I wish to go with Cortés to these rich lands." There is no doubt that some kinsman of the Governor had given gold pieces to the buffoon to utter these malicious sayings, passing them off as witty. However, this all came true, and it is said that madmen do sometimes hit the mark in their speeches.

---

[1] De muy buena tinta = most efficiently.

Truly Hernando Cortés was chosen to exalt our holy faith and to serve his Majesty, as I will tell later on.

Before going any further I wish to say that the valiant and energetic Hernando Cortés was a gentleman by birth (hijo-d'algo) by four lines of descent. The first through the Cortéses, for so his father Martin Cortés was named, the second through the Pizarros, the third through the Monroys and the fourth through the Altamiranos. Although he was such a valiant, energetic and daring captain, I will not from now on, call him by any of these epithets of valiant, or energetic, nor will I speak of him as Marqués del Valle, but simply as Hernando Cortés. For the name Cortés alone was held in as high respect throughout the Indies as well as in Spain, as was the name of Alexander in Macedonia, and those of Julius Caesar and Pompey and Scipio among the Romans, and Hannibal among the Carthaginians, or in our own Castille the name of Gonzalo Hernández, the Great Captain. And the valiant Cortés himself was better pleased not to be called by lofty titles but simply by his name, and so I will call him for the future. And now I must cease talking of this, and relate in the next chapter what he undertook and accomplished about the preparation of his fleet.

CHAPTER XX.

How Cortés prepared and continued the arrangements necessary
for the dispatch of the fleet.

As soon as Hernando Cortés had been appointed General in the way I have related, he began to search for all sorts of arms, guns, powder and crossbows and every kind of warlike stores which he could get together, and all sorts of articles to be used for barter, and other things necessary for the expedition.

Moreover he began to adorn himself and be more careful of his appearance than before, and he wore a plume of feathers with a medal, and a gold chain, and a velvet cloak trimmed with knots of gold, in fact he looked like a gallant and courageous Captain.   However, he had no money to defray the expenses I have spoken about, for at that time he was very poor and much in debt, although he had a good *encomienda* of Indians who were getting him a return from his gold mines, but he spent all of it on his person and on finery for his wife whom he had recently married, and on entertaining some guests who had come to visit him.   For he was affable in his manner and a good talker, and he had twice been chosen *Alcalde*[1] of the town of Santiago Baracoa where he had settled, and in that country it is esteemed a great honour to be chosen as *Alcalde*.

When some merchant friends of his named Jaime Tria, Jerónimo Tria and Pedro de Jerez saw that he had obtained this command as Captain General, they lent him four thousand gold dollars in coin and gave him merchandise worth another four thousand dollars secured on his Indians and estates. Then he ordered two standards and banners to be made, worked in gold with the royal arms and a cross on each side with a legend which said, "Comrades, let us follow the sign of the holy Cross with true faith, and through it we shall conquer." And he ordered a proclamation to be made with the sound of drums and trumpets in the name of His Majesty and by Diego Velásquez in the King's name, and in his own as Captain General, to the effect that whatsoever person might wish to go in his company to the newly discovered lands to conquer them and to settle there, should receive his share of the gold, silver and riches which might be gained

---

[1] Alcalde = Mayor.

and an *encomienda* of Indians after the country had been pacified, and that to do these things Diego Velásquez held authority from His Majesty.

Although he put in the proclamation this about the authority of Our Lord the King, the Chaplain, Benito Martínez, had not yet arrived from Spain with the Commission which Diego Velásquez had sent him to obtain, as I have already mentioned in a former chapter.

When this news was known throughout Cuba, and Cortés had written to all his friends in the different towns begging them to get ready to come with him on this expedition, some of them sold their farms so as to buy arms and horses, others began to prepare cassava bread and to salt pork for stores, and to make quilted cotton armour, and they got ready what was necessary as well as they could.

We assembled at Santiago de Cuba, whence we set out with the fleet more than three hundred and fifty soldiers in number. From the house of Velásquez there came Diego de Ordás, the chief Mayordomo, whom Velásquez himself sent with orders to keep his eyes open and see that no plots were hatched in the fleet, for he was always distrustful of Cortés although he concealed his fears. There came also Francisco de Morla and an Escobar, whom we called The Page, and a Heredia, and Juan Ruano and Pedro Escudero, and Martin Ramos de Lares, and many others who were friends and followers of Diego Velásquez; and I place myself last on the list for I also came from the house of Diego Velásquez, for he was my kinsman.

I have put down here the names of these soldiers from memory, later on, at the proper time and place I will record all those who went in the fleet whose names I can call to mind, and say from what part of Spain they came.

Cortés worked hard to get his fleet under way and hastened on his preparations, for already envy and malice had taken possession of the relations of Diego Velásquez who were affronted because their kinsman neither trusted them nor took any notice of them and because he had given charge and command to Cortés, knowing that he had looked upon him as a great enemy only a short time before, on account of his marriage, already mentioned by me; so they went about grumbling at their kinsman Diego Velásquez and at Cortés, and by every means in their power they worked on Diego Velásquez to induce him to revoke the commission.

Now Cortés was advised of all this, and for that reason never left the Governor's side, and always showed himself to be his zealous servant, and kept on telling him that, God willing, he was going to make him a very illustrious and wealthy gentleman in a very short time. Moreover Andrés de Duero was always advising Cortés to hasten the embarkation of himself and his soldiers, for Diego Velásquez was already changing his mind owing to the importunity of his family.

When Cortés knew this he sent orders to his wife that all provisions of food which he wished to take and any other gifts (such as women usually give to their husbands when starting on such an expedition) should be sent at once and placed on board ship.

He had already had a proclamation made that on that day by nightfall all ships, Captains, pilots and soldiers should be on board and no one should remain on shore. When Cortés had seen all his company embarked he went to take leave of Diego Velásquez, accompanied by his great friends and many other gentlemen, and all the most distinguished citizens of that town.

After many demonstrations and embraces of Cortés by the Governor, and of the Governor by Cortés, he took his leave. The next day very early after having heard Mass we went to our ships, and Diego Velásquez himself accompanied us, and again they embraced with many fair speeches one to the other until we set sail.

A few days later, in fine weather, we reached the Port of Trinidad where we brought up in the harbour and went ashore, and nearly all the citizens of that town came out to meet us; and entertained us well.

Here in this story will be seen all the opposition which Cortés met with, and how what happened differed entirely from the account given by Gómara in his history.

NOTE.—This account differs very considerably from that given by Las Casas (Lib. III, cap. cxv). It appears that Diego Velásquez had already determined to take the command from Cortés, "at once on the very night that he became aware of what was going on, as soon as Diego Velásquez was in bed, and all those who belonged to [him,] Cortés, had left the Palace, he went in the profound silence of the night in the utmost haste to awaken the rest of his friends telling them that it was advisable to embark at once. Taking with him a company sufficient to defend his person, he immediately went off to the slaughter house and, although it troubled the contractor who had to supply the whole town with meat, he took it all away without leaving a single cow, pig, or sheep, and had it carried to the ships, exclaiming, but not out loud, for it might perhaps have cost him his life, that they could lay the blame on him [Cortés] for not supplying meat to the town. Then Cortés took off a small golden chain that he wore round his neck and gave it to the contractor or butcher, *and this Cortés told me himself.*

"Cortés at once went on board ship with all the people that he could arouse without noise. Many of the people who had agreed to go with him and who really went were already on board.

"When he was gone either the butcher or others who knew of his departure advised Diego Velásquez that Cortés was gone and was already on board ship. Diego Velásquez got up and mounted his horse, and all the people of the city, in a state of astonishment, accompanied him to the landing place by the sea at daybreak. When Cortés saw him he ordered a boat to be got ready with cannon, guns, muskets and crossbows, and all the necessary arms, and accompanied by the men he could trust best, with his magistrate's wand [in his hand] he came within crossbow shot of the land and there stopped. Diego Velásquez said to him ' How is it, compadre,[1] that you are going off like this ? Is this the right way to take leave of me ?' Cortés replied 'Señor, may your Excellency pardon me, but these things and the like are done before they are thought about, I am at your Excellency's orders.' Diego Velásquez had nothing to say when he saw his infidelity and shamelessness. Cortés ordered the boat's head to be turned and went back to the ships, and ordered the sails to be hoisted in all haste [and] on the 18th Nov. 1518 [he set out] with very little food for the ships were not yet fully laden."

CHAPTER XXI.

What Cortés did when he arrived at the town of Trinidad and concerning the soldiers who there joined him to go in his company,
and other things that happened.

THE leading inhabitants of that town soon provided quarters for Cortés and all of us among their neighbours. Cortés was lodged in the house of Captain Juan de Grijalva, and he ordered his standard and the Royal pennant to be set up in front of his quarters and issued a proclamation as he had done in Santiago, and ordered search to be made for all sorts of arms, and food and other necessaries to be purchased.

From that town there came to join us five brothers, namely Pedro de Alvarado and Jorge de Alvarado, and Gonzalo and Gómez, and Juan de Alvarado the elder, who was a bastard. The Captain Pedro de Alvarado has often been mentioned by me already. There also joined us from this town Alonzo de Ávila, who went as a Captain in Grijalva's expedition, and Juan de Escalante and Pedro Sanchez Farfan, and Gonzalo Mejía who later on became treasurer in Mexico, and a certain Baena and Juanes of Fuenterrabia, and Lares, the good horseman, so called because there was another Lares, and Cristóbal de Olid, the Valiant, who was Maestro de Campo during the

---

[1] Compadre = friend, crony.

Mexican wars, and Ortis the Musician, and Gaspar
Sanchez, nephew of the treasurer of Cuba, and Diego de
Pineda or Pinedo, and Alonzo Rodríguez, who owned
some rich gold mines, and Bartolomé García and other
gentlemen whose names I do not remember, all persons of
quality.

From Trinidad Cortés wrote to the town of Santispíritus
which was eighteen leagues distant, informing all the
inhabitants that he was setting out on this expedition in
His Majesty's service, adding fair words and inducements
to attract many persons of quality who had settled in that
town, among them Alonzo Hernándes Puertocarrero cousin
of the Count of Medellin, and Gonzalo de Sandoval who
became later on, in Mexico, *Alguazil Mayor*,[1] and for eight
months was Governor of New Spain and Juan Velásquez de
Leon came, a kinsman of Diego Velásquez, and Rodrigo
Reogel, and Gonzalo Lópes de Jimena, and his brother, and
Juan Sedeño also came. This Juan Sedeño was a settler in
the town, I mention this because we had two others of the
name Juan Sedeño in the fleet. All these distinguished
persons whom I have named came from the town of Santispíritus to Trinidad where Cortés was staying, and when
he heard that they were coming he went out to meet them
with all the soldiers of his company and received them
with great cordiality and they treated him with the highest
respect.

All these settlers whom I have named possessed farms
near the town where they made Cassava bread and kept
herds of swine, and each one endeavoured to contribute as
much food as he could.

We continued to enlist soldiers and to buy horses, which
at that time were both scarce and costly, and as that
gentleman already mentioned by me, Alonzo Hernándes

---

[1] Chief Constable.

Puertocarrero, neither possessed a horse nor the where-
withal to buy one, Hernando Cortés bought him a gray
mare, and paid for it with some of the golden knots off the
velvet cloak which as I have said he had had made at
Santiago de Cuba.

At that very time a ship arrived in port from Havana,
which a certain Juan Sedeño, a settler at Havana, was
taking, freighted with Cassava bread and salt pork to sell
at some gold mines near Santiago de Cuba.

Juan Sedeño landed and went to pay his respects to
Cortés, and after a long conversation Cortés bought the
ship and the pork and bread on credit, and it all came
with us. So we already had eleven ships and thank God
all was going well with us.

Meanwhile Diego Velásquez had sent letters and commands for the fleet to be detained and Cortés to be sent
to him as a prisoner.

<hr />

CHAPTER XXII.

How the Governor Diego Velásquez sent two of his servants post
    haste to the town of Trinidad with orders and authority to cancel
    the appointment of Cortés, detain the fleet, arrest Cortés and
    send him as a prisoner to Santiago.

I MUST go back a little from our story, to say that after
we had set out from Santiago de Cuba with all the ships,
in the way I have already related, so many things were
said to Diego Velásquez against Cortés, that he was forced
to change his mind, for they told him that Cortés was
already in rebellion, and that he left the port by stealth,
and that he had been heard to say that although Diego
Velásquez and his relations might regret it, he intended to
be Captain and that was the reason why he had embarked

all his soldiers by night, so that if any attempt were made
to detain him by force he might set sail; they also said
that Andrés de Duero, the Secretary, and the Accountant
Amador de Lares had deceived Diego Velásquez on
account of arrangements made between them and Cortés.
Those who took the leading part in persuading Diego
Velásquez to revoke the authority he had given to Cortés
were some members of the Velásquez family and an old
man named Juan Millan whom some called the astrologer,
but others said he had a touch of madness because he
acted without reflection, and this old man kept repeating
to Diego Velásques " Take care, Sir, for Cortés will take
vengeance on you for putting him in prison,[1] and as he is
sly and determined he will ruin you if you do not prevent
it at once."

And Velásquez listened to these speeches, and was
always haunted by suspicions, so without delay he sent
two messengers whom he trusted, with orders and instructions to Francisco Verdugo, the Chief Alcalde of Trinidad,
who was his brother-in-law, and wrote letters to other
friends and relations, to the effect that on no account
should the fleet be allowed to sail, and he said in his
orders that Cortés should be detained or taken prisoner as
he was no longer its captain, for he had revoked his
commission and given it to Vasco Porcallo. The messengers
also carried letters to Diego de Ordás and Francisco de
Morla and other dependents of his begging them not to
allow the fleet to sail.

When Cortés heard of this, he spoke to Ordás and
Francisco Verdugo and to all the soldiers and settlers at
Trinidad, whom he thought would be against him and in
favour of the instructions, and he made such speeches and

---

[1] This refers to an earlier incident in the relations between Cortés
and Diego Velásquez.

promises to them that he brought them over to his side. Diego Ordás himself spoke at once to Francisco Verdugo, the Alcalde Mayor advising him to have nothing to do with the affair but to hush it up, and bade him note that up to that time they had seen no change in Cortés, on the contrary that he showed himself to be a faithful servant of the Governor, and that if Velásquez wished to impute any evil to him in order to deprive him of the command of the fleet, it was as well to remember that Cortés had many men of quality among his friends, who were unfriendly to Velásquez because he had not given them good grants of Indians. In addition to this, that Cortés had a large body of soldiers with him and was very powerful and might sow strife in the town, and perhaps the soldiers might sack the town and plunder it, and do even worse damage.

So the matter was quietly dropped and one of the messengers who brought the letters and instructions, named Pedro Lazo de la Vega joined our company, and by the other messenger Cortés sent a letter to Diego Velásquez written in a very friendly manner, saying that he was amazed at His Honour having come to such a decision, that his desire was to serve God and his Majesty, and to obey him as His Majesty's representative, and that he prayed him not to pay any more attention to what was said by the gentlemen of his family, nor to change his mind on account of the speeches of such an old lunatic as Juan Millan. He also wrote to all his friends and especially to his partners Duero and the Treasurer.

When these letters had been written Cortés ordered all the soldiers to polish up their arms, and he ordered the blacksmiths in the town to make head pieces, and the cross bowmen to overhaul their stores and make arrows, and he also sent for the two blacksmiths and persuaded them to accompany us, which they did. We were ten days

G

in that town. Here I will leave off and go on to tell how we embarked for Havana.

However, I wish first to point out to my readers how different this is from the story of Francisco Gómara who says that Diego Velásquez sent to Ordás telling him to invite Cortés to dinner on board a ship, and then to carry him off as a prisoner to Santiago, and makes other statements calculated to mislead in his history, but, so as not to become prolix, I will leave them to the judgment of interested readers.

CHAPTER XXIII.

How the Captain Hernando Cortés with all the soldiers sailed along the south coast to the port of Havana,[1] and how another ship was sent along the north coast to the same port, and what else took place.

WHEN Cortés saw that there was nothing more to be done at the town of Trinidad he summoned all the soldiers who had assembled there to go with him * * * * * (Pedro) de Alvarado that he should go by land to Havana[2] * * * * * to pick up some soldiers who lived on farms along the road, and I went in his company. Cortés also sent a gentleman named Juan de Escalante, a great friend of his, in a ship along the north coast, and he sent all the horses by land. When

---

[1] This was on the south coast, not the present port of Havana on the north coast, which must have been about thirty miles distant. Cortés and his fleet sailed along the south coast of Cuba, and the "San Sebastian" and the vessel commanded by Juan de Escalante were the only vessels on the north side of the Island.

[2] The Alonzo Remón edition says "he summoned all the gentlemen and soldiers who had assembled there to go with him either to embark on the ships which were in port on the south coast, or if they preferred it to go by land to Havana with Pedro de Alvarado who was going to pick up some soldiers who lived on farms along the road."

all this had been done Cortés went on board the flagship
to set sail with all the fleet for Havana.

It appears that the ships of the Convoy did not see the
flagship in which Cortés had embarked, for it was night
time and they went on to the port [of Havana]. We also
arrived by land at the town of Havana with Pedro de
Alvarado, and the ship in which Juan de Escalante had
come along the north coast had already arrived, and all
the horses which had been sent by land, but Cortés did
not appear, and no one knew where he was delayed.
Five days passed without news of his ship and we began
to wonder whether he had been lost on the *Jardines*, ten
or twelve miles from Havana near the Isle of Pines where
there are many shallows. We all agreed that three of the
smaller vessels should go in search of Cortés, and in preparing the vessels and in debates whether this or the other
man—Pedro or Sancho—should go, two more days went
by and Cortés did not appear. Then parties began to be
formed, and we all played the game of " Who shall be
Captain until Cortés comes ? " And the man who took
the lead in this was Diego de Ordás, as the chief Mayordomo of Velásquez, who had been sent by the Governor
merely to look after the fleet and see that there should be
no mutiny.

Let us leave this subject and return to Cortés who, as I
have already said, had embarked on the largest ship of
the fleet, and in the neighbourhood of the Isle of Pines, or
near the *Jardines*, where there are many shallows, the ship
ran aground and remained there hard and fast and could
not be floated.

Cortés ordered all the cargo which could be removed to
be taken ashore in the boat, for there was land near by
where it could be stored, and when it was seen that the
ship was floating and could be moved, she was taken into
deeper water and was laden again with the cargo which

had been taken ashore, sail was then set and the voyage continued to the port of Havana.

When Cortés arrived nearly all of us gentlemen and soldiers who were awaiting him were delighted at his coming, all except some who had hoped to be Captains, for the game of choosing captains came to an end.

As soon as we had lodged Cortés in the house of Pedro Barba, who was the lieutenant of Diego Velásquez in that town, he ordered the standards to be brought out and placed in front of the buildings in which he was lodged and ordered proclamation to be made, as he had done before.

From the Havana there came the Hidalgo Francisco Montejo very often mentioned by me, who after the conquest of Mexico was appointed Governor and Adelantado of Yucatan, and there also came Diego de Soto of Toro who was Mayordomo to Cortés in Mexico, and a certain Angulo y Garcicaro, and Sebastian Rodríguez and a Pacheco and a somebody Gutierrez, and a Rójas (not Rójas el Rico) and a youth named Santa Clara, and two brothers called the Martínez del Freginal, and a Juan de Najara (I don't mean the deaf one who played Pelota[1] in Mexico), all persons of quality, not counting other soldiers whose names I cannot remember.

When Cortés beheld all these Hidalgos collected together he was greatly pleased. He sent a ship to the Cape of Guaniguanico, to an Indian town there, where they made Cassava bread and kept many pigs, to have her laden with salt pork, for the farm belonged to the Governor Diego Velásquez,[2] and he sent Diego de Ordás

---

[1] A ball game.

[2] In a conversation with Las Casas in the year 1542, Cortés, speaking of this expedition, laughingly remarked, " A mi fé, anduve por alli como un gentil corsario."   " By my faith I went about there like an excellent robber." (Las Casas, *Hist. de Indias*, Lib. III, cap. cxvi).

who was the chief Mayordomo of the property of Velásquez in command of the ship, as he wished to get him out of the way, for he knew that Diego de Ordás did not show himself to be very well disposed towards him at the time when his ship went ashore near the Isle of Pines and the question arose as to who should be chosen captain. So in order to avoid disputes with him he sent Diego de Ordás off with orders that after freighting the ship with supplies of food, he should remain at the port of Guaniguanico until he was joined by the other ship which was going along the north coast, and then that the two should sail together for Cozumel, but that [in case of any change of plans] he would send Indians in canoes to advise him what was to be done.

I must not forget to say that Francisco de Montejo and all the other settlers at Havana sent on board great stores of Cassava bread and salt pork, for other provisions were not to be had.

Cortés now ordered all the artillery, which consisted of ten brass guns and some falconets, to be brought out of the ships, and gave them in charge of an artilleryman named Mesa, and of a levantine named Arbenga, and a certain Juan Catalan, with orders to have them thoroughly cleaned and tested, and to see that the balls and powder were in readiness, and he gave them wine and vinegar with which to clean them. He gave the gunners as a companion a certain Bartolomé de Usagre. He also ordered that the crossbows with their cords, nuts, and other necessaries should be overhauled, and that they should be tested at a target, so as to see how far each of them would carry.

As in the country round Havana there is much cotton, we made well padded armour for ourselves, which is most necessary when fighting Indians, on account of the great use they make of darts, arrows and lances, and stones which fall on one like hail.

It was here in Havana that Cortés began to organize a household and to be treated as a Lord. The first Marshal of the household,[1] whom he appointed was a certain Guzman who soon afterwards died or was killed by the Indians (this was not Cristóbal de Guzman, the Mayordomo of Cortés who took Guatemoc[2] prisoner during the war in Mexico) and he had as *camarero*[3] Rodrigo Ranguel, and for Mayordomo, Juan de Cáceres who became a rich man after the conquest of Mexico.

When all this was settled we got ready to embark and the horses were divided among all the ships, and mangers were made for them and a store of maize and hay put on board. I will now call to mind all the mares and horses that were shipped :—

The Captain Cortés :—A vicious dark chestnut horse, which died as soon as we arrived at San Juan de Ulúa.

Pedro de Alvarado and Hernando López de Ávila :—a very good sorrel mare, good both for sport and as a charger. When we arrived at New Spain Pedro de Alvarado bought the other half share in the mare or took it by force.

Alonzo Hernández Puertocarrero :—a grey mare, a very good charger which Cortés bought for him with his gold buttons.

Juan Velásquez de Leon :—A very powerful gray mare which we called "La Rabona,"[4] very handy and a good charger.

Cristóval de Olid :—a dark chestnut horse, fairly good.

Francisco de Montejo and Alonzo de Ávila :—a parched sorrel horse, no use for warfare.

---

[1] Maestresala = the chief waiter in a nobleman's household.
[2] Guatemuz in the original.
[3] *Camarero* = chamberlain.
[4] La Rabona = the bob-tailed.

Francisco de Morla :—a dark chestnut horse, very fast and very easily handled.

Juan de Escalante :—a light chestnut horse with three white stockings, not much good.

Diego de Ordás, a gray mare, barren, tolerably good, but not fast.

Gonzalo Domínguez :—a wonderfully good horseman ; a very good dark chestnut horse, a grand galloper.

Pedro González de Trujillo :—a good chestnut horse, all chestnut, a very good goer.

Moron, a settler at Bayamo :—a dappled horse with stockings on the forefeet, very handy.

Baena : a settler at Trinidad :—a dappled horse almost black, no good for anything.

Lares, a very good horseman :—an excellent horse of rather light chestnut colour, a very good goer.

Ortiz the musician and Bartolomé García, who once owned gold mines :—a very good dark horse called "El Arriero,"[1] this was one of the best horses carried in the fleet.

Juan Sedeño, a settler at Havana :—a chestnut mare which foaled on board ship.

This Juan Sedeño passed for the richest soldier in the fleet, for he came in his own ship with the mare, and a negro and a store of cassava bread and salt pork, and at that time horses and negroes were worth their weight in gold, and that is the reason why more horses were not taken, for there were none to be bought. I will leave off here and tell what next happened to us, when we were just about to embark.

---

[1] *El arriero* = the muleteer, carrier.

CHAPTER XXIV.

How Diego Velásquez sent a servant named Gaspar de Garnica with orders and instructions that in any case Cortés should be arrested and the fleet taken from him, and what was done about it.

To make my story clear, I must go back and relate that when Diego Velásquez knew for certain that his lieutenant and brother-in-law Francisco Verdugo who was stationed at the town of Trinidad not only refused to compel Cortés to leave the fleet, but, together with Diego de Ordás, had helped him to get away, they say that he was so angry that he roared with rage and told his secretary Andrés de Duero and the Treasurer Amador de Lares that they had deceived him by the agreement they had made, and that Cortés was mutinous. He made up his mind to send a servant with letters and orders to Pedro Barba, his lieutenant at Havana, and wrote very graciously to all his friends who were settlers in that town, and to Diego de Ordás and to Juan Velásquez de Leon who were his friends and kinsmen praying them neither for good nor ill to let the fleet get away, and to seize Cortés at once and send him under a strong guard to Santiago de Cuba.

On the arrival of Garnica (that was the name of the man who brought the letters and orders to Havana) it was known at once what he had brought with him, for by the same messenger Cortés was advised of what Velásquez was doing. It happened in this way :—it appears that a friar of the Order of Mercy, who gave himself out to be a follower of Velásquez, was in the Governor's company at the time, and he wrote a letter to another friar of his order named Bartolomé del Olmedo, who was with us, and in that letter, written by the friar, Cortés was informed by his two associates, Andrés de Duero and the treasurer of all that had happened.

To go back to my story :—As Cortés had sent away Diego de Ordás in a ship to collect stores, there was no one to oppose him except Juan Velásquez de Leon, and as soon as Cortés spoke to him he brought him over to his side,—all the more easily because Juan Velásquez was put out with his kinsman for not giving him a good grant of Indians.

Not one of the others to whom Diego Velásquez had written favoured his proposal, indeed one and all declared for Cortés, the lieutenant Pedro Barba above all. In addition to this the Alvarados, Alonzo Hernández Puerto-carrero, Francisco de Montejo, Cristóval de Olid, Juan de Escalante, Andrés de Monjaraz, and his brother Gregorio de Monjaraz and all of us would have given our lives for Cortés. So that if in the Town of Trinidad the orders of Velásquez were slighted, in the town of Havana they were absolutely ignored.

By this same Garnica, the lieutenant Pedro Barba wrote to Diego Velásquez that he did not dare to seize Cortés as he was too strongly supported by soldiers, and he was afraid lest Cortés should sack and plunder the town and carry off all the settlers along with him ; that from all that he had gathered Cortés was the Governor's faithful servant and would not dare to be anything else. Cortés also wrote to Velásquez in the agreeable and complimentary terms which he knew so well how to use, and told him that he should set sail next day and that he remained his humble servant.

CHAPTER XXV.

How Cortés set sail with all his company of Gentlemen and soldiers
for the Island of Cozumel and what happened there.

THERE was to be no parade of the forces until we arrived
at Cozumel. Cortés ordered the horses to be taken on
board ship, and he directed Pedro de Alvarado to go along
the North coast in a good ship named the *San Sebastian*,
and he told the pilot who was in charge to wait for him at
Cape San Antonio as all the ships would meet there and
go in company to Cozumel. He also sent a messenger to
Diego de Ordás, who had gone along the North Coast
to collect supplies of food with orders to do the same and
await his coming.

On the 10th February 1519, after hearing Mass, they set
sail along the south coast with nine ships and the company
of gentlemen and soldiers whom I have mentioned, so that
with the two ships absent on the north coast there were
eleven ships in all, including that which carried Pedro de
Alvarado with seventy soldiers and I travelled in his
company.

The Pilot named Camacho who was in charge of our
ship paid no attention to the orders of Cortés and went
his own way and we arrived at Cozumel two days before
Cortés and anchored in the port which I have often
mentioned when telling about Grijalva's expedition.

Cortés had not yet arrived, being delayed by the ship
commanded by Francisco de Morla having lost her rudder
in bad weather, however she was supplied with another
rudder by one of the ships of the fleet,[1] and all then came
on in company.

---

[1] Blotted out in the original MS. "They turned back looking
for the rudder in the sea and they found it and put it in its place, so
that they were soon able to navigate the ship."—G. G.

To go back to Pedro de Alvarado. As soon as we arrived in port we went on shore with all the soldiers to the town of Cozumel, but we found no Indians there as they had all fled. So we were ordered to go on to another town about a league distant, and there also the natives had fled and taken to the bush, but they could not carry off their property and left behind their poultry and other things and Pedro de Alvarado ordered forty of the fowls to be taken. In an Idol house there were some altar ornaments made of old cloths and some little chests containing diadems, Idols, beads and pendants of gold of poor quality, and here we captured two Indians and an Indian woman, and we returned to the town where we had disembarked.

While we were there Cortés arrived with all the fleet, and after taking up his lodging the first thing he did was to order the pilot Camacho to be put in irons for not having waited for him at sea as he had been ordered to do. When he saw the town without any people in it, and heard that Pedro de Alvarado had gone to the other town and had taken fowls and cloths and other things of small value from the Idols, and some gold which was half copper, he showed that he was very angry both at that and at the pilot not having waited for him, and he reprimanded Pedro de Alvarado severely, and told him that we should never pacify the country in that way by robbing the natives of their property, and he sent for the two Indians and the woman whom we had captured, and through Melchorejo, (Julianillo his companion was dead) the man we had brought from Cape Catoche who understood the language well, he spoke to them telling them to go and summon the Caciques and Indians of their town, and he told them not to be afraid, and he ordered the gold and the cloths and all the rest to be given back to them, and for the fowls (which had already been eaten) he ordered them to be given beads and little bells, and in addition he gave to each Indian a Spanish shirt. So they went off to summon the lord of the town, and the next day the Cacique and all his people arrived, women and children and all the inhabitants of the town, and they went about among us as though they had been used to us all their lives, and Cortés ordered us not to annoy them in any way. Here in this Island Cortés began to rule energetically, and Our Lord so favoured him that whatever he put his hand to it turned out well for him, especially in pacifying the people and towns of these lands, as we shall see further on.

CHAPTER XXVI.

How Cortés reviewed all his army and what else happened to us.

WHEN we had been in Cozumel three days Cortés ordered a muster of his forces so as to see how many of us there were, and he found that we numbered five hundred and eight, not counting the shipmasters, pilots and sailors, who numbered about one hundred. There were sixteen horses and mares all fit to be used for sport or as chargers.

There were eleven ships both great and small, and one a sort of launch which a certain Gines Nortes brought laden with supplies.

There were thirty two cross bowmen and thirteen musketeers;—*escopeteros*, as they were then called and [1] brass guns, and four falconets, and much powder and ball. About the number of cross bowmen my memory

------

[1] Blotted out in the original MS. is the word "ten."—G. G.

does not serve me very well, but it is not material to my story.

After the review Cortés ordered Mesa surnamed "the gunner" and Bartolomé de Usagre and Arbenga and a certain Catalan who were all artillerymen, to keep their guns clean and in good order, and the ammunition ready for use. He appointed Francisco de Orozco, who had been a soldier in Italy to be captain of the Artillery. He likewise ordered two crossbowmen named Juan Benítez and Pedro del Guzman the crossbowman, who were masters of the art of repairing crossbows, to see that every crossbow had two or three [spare] nuts and cords and fore cords and to be careful to keep them stored and to have smoothing tools and *inguijuela*[1] and [to see] that the men should practice at a target. He also ordered all the horses to be kept in good condition.

I don't know why I should expend so much ink in telling about these preparations of arms and the rest of it, for in truth Cortés was most vigilant about everything.

CHAPTER XXVII.

How Cortés came to know that the Indians of Cape Catoche held two Spaniards in captivity, and what he did about it.

As Cortés was most diligent in all matters, he sent for me and a Biscayan named Martin Ramos, and asked us what we thought about those words which the Indians of Campeche had used when we went there with Francisco Hernández de Córdova, when they cried out "Castilan, Castilan" as I have already stated in the chapter which treats of that expedition. We again related to Cortés all that we had seen and heard about the matter, and he said

---

[1] Probably some technical term now obsolete.

that he also had often thought about it, and that perhaps there might be some Spaniards living in the country, and added " It seems to me that it would be well to ask these Caciques of Cozumel if they know anything about them." So through Melchorejo, the man from Cape Catoche, who already understood a little Spanish and knew the language of Cozumel very well, all the chiefs were questioned, and every one of them said that they had known of certain Spaniards and gave descriptions of them, and said that some Caciques, who lived about two days' journey inland, kept them as slaves, and that here in Cozumel were some Indian traders who spoke to them only a few days ago. We were all delighted at this news, and Cortés told the Caciques that they must go at once and summon the Spaniards, taking with them letters, (which in the Indian language they call *amales*) and he gave shirts to the Caciques and Indians who went with the letters and spoke reassuringly to them, and told them that when they returned he would give them some more beads.   The Cacique advised Cortés to send a ransom to the owners who held these men as slaves, so that they should be allowed to come, and Cortés did so, and gave to the messengers all manner of beads.   Then he ordered the two smallest vessels to be got ready (one of them was little larger than a launch) and twenty men with guns and crossbows, under the command of Diego de Ordás, and he sent them off to the coast near Cape Catoche where the larger vessel was to wait for eight days while the smaller vessel should go backwards and forwards and bring news of what was being done, for the land of Cape Catoche was only four leagues distant, and the one country could be seen from the other.

In the letter Cortés said :—" Gentlemen and brothers, here in Cozumel I have learnt that you are captives in the hands of a Cacique, and I pray you that you come here to Cozumel at once, and for this purpose I have sent a ship

with soldiers, in case you have need of them, and a ransom
to be paid to those Indians with whom you are living.
The ship will wait eight days for you.   Come in all haste,
and you will be welcomed and protected.   I am here at
this Island with five hundred soldiers and eleven ships, in
which I go on, please God, to a town called Tabasco or
Potonchan."

The two vessels were soon despatched with the two
Indian traders from Cozumel who carried the letters, and
they crossed the strait in three hours and the messengers
with the letters and ransom were landed.   In two days
the letters were delivered to a Spaniard named Jerónimo
de Aguilar, for that we found to be his name, and so
I shall call him in future.   When he had read the letter
and received the ransom of beads which we had sent to
him he was delighted, and carried the ransom to the
Cacique his master, and begged leave to depart, and the
Cacique at once gave him leave to go wherever he pleased.
Aguilar set out for the place, five leagues distant, where
his companion Gonzalo Guerrero was living, but when he
read the letter to him he answered, " Brother Aguilar, I
am married and have three children and the Indians look
on me as a Cacique and captain in wartime,—You go and
God be with you, but I have my face tatooed and my ears
pierced, what would the Spaniards say should they see me
in this guise ? and look how handsome these boys of mine
are, for God's sake give me those green beads you have
brought and I will give the beads to them and say that
my brothers have sent them from my own country."   And
the Indian wife of Gonzalo spoke to Aguilar in her own
tongue very angrily and said to him, " What is this slave
coming here for talking to my husband,—go off with you,
and don't trouble us with any more words."

Then Aguilar reminded Gonzalo that he was a Christian
and said that he should not imperil his soul for the sake of

an Indian woman, and as for his wife and children he could
take them with him if he did not wish to desert them
But by no words or admonishments could he be persuaded
to come.   It appears that Gonzalo Guerrero was a sailor
and a native of Palos.

When Jerónimo de Aguilar saw that Gonzalo would not
accompany him he went at once, with the two Indian
messengers, to the place where the ship had been awaiting
his coming, but when he arrived he saw no ship for she had
already departed.   The eight days during which Ordás
had been ordered to await and one day more had already
expired, and seeing that Aguilar had not arrived Ordás
returned to Cozumel without bringing any news about that
for which he had come.

When Aguilar saw that there was no ship there he
became very sad, and returned to his master and to the
town where he usually lived.

Now I will leave this and say that when Cortés saw
Ordás return without success or any news of the Spaniards
or Indian messengers he was very angry, and said haughtily
to Ordás that he thought that he would have done better
than to return without the Spaniards or any news of them,
for it was quite clear that they were prisoners in that
country.

At that moment it happened that some sailors called
the Peñates,[1] natives of Gibraleon,[2] had stolen some pieces
of salt pork from a soldier named Berrio and would not
return them, so Berrio complained to Cortés and the
sailors were put on oath, and they perjured themselves,
but in the enquiry the fact of the theft was proved, and
that the pork had been divided among seven sailors, and
Cortés ordered four of them to be flogged, in spite of the
appeals of some of the Captains.

---

[1] Peñates = rock men.   [2] Gibraltar.

Here I must leave both this matter of the sailors and
that of Aguilar, and keep the story of our journey up
to date and tell how many Indians both the natives of the
towns near Cape Catoche and those from other parts of
Yucatan came on pilgrimages to the Island of Cozumel, for
it appeared that there were some very hideous idols kept
in a certain oratory on Cozumel to which it was the custom
of the people of the land to offer sacrifices at that season.
One morning the courtyard of the oratory where the Idols
were kept was crowded with Indians, and many of them
both men and women were burning a resin like our incense.
As this was a new sight to us we stood round watching it
with attention, and presently an old Indian with a long
cloak, who was the priest of the Idols (and I have already
said that the priests in New Spain are called *Papas*) went
up on the top of the oratory and began to preach to the
people. Cortés and all of us were wondering what would
be the result of that black sermon. Cortés asked Melchorejo, who understood the language well, what the old
Indian was saying, for he was informed that he was preach-
ing evil things, and he sent for the Cacique and all the
principal chiefs and the priest himself, and, as well as he
could through the aid of our interpreter, he told them
that if we were to be brothers they must cast those most
evil Idols out of their temple, for they were not gods at all
but very evil things which led them astray and could lead
their souls to hell. Then he spoke to them about good
and holy things, and told them to set up in the place of
their Idols an image of Our Lady which he gave them, and
a cross, which would always aid them and bring good
harvests and would save their souls, and he told them in a
very excellent way other things about our holy faith.

The Priest and the Caciques answered that their forefathers had worshipped those Idols because they were
good, and that they did not dare to do otherwise, and that

H

if we cast out their Idols we would see how much harm it would do us, for we should be lost at sea. Then Cortés ordered us to break the Idols to pieces and roll them down the steps,[1] and this we did; then he ordered lime to be brought, of which there was a good store in the town, and Indian masons, and he set up a very fair altar on which we placed the figure of Our Lady; and he ordered two of our party named Alonzo Yáñez and Álvaro López who were carpenters and joiners to make a cross of some rough timber which was there, and it was placed in a small chapel near the altar and the priest named Juan Díaz said mass there, and the Cacique and the heathen priest and all the Indians stood watching us with attention.

The Caciques in this Island of Cozumel are called Calachiones as I have already said when telling about our doings at Potonchan. Now I will leave off here, and will go on to tell how we embarked on board ship.

CHAPTER XXVIII.

How Cortés allotted the ships and appointed captains to go in them, and gave instructions to the pilots and arranged lantern signals for the night time, and what else happened to us.

CORTÉS himself took command of the flagship, Pedro de Alvarado and his brothers took charge of the *San Sebastian*, a very good ship, and the commands of the other ships were given to Alonso Hernández Puertocarrero, Francisco de Montejo, who had a good ship, Cristóval de Olid, Diego de Ordás, Juan Velásquez de Leon, Juan de Escalante,

------

[1] In the "Itinerary of Grijalva" a temple or oratory of the Idols is thus described:—"It was eighteen steps (of a stairway) in height and the base was solid, and the measurement round it was one hundred and eighty feet. On the top of this was a small tower the height of two men one above the other and inside were certain figures and bones and *Cenis* which are the Idols which they worship."

Francisco de Morla, the Page Escobar, and the smallest vessel of all, a launch, was commanded by Gines Nortes. Each ship had its pilot; Anton de Alaminos was Pilot in Chief, and instructions were given about the course to be steered and other matters, and about the lantern signals for the night time.

Cortés took leave of the Caciques and priests and confided to their care the Image of Our Lady and told them to reverence the cross and keep it clean and wreathed with flowers and they would see what advantage they would gain by so doing, and the Indians replied that they would do so, and they brought four fowls and two jars of honey and they embraced him.

We embarked and set sail on a day in the Month of March 1519, and went on our way in fair weather. At ten o'clock that same morning loud shouts were given from one of the ships, which tried to lay to, and fired a shot so that all the vessels of the fleet might hear it, and when Cortés heard this he at once checked the flagship and seeing the ship commanded by Juan de Escalante bearing away and returning towards Cozumel, he cried out to the other ships which were near him "What is the matter? What is the matter?" And a soldier named Luis de Zaragoza answered that Juan de Escalante's ship with all the Cassava bread on board was sinking, and Cortés cried, "Pray God that we suffer no such disaster," and he ordered the Pilot Alaminos to make signal to all the other ships to return to Cozumel. So this same day we returned to the port whence we had sailed, and sent the Cassava bread on shore, and we found the image of Our Lady and the Cross well cared for with incense burning in front of it, and this pleased us greatly. The Cacique and priests came to speak to Cortés and asked why we had returned, and he replied, because one of the ships was leaking and we wished to caulk her, and he asked them to

come in their canoes and help the ships boats to bring the
Cassava bread on shore, and this they did.

We were four days repairing the ship. Now I will stop
writing about this, and will relate how the Spaniard named
Aguilar who was a prisoner among the Indians heard
of our return, and what else happened.

CHAPTER XXIX.

How the Spaniard named Jerónimo de Aguilar, who was a prisoner
among the Indians, heard that we had returned to Cozumel and
came to us, and what else took place.

WHEN the Spaniard who was a prisoner among the
Indians, knew for certain that we had returned to Cozumel
with the ships, he was very joyful and gave thanks to God,
and he came in all haste with the two Indians who had
carried the letters and ransom, and embarked in a canoe,
and as he was able to pay well with the green beads
we had sent him, he soon hired a canoe and six Indian
rowers, and they rowed so fast that, meeting no head wind,
in a very short time they crossed the strait between the
two shores, which is a distance of about four leagues.

When they arrived on the coast of Cozumel and were
disembarking, some soldiers who had gone out hunting
(for there were wild pigs on the island) told Cortés that a
large canoe, which had come from the direction of Cape
Catoche, had arrived near the town. Cortés sent Andrés
de Tápia and two other soldiers to go and see, for it was a
new thing for Indians to come fearlessly in large canoes
into our neighbourhood. So they set out, and as soon as
the Indians who came in the canoe which Aguilar had
hired caught sight of the Spaniards, they were frightened
and wished to get back into the canoe and flee away.
Aguilar told them in their own language not to be afraid,

that these men were his brothers. When Andrés de Tápia saw that they were only Indians (for Aguilar looked neither more nor less than an Indian), he at once sent word to Cortés by a Spaniard that they were Cozumel Indians who had come in the canoe. As soon as the men had landed, the Spaniard in words badly articulated and worse pronounced, cried *Dios y Santa Maria de Sevilla,* and Tápia went at once to embrace him. The other soldier who had accompanied Tápia when he saw what had happened, promptly ran to Cortés to beg a reward for the good news, for it was a Spaniard who had come in the canoe, and we were all delighted when we heard it.

Tápia soon brought the Spaniard to Cortés, but before he arrived where Cortés was standing, several Spaniards asked Tápia where the Spaniard was? although he was walking by his side, for they could not distinguish him from an Indian as he was naturally brown and he had his hair shorn like an Indian slave, and carried a paddle on his shoulder, he was shod with one old sandal and the other was tied to his belt, he had on a ragged old cloak, and a worse loin cloth with which he covered his nakedness, and he had tied up, in a bundle in his cloak, a Book of Hours, old and worn. When Cortés saw him in this state, he too was deceived like the other soldiers, and asked Tápia " Where is the Spaniard ?" On hearing this, the Spaniard squatted down on his haunches as the Indians do and said " I am he." Cortés at once ordered him to be given a shirt and doublet and drawers and a cape and sandals, for he had no other clothes, and asked him about himself and what his name was and when he came to this country. The man replied, pronouncing with difficulty, that he was called Jerónimo de Aguilar, a native of Ecija, and that he had taken holy orders, that eight years had passed since he and fifteen other men and two women left Darien for the Island of Santo Domingo, where he had

some disputes and a law-suit with a certain Enciso y
Valdívia, and he said that they were carrying ten thousand
gold dollars and the legal documents of the case, and that
the ship in which they sailed, struck on the *Alacranes* so
that she could not be floated, and that he and his companions and the two women got into the ship's boat,
thinking to reach the Island of Cuba or Jamaica, but that
the currents were very strong and carried them to this
land, and that the Calachiones of that district had divided
them among themselves, and that many of his companions
had been sacrificed to the Idols, and that others had died
of disease, and the women had died of overwork only a
short time before, for they had been made to grind corn ;
that the Indians had intended him for a sacrifice, but that
one night he escaped and fled to the Cacique with whom
since then he had been living (I don't remember the name
that he gave) and that none were left of all his party except
himself and a certain Gonzalo Guerrero, whom he had gone
to summon, but he would not come.

When Cortés heard all this, he gave thanks to God,
and said that he would have him well looked after and
rewarded. He questioned Aguilar about the country and
the towns, but Aguilar replied that having been a slave,
he knew only about hewing wood and drawing water and
digging in the fields, that he had only once travelled as far
as four leagues from home when he was sent with a load,
but, as it was heavier than he could carry, he fell ill, but
that he understood that there were very many towns.
When questioned about Gonzalo Guerrero, he said that he
was married and had three sons, and that his face was
tattooed and his ears and lower lip were pierced, that he
was a seaman and a native of Palos, and that the Indians
considered him to be very valiant ; that when a little more
than a year ago a captain and three vessels arrived at
Cape Catoche, (it seems probable that this was when we

came with Francisco Hernández de Córdova) it was at the suggestion of Guerrero that the Indians attacked them, and that he was there himself in the company of the Cacique of the large town, whom I have spoken about when describing the expedition of Francisco Hernández de Córdova. When Cortés heard this he exclaimed " I wish I had him in my hands for it will never do to leave him here."

When the Caciques of Cozumel found out that Aguilar could speak their language, they gave him to eat of their best, and Aguilar advised them always to respect and revere the holy image of Our Lady and the Cross, for they would find that it would benefit them greatly.

On the advice of Aguilar the Caciques asked Cortés to give them a letter of recommendation, so that if any other Spaniards came to that port they would treat the Indians well and do them no harm, and this letter was given to them. After bidding the people good-bye with many caresses and promises we set sail for the Rio de Grijalva.

This is the true story of Aguilar, and not the other which the historian Gómara has written; however, I am not surprised that what he says is news to me. Now I must go on with my story.

CHAPTER XXX.

How we again embarked and made sail for the Rio de Grijalva, and what happened to us on the voyage.

ON the 4th March 1519, with the good fortune to carry such a useful and faithful interpreter along with us, Cortés gave orders for us to embark in the same order as we had followed before we ran back to Cozumel, under the same instructions and with the same lantern signals by night.

We sailed along in good weather, until at nightfall a head wind struck us so fiercely that the ships were dispersed and there was great danger of being driven ashore. Thank God, by midnight the weather moderated, and as soon as dawn broke the ships got together again, excepting the vessel under the command of Juan Velásquez de Leon. We went on our way and up to midday had seen nothing of the missing vessel which distressed us all as we feared she had been lost on a shoal. When the whole day had passed and she did not appear Cortés told the pilot Alaminos that it was no good going on any further without news of the missing ship, so the pilot made signal for all the vessels to lay to, and wait to see if by chance the storm had driven her into some bay whence she could not get out again against a head wind. However, when she still failed to appear, the pilot said to Cortés, "Sir, I feel certain that she put into a sort of port or bay which we have already passed, and that a head wind keeps her there, for the pilot on board of her is Juan Álvarez el Manquillo who was with Francisco Hernández de Córdova and again with Grijalva and he knows that port." So it was agreed that the whole fleet should go back and search for the missing ship, and we found her at anchor in the bay of which the pilot had spoken, which was a great relief to us all. We stayed in that bay for a day and we lowered two boats and the pilot and a Captain called Francisco de Lugo went on shore and found farms and maize plantations, and some places where the Indians made salt, and there were four *Cues* which are the houses of their Idols, and there were many Idols in them, nearly all of them figures of tall

TEMPLE ON THE ISLA DE LAS MUGERES.

Drawn by Miss Annie Hunter from a photograph by W. H. Holmes and a drawing by F. Catherwood.

Reproduced for the Hakluyt Society by Donald Macbeth, 1908.

women so that we called that place the *Punta de las Mugeres*.[1]

I remember that Aguilar said that the town where he was held in slavery was near these farms and that he had come there with a load, and his master had taken him there, and that he fell ill on account of the weight of the load, and he said that the town where Gonzalo Guerrero lived was not far off, and that there was some gold in all the towns, but it did not amount to much; that if we liked he would guide us to the towns, and advised us to go there. Cortés replied, laughing, that we were not after such small game, but to serve God and the King.

Soon afterwards Cortés ordered a Captain named Escobar to go in the vessel under his command, which was a fast sailer and drew little water, to the Boca de Términos and to examine the place thoroughly and find out if it would be a good port for a settlement, and if game were plentiful there as he had been told it was. That after he had examined the place he should put up some sign and break down some trees at the mouth of the harbour, or that he should write a letter and place it where we could see it from either side of the harbour, so that we should know that he had gone in there; or that, after examining the port he should beat up to windward and await the fleet at sea. This order was given on the

---

[1] Punta de las Mugeres = the cape of the women. The Island which forms the bay is still called Isla de las Mugeres. Bernal Díaz says nothing about this locality in his description of the two earlier voyages, but the author of the *Itinerario* says that Grijalva observed it, after leaving Cozumel :—"We made sail and went towards the Island of Yucatan along the North Coast, and as we coasted along we came to a beautiful tower on a point, which is said to be inhabited by women who live without men. One might believe them to be a race of Amazons." As Grijalva could not possibly have had any information on the subject, it seems to show that the *Itinerario* was written at a later date than is usually assigned to it, and gave this explanation to account for the name given to the locality by Cortés.

advice of the pilot, so that when we arrived at the Boca de Términos with the fleet we should not be delayed by going into port.

So Escobar left us and went to the Puerto de Términos and did all that he was told to do, and he found the lurcher which had been left there in Grijalva's time, and she was fat and sleek. Escobar said that when the lurcher saw the ship come into port she wagged her tail and showed other signs of delight, and came at once to the soldiers and went with them on board the ship.

After carrying out his orders Escobar put to sea again and awaited the fleet, and it appears that with the south wind that was blowing he was not able to lay to but was driven out to sea.

To go back to our fleet; we remained at the Punta de las Mugeres until the next day when we put to sea with a good breeze off the land and went on until we arrived at the Boca de Términos, but, as we did not meet Escobar, Cortés ordered a boat to be lowered, and with ten crossbowmen went to look for him in the Boca de Términos, or to see if there was any signal or letter. They soon found trees that had been cut down, and a letter in which Escobar said that the harbour was a good one, that the land was fertile, and that there was an abundance of game, and he told about the lurcher. However, the pilot Alaminos told Cortés that we had better keep on our course, for with the wind from the south Escobar must have been driven out to sea, but that he would not be far off as he would lie close to the wind. But Cortés was anxious lest some accident had befallen him, so he ordered the sheets to be slacked away and we soon came up to Escobar who made his report to Cortés and told him why he could not await his coming.

While this was taking place we arrived near Potonchan

[Chanpoton] and Cortés ordered the Pilot to drop anchor in the bay, but the Pilot replied that it was a bad port, for the tide ran out so far that the ships had to be brought up more than two leagues from the shore. Cortés had a mind to give the Indians a lesson on account of the defeat they had inflicted on Francisco Hernández de Córdova and Grijalva, and many of us soldiers who had been in those battles begged him to go in, and not to leave without giving the Indians a good chastisement, even if it did detain us two or three days. But the Pilot Alaminos and the other pilots contended that if we should go in it might, with a head wind, be eight days before we could get out again; that we had a fair wind now for Tabasco and could get there in two days. So we passed on and after three days sail arrived at the Rio de Grijalva called in the Indian language the Tabasco River, and what happened to us there and the attack that was made on us I will go on to relate.

CHAPTER XXXI.

How we arrived at the Rio de Grijalva, which in the language of the Indians is called Tabasco, of the attack the Indians made on us, and what else happened to us with them.

ON the 12th March, 1519, we arrived with all the fleet at the Rio de Grijalva, which is also called Tabasco, and as we already knew from our experience with Grijalva that vessels of large size could not enter into the river, the larger vessels were anchored out at sea, and from the smaller vessels and boats all the soldiers were landed at the Cape of the Palms (as they were in Grijalva's time) which was about half a league distant from the town of

Tabasco.[1] The river, the river banks and the mangrove
thickets were swarming with Indians, at which those of
us who had not been here in Grijalva's time were much
astonished.

In addition to this there were assembled in the town
more than twelve thousand warriors[2] all prepared to make
war on us, for at this time the town was of considerable
importance and other large towns were subject to it
and they had all made preparation for war and were
well supplied with the arms which they are accustomed
to use.

The reason for this was that the people of Potonchan[3]
and Lázaro and the other towns in that neighbourhood
had looked upon the people of Tabasco as cowards, and
had told them so to their faces, because they had given

---

[1] The large town which the author here calls Tabasco appears
originally to have been called Potonchan ; it was renamed by the
Spaniards Santa Maria de la Victoria ; it was later on called Tabasco,
and it soon fell into ruin and disappeared altogether, its place as
a port being taken by Frontera on the other side of the river.
In the *Relacion de la Villa de Santa Maria de la Victoria*, 1579
(*Relaciones de Yucatan*, vol. ii, p. 341), we find : "This river and port is
at 18° 30' (N. Lat.), where this town was established about a league
from the mouth of the river on a *placel** of water which is formed on
the north side, and on a branch of the river which leads to a town
called Taxagual, of fifteen households (*vecinos*) more or less, which is
three leagues from this town and one league away from the river. The
land of this town [Santa Maria] is sterile because it is built on sand
and swamps. This branch of the river turns to the south-west, and
into it enter swamps and lagoons, and it has many deep places
(*bajos*). The barques and frigates anchor in this branch of the river
when they come to this town to load or unload at the foot of the Cross
which is at the end of the street and the mound on which it stands."
See also Note to Chapter III. In the *American Antiquarian* for
September, 1896, Dr. Daniel Brinton published an article on "The
Battle and the Ruins of Cintla," taken principally from notes made
by the late Dr. C. H. Berendt, who visited and surveyed the ruins in
March and April, 1869.

[2] Blotted out in the original : "twenty eight thousand."

[3] Chanpoton.

---

* "Sobre un placel de Agua que se hace de la parte del Norte" = on
a sandbank which has formed to the north of the water (?).

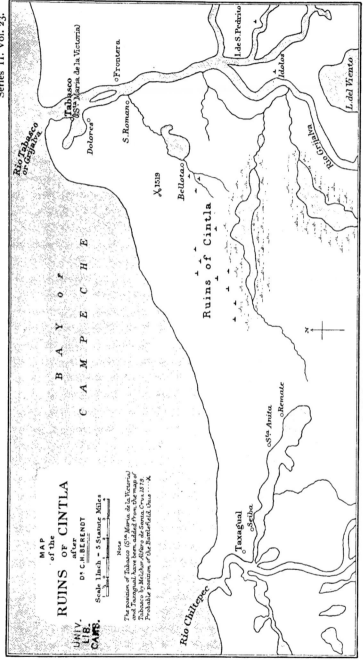

UNIV.
LIB.
CAMB.

MAP
of the
RUINS of CINTLA
after
Dᶜ C. H. BERENDT

Scale 1 Inch = 5 Statute Miles

Note

The position of Tabasco (Sᵗᵃ Maria de la Victoria)
and Taxagual have been added from the map of
Tabasco by Melchor Alfaro de Santa Cruz 1579.
Probable position of the Battlefield thus ···X

Rio Tabasco
or Grijalva

B A Y   O F

C A M P E C H E

Tabasco
(Sᵗᵃ Maria de la Victoria)

oFrontera

Doloreso

S.Romano

X 1519

Bellotao

I. de S. Pedrito

Idolos

Rio Grijalva

L. del Viento

Ruins of Cintla

N

oSᵗᵃ Anita

oRemate

Taxagual

oSeiba

Rio Chiltepec

Grijalva the gold jewels which I have spoken about in an earlier chapter, and they said that they were too faint hearted to attack us although they had more towns and more warriors than the people of Potonchan and Lázaro. This they said to annoy them and added that they in their towns had attacked us and killed fifty six of us. So on account of these taunts which had been uttered, the people of Tabasco had determined to take up arms.

When Cortés saw them drawn up ready for war he told Aguilar the interpreter, who spoke the language of Tabasco well,[1] to ask the Indians who passed near us, in a large canoe and who looked like chiefs, what they were so much disturbed about, and to tell them that we had not come to do them any harm, but were willing to give them some of the things we had brought with us and to treat them like brothers, and we prayed them not to begin a war as they would regret it, and much else was said to them about keeping the peace. However, the more Aguilar talked to them the more violent they became, and they said that they would kill us all if we entered their town, and that it was fortified all round with fences and barricades of large trunks of trees.

Aguilar spoke to them again and asked them to keep the peace, and allow us to take water and barter our goods with them for food, and permit us to tell the Calachones[2] things which would be to their advantage and to the service of God our Lord, but they still persisted in saying that if we advanced beyond the palm trees they would kill us.

When Cortés saw the state of affairs he ordered the

---

[1] These people were Tzendals, a branch of the Maya stock, and Aguilar, who spoke Maya, could understand and speak to them.

[1] Çalachiones?

boats and small vessels to be got ready and ordered three
cannon to be placed in each boat and divided the crossbowmen and musketeers among the boats. We remembered that when we were here with Grijalva we had found
a narrow path which ran across some streams from the
palm grove to the town, and Cortés ordered three soldiers
to find out in the night if that path ran right up to the
houses, and not to delay in bringing the news, and these
men found out that it did lead there. After making a
thorough examination of our surroundings the rest of the
day was spent in arranging how and in what order we
were to go in the boats.

The next morning we had our arms in readiness and
after hearing mass Cortés ordered the Captain Alonzo de
Avila and a hundred soldiers among whom were ten
crossbowmen, to go by the little path which led to the
town, and, as soon as he heard the guns fired, to attack
the town on one side while he attacked it on the other.
Cortés himself and all the other Captains and soldiers
went in the boats and light draft vessels up the river.
When the Indian warriors who were on the banks and
among the mangroves saw that we were really on the
move, they came after us with a great many canoes with
intent to prevent our going ashore at the landing place,
and the whole river bank appeared to be covered with
Indian warriors carrying all the different arms which
they use, and blowing trumpets and shells and sounding
drums. When Cortés saw how matters stood he ordered
us to wait a little and not to fire any shots from guns
or crossbows or cannon, for as he wished to be justified
in all that he might do he made another appeal to the
Indians through the interpreter Aguilar, in the presence
of the King's Notary, Diego de Godoy, asking the Indians
to allow us to land and take water and speak to them
about God and about His Majesty, and adding that should

they make war on us, that if in defending ourselves some
should be killed and others hurt, theirs would be the fault
and the burden and it would not lie with us, but they
went on threatening that if we landed they would kill us.

Then they boldly began to let fly arrows at us, and
made signals with their drums, and like valiant men they
surrounded us with their canoes, and they all attacked us
with such a shower of arrows that they kept us in the
water in some parts up to our waists. As there was much
mud and swamp at that place we could not easily get
clear of it, and so many Indians fell on us, that what
with some hurling their lances with all their might and
others shooting arrows at us, we could not reach the land
as soon as we wished.

While Cortés was fighting he lost a shoe in the mud and
could not find it again, and he got on shore with one foot
bare. Presently someone picked the shoe out of the mud
and he put it on again.

While this was happening to Cortés, all of us Captains
as well as soldiers, with the cry of "Santiago," fell upon
the Indians and forced them to retreat, but they did not fall
back far, as they sheltered themselves behind great barriers
and stockades formed of thick logs until we pulled them
apart and got to one of the small gateways of the town.
There we attacked them again, and we pushed them along
through a street to where other defences had been erected,
and there they turned on us and met us face to face and
fought most valiantly, making the greatest efforts, shouting
and whistling and crying out "al calacheoni", "al calacheoni", which in their language meant an order to kill or
capture our Captain. While we were thus surrounded by
them Alonzo de Ávila and his soldiers came up.

As I have already said they came from the Palm grove
by land and could not arrive sooner on account of the
swamps and creeks. Their delay was really unavoidable,

just as we also had been delayed over the summons of the
Indians to surrender, and in breaking openings in the
barricades, so as to enable us to attack them.   Now we all
joined together to drive the enemy out of their strong-
holds, and we compelled them to retreat, but like brave
warriors they kept on shooting showers of arrows and
fire-hardened darts, and never turned their backs on us
until [we gained] a great court with chambers and large
halls, and three Idol houses, where they had already
carried all the goods they possessed.   Cortés then ordered
us to halt, and not to follow on and overtake the enemy in
their flight.

There and then Cortés took possession of that land for
His Majesty, performing the act in His Majesty's name.
It was done in this way ; he drew his sword and as a sign
of possession he made three cuts in a huge tree called a
Ceiba, which stood in the court of that great square, and
cried that if any person should raise objection, that he
would defend the right with the sword and shield which
he held in his hands.

All of us soldiers who were present when this happened
cried out that he did right in taking possession of the land
in His Majesty's name, and that we would aid him should
any person say otherwise.   This act was done in the
presence of the Royal Notary.   The partizans of Diego
Velásquez chose to grumble at this act of taking possession.[1]

I call to mind that in that hard fought attack which the
Indians made on us, they wounded fourteen soldiers, and

---

[1] This was the first overt act showing the intention of Cortés to free
himself from the control of Velásquez and place himself directly under
the protection of his sovereign, a policy which was consummated a
few weeks later on the sands at Vera Cruz.   Had Cortés intended to
continue his subservience to Diego Velásques, his name would have
been used in the formal act of taking possession as it had been used
in the proclamations made by Cortés in Cuba.

they gave me an arrow wound in the thigh, but it was only a slight wound ; and we found eighteen Indians dead in the water where we disembarked.

We slept there [in the great square] that night with guards and sentinels on the alert. I will stop here and go on to tell what more happened.

NOTE.—The Carta de Vera Cruz says that the Indians then sent a deputation and a small present to Cortés, but still insisted that the Spaniards should leave the country. Cortés demanded food for his men, and the Indians promised to send it. Cortés then waited for two days, and as no Indians with food made their appearance he sent out the foraging expeditions described in the following Chapter.

CHAPTER XXXII.

How Cortés ordered two of his Captains each with a hundred soldiers to go and examine the country further inland, and what happened to us.

THE next morning Cortés ordered Pedro de Alvarado to set out in command of a hundred soldiers, fifteen of them with guns and crossbows, to examine the country inland for a distance of two leagues, and to take Melchorejo the interpreter from Cape Catoche in his company. When Melchorejo was looked for he could not be found as he had run off with the people of Tabasco, and it appears that the day before he had left the Spanish clothes that had been given to him hung up in the palm grove, and had fled by night in a canoe. Cortés was much annoyed at his flight, fearing that he would tell things to his fellow countrymen to our disadvantage,—well, let him go as a bit of bad luck, and let us get back to our story. Cortés also sent the Captain Francisco de Lugo, in another direction, with a hunded soldiers, twelve of them musketeers and crossbowmen, with instructions not to go beyond two leagues and to return to the camp to sleep.

I

When Francisco de Lugo and his company had marched about a league from camp he came on a great host of Indian archers carrying lances and shields, drums and standards and they made straight for our company of soldiers and surrounded them on all sides.   They were so numerous and shot their arrows so deftly that it was impossible to withstand them, and they hurled their fire-hardened darts and cast stones from their slings in such numbers that they fell like hail, and they attacked our men with their two-handed knife-like swords.[1]   Stoutly as Francisco de Lugo and his soldiers fought, they could not ward off the enemy, and when this was clear to them, while still keeping a good formation, they began to retreat towards the camp.   A certain Indian, a swift and daring runner, had been sent off to the camp to beg Cortés to come to their assistance, meanwhile Francisco de Lugo by careful management of his musketeers and crossbowmen, some loading while others fired, and by occasional charges was able to hold his own against all the squadrons attacking him.

Let us leave him in the dangerous situation I have described and return to Captain Pedro de Alvarado, who after marching about a league came on a creek which was very difficult to cross, and it pleased God our Lord so to lead him that he should return by another road in the direction where Francisco de Lugo was fighting.   When he heard the reports of the muskets and the great din of drums and trumpets, and the shouts and whistles of the Indians, he knew that there must be a battle going on, so with the greatest haste but in good order he ran towards the cries and shots and found Captain Francisco de Lugo and his men fighting with their faces to the enemy, and five of the enemy lying dead.   As soon as he joined forces

---

[1] Macanas or Maquahuitls—edged with flint or obsidian.

with Francisco de Lugo they turned on the Indians and
drove them back, but they were not able to put them
to flight, and the Indians followed our men right up to
the camp.

In like manner other companies of warriors had attacked
us where Cortés was guarding the wounded, but we soon
drove them off with our guns, which laid many of them
low, and with our good sword play.

When Cortés heard of Francisco de Lugo's peril from
the Cuban Indian who came to beg for help, we promptly
went to his assistance, and we met the two captains with
their companies about half a league from the camp. Two
soldiers of Francisco de Lugo's company were killed and
eight wounded, and three of Pedro de Alvarado's company
were wounded. When we arrived in camp we buried the
dead and tended the wounded, and stationed sentinels and
kept a strict watch.

In those skirmishes we killed fifteen Indians and captured three, one of whom seemed to be a chief, and through
Aguilar, our interpreter, we asked them why they were so
mad as to attack us, and that they could see that we
should kill them if they attacked us again. Then one of
these Indians was sent with some beads to give to the
Caciques to bring them to peace, and that messenger told
us that the Indian Melchorejo whom we had brought from
Cape Catoche, went to the chiefs the night before and
counselled them to fight us day and night and said that
they would conquer us as we were few in number; so
it turned out that we had brought an enemy with us
instead of a help.

This Indian whom we despatched with the message
went off and never returned. From the other two Indian
prisoners Aguilar the interpreter learnt for certain that by
the next day the Caciques from all the neighbouring towns
of the province would have assembled with all their forces

ready to make war on us, and that they would come and
surround our camp, for that was Melchorejo's advice to
them.

I must leave off here, and will go on to tell what we did
in the matter.

CHAPTER XXXIII.

How Cortés told us all to get ready by the next day to go in search of
the Indian host, and ordered the horses to be brought from the
ships, and what happened in the battle which we fought.

As soon as Cortés knew for certain that the Indians
intended to make war on us, he ordered all the horses to
be landed from the ships without delay, and the crossbowmen and musketeers and all of us soldiers, even those
who were wounded, to have our arms ready for use.

When the horses were brought on shore they were very
stiff and afraid to move, for they had been many days on
board ship, but the next day they moved quite freely.

At that time it happened that six or seven soldiers,
young men and otherwise in good health, suffered from
pains in their loins, so that they could not stand on their
feet and had to be carried on men's backs. We did not
know what this sickness came from, some say that they
fell ill on account of the [quilted] cotton armour which
they never took off, but wore day and night, and because
in Cuba they had lived daintily and were not used to hard
work, so in the heat they fell ill. Cortés ordered them not
to remain on land but to be taken at once on board ship.

The best horses and riders were chosen to form the
cavalry, and the horses had little bells attached to their
breastplates. The men were ordered not to stop to spear
those who were down, but to aim their lances at the faces
of the enemy.

Thirteen gentlemen were chosen to go on horseback with Cortés in command of them, and I here record their names : — Cortés, Cristóval de Olíd, Pedro de Alvarado, Alonzo Hernández Puertocarrero, Juan de Escalante, Francisco de Montejo, and Alonzo de Ávila to whom was given the horse belonging to Ortiz the musician and Bartolomé García, for neither of these men were good horsemen, Juan Velásquez de Leon, Francisco de Morla, and Lares the good horseman (I call him so because there was another Lares), Gonzalo Domínguez, an excellent horseman, Moron of Bayamo, and Pedro González of Trujillo. Cortés selected all these gentlemen and went himself as their captain.

Cortés ordered Mesa the artilleryman to have his guns ready, and he placed Diego de Ordás in command of us foot soldiers and he also had command of the musketeers and bowmen, for he was no horseman.

Very early the next day which was the day of Nuestra Señora de Marzo[1] after hearing mass, which was said by Fray Bartolomé de Olmedo, we formed in order under our standard bearer, who at that time was Antonio de Villaroel the husband of Isabel de Ojeda, who afterwards changed his name to Antonio Serrano de Cardona, and marched to some large savannas where Francisco de Lugo and Pedro de Alvarado had been attacked, about a league distant from the camp we had left ; and that savanna and township was called Cintla, and was subject to Tabasco.

Cortés [and the horsemen] were separated a short distance from us on account of some swamps which could not be crossed by the horses, and as we were marching along in the way I have said, we came on the whole force of Indian warriors who were on the way to attack us in our

---

[1] Lady-day, 25th March.

camp. It was near the town of Cintla that we met them on an open plain. So it happened that those warriors were looking for us with the intention of attacking us, and we were looking for them for the very same purpose. I must leave off here, and will go on to tell what happened in the battle, and one may well call it a battle, as will be seen further on.

CHAPTER XXXIV.

How all the Caciques of Tabasco and its dependencies atttacked us, and what came of it.

I HAVE already said how we were marching along when we met all the forces of the enemy which were moving in search of us, and all the men wore great feather crests and they carried drums and trumpets, and their faces were coloured black and white, and they were armed with large bows and arrows, lances and shields and swords shaped like our two-handed swords, and many slings and stones and fire-hardened javelins, and all wore quilted cotton armour. As they approached us their squadrons were so numerous that they covered the whole plain, and they rushed on us like mad dogs completely surrounding us, and they let fly such a cloud of arrows, javelins and stones that on the first assault they wounded over seventy of us, and fighting hand to hand they did us great damage with their lances, and one soldier[1] fell dead at once from an arrow wound in the ear, and they kept on shooting and wounding us.[2] With our muskets and crossbows and with

---

[1] Alonzo Remón Edition says "a soldier named Saldaña."

[2] Carta de Vera Cruz says that only twenty were wounded in all, and that no one died of their wounds. Gomara says seventy were wounded.

good sword play we did not fail as stout fighters, and
when they came to feel the edge of our swords little by
little they fell back, but it was only so as to shoot at
us in greater safety.   Mesa, our artilleryman, killed many
of them with his cannon, for they were formed in great
squadrons and they did not open out so that he could fire
at them as he pleased, but with all the hurts and wounds
which we gave them, we could not drive them off.   I said
to Diego de Ordás " it seems to me that we ought to close
up and charge them," for in truth they suffered greatly
from the strokes and thrusts of our swords, and that was
why they fell away from us, both from fear of these
swords, and the better to shoot their arrows and hurl their
javelins and the hail of stones.   Ordás replied that it was
not good advice, for there were three hundred Indians to
every one of us, and that we could not hold out against
such a multitude,—so there we stood enduring their attack.
However, we did agree to get as near as we could to them,
as I had advised Ordás, so as to give them a bad time
with our swordsmanship, and they suffered so much from
it that they retreated towards a swamp.

During all this time Cortés and his horsemen failed to
appear, although we greatly longed for him, and we feared
that by chance some disaster had befallen him.

I remember that when we fired shots the Indians gave
great shouts and whistles and threw dust and rubbish into
the air so that we should not see the damage done to
them, and they sounded their trumpets and drums and
shouted and whistled and cried " Alala! alala!"

Just at this time we caught sight of our horsemen,
and as the great Indian host was crazed with its attack on
us, it did not at once perceive them coming up behind
their backs, and as the plain was level ground and the
horsemen were good riders, and many of the horses were
very handy and fine gallopers, they came quickly on the

enemy and speared them as they chose. As soon as we saw the horsemen we fell on the Indians with such energy that with us attacking on one side and the horsemen on the other, they soon turned tail. The Indians thought that the horse and its rider was all one animal, for they had never seen horses up to this time.

The savannas and fields were crowded with Indians running to take refuge in the thick woods near by.

After we had defeated the enemy Cortés told us that he had not been able to come to us sooner as there was a swamp in the way, and he had to fight his way through another force of warriors before he could reach us, and three horsemen and five horses had been wounded.

As soon as the horsemen had dismounted under some trees and houses, we returned thanks to God for giving us so complete a victory.

As it was Lady day we gave to the town which was afterwards founded here the name of Santa Maria de la Victoria, on account of this great victory being won on Our Lady's day. This was the first battle that we fought under Cortés in New Spain.

After this we bound up the hurts of the wounded with cloths, for we had nothing else, and we doctored the horses by searing their wounds with the fat from the body of a dead Indian which we cut up to get out the fat, and we went to look at the dead lying on the plain and there were more than eight hundred of them, the greater number killed by thrusts, the others by the cannon, muskets and crossbows, and many were stretched on the ground half dead. Where the horsemen had passed, numbers of them lay dead or groaning from their wounds. The battle lasted over an hour, and the Indians fought all the time like brave warriors, until the horsemen came up.

We took five prisoners, two of them Captains. As it was late and we had had enough of fighting, and we had not eaten anything, we returned to our camp. Then we buried the two soldiers who had been killed, one by a wound in the ear, and the other by a wound in the throat, and we seared the wounds of the others and of the horses with the fat of the Indian, and after posting sentinels and guards, we had supper and rested.

It is on this occasion that Francisco López de Gomara says that Francisco de Morla set out on a dapple gray horse before Cortés and the other horsemen arrived, and that the sainted apostles Señor Santiago and Señor San Pedro appeared. I say that all our doings and our victories are at the hands of our Lord Jesus Christ, and that in this battle there were so many Indians to every one of us that they could have blinded us with the dust they raised but for the pity of God who always helped us. It may be that as Gomara says the Glorious Apostles Señor Santiago and Señor San Pedro came to our aid and that I, being a sinner was not worthy to behold them. What I saw was Francisco de Morla, on a chestnut horse, who came up at the same time as Cortés, and it seems to me that now as I write I can see again with these sinful eyes all that battle in the very way that it took place, and although I am a poor sinner and not worthy to see either of those glorious apostles, there were there in our company over four hundred soldiers and Cortés himself and many other gentlemen, and it would have been talked about, and evidence would have been taken, and a church would have been built when the town was founded, and the town would have been named Santiago de la Victoria, or San Pedro de la Victoria instead of Santa Maria de la Victoria. If it was as Gomara says we must have all been very bad Christians, when our Lord God sent his holy Apostle to us, not to recognise the great favour that he was showing to us, and not daily to have venerated that church. I wish to God it were as the historian Gomara says, but, until I read

his history, one never heard about it among the conquistadores who were there at the time.

I will leave off here and go on to tell what else happened
to us.

CHAPTER XXXV.

How Cortés sent to summon all the Caciques of those provinces and what was done about it.

I HAVE already said that we captured five Indians during
the battle of whom two were captains. When Aguilar
spoke to these men he found out from what they said that
they were fit persons to be sent as messengers, and he
advised Cortés to free them, so that they might go and talk
to the Caciques of the town and any others they might see.
These two messengers were given green and blue beads,
and Aguilar spoke many pleasant and flattering words
to them, telling them that they had nothing to fear as
we wished to treat them like brothers, that it was their own
fault that they had made war on us, and that now they had
better collect together all the Caciques of the different
towns as we wished to talk to them, and he gave them
much other advice in a gentle way so as to gain their good
will.   The messengers went off willingly and spoke to the
Caciques and chief men, and told them all we wished them
to know about our desire for peace.

When our envoys had been listened to, it was settled
among them that fifteen Indian slaves, all with stained
faces and ragged cloaks and loin cloths, should at once
be sent to us with fowls and baked fish and maize cakes.
When these men came before Cortés he received them
graciously, but Aguilar the interpreter asked them rather
angrily why they had come with their faces in that state,
that it looked more as though they came to fight than to
treat for peace; and he told them to go back to the

Caciques and inform them, that if they wished for peace in the way we offered it, chieftains should come and treat for it, as was always the custom, and that they should not send slaves. But even these painted faced slaves were treated with consideration by us and blue beads were sent by them in sign of peace, and to soothe their feelings.

The next day thirty Indian Chieftains, clad in good cloaks, came to visit us and brought fowls, fish, fruit and maize cakes, and asked leave from Cortés to burn and bury the bodies of the dead who had fallen in the recent battles, so that they should not smell badly or be eaten by lions and tigers. Permission was at once given them and they hastened to bring many people to bury and burn the bodies according to their customs.

Cortés learnt from the Caciques that over eight hundred men were missing, not counting those who had been carried off wounded.[1]

They said that they could not tarry with us either to discuss the matter or make peace, for on the morrow the chieftains and leaders of all the towns would have assembled, and that then they would agree about a peace.

As Cortés was very sagacious about everything, he said, laughing, to us soldiers who happened to be in his company, " Do you know, gentlemen, that it seems to me that the Indians are terrified at the horses and may think that they and the cannon alone make war on them. I have thought of something which will confirm this belief, and that is to bring the mare belonging to Juan Sedeño, which foaled the other day on board ship, and tie her up where I am now standing and also to bring the stallion of Ortiz the musician, which is very excitable, near enough to scent the mare, and when he has scented her to lead

---

[1] The Carta de Vera Cruz says the Indians were 40,000 in number and that they lost 220 killed.

each of them off separately so that the Caciques who are coming shall not hear the horse neighing as they approach, not until they are standing before me and are talking to me." We did just as Cortés ordered and brought the horse and mare, and the horse soon detected the scent of her in Cortés's quarters. In addition to this Cortés ordered the largest cannon that we possessed to be loaded with a large ball and a good charge of powder.

About mid-day forty Indians arrived, all of them Caciques of good bearing, wearing rich mantles such as are used by them. They saluted Cortés and all of us, and brought incense and fumigated all of us who were present, and they asked pardon for their past behaviour, and said that henceforth they would be friendly.

Cortés, through Aguilar the Interpreter, answered them in a rather grave manner, as though he were angry, that they well knew how many times he had asked them to maintain peace, that the fault was theirs, and that now they deserved to be put to death, they and all the people of their towns, but that as we were the vassals of a great King and Lord named the Emperor Don Carlos, who had sent us to these countries, and ordered us to help and favour those who would enter his royal service, that if they were now as well disposed as they said they were, that we would take this course, but that if they were not, some of those *Tepustles* would jump out and kill them (they call iron *Tepustle* in their language) for some of the *Tepustles* were still angry because thay had made war on us. At this moment the order was secretly given to put a match to the cannon which had been loaded, and it went off with such a thunderclap as was wanted, and the ball went buzzing over the hills, and as it was mid-day and very still it made a great noise, and the Caciques were terrified on hearing it. As they had never seen anything like it they believed what Cortés had told them was true.

Then Cortés told them, through Aguilar, not to be afraid for he had given orders that no harm should be done to them.

Just then the horse that had scented the mare was brought and tied up not far distant from where Cortés was talking to the Caciques, and, as the mare had been tied up at the place where Cortés and the Indians were talking, the horse began to paw the ground and neigh and become wild with excitement, looking all the time towards the Indians and the place whence the scent of the mare had reached him, and the Caciques thought that he was roaring at them and they were terrified. When Cortés observed their state of mind, he rose from his seat and went to the horse and told two orderlies to lead it far away, and said to the Indians that he had told the horse not to be angry as they were friendly and wished to make peace.

While this was going on there arrived more than thirty Indian carriers, whom the natives call *Tamenes*, who brought a meal of fowls and fish and fruits and other food, and it appears that they had lagged behind and could not reach us at the same time as the Caciques.

Cortés had a long conversation with these chieftains and Caciques and they told him that they would all come on the next day and would bring a present and would discuss other matters, and then they went away quite contented.

And there I will leave them until the next day.

CHAPTER XXXVI.

How all the Caciques and Calachonis from the Rio de Grijalva came
and brought a present, and what took place about it.

EARLY the next morning, the 15th March, 1519,[1] many
Caciques and chiefs of Tabasco and the neighbouring
towns arrived and paid great respect to us all, and they
brought a present of gold, consisting of four diadems and
some gold lizards, and two [ornaments] like little dogs, and
earrings, and five ducks, and two masks[2] with Indian faces,
and two gold soles for sandals, and some other things of
little value. I do not remember how much the things were
worth; and they brought cloth, such as they make and
wear, which was quilted stuff. My readers will have heard
from those who know that province that there is nothing
of much value in it.

This present, however, was worth nothing in comparison
with the twenty women that were given us, among them
one very excellent woman called Doña Marina, for so she
was named when she became a Christian. I will leave off
talking about her and the other women who were brought
to us, and will tell how Cortés received this present with
pleasure and went aside with all the Caciques, and with
Aguilar, the interpreter, to hold converse, and he told
them that he gave them thanks for what they had brought
with them, but there was one thing that he must ask
of them, namely, that they should re-occupy the town
with all their people, women and children, and he wished
to see it repeopled within two days, for he would
recognize that as a sign of true peace. The Caciques

---

[1] This is evidently an error, as Bernal Díaz has already stated that
the Battle of Cintla was fought on Lady day, the 25th March.

[2] In the text "dos figuras de Caras de Indios."

sent at once to summon all the inhabitants with their women and children and within two days they were again settled in the town.

One other thing Cortés asked of the chiefs and that was to give up their idols and sacrifices, and this they said they would do, and, through Aguilar, Cortés told them as well as he was able about matters concerning our holy faith, how we were Christians and worshipped one true and only God, and he showed them an image of Our Lady with her precious Son in her arms and explained to them that we paid the greatest reverence to it as it was the image of the Mother of our Lord God who was in heaven. The Caciques replied that they liked the look of the great Teleciguata (for in their language great ladies are called Teleciguatas) and [begged] that she might be given them to keep in their town, and Cortés said that the image should be given to them and ordered them to make a well-constructed altar, and this they did at once.

The next morning, Cortés ordered two of our carpenters, named Alonzo Yañez and Alvaro López, to make a very tall cross.

When all this had been settled Cortés asked the Caciques what was their reason for attacking us three times when we had asked them to keep the peace ; the chief replied that he had already asked pardon for their acts and had been forgiven, that the Cacique of Chanpoton, his brother, had advised it, and that he feared to be accused of cowardice, for he had already been reproached and dishonoured for not having attacked the other captain who had come with four ships, (he must have meant Juan de Grijalva) and he also said that the Indian whom we had brought as an Interpreter, who escaped in the night, had advised them to attack us both by day and night.

Cortés then ordered this man to be brought before him without fail, but they replied that when he saw that the battle was going against them, he had taken to flight, and they knew not where he was although search had been made for him; but we came to know that they had offered him as a sacrifice because his counsel had cost them so dear.

Cortés also asked them where they procured their gold and jewels, and they replied, from the direction of the setting sun, and said "Culua" and "Mexico," and as we did not know what Mexico and Culua meant we paid little attention to it.

Then we brought another interpreter named Francisco, whom we had captured during Grijalva's expedition, who has already been mentioned by me, but he understood nothing of the Tabasco language only that of Culua[1] which is the Mexican tongue. By means of signs he told Cortés that Culua was far ahead, and he repeated "Mexico" which we did not understand.

So the talk ceased until the next day when the sacred image of Our Lady and the Cross were set up on the altar and we all paid reverence to them, and Padre Fray Bartolomé de Olmedo said mass and all the Caciques and chiefs were present and we gave the name of Santa Maria de la Victoria to the town, and by this name the town of Tabasco is now called. The same friar, with Aguilar as interpreter, preached many good things about our holy faith to the twenty Indian women who had been given us, telling them not to believe in the Idols which they had been wont to trust in, for they were evil things and not gods, and that they should offer no more sacrifices to them for they would lead them astray, but that they should worship our Lord Jesus Christ, and immediately afterwards they were baptized. One Indian lady who was given to us here was christened Doña Marina, and she was truly a great chief-

---

[1] The word in the text is Cuba, but clearly it must be intended for Culua, as is shown in the context.

tainess and the daughter of great Caciques and the mistress of vassals, and this her appearance clearly showed. Later on I will relate why it was and in what manner she was brought here.

I do not clearly remember the names of all the other women, and it is not worth while to name any of them ; however, they were the first women to become Christians in New Spain.

Cortés allotted one of them to each of his captains and Doña Marina, as she was good looking and intelligent and without embarrassment, he gave to Alonzo Hernández Puertocarrero, who I have already said was a distinguished gentleman, and cousin of the Count of Medellin. When Puertocarrero went to Spain, Doña Marina lived with Cortés, and bore him a son named Don Martin Cortés.

We remained five days in this town, to look after the wounded and those who were suffering from pain in the loins, from which they all recovered. Furthermore, Cortés drew the Caciques to him by kindly converse, and told them how our master the Emperor, whose vassals we were, had under his orders many great lords, and that it would be well for them also to render him obedience, and that then, whatever they might be in need of, whether it was our protection or any other necessity, if they would make it known to him, no matter where he might be, he would come to their assistance.

The Caciques all thanked him for this, and thereupon all declared themselves the vassals of our great Emperor. These were the first vassals to render submission to His Majesty in New Spain.

Cortés then ordered the Caciques to come with their women and children early the next day, which was Palm Sunday, to the altar, to pay homage to the holy image of Our Lady and to the Cross, and at the same time Cortés ordered them to send six Indian carpenters to accompany

K

our carpenters to the town of Cintla where our Lord God was pleased to give us victory in the battle which I have described, there to cut a cross on a great tree called a Ceiba which grew there, and they did it so that it might last a long time, for as the bark is renewed the cross will show there for ever.   When this was done he ordered the Indians to get ready all the canoes that they owned to help us to embark, for we wished to set sail on that holy day because the pilots had come to tell Cortés that the ships ran a great risk from a *Norther* which is a dangerous gale.

The next day, early in the morning, all the Caciques and chiefs came in their canoes with all their women and children and stood in the court where we had placed the church and cross, and many branches of trees had already been cut ready to be carried in the procession.   Then the Caciques beheld us all, Cortés, as well as the captains, and every one of us marching together with the greatest reverence in a devout procession, and the Padre de la Merced and the priest, Juan Diaz, clad in their vestments, said mass, and we paid reverence to and kissed the Holy Cross, while the Caciques and Indians stood looking on at us.

When our solemn festival was over the chiefs approached and offered Cortés ten fowls, and baked fish and vegetables, and we took leave of them, and Cortés again commended to their care the Holy image and the sacred crosses and told them always to keep the place clean and well swept and to deck the cross with garlands and to reverence it, and then they would enjoy good health and bountiful harvests.

It was growing late when we got on board ship and the next day, Monday, we set sail in the morning and with a fair wind laid our course for San Juan de Ulúa, keeping close in shore all the time

As we sailed along in the fine weather, we soldiers who knew the coast would say to Cortés, "Señor, over there is La Rambla, which the Indians call Ayagualulco," and soon afterwards we arrived off Tonalá which we called San Antonio, and we pointed it out to him. Further on we showed him the great river of Coatzacoalcos, and he saw the lofty snow capped mountains, and then the Sierra of San Martin, and further on we pointed out the split rock, which is a great rock standing out in the sea with a mark on the top of it which gives it the appearance of a seat. Again further on we showed him the Rio de Alvarado, which Pedro de Alvarado entered when we were with Grijalva, and then we came in sight of the Rio de Banderas, where we had gained in barter the sixteen thousand dollars, then we showed him the Isla Blanca, and told him where lay the Isla Verde, and close in shore we saw the Isla de Sacrificios where we found the altars and the Indian victims in Grijalva's time ; and at last our good fortune brought us to San Juan de Ulúa soon after midday on Holy Thursday.

I remember that a gentleman, Alonzo Hernández Puertocarrero came up to Cortés and said : " It seems to me, sir, that these gentlemen who have been twice before to this country are saying to you :—

Cata Francia, Montesinos.	Behold France, Montesinos.
Cata Paris la ciudad.	Look at Paris, the city.
Cata las aguas de Duero	See the waters of the Duero
Do van a dar en la Mar.	Flowing to the sea.

I say that you are looking on rich lands, may you know how to govern them well!"

Cortés knew well the purpose for which these words were said, and answered : "Let God give us the good fortune in fighting which He gave to the Paladin Roldan, and with Your Honour and the other gentlemen for leaders, I shall know well how to manage it."

Let us leave off here, for this is what took place and Cortés did not go into the Rio de Alvarado, as Gomara says he did.

CHAPTER XXXVII.

Showing that Doña Marina was a *Cacica* and the daughter of persons of high rank, and was the mistress of towns and vassals, and how it happened that she was taken to Tabasco.

BEFORE telling about the great Montezuma and his famous City of Mexico and the Mexicans, I wish to give some account of Doña Marina, who from her childhood had been the mistress and Cacica of towns and vassals. It happened in this way:

Her father and mother were chiefs and Caciques of a town called Paynala, which had other towns subject to it, and stood about eight leagues from the town of Coatza-coalcos. Her father died while she was still a little child, and her mother married another Cacique, a young man, and bore him a son. It seems that the father and mother had a great affection for this son and it was agreed between them that he should succeed to their honours when their days were done. So that there should be no impediment to this, they gave the little girl, Doña Marina, to some Indians from Xicalango[1] and this they did by night so as to escape observation, and they then spread the report that she had died, and as it happened at this time that a child of one of their Indian slaves died they gave out that it was their daughter and the heiress who was dead.

The Indians of Xicalango gave the child to the people of Tabasco, and the Tabasco people gave her to Cortés. I myself knew her mother, and the old woman's son and

---

[1] Xicalango, on the southern side of the Laguna de Términos, was an outlying stronghold of the Aztec Empire. (See *Relacion de Melchor de Sta. Cruz.*)

her half-brother, when he was already grown up and ruled the town jointly with his mother, for the second husband of the old lady was dead. When they became Christians, the old lady was called Marta and the son Lázaro. I knew all this very well because in the year 1523 after the conquest of Mexico and the other provinces, when Cristóval de Olid revolted in Honduras, and Cortés was on his way there, he passed through Coatzacoalcos and I and the greater number of the settlers of that town accompanied him on that expedition as I shall relate in the proper time and place. As Doña Marina proved herself such an excellent woman and good interpreter throughout the wars in New Spain, Tlascala and Mexico (as I shall show later on) Cortés always took her with him, and during that expedition she was married to a gentleman named Juan Jaramillo at the town of Orizaba, before certain witnesses, one of whom was named Aranda, a settler in Tabasco and this man told [me] about the marriage (not in the way the historian Gomara relates it).

Doña Marina was a person of the greatest importance and was obeyed without question by the Indians throughout New Spain.

When Cortés was in the town of Coatzacoalcos he sent to summon to his presence all the Caciques of that province in order to make them a speech about our holy religion, and about their good treatment, and among the Caciques who assembled was the mother of Doña Marina and her half-brother, Lázaro.

Some time before this Doña Marina had told me that she belonged to that province and that she was the mistress of vassals, and Cortés also knew it well, as did Aguilar, the interpreter. In such a manner it was that mother, daughter and son came together, and it was easy enough to see that she was the daughter from the strong likeness she bore to her mother.

These relations were in great fear of Doña Marina, for they thought that she had sent for them to put them to death, and they were weeping.

When Doña Marina saw them in tears, she consoled them and told them to have no fear, that when they had given her over to the men from Xicalango, they knew not what they were doing, and she forgave them for doing it, and she gave them many jewels of gold, and raiment, and told them to return to their town, and said that God had been very gracious to her in freeing her from the worship of idols and making her a Christian, and letting her bear a son to her lord and master Cortés and in marrying her to such a gentleman as Juan Jaramillo, who was now her husband. That she would rather serve her husband and Cortés than anything else in the world, and would not exchange her place to be Cacica of all the provinces in New Spain.

All this which I have repeated here I know for certain (and I swear to it.)[1]

This seems to me very much like what took place between Joseph and his brethren in Egypt when they came into his power over the matter of the wheat. It is what actually happened and not the story which was told to Gomara, who also says other things which I will leave unnoticed.

To go back to my subject: Doña Marina knew the language of Coatzacoalcos, which is that common to Mexico, and she knew the language of Tabasco, as did also Jerónimo de Aguilar, who spoke the language of Yucatan and Tabasco, which is one and the same. So that these two could understand one another clearly, and Aguilar translated into Castilian for Cortés.

---

[1] The words in brackets are blotted out in the original MS. —G. G.

This was the great beginning of our conquests and thus, thanks be to God, things prospered with us. I have made a point of explaining this matter, because without the help of Doña Marina we could not have understood the language of New Spain and Mexico.

Here I will leave off, and go on later to tell how we disembarked in the Port of San Juan de Ulúa.

BOOK III.

THE MARCH INLAND.

CHAPTER XXXVIII.

How we arrived with all the ships at San Juan de Ulúa, and what happened there.

N Holy Thursday, the anniversary of the Last Supper of Our Lord, in the year 1519, we arrived with all the fleet at the Port of San Juan de Ulúa, and as the Pilot Alaminos knew the place well from having come there with Juan de Grijalva he at once ordered the vessels to drop anchor where they would be safe from the northerly gales. The flagship hoisted her royal standards and pennants, and within half an hour of anchoring, two large canoes (which in those parts are called piraguas) came out to us, full of Mexican Indians. Seeing the big ship with the standards flying they knew that it was there they must go to speak with the captain ; so they went direct to the flagship and going on board asked who was the Tatuan[1] which in their language means the chief. Doña Marina who understood the language well, pointed him out. Then the Indians paid many marks

---

[1] Tlatoan.

of respect to Cortés, according to their usage, and bade
him welcome, and said that their lord, a servant of the
great Montezuma, had sent them to ask what kind of men
we were and of what we were in search, and added that if
we were in need of anything for ourselves or the ships, that
we should tell them and they would supply it. Our Cortés
thanked them through the two interpreters, Aguilar and
Doña Marina, and ordered food and wine to be given them
and some blue beads, and after they had drunk he told
them that we came to see them and to trade with them
and that our arrival in their country should cause them no
uneasiness but be looked on by them as fortunate. The
messengers returned on shore well content, and the next
day, which was Good Friday, we disembarked with the
horses and guns, on some sand hills which rise to a
considerable height, for there was no level land, nothing
but sand dunes; and the artilleryman Mesa placed the
guns in position to the best of his judgment. Then we set
up an altar where mass was said and we made huts
and shelters for Cortés and the captains, and three hundred
of the soldiers brought wood and made huts for themselves
and we placed the horses where they would be safe and in
this way was Good Friday passed.

The next day, Saturday, Easter Eve, many Indians
arrived sent by a chief who was a governor under Montezuma, named Pitalpitoque[1] (whom we afterwards called
Ovandillo), and they brought axes and dressed wood for
the huts of the captain Cortés and the other ranchos near to
it, and covered them with large cloths on account of the
strength of the sun, for as it was in Lent the heat was very
great—and they brought fowls and maize cakes and plums,
which were then in season, and I think that they brought

---

[1] Pitalpitoque = Cuitlalpitoc, who had been sent as an ambassador
to meet Grijalva.   See *Orozco y Berra*, pp. 44 and 132, vol. iv.

some gold jewels, and they presented all these things to Cortés ; and said that the next day a governor would come and would bring more food. Cortés thanked them heartily and ordered them to be given certain articles in exchange with which they went away well content. The next day, Easter Sunday, the governor whom they spoke of arrived. His name was Tendile,[1] a man of affairs, and he brought with him Pitalpitoque who was also a man of importance amongst the natives and there followed them many Indians with presents of fowls and vegetables. Tendile ordered these people to stand aside on a hillock and with much humility he made three obeisances to Cortés according to their custom,[2] and then to all the soldiers who were standing around. Cortés bade them welcome through our interpreters and embraced them and asked them to wait, as he wished presently to speak to them. Meanwhile he ordered an altar to be made as well as it could be done in the time, and Fray Bartolomé de Olmedo, who was a fine singer, chanted Mass, and Padre Juan Diaz[3] assisted, and the two governors and the other chiefs who were with them looked on. When Mass was over, Cortés and some of our captains and the two Indian officers of the great Montezuma dined together. When the tables had been cleared away—Cortés went aside with the two Caciques and our two interpreters and explained to them that we were Christians and vassals of the greatest lord on earth, called the Emperor Don Carlos, who had many great princes as his vassals and servants, and that it was at his orders that we had come to this country, because for many years he had heard rumours

---

[1] Teuhtlilli, Governor of Cuetlaxtla (Cotaxtla of modern maps).

[2] Blotted out in the original—"and they brought much incense on live coals in pottery brasiers."—G. G.

[3] Blotted out in the original—"and other soldiers who helped him."—G. G.

about the country and the great prince who ruled it. That he wished to be friends with this prince and to tell him many things in the name of the Emperor which things, when he knew and understood them, would please him greatly. Moreover he wished to trade with their prince and his Indians in good friendship, and he wanted to know where this prince would wish that they should meet so that they might confer together. Tendile replied somewhat proudly, and said—" You have only just now arrived and you already ask to speak with our prince ; accept now this present which we give you in his name, and afterwards you will tell me what you think fitting." With that he took out a *petaca*—which is a sort of chest, many articles of gold beautifully and richly worked and ordered ten loads of white cloth made of cotton and feathers to be brought, wonderful things to see, and there were other things which I do not remember, besides quantities of food consisting of fowls of the country,[1] fruit and baked fish. Cortés received it all with smiles in a gracious manner and gave in return, beads of twisted glass and other small beads from Spain, and he begged them to send to their towns to ask the people to come and trade with us as he had brought many beads to exchange for gold, and they replied that they would do as he asked. As we afterwards found out, these two men, Tendile and Pitalpitoque, were the governors of the provinces named Cotustan, Tustepeque,[2] Guazpaltepeque and Tatalteco, and of some other townships lately conquered. Cortés then ordered his servants to bring an arm-chair, richly carved and inlaid and some *margaritas*,[3] stones with many [intricate] designs in them, and a string

---

[1] Turkeys, Huajolotes (Mex.).

[2] Cotaxtla, Tuxtepec.

[3] Piedras margaritas, possibly margajita ; probably mossagate or lapis lazuli.

of twisted glass beads[1] packed in cotton scented with musk
and a crimson cap with a golden medal engraved with
a figure of St. George on horseback, lance in hand, slaying
the dragon, and he told Tendile that he should send
the chair to his prince Montezuma (for we already knew
that he was so called) so that he could be seated in it when
he, Cortés, came to see and speak with him, and that
he should place the cap on his head, and that the stones
and all the other things were presents from our lord
the King, as a sign of his friendship, for he was aware that
Montezuma was a great prince, and Cortés asked that
a day and a place might be named where he could go
to see Montezuma. Tendile received the present and said
that his lord Montezuma was such a great prince that
it would please him to know our great King and that
he would carry the present to him at once and bring back
a reply.

It appears that Tendile brought with him some clever
painters such as they had in Mexico and ordered them
to make pictures true to nature of the face and body of
Cortés and all his captains, and of the soldiers, ships, sails
and horses, and of Doña Marina and Aguilar, even of the
two greyhounds, and the cannon and cannon balls, and all
of the army we had brought with us, and he carried
the pictures to his master. Cortés ordered our gunners
to load the lombards with a great charge of powder so that
they should make a great noise when they were fired
off, and he told Pedro de Alvarado that he and all the
horsemen should get ready so that these servants of
Montezuma might see them gallop and told them to attach
little bells to the horses' breastplates. Cortés also mounted
his horse and said—" It would be well if we could gallop
on these sand dunes but they will observe that even when

---

[1] Diamantes torcidos.

on foot we get stuck in the sand—let us go out to the
beach when the tide is low and gallop two and two ;"—
and to Pedro de Alvarado whose sorrel coloured mare was
a great galloper, and very handy, he gave charge of all the
horsemen.

All this was carried out in the presence of the two
ambassadors, and so that they should see the cannon fired,
Cortés made as though he wished again to speak to them
and a number of other chieftains, and the lombards were
fired off, and as it was quite still at that moment, the
stones went flying through the forest resounding with a
great din, and the two governors and all the other Indians
were frightened by things so new to them, and ordered the
painters to record them so that Montezuma might see. It
happened that one of the soldiers had a helmet half gilt but
somewhat rusty and this Tendile noticed, for he was the
more forward of the two ambassadors, and said that he
wished to see it as it was like one that they possessed which
had been left to them by their ancestors of the race from
which they had sprung, and that it had been placed on the
head of their god—Huichilobos,[1] and that their prince
Montezuma would like to see this helmet. So it was given
to him, and Cortés said to them that as he wished to know
whether the gold of this country was the same as that we
find in our rivers, they could return the helmet filled with
grains of gold so that he could send it to our great
Emperor. After this, Tendile bade farewell to Cortés and
to all of us and after many expressions of regard from
Cortés he took leave of him and said that he would return
with a reply without delay. After Tendile had departed
we found out that besides being an Indian employed in
matters of great importance, Tendile was the most active
of the servants whom his master, Montezuma, had in

---

[1] Huitzilopochtli.

his employ, and he went with all haste and narrated everything to his prince, and showed him the pictures which had been painted and the present which Cortés had sent.   When the great Montezuma gazed on it he was struck with admiration and received it on his part with satisfaction.   When he examined the helmet and that which was on his Huichilobos, he felt convinced that we belonged to the race which, as his forefathers had foretold would come to rule over that land.   It is here that the historian Gomara relates many things which were not told to him correctly.

I will leave off here, and then go on to say what else happened.

CHAPTER XXXIX.

How Tendile went to report to his Prince Montezuma and to carry the present, and what we did in our camp.

WHEN Tendile departed with the present which the Captain Cortés gave him for his prince Montezuma, the other governor, Pitalpitoque, stayed in our camp and occupied some huts a little distance from ours, and they brought Indian women there to make maize bread, and brought fowls and fruit and fish, and supplied Cortés and the captains who fed with him.   As for us soldiers, if we did not hunt for shell fish on the beach, or go out fishing, we did not get anything.

About that time, many Indians came from the towns already mentioned by me over which these two servants of Montezuma were governors, and some of them brought gold and jewels of little value, and fowls to exchange with us for our goods, which consisted of green beads and clear glass beads and other articles, and with this we managed to supply ourselves with food.   Almost all the soldiers had brought things for barter, as we learnt in Grijalva's time that it was a good thing to bring beads—and in this manner six or seven days passed by.

Then one morning, Tendile arrived with more than one hundred laden Indians, accompanied by a great Mexican Cacique, who in his face, features and appearance bore a strong likeness to our Captain Cortés and the great Montezuma had sent him purposely, for it is said that when Tendile brought the portrait of Cortés all the chiefs who were in Montezuma's company said that a great chief named Quintalbor looked exactly like Cortés and that was the name of the Cacique who now arrived with Tendile; and as he was so like Cortés we called them in camp "our Cortés" and "the other Cortés." To go back to my story, when these people arrived and came before our Captain they first of all kissed the earth[1] and then fumigated him and all the soldiers who were standing around him, with incense which they brought in brasiers of pottery. Cortés received them affectionately and seated them near himself, and that chief who came with the present (who I have already said was named Quintalbor) had been appointed spokesman together with Tendile. After welcoming us to the country and after many courteous speeches had passed he ordered the presents which he had brought to be displayed, and they were placed on mats which they call petates over which were spread cotton cloths.[2] The first article presented was a wheel like a sun, as big as a cart-wheel, with many sorts of pictures on it, the whole of fine gold, and a wonderful thing to behold, which those who afterwards weighed it said was worth more than ten thousand dollars. Then another wheel was presented of greater size made of silver of great brilliancy in

---

[1] On seeing Don Hernando Cortés they made the usual obeisance, placing the forefinger (*dedo mayor*) of the right hand on the ground and raising it to the mouth. (*Orozco y Berra*, vol. iv, p. 127.)

[2] See Appendix A.   Montezuma's gifts to Cortés.

imitation of the moon with other figures shown on it, and this was of great value as it was very heavy—and the chief brought back the helmet full of fine grains of gold, just as they are got out of the mines, and this was worth three thousand dollars. This gold in the helmet was worth more to us than if it had contained $20,000, because it showed us that there were good mines there. Then were brought twenty golden ducks, beautifully worked and very natural looking, and some [ornaments] like dogs, of the kind they keep, and many articles of gold worked in the shape of tigers and lions and monkeys, and ten collars beautifully worked and other necklaces ; and twelve arrows and a bow with its string, and two rods like staffs of justice, five palms long, all in beautiful hollow work of fine gold. Then there were presented crests of gold and plumes of rich green feathers, and others of silver, and fans of the same materials, and deer copied in hollow gold and many other things that I cannot remember for it all happened so many years ago. And then over thirty loads of beautiful cotton cloth were brought worked with many patterns and decorated with many coloured feathers, and so many other things were there that it is useless my trying to describe them for I know not how to do it. When all these things had been presented, this great Cacique Quintalbor and Tendile asked Cortés to accept this present with the same willingness with which his prince had sent it, and divide it among the *teules*[1] and men who accompanied him. Cortés received the present with delight and then the ambassadors told Cortés that they wished to repeat what their prince, Montezuma, had sent them to say. First of all they told him that he was pleased that such valiant men, as he had heard that we

---

[1] *Teules*, "for so they call the Idols which they worship." See p. 172.

were, should come to his country, for he knew all about
what we had done at Tabasco, and that he would much
like to see our great emperor who was such a mighty prince
and whose fame was spread over so many lands, and that
he would send him a present of precious stones ; and that
meanwhile we should stay in that port ; that if he could
assist us in any way he would do so with the greatest
pleasure ; but as to the interview, they should not worry
about it ; that there was no need for it and they (the
ambassadors) urged many objections.   Cortés kept a good
countenance, and returned his thanks to them, and with
many flattering expressions gave each of the ambassadors
two holland shirts and some blue glass beads and other
things, and begged them to go back as his ambassadors to
Mexico and to tell their prince, the great Montezuma, that
as we had come across so many seas, and had journeyed
from such distant lands solely to see and speak with him
in person, that if we should return thus, that our great king
and lord would not receive us well, and that wherever their
prince Montezuma might be we wished to go and see him
and do what he might order us to do.   The ambassadors
replied that they would go back and give this message to
their prince, but as to the question of the desired interview
—they considered it superfluous.   By these ambassadors
Cortés sent what our poverty could afford as a gift to
Montezuma : a glass cup of Florentine ware, engraved with
trees and hunting scenes and gilt, and three holland shirts
and other things, and he charged the messengers to bring
a reply.   The two governors set out and Pitalpitoque
remained in camp ; for it seems that the other servants of
Montezuma had given him orders to see that food was
brought to us from the neighbouring towns.   Here I will
leave off, and then go on to tell what happened in our
camp.

L

CHAPTER XL.

How Cortés sent to look for another harbour and site where to make
a settlement, and what was done about it.

AS soon as the messengers had been sent off to Mexico,
Cortés despatched two ships to go and explore the coast
further along, and placed Francisco de Montejo in command of them and ordered him to follow the course
we had taken with Grijalva (for Montejo had accompanied
us during Grijalva's expedition) and to seek out a safe
harbour, and search for lands where we could settle, for it
was clear that we could not settle on those sand dunes,
both on account of the mosquitoes and the distance from
other towns.   Cortés ordered Alaminos and Juan Álvarez
el Manquillo to go as pilots as they knew the route, and
told them to sail as far along the coast as was possible in
ten days.   They did as they were told and arrived at the
Rio Grande, which is close to Panuco,[1] which we had
reached during the expedition under the Captain Juan de
Grijalva.   They were not able to proceed any further
on account of the strong currents.   Seeing how difficult
the navigation had become, they turned round and made
for San Juan de Ulúa, without having made any further
progress, or having anything to tell us, beyond the news
that, twelve leagues away, they had seen a town looking
like a fortified harbour which was called Quiahuitztlan, and
that near that town was a harbour where the pilot Alaminos
thought that the ships would be safe from the northerly
gales.   He gave to it an ugly name, that of Bernal, for it
is like another harbour in Spain of that name.   In these
comings and goings Montejo was occupied ten or twelve
days.

---

[1] The expedition under Grijalva did not pass beyond Cape Rojo.

I must now go back to say that the Indian Pitalpitoque, who remained behind to look after the food, slackened his efforts to such an extent that no provisions reached the camp and we were greatly in need of food, for the cassava turned sour from the damp and rotted and became foul with weevils and if we had not gone hunting for shell fish we should have had nothing to eat.   The Indians who used to come bringing gold and fowls for barter, did not come in such numbers as on our first arrival and those who did come were very shy and cautious and we began to count the hours that must elapse before the return of the messengers who had gone to Mexico.   We were thus waiting when Tendile returned accompanied by many Indians, and after having paid their respects in the usual manner by fumigating Cortés and the rest of us with incense, he presented ten loads of fine rich feather cloth, and four chalchihuites, which are green stones of very great value, and held in the greatest esteem among the Indians, more than emeralds are by us, and certain other gold articles.   Not counting the chalchihuites, the gold alone was said to be worth three thousand dollars.   Then Tendile and Pitalpitoque approached (the other great cacique, Quintalbor, fell ill on the road and did not return) and those two governors went aside with Cortés and Doña Marina and Aguilar, and reported that their prince Montezuma had accepted the present and was greatly pleased with it, but as to an interview, that no more should be said about it; that these rich stones of chalchihuite should be sent to the great Emperor as they were of the highest value, each one being worth more and being esteemed more highly than a great load of gold, and that it was not worth while to send any more messengers to Mexico.   Cortés thanked the messengers and gave them presents, but it was certainly a disappointment to him to be told so distinctly that we could not see Montezuma, and he said to some soldiers who happened to be standing near : " Surely this must be a great and rich prince, and some day, please God, we must go and see him"—and the soldiers answered : " We wish that we were already living with him !"

Let us now leave this question of visits and relate that it was now the time of the Ave Maria, and at the sound of a bell which we had in the camp we all fell on our knees before a cross placed on a sand hill and said our prayers of the Ave Maria before the cross. When Tendile and Pitalpitoque saw us thus kneeling, as they were very intelligent, they asked what was the reason that we humbled ourselves before a tree cut in that particular way. As Cortés heard this remark he said to the Padre de la Merced who was present : " It is a good opportunity, father, as we have good material at hand, to explain through our interpreters matters touching our holy faith." And then he delivered a discourse to the Caciques so fitting to the occasion that no good theologian could have bettered it. After telling them that we were Christians and relating all the matters pertaining to our holy religion, he told them that their idols were not good but evil things which would take flight at the presence of that sign of the cross, for on a similar cross the Lord of Heaven and earth and all created things suffered passion and death ; that it is He whom we adore and in whom we believe, our true God, Jesus Christ, who had been willing to suffer and die in order to save the whole human race ; that the third day He rose again and is now in heaven ; and that by Him we shall all be judged. Cortés said many other things very well expressed, which they thoroughly understood, and they replied that they would report them to their prince Montezuma. Cortés also told them that one of the objects for which our great Emperor had sent us to their countries was to abolish human sacrifices, and the other

evil rites which they practised and to see that they did not
rob one another, or worship those curséd images.   And
Cortés prayed them to set up in their city, in the temples
where they kept the idols which they believed to be gods, a
cross like the one they saw before them, and to set up
in the same place an image of Our Lady, which he would
give them, with her precious son in her arms, and they
would see how well it would go with them, and what our
God would do for them.   However, as many other arguments were used and as I do not know how to write them
all out at length I will leave the subject and recall to mind
that on this latest visit many Indians came with Tendile,
who were wishing to barter articles of gold, which, however, were of no great value.   So all the soldiers set about
bartering, and the gold which we gained by this barter we
gave to the sailors who were out fishing in exchange for
their fish so as to get something to eat, for otherwise
we often underwent great privations through hunger.
Cortés was pleased at this although he pretended not to
see what was going on, and many of the servants and
friends of Diego Velásquez asked him why he did not
prevent us from bartering.   What happened about this
I will tell later.

CHAPTER XLI.

What was done about the bartering for gold, and other things that took place in camp.

WHEN the friends of Diego Velásquez saw that some of
us soldiers were bartering for gold, they asked Cortés why
he permitted it, and said that Diego Velásquez did not
send out the expedition in order that the soldiers should
carry off most of the gold, and that it would be as well to
issue an order that for the future no gold should be

bartered for by anyone but Cortés himself and that all the gold already obtained should be displayed so that the royal fifth might be taken from it, and that some suitable person should be placed in charge of the treasury.

To all this Cortés replied that all they said was good, and that they themselves should name that person, and they chose Gonzalo Mejia. When this had been done, Cortés turned to them with angry mien and said : "Observe, gentlemen, that our companions are suffering great hardships from want of food, and it is for this reason that we ought to overlook things, so that they may all find something to eat ; all the more so as the amount of gold they bargain for is but a trifle,—and God willing, we are going to obtain a large amount of it. However, there are two sides to everything ; the order has been issued that bartering for gold shall cease, as you desired ; we shall see next what we will get to eat."

This is where the historian, Gomara, states that Cortés did this so that Montezuma might think that we cared nothing for gold, but he (Gomara) was not well informed, for ever since the event of Grijalva's visit to the Rio de Banderas, Montezuma must have understood well enough, and even more so when we sent the helmet to him with a request that it should be filled with gold grains from the mines, besides they had seen us bargaining and the Mexicans were not the sort of people to misunderstand the meaning of it all.

Let us drop this subject then, which Gomara says he knows about because "they told him so" and I will go on to relate how, one morning, we woke up to find not a single Indian in any of their huts, neither those who used to bring the food, nor those who came to trade, nor Pital-pitoque himself ; they had all fled without saying a word. The cause of this, as we afterwards learned, was that Montezuma had sent orders to avoid further conversation

with Cortés and those in his company ; for it appears that
Montezuma was very much devoted to his idols, named
Tezcatepuca, and Huichilobos, the latter the god of war,
and Tezcatepuca, the god of hell ; and daily he sacrificed
youths to them so as to get an answer from the gods as to
what he should do about us ; for Montezuma had already
formed a plan, if we did not go off in the ships, to get us
all into his power, and to raise a breed of us[1] and also
to keep us for sacrifice.   As we afterwards found out, the
reply given by the gods was that he should not listen to
Cortés, nor to the message which he sent about setting
up a cross and an image of Our Lady, and that such
things should not be brought to the city.   This was the
reason why the Indians left our camp without warning.
When we heard the news we thought that they meant
to make war on us, and we were very much on the alert.
One day, as I and another soldier were stationed on some
sand dunes keeping a look out, we saw five Indians coming
along the beach, and so as not to raise a scare in camp over
so small a matter, we permitted them to approach.   When
they came up to us with smiling countenances they paid
us homage according to their custom, and made signs that
we should take them into camp.   I told my companion to
remain where he was and I would accompany the Indians,
for at that time my feet were not as heavy as they are now
that I am old, and when we came before Cortés the Indians
paid him every mark of respect and said : *Lope luzio, lope
luzio*—which in the Totonac language means: " prince
and great lord."   These men had large holes in their lower
lips, some with stone disks in them spotted with blue, and
others with thin leaves of gold.   They also had their ears
pierced with large holes in which were placed disks of

---

[1] Blotted out in the original MS.—With which to make war.
—G. G.

stone or gold, and in their dress and speech they differed
greatly from the Mexicans who had been staying with us.
When Doña Marina and Aguilar, the Interpreters, heard
the word *Lope luzio* they did not understand it, and Doña
Marina asked in Mexican if there were not among them
Nahuatatos, that is, interpreters of the Mexican language,
and two of the five answered yes, that they understood and
spoke it, and they bade us welcome and said that their chief
had sent them to ask who we might be, and that it would
please him to be of service to such valiant men, for it
appeared that they knew about our doings at Tabasco and
Potonchan, and they added that they would have come to
see us before but for fear of the people of Culua who had
been with us, (by Culua they meant Mexicans, as we might
say Cordovans, or rustics) and that they knew that three
days ago they had fled back to their own country, and
in the course of their talk Cortés found out that Montezuma had opponents and enemies, which he was delighted
to hear, and after flattering these five messengers and
giving them presents he bade them farewell, asking them
to tell their chief that he would very soon come and pay
them a visit.   From this time on we called those Indians
the *Lope luzios*.   I must leave them now and go on to say
that in those sand dunes where we were camped there were
always many mosquitos, both long-legged ones and small
ones which are called *xexenes* which are worse than the
large ones, and we could get no sleep on account of them.
We were very short of food and the cassava bread was
disappearing, and what there was of it was very damp and
foul with weevils.   Some of the soldiers who possessed
Indians in the Island of Cuba were continually sighing for
their homes, especially the friends and servants of Diego
Valásquez.   When Cortés noted the state of affairs and the
wishes of these men he gave orders that we should go
to the fortified town which had been seen by Montejo and

the pilot, Alaminos, named Quiahuitztlan where the ships would be under the protection of the rock which I have mentioned. When arrangements were being made for us to start, all the friends, relations and servants of Diego Velásquez asked Cortés why he wanted to make that journey without having any provisions, seeing that there was no possibility of going on any further and that over thirty five soldiers had already died in camp from wounds inflicted at Tabasco, and from sickness and hunger ; that the country we were in was a great one and the settlements very thickly peopled and that any day they might make war on us ; that it would be much better to return to Cuba and account to Diego Velásquez for the gold gained in barter, which already amounted to a large sum, and the great presents from Montezuma, the sun and the silver moon and the helmet full of golden grains from the mines, and all the cloths and jewels already mentioned by me. Cortés replied to them that it was not good advice to recommend our going back without reason ; that hitherto we could not complain of our fortune and should give thanks to God who was helping us in everything, and as for those who had died, that that always happened in wars and under hardship ; that it would be as well to find out what the country contained ; that meanwhile we could eat the maize and other food held by the Indians and by the neighbouring towns, unless our hands had lost their cunning. With this reply, the partisans of Diego Velásquez were somewhat, but not wholly appeased, for there were already cliques formed in camp who discussed the return to Cuba. I will leave off here and then go on to say what happened.

CHAPTER XLII.

How we raised Hernando Cortés to the post of Captain General and
   Chief Justice, until His Majesty's wishes on the matter should be
   known, and what was done about it.

I HAVE already said that the relations and friends of Diego
Velásquez were going about the camp raising objections
to our going on any further and insisting that we should
return at once from San Juan de Ulúa to the Island of
Cuba.   It appears that Cortés had already talked the
matter over with Alonzo Hernández Puertocarrero, and
Pedro de Alvarado and his four brothers, Jorge, Gonzalo,
Gómez and Juan, and with Cristóbal de Olid, Alonzo
de Ávila, Juan de Escalante, Francisco de Lugo, and with
me and other gentlemen and captains, and suggested that
we should beg of him to be our captain.   Francisco de
Montejo understood what was going on and was on the
watch.   One night, after midnight, Alonzo Hernández
Puertocarrero, Juan de Escalante and Francisco de Lugo,
came to my hut.   Francisco de Lugo and I came from the
same country and were distant kinsmen.   They said to
me : " Señor Bernal Díaz, come out with your arms and go
the rounds ; we will accompany Cortés who is just now
going the rounds."   When I was a little distance from the
hut they said to me : " Look to it, sir, that you keep secret
for a time what we wish to tell you, for it is a matter
of importance, and see that your companions in your hut
know nothing about it, for they are of the party of Diego
Velásquez."   What they said to me was: " Sir, does it
seem to you to be right that Hernando Cortés should have
deceived us all in bringing us here, he having proclaimed
in Cuba that he was coming to settle, and now we find out
that he has no power to do so, but only to trade, and they
want us to return to Santiago de Cuba with all the gold

that has been collected, and we shall lose our all, for will not Diego Velásquez take all the gold as he did before? Look, sir, counting this present expedition, you have already come to this country three times, spending your own property and contracting debts and risking your life many times with the wounds you have received. Many of us gentlemen who know that we are your honour's friends wish you to understand that this must not go on ; that this land must be settled in the name of His Majesty, and by Hernando Cortés in His Majesty's name, while we await the opportunity to make it known to our lord the King in Spain. Be sure, sir, to cast your vote so that all of us unanimously and willingly choose him captain, for it will be a service to God and our lord the King." I replied that it was not a wise decision to return to Cuba and that it would be a good thing for the country to be settled and that we should choose Cortés as General and Chief Justice until his Majesty should order otherwise. This agreement passed from soldier to soldier and the friends and relations of Diego Velásquez, who were more numerous than we were, got to know of it, and with over-bold words asked Cortés why he was craftily arranging to remain in this country instead of returning to render an account of his doings to the man who had sent him as captain, and they told him that Diego Velásquez would not approve of it, and that the sooner we embarked the better ; that there was no use in his subterfuges and secret meetings with the soldiers, for we had neither supplies nor men, nor any possibility of founding a settlement. Cortés answered without a sign of anger, and said that he agreed with them ; that he would not go against the instructions and notes which he had received from Diego Velásquez, and he issued an order for us all to embark on the following day, each one in the ship in which he had come. We who had made the agreement answered that it was not fair to deceive us so, that in Cuba he had proclaimed that he was coming to make a settlement, whereas he had only come to trade; and we demanded on behalf of our Lord God and of His Majesty that he should at once form a settlement and give up any other plan, because that would be of the greatest benefit and service to God and the King; and they placed many other well-reasoned arguments before him saying that the natives would never let us land again as they had done this time, and that as soon as a settlement was made in the country soldiers would gather in from all the islands to give us help and that Velásquez had ruined us all by stating publicly that he had received a decree from His Majesty to form a settlement, the contrary being the case; that we wished to form a settlement, and to let those depart who desired to return to Cuba. So Cortés agreed to it, although he pretended to need much begging, as the saying goes: "You are very pressing, and I want to do it,"[1]—and he stipulated that we should make him Chief Justice and Captain General, and the worst of all that we conceded was that we should give him a fifth of all the gold which should be obtained, after the royal fifth had been deducted, and then we gave him the very fullest powers in the presence of the King's Notary, Diego de Godoy, embracing all that I have here stated. We at once set to work to found and settle a town, which was called the "Villa rica de la Vera Cruz" because we arrived on Thursday of the (last) supper and landed on "Holy Friday of the Cross" and "rich" because of what that gentleman said, as I have related in a former chapter (XXVI) who approached Cortés and said to him: "Behold rich lands! May you know how to govern them well!" and what he wanted to say was—"May you

---

[1] "Tu me lo ruegas y yo me lo quiero."

remain as their Captain General." That gentleman was Alonzo Hernández Puertocarrero.

To go back to my story : as soon as the town was founded we appointed alcaldes and regidores ; the former were Alonzo Hernández Puertocarrero and Francisco Montejo. In the case of Montejo, it was because he was not on very good terms with Cortés that Cortés ordered him to be named as Alcalde, so as to place him in the highest position. I need not give the names of the Regidores, for it is no use naming only a few of them ; but I must mention the fact that a pillory was placed in the Plaza and a gallows set up outside the town. We chose Pedro de Alvarado as captain of expeditions and Cristóbal de Olid as Maestro de Campo.[1] Juan de Escalante was chosen chief Alguacil ;[2] Gonzalo Mejia, treasurer, and Alonzo de Ávila accountant. A certain Corral was named as Ensign, because Villaroel who had been Ensign was dismissed from the post on account of some offence (I do not exactly know what) he had given Cortés about an Indian woman from Cuba: Ochoa, a Biscayan, and Alonzo Romero were appointed Alguaciles of the Camp.[3]

It will be said that I have made no mention of the Captain Gonzalo de Sandoval, he of whom our lord the Emperor has heard such reports, who was such a renowned captain that he ranked next to Cortés[4] in our estimation. I say this was because at that time he was a youth, and we did not take such count of him and of other valiant captains until we saw him grow in worth in such a way that Cortés and all the soldiers held him in the same esteem as Cortés himself, as I shall tell later on.

---

[1] Maestro de Campo = Quartermaster.
[2] Alguacil Mayor = High Constable.
[3] Alguacil del Real = Constables and storekeepers.
[4] Blotted out in the original : "y Pedro de Alvarado."—G. G.

mained prisoners for some days, in chains and under guard.

I will go on to tell how Pedro de Alvarado made an expedition to a town in the neighbourhood. Here the chronicler, Gomara, in his history gives quite a wrong account of what happened, and whoever reads his history will see that his story is greatly exaggerated, had he been correctly informed he would have related what [really] took place.

CHAPTER XLIV.

How it was arranged to send Pedro de Alvarado inland to look for maize and other supplies and what else happened.

WHEN all that I have related had been settled and done with, it was arranged that Pedro de Alvarado should go inland to some towns which we had been told were near by and see what the country was like and bring back maize and some sort of supplies, for there was a great want of food in camp. Alvarado took one hundred soldiers with him, among them fifteen crossbowmen and six musketeers. More than half his soldiers were partisans of Diego Velás-quez. All Cortés' party remained with him for fear there should be any further disturbance or tricks played or any rising against him, until things became more settled.

Alvarado went first to some small towns subject to another town called Cotastan,[1] where the language of Culua was spoken. This name, Culua, in this country means the common language of the partisans of Mexico and Montezuma ; so that in all that country when Culua is mentioned, it means people vassal and subject to Mexico, and must be thus understood, just as we should speak of the Romans and their allies.

---

[1] Cotaxtla.

When Pedro de Alvarado reached these towns he found that they had all been deserted that same day, and he found in the *cues* bodies of men and boys who had been sacrificed, and the walls and altars stained with blood and the hearts placed as offerings before the Idols. He also found the stones on which the sacrifices were made and the stone knives with which to open the chest so as to take out the heart.

Pedro de Alvarado said that he found most of the bodies without arms or legs, and that he was told by some Indians that they had been carried off to be eaten, and our soldiers were astounded at such great cruelty. I will not say any more of the number of sacrifices, although we found the same thing in every town we afterwards entered, and I will go back to Pedro de Alvarado and say that he found the towns well provisioned but deserted that very day by their inhabitants, so that he could not find more than two Indians to carry maize, and each soldier had to load himself with poultry and vegetables, and he returned to camp without doing any other damage (although he had good opportunity for doing it) because Cortés had given orders to that effect, so that there should be no repetition of what happened at Cozumel.

We were pleased enough in camp even with the little food that had been brought, for all evils and hardships disappear when there is plenty to eat.

Here it is that the historian, Gomara, says that Cortés went inland with four hundred soldiers. He was misinformed, for the first to go was [Alvarado] as I have stated here, and no other.

To go back to my story: As Cortés was most energetic in every direction, he managed to make friends with the partisans of Diego Velásquez, for, with that solvent of hardness, presents of gold from our store to some, and promises to others, he brought them over to his side, and

M

took them out of prison; all except Juan Velásquez de Leon and Diego de Ordás, who were in irons on board ship. These, too, he let out of prison after a few days, and made good and true friends of them as will be seen further on,—and all through gold which is such a pacifier!

When everything had been settled, we arranged to go to the fortified town already mentioned by me, which was called Quiahuitztlan. The ships were to go to the rock and harbour which was opposite that town, about a league distant from it. I remember that as we marched along the coast we killed a large fish which had been thrown up high and dry by the sea. When we arrived at the river where Vera Cruz is now situated[1] we found the water to be deep, and we crossed over it in some broken canoes like troughs, and others crossed by swimming, or on rafts.

Then we came on some towns subject to the large town named Cempoala, whence came the five Indians with the golden labrets, who I have already said came as messengers to Cortés at the sand dunes, and whom we called *Lope luzios*. We found some idol houses and places of sacrifice, and blood splashed about, and incense used for fumigation and other things belonging to the idols, and stones with which they made the sacrifices, and parrots' feathers and many paper books doubled together in folds like Spanish cloth; but we found no Indians, they having already fled, for as they had never before seen men like us, nor horses, they were afraid.

We slept there that night, and went without supper, and next day, leaving the coast, we continued our march inland towards the west, without knowing the road we were taking, and we came on some good meadows called *savanas* where deer were grazing, and Pedro de Alvarado rode after one on his sorrel mare and struck at it with his

---

[1] The third site, now known as La Antigua.

lance and wounded it, but it got away into the woods and could not be caught.

While this was happening we saw twelve Indians approaching, inhabitants of the farms where we had passed the night. They came straight from their Cacique, and brought fowls and maize cakes, and they said to Cortés, through our interpreters, that their chief had sent the fowls for us to eat, and begged us to come to his town, which was, according to the signs they made, distant one sun's (that is one day's) march.

Cortés thanked them and made much of them, and we continued our march and slept in another small town, where also many sacrifices had been made, but as my readers will be tired of hearing of the great number of Indian men and women whom we found sacrificed in all the towns and roads we passed, I shall go on with my story without stopping to say any more about them.

They gave us supper at the little town and we learnt that the road to Quiahuitztlan, which I have already said is a fortress, passed by Cempoala. I will go on to say how we entered Cempoala.

CHAPTER XLV.

How we entered Cempoala, which at that time was a very fine town and what happened to us there.

WE slept at the little town where the twelve Indians I have mentioned had prepared quarters for us, and after being well informed about the road which we had to take to reach the town on the hill, very early in the morning we sent word to the Caciques of Cempoala that we were coming to their town and that we hoped they would approve. Cortés sent six of the Indians with this message and kept the other six as guides. He also ordered the guns, muskets and crossbows to be kept ready for use, and sent scouts on ahead on the look out, and the horsemen and all the rest of us were kept on the alert, and in this way we marched to within a league of the town. As we approached, twenty Indian chieftains came out to receive us in the name of the Cacique, and brought some cones made of the roses of the country with a delicious scent, which they gave to Cortés and those on horseback with every sign of friendliness, and they told Cortés that their Lord was awaiting us at our apartments, for, as he was a very stout and heavy man, he could not come out to receive us himself. Cortés thanked them and we continued our march, and as we got among the houses and saw what a large town it was, larger than any we had yet seen, we were struck with admiration. It looked like a garden with luxuriant vegetation, and the streets were so full of men and women who had come to see us, that we gave thanks to God at having discovered such a country.

Our scouts, who were on horseback, reached a great plaza with courts, where they had prepared our quarters, and it seems that during the last few days they had been whitewashed and burnished, a thing they knew well how to do, and it seemed to one of the scouts that this white surface which shone so brightly must be silver and he came back at full speed to tell Cortés that the walls of the houses were made of silver! Doña Marina and Aguilar said that it must be plaster or lime and we had a good laugh over the man's silver and excitement and always afterwards we told him that everything white looked to him like silver. I will leave our jokes and say that we reached the buildings, and the fat Cacique came out to receive us in the court. He was so fat that I shall call him by this name ; and he made deep obeisance to Cortés and fumigated him, as is their custom, and Cortés embraced him and we were lodged in fine and large apartments that held us all, and they gave us food and brought some baskets of plums which were very plentiful at that season, and maize cakes, and as we arrived ravenous and had not seen so much food for a long time, we called the town Villa Viciosa ; and others called it Sevilla.

Cortés gave orders that none of the soldiers should leave the plaza and that on no account should they give any offence to the Indians. When the fat Cacique heard that we had finished eating he sent to tell Cortés that he wished to come and visit him ; and he came in company with a great number of Indian chieftains, all wearing large gold labrets and rich mantles. Cortés left his quarters to go out and meet them, and embraced the Cacique with great show of caressing and flattery, and the fat Cacique ordered a present to be brought which he had prepared, consisting of gold, jewels and cloths ; but although it did not amount to much and was of little value he said to Cortés : " *Lope luzio, Lope luzio,* accept this in good part ; if I had more I would give it to you ! " I have already said that in the Totonac language *Lope luzio* means Señor or great lord.

Cortés replied through Doña Marina and Aguilar that he would pay for the gift in good works, and that if the Cacique would tell him what he wanted to be done that he would do it for them for we were the vassals of a great prince, the Emperor Don Carlos, who ruled over many kingdoms and countries, and had sent us to redress grievances and punish evil doers, and to put an end to human sacrifices. And he explained to them many things touching our holy religion. When the fat Cacique heard this, he sighed, and complained bitterly of the great Montezuma and his governors saying that he had recently been brought under his yoke; that all his golden jewels had been carried off, and he and his people were so grievously

oppressed, that they dared do nothing without Montezuma's orders, for he was the Lord over many cities and
countries and ruled over countless vassals and armies
of warriors.

As Cortés knew that he could not attend at that time to
the complaints which they made, he replied that he would
see to it that they were relieved of their burdens, that
he was now on the way to visit his *Acales* (for so they
call the ships in the Indian language) and take up his
residence and make his headquarters in the town of
Quiahuitztlan, and that as soon as he was settled there he
would consider the matter more thoroughly. To this
the fat Cacique replied that he was quite satisfied that it
should be so.

The next morning we left Cempoala, and there were
awaiting our orders over four hundred Indian carriers, who
are here called *tamenes* who carry fifty pounds weight on
their backs and march five leagues with it. When we saw
so many Indians to carry burdens we rejoiced, as before
this, those of us who had not brought Indians with us from
Cuba had to carry knapsacks on our own backs. And
only six or seven Cubans had been brought in the fleet,
and not a great number as Gomara asserts. Doña Marina
and Aguilar told us that in these parts in times of peace
the Caciques are bound to furnish *tamenes* to carry burdens,
as a matter of course, and from this time forward wherever
we went we asked for Indians to carry loads.

Cortés took leave of the fat Cacique, and on the following
day we set out on our march and slept at a little town
which had been deserted near to Quiahuitztlan, and the
people of Cempoala brought us food. The historian,
Gomara, says that Cortés remained many days in Cempoala
and planned a league and rebellion against Montezuma,
but he was not correctly informed, because, as I have said,
we left Cempoala on the following morning, and where the

rebellion was planned and what was the reason of it, I will relate further on.

I will pause here and go on to tell how we entered Quiahuitztlan.

CHAPTER XLVI.

How we entered Quiahuitztlan, which was a fortified town, and were peaceably received.

THE next day about ten o'clock we reached the fortified town called Quiahuitztlan, which stands amid great rocks and lofty cliffs and if there had been any resistance it would have been very difficult to capture it. Expecting that there would be fighting we kept a good formation with the artillery in front and marched up to the fortress in such a manner that if anything had happened we could have done our duty.

At this time, Alonzo de Ávila was acting as captain, and as he was arrogant and bad tempered, when a soldier named Hernando Alonzo de Villanueva failed to keep his place in the ranks, he gave him a thrust with a lance in his arm which maimed him ; and after this Hernando Alonzo de Villanueva was always called " El Manquillo."[1] It will be said that I am always turning aside to tell old stories, so I must leave off and go on to say that we went half way through the town without meeting a single Indian to speak to, at which we were very much surprised, for they had fled in fear that very day when they had seen us climbing up to their houses. When we had reached the top of the fortress in the plaza near by where they had their *cues* and great idol houses, we saw fifteen Indians awaiting us all clad in good mantles, and each one with a brasier in his hand

---

[1] El Manquillo = the one armed or the maimed.

containing incense, and they came to where Cortés was
standing and fumigated him and all the soldiers who were
standing near and with deep obeisances they asked pardon
for not coming out to meet us, and assured us that we
were welcome and asked us to rest. And they said that
they had fled and kept out of the way until they could see
what sort of things we were, for they were afraid of us and
of our horses, but that night they would order all the people
to come back to the town.

Cortés displayed much friendship toward them and told
them many things about our holy religion; this we were
always in the habit of doing wherever we might go. And
he told them that we were the vassals of our great
Emperor, Don Carlos, and he gave them some green beads
and other trifles from Spain, and they brought fowls and
maize cakes. While we were talking, someone came to
tell Cortés that the fat Cacique from Cempoala was coming
in a litter carried on the shoulders of many Indian chieftains. When the fat Cacique arrived he, together with the
Cacique and chiefs of the town addressed Cortés, relating
their many causes of complaint against Montezuma and
telling him of his great power, and this they did with such
sighs and tears that Cortés and those who were standing
with him were moved to pity. Besides relating the way
that they had been brought into subjection, they told us
that every year many of their sons and daughters were
demanded of them for sacrifice, and others for service in
the houses and plantations of their conquerors; and they
made other complaints which were so numerous that I
do not remember them all; but they said that Montezuma's
tax gatherers carried off their wives and daughters if they
were handsome and ravished them, and this they did
throughout the land where the Totonac language was
spoken, which contained over thirty towns.

Cortés consoled them as well as he was able through our

interpreters and said he would help them all he could, and
would prevent these robberies and offences, as it was for
that our lord the Emperor had sent us to these parts,
and that they should have no anxiety, for they would soon
see what we would do in the matter ; and they seemed to
gather some satisfaction from this assurance but their
hearts were not eased on account of the great fear they
had of the Mexicans.

While this conversation was going on, some Indians from
the town came in great haste to tell the Caciques who
were talking to Cortés, that five Mexicans, who were
Montezuma's tax gatherers, had just arrived. When they
heard the news they turned pale and trembled with fear,
and leaving Cortés alone they went off to receive the
Mexicans, and in the shortest possible time they had
decked a room with flowers, and had food cooked for the
Mexicans to eat, and prepared plenty of cacao, which is
the best thing they have to drink.

When these five Indians entered the town, they came to
the place where we were assembled, where were the houses
of the Cacique and our quarters, and approaching us with
the utmost assurance and arrogance, without speaking to
Cortés or to any of us, they passed us by. Their cloaks
and loin cloths were richly embroidered (for at that time
they wore loin cloths), and their shining hair was gathered
up as though tied on their heads, and each one was
smelling the roses that he carried, and each had a crooked
staff in his hand. Their Indian servants carried fly-whisks,
and they were accompanied by many of the chief men
of the other Totonac towns, who until they had shown them
to their lodgings and brought them food of the best, never
left them.

As soon as they had dined they sent to summon the
fat Cacique and the other chiefs, and scolded them for
entertaining us in their houses, for now they would have to

noised it abroad, for each one returned to his own town
to deliver the order and relate what had happened.

When they witnessed deeds so marvellous and of such
importance to themselves they said that no human beings
would dare to do such things, and that it was the work of
Teules, for so they call the idols which they worship, and
for this reason from that time forth, they called us Teules,
which, as I have already explained, is as much as to say
that we were either gods or demons.   When in the course
of my story I may use the word *Teule* in matters connected
with our persons, let it be understood that we (Spaniards)
are meant.

I must go back to tell about the prisoners.   It was the
advice of all the Caciques that they should be sacrificed so
that none of them could return to Mexico to tell the story;
but when Cortés heard this he said that they should not
be killed, and that he would take charge of them, and
he set some of our soldiers to guard them.   At midnight,
Cortés sent for these soldiers who were in charge and said
to them : " See to it that two of the prisoners are loosened
[the two] that appear to you the most intelligent, in such a
way that the Indians of this town shall know nothing about
it."   And he told them to bring the prisoners to his
lodging.   When the prisoners came before him, he asked
them through our interpreters why they were prisoners and
what country they came from, as though he knew nothing
about them.   They replied that the Caciques of Cempoala
and of this town, with the aid of their followers and ours,
had imprisoned them, and Cortés answered that he knew
nothing about it, and was sorry for it, and he ordered food
to be brought them and talked in a very friendly manner
to them, and told them to return at once to their lord
Montezuma and tell him that we were all his good friends
and entirely at his service, and that lest any harm should
happen to them he had taken them from their prison, and

had quarrelled with the Caciques who had seized them and that anything he could do to serve them he would do with the greatest good will, and that he would order the three Indians their companions who were still held prisoners to be freed and protected. That they two should go away at once and not turn back to be captured and killed.

The two prisoners replied that they valued his mercy and said they still had fear of falling into the hands of their enemies, as they were obliged to pass through their territory. So Cortés ordered six sailors to take them in a boat during the night a distance of four leagues and set them on friendly ground beyond the frontier of Cempoala. When the morning came and the Caciques of the town and the fat Cacique found that the two prisoners were missing they were all the more intent on sacrificing those that remained, if Cortés had not put it out of their power and pretended to be enraged at the loss of the two who had escaped. He ordered a chain to be brought from the ships and bound the prisoners to it, and then ordered them to be taken on board ship, saying that he himself would guard them, as such bad watch had been kept over the others. When they were once on board he ordered them to be freed from their chains and with friendly words he told them that he would soon send them back to Mexico.

I must leave this subject and say that when this was done, all the Caciques of this town and of Cempoala, and all the other Totonac chiefs who had assembled, asked Cortés what was to be done, and that all the force of the great Montezuma and of Mexico would descend upon them and they could not escape death and destruction.

Cortés replied with the most cheerful countenance that he and his brothers who were here with him would defend them and would kill anyone who wished to molest them. Then the Caciques and other townsmen vowed one and all that they would stand by us in everything we ordered them to do and would join their forces [with ours] against Montezuma and all his allies. Then, in the presence of Diego de Godoy, the scribe, they pledged obedience to his Majesty and messengers were sent to relate all that had happened to the other towns in that province. And as they no longer paid any tribute and no more tax gatherers appeared there was no end to the rejoicing at being rid of that tyranny.

Now, I will leave this incident and tell how we agreed to descend to the plain to some fields where we began to build a fort. This is what really took place and not the story that was told to the historian Gomara.[1]

CHAPTER XLVIII.

How we determined to found " La Villa Rica de la Vera Cruz" and to build a fort in some meadows near the salt marshes, and close to the harbour with the ugly name [Bernal] where our ships were at anchor, and what we did there.

As soon as we had made this federation and friendship with more than twenty of the hill towns, known as [the towns of] the Totonacs, which at this time rebelled against the great Montezuma, and gave their allegiance to His Majesty, and offered to serve us—we determined with their ready help at once to found the Villa Rica de la Vera Cruz on a plain half a league from this fortress-like town, called Quiahuitztlan, and we laid out plans of a church, market-place and arsenals, and all those things that are needed for a town, and we built a fort, and from the laying of the foundations until the walls were high enough to receive

---

[1] Blotted out in the original MS. " No matter how eloquently he may relate it."—G. G.

the woodwork, loopholes, watch-towers, and barbicans, we
worked with the greatest haste.

Cortés himself was the first to set to work to carry out
the earth and stone on his back, and to dig foundations,
and all his captains and soldiers followed his example;
and we kept on labouring [without pause] so as to finish
the work quickly, some of us digging foundations and
others building walls,[1] carrying water, working in the lime
kilns, making bricks and tiles, or seeking for food. Others
worked at the timber, and the blacksmiths, for we had two
blacksmiths with us, made nails. In this way we all
laboured without ceasing, from the highest to the lowest;
the Indians helping us, so that the church and some of the
houses were soon built and the fort almost finished.

While we were thus at work, it seems that the great
Montezuma heard the news in Mexico about the capture of
his tax gatherers and the rebellion against his rule, and
how the Totonac towns had withdrawn their allegiance and
risen in revolt. He showed much anger against Cortés
and all of us, and had already ordered a great army of
warriors to make war on the people who had rebelled
against him, and not to leave a single one of them alive.
He was also getting ready to come against us with a great
army with many companies.

Just at this moment there arrived two Indian prisoners
whom Cortés had ordered to be set free, as I have related
in the last chapter, and when Montezuma knew that it was
Cortés who had taken them out of prison and had sent
them to Mexico,—and when he heard the words and
promises which he had sent them to report, it pleased our
Lord God that his anger was appeased, and he resolved to
send and gather news of us. For this purpose he despatched
his two young nephews under the charge of four old men

---

[1] Tapias = walls made of earth stamped into a mould.

who were Caciques of high rank, and sent with them a present of gold and cloth, and told his messengers to give thanks to Cortés for freeing his servants.

On the other hand, he sent many complaints, saying that it was owing to our protection that those towns had dared to commit such a great treason as to refuse to pay him tribute and to renounce their allegiance to him, and that now, having respect for what he knew to be true—that we were those whom his ancestors had foretold were to come to their country, and must therefore be of his own lineage, how was it that we were living in the houses of these traitors? He did not at once send to destroy them, but the time would come when they would not brag of such acts of treason.

Cortés accepted the gold and the cloth, which was worth more than two thousand dollars, and he embraced the envoys and gave as an excuse that he and all of us were very good friends of the Lord Montezuma, and that it was as his servant that he still kept guard over the three tax gatherers, and he sent at once to have them brought from the ships—where they had been well treated and well clothed, and he delivered them up to the messengers.

Then Cortés, on his part, complained greatly of Montezuma, and told the envoys how the Governor, Pitalpitoque, had left the camp one night without giving him notice, which was not well done and that he believed and felt certain that the Lord Montezuma had not authorized any such meanness, and that it was on account of this that we had come to these towns where we were now residing and where we had been well treated by the inhabitants. And he prayed him to pardon the disrespect of which the people had been guilty. As to what he said about the people no longer paying tribute, they could not serve two masters and during the time we had been there they had rendered service to us in the name of our Lord and King; but as he, Cortés, and all his brethren were on their way to visit him, and place themselves at his service, that when we were once there, then his commands would be attended to.

When this conversation and more of the same nature was over, Cortés ordered blue and green glass beads to be given to the two youths, who were Caciques of high rank, and to the four old men who had come in charge of them, who were also chieftains of importance, and paid them every sign of honour. And as there were some good meadows in the neighbourhood, Cortés ordered Pedro de Alvarado who had a good and very handy sorrel mare, and some of the other horsemen, to gallop and skirmish before the Caciques, who were delighted at the sight of their galloping, and they then took leave of Cortés and of all of us well contented, and returned to Mexico.

About this time Cortés' horse died, and he bought or was given another called "El Arriero," a dark chestnut which belonged to Ortiz, the musician, and Bartolomé Garcia, the miner ; it was one of the best of the horses that came in the fleet.

I must stop talking about this, and relate that as these towns of the sierra, our allies, and the town of Cempoala had hitherto been very much afraid of the Mexicans, believing that the great Montezuma would send his great army of warriors to destroy them, when they saw the kinsmen of the great Montezuma arriving with the presents I have mentioned, and paying such marked respect to Cortés and to all of us, they were fairly astounded and the Caciques said to one another that we must be Teules for Montezuma had fear of us, and had sent us presents of gold. If we already had reputation for valour, from this time forth it was greatly increased. But I must leave off here and go on to say what the fat Cacique and his friends were about.

CHAPTER XLIX.

How the fat Cacique and other chieftains came to complain to Cortés, that in a fortified town named Cingapacinga,[1] there was a garrison of Mexicans which did them much damage, and what was done about it.

As soon as the Mexican messengers had departed, the fat Cacique with many other friendly chieftains, came to beg Cortés to go at once to a town named Cingapacinga, two days' journey from Cempoala (that is about eight or nine leagues)—as there were many warriors of the Culuas, or Mexicans, assembled there, who were destroying their crops and plantations, and were waylaying and ill-treating their vassals, and doing other injuries. Cortés believed the story as they told it so earnestly. He had promised that he would help them, and would destroy the Culuas and other Indians who might annoy them, and noting with what importunity they pressed their complaints, he did not know what to answer them, unless it were to say that he would willingly go, or send some soldiers under one of us, to turn these Mexicans out. As he stood there thinking the matter over, he said laughingly to some of us companions who were with him : " Do you know, gentlemen, that it seems to me that we have already gained a great reputation for valour throughout this country and that from what they saw us do in the matter of Montezuma's tax-gatherers, the people here take us for gods or beings like their idols. I am thinking that so as to make them believe that one of us is enough to defeat those Indian warriors, their enemies, who they say are occupying the town with the fortress, that we will send Heredia against

---

[1] Not marked on the modern maps. Orozco y Berra (vol. iv, p. 163) says that it no longer exists, but that he found it marked in a MS. map of Patiño under the name of Tizapanecingo, eight or nine leagues N.W. of Cempoala.

them." Now, this old man was a Biscayan musketeer who
had a bad twitch in his face, a big beard, a face covered
with scars, and was blind of one eye and lame of one leg.

Cortés sent for him and said : " Go with these Caciques
to the river which is a quarter of a league distant, and
when you get there, stop to drink and wash your hands,
and fire a shot from your musket, and then I will send
to call you back. I want this to be done because the
people here think that we are gods, or at least they have
given us that name and reputation, and as you are ugly
enough, they will believe that you are an idol." Heredia
did what he was told, for he was an intelligent and clever
man who had been a soldier in Italy, and Cortés sent for
the fat Cacique and the other chieftains, who were waiting
for his help and assistance, and said to them : " I am
sending this brother of mine with you to kill or expel all
the Culuas from this town you speak of, and to bring me
here as prisoners all who refuse to leave." The Caciques
were surprised when they heard this and did not know
whether to believe it or not, but seeing that Cortés never
changed his face, they believed that what he told them was
true. So old Heredia shouldered his musket and set out
with them, and he fired shots into the air as he went
through the forest so that the Indians might see and hear
him. And the Caciques sent word to the other towns that
they were bringing along a Teule to kill all the Mexicans
who were in Cingapacinga. I tell this story here merely
as a laughable incident, and to show the wiles of Cortés.
When Cortés knew that Heredia had reached the river
that he had been told about, he sent in haste to call
him back, and when old Heredia and the Caciques had
returned, he told them that on account of the good will he
bore them that he, Cortés himself, would go in person with
some of his brethren to afford them the help they needed
and visit the country and fortresses ; and he ordered them

at once to bring one hundred Indian carriers to transport the *tepusques*, that is, the cannon, and they came early the next morning, and we set out that same day with four hundred men and fourteen horsemen, and crossbowmen and musketeers who were all ready. Certain soldiers belonging to the party of Diego Velásquez refused to go and told Cortés that he could set out with those who were willing, but that they wished to go back to Cuba.

What was done about this I will tell in the next chapter.

CHAPTER L.

How certain soldiers, partisans of Diego Velásquez, seeing that we positively intended to make settlements, and establish peace in the towns, said that they did not want to go on any expedition, but wished to return to the Island of Cuba.

YOU have already heard me tell in the preceding chapter how Cortés had undertaken to go to a town named Cingapacinga, and take with him four hundred soldiers and fourteen horsemen and musketeers and crossbowmen, and we took good care to make certain soldiers of the party of Diego Velásquez go with us. When the officers went to warn them to get their arms ready, and those who had them to bring their horses, they answered haughtily that they did not want to go on any expedition but back to their farms and estates in Cuba ; that they had already lost enough through Cortés having enticed them from their homes, and that he had promised them on the sand dunes that whosoever might wish to leave, that he would give them permission to do so and a ship and stores for the voyage ; and for that reason there were now seven soldiers all ready to return to Cuba. When Cortés heard this he sent to summon these men before him, and when he asked them why they were doing such a mean thing they replied somewhat indignantly and said that they wondered at his honour, with so few soldiers under his command, wishing to settle in a place where there were reported to be such thousands of Indians and such great towns ; that. as for themselves, they were invalids and could hardly crawl from one place to another and that they wished to return to their homes and estates in Cuba, and they asked him to grant them leave to depart as he had promised that he would do. Cortés answered them gently that it was true that he had promised it, but that they were not doing their duty in deserting from their captain's flag. And then he ordered them to embark at once without any delay and assigned a ship to them and ordered them to be furnished with cassava bread and a jar of oil and such other supplies as we possessed.

One of these soldiers, a certain Moron, a native of the town of Bayamo, owned a good dappled (gray) horse, with stockinged fore-feet, and he sold it a good bargain to Juan Ruano in exchange for some property which Juan Ruano had left in Cuba.

When these people were ready to set sail, all of us comrades, and the Alcaldes and Regidores of our town of Villa Rica, went and begged Cortés on no account to allow anyone to leave the country, for, in the interest of the service of our Lord God and His Majesty, any person asking for such permission should be considered as deserving the punishment of death, in accordance with military law, as a deserter from his captain and his flag in time of war and peril, especially in this case when, as they had stated, we were surrounded by such a great number of towns peopled by Indian warriors.

Cortés acted as though he wished to give them leave to depart, but in the end he revoked the permission and they remained baffled, and even ashamed of themselves ; however Moron had sold his horse and Juan Ruano, who had possession of it, did not want to give it back again; but Cortés arranged all this and we set out on our expedition to Cingapacinga.

CHAPTER LI.

What happened to us at Cingapacinga, and how, on our return by way of Cempoala, we demolished the idols; and other things that happened.

As soon as the seven men who wished to return to Cuba had calmed down, we set out with the force of horsemen and foot soldiers already mentioned, and slept that night at the town of Cempoala. Two thousand Indian warriors divided into four commands, were all ready to accompany us, and on the first day we marched five leagues in good order. The next day, a little after dusk[1] we arrived at some farms near to the town of Cingapacinga, and the natives of the town heard the news of our coming. When we had already begun the ascent to the fortress and houses which stood amid great cliffs and crags, eight Indian chieftains and priests came out to meet us peacefully and asked Cortés with tears, why he wished to kill and destroy them when they had done nothing to deserve it; that we had the reputation of doing good to all and of relieving those who had been robbed, and we had imprisoned the tax gatherers of Montezuma; that these Cempoala Indians who accompanied us were hostile to them on account of old enmities over the land claims and boundaries, and under our protection they had come to kill and rob them. It was true, they said, that there was formerly a Mexican garrison in the town, but that they had left for their own country a few days earlier when they heard that we had

---

[1] A poco mas de Visperas.

taken the other tax gatherers prisoners, and they prayed us not to let the matter go any further, but to grant them protection. When Cortés thoroughly understood what they had said through our interpreters, Doña Marina and Aguilar, without delay he ordered Captain Pedro de Alvarado, and the quartermaster Cristovól de Olid, and all of us comrades who were with him, to restrain the Indians of Cempoala and prevent them from advancing; and this we did. But although we made haste to stop them, they had already begun to loot the farms. This made Cortés very angry and he sent for the captains who had command of the Cempoala warriors, and with angry words and serious threats, he ordered them to bring the Indian men and women and cloths and poultry that they had stolen from the farms, and forbade any Cempoala Indian to enter the town, and said that for having lied and for having come under our protection merely to rob and sacrifice their neighbours, they were deserving of death, and that our Lord and King, whose servants we were, had not sent us to these countries to commit such indignities, and that they should keep their eyes wide open in order that such a thing did not happen again, otherwise he would not leave one of them alive. Then the Caciques and captains of the Cempoalans brought to Cortés everything they had seized, both Indian men and women and poultry, and he gave them all back to their owners and with a face full of wrath he turned [to the Cempoalans] and ordered them to retire and sleep in the fields—and this they did.

When the caciques and priests[1] of that town saw how just we were [in our dealings] and heard the affectionate words that Cortés spoke to them through our interpreters, including matters concerning our holy religion which it was always our custom to explain, and his advice to them

---

[1] Papas.

to give up human sacrifices and robbing one another, and the filthy practice of sodomy, and the worship of their curséd Idols, and much other good counsel which he gave them, they showed such good will towards us that they at once sent to call together the people of the neighbouring towns, and all gave their fealty to his Majesty.

They soon began to utter many complaints against Montezuma, just as the people of Cempoala had done when we were at the town of Quiahuitztlan. On the next morning Cortés sent to summon the captains and caciques of Cempoala, who were waiting in the fields to know what we should order them to do, and still in terror of Cortés on account of the lies they had told him. When they came before him he made them make friends with the people of the town, a pact which was never broken by any of them.

Then we set out for Cempoala by another road and passed through two towns friendly to Cingapacinga, where we rested, for the sun was very hot and we were wearied with carrying our arms on our backs. A soldier, (a something) de Mora, a native of Ciudad-Rodrigo, took two chickens from an Indian house in one of the towns, and Cortés who happened to see it, was so enraged at that soldier for stealing chickens in a friendly town before his very eyes, that he immediately ordered a halter to be put around his neck, and he would have been hanged there if Pedro de Alvarado, who chanced to be near Cortés, had not cut the halter with his sword when the poor soldier was half dead. I call this story to mind here to show my curious readers, and even the priests who nowadays have charge of administering the holy sacraments and teaching the doctrine to the natives of the country, that because the poor soldier stole two fowls in a friendly town, it nearly cost him his life, so that they can see how one ought to act towards the Indians, and not seize their

property. This same soldier was killed later on in a battle
fought on a rocky height in the province of Guatemala.

To go on with my story—when we had left those towns
in peace and continued our march towards Cempoala, we
met the fat cacique and other chiefs waiting for us in some
huts with food, for although they were Indians, they saw
and understood that justice is good and sacred, and that
the words Cortés had spoken to them, that we had come to
right wrongs and abolish tyranny, were in conformity with
what had happened on that expedition, and they were
better affected towards us than ever before.

We slept the night in those huts, and all the caciques
bore us company all the way to our quarters in their town.
They were really anxious that we should not leave their
country, as they were fearful that Montezuma would send
his warriors against them, and they said to Cortés that as
we were already their friends, they would like to have us
for brothers, and that it would be well that we should take
from their daughters, so as to have children by them ; and
to cement our friendship, they brought eight damsels, all
of them daughters of caciques, and gave one of these
cacicas, who was the niece of the fat cacique, to Cortés ;
and one, who was the daughter of another great cacique,
(called Cuesco in their language,) was given to Alonzo
Hernández Puertocarrero. All eight of them were clothed
in the rich garments of the country, beautifully ornamented
as is their custom. Each one of them had a golden collar
around her neck and golden ear-rings in her ears, and they
came accompanied by other Indian girls who were to serve
as their maids. When the fat cacique presented them, he
said to Cortés : " Tecle, (which in their language means
Lord)—these seven women are for your captains, and this
one, who is my niece, is for you, and she is the señora of
towns and vassals." Cortés received them with a cheerful
countenance and thanked the caciques for the gift, but he

said that before we could accept them and become brothers, they must get rid of those idols which they believed in and worshipped, and which kept them in darkness, and must no longer offer sacrifices to them, and that when he could see those cursed things thrown to the ground and an end put to sacrifices that then our bonds of brotherhood would be most firmly tied.   He added that these damsels must become Christians before we could receive them, and the people must free themselves from sodomy, for there were boys dressed like women who went about for gain by that cursed practice, and every day we saw sacrificed before us three, four or five Indians whose hearts were offered to the idols and their blood plastered on the walls, and the feet, arms and legs of the victims were cut off and eaten, just as in our country we eat beef brought from the butchers. I even believe that they sell it by retail in the *tianguez*[1] as they call their markets. Cortés told them that if they gave up these evil deeds and no longer practiced them, not only would we be their friends, but we would make them lords over other provinces.   All the caciques, priests, and chiefs replied that it did not seem to them good to give up their idols and sacrifices and that these gods of theirs gave them health and good harvests and everything of which they had need ; and that as for sodomy, measures would be taken to put a stop to it so that it should no longer be practiced.

When Cortés and all of us who had seen so many cruelties and infamies which I have mentioned heard that disrespectful answer, we could not stand it, and Cortés spoke to us about it and reminded us of certain good and holy doctrines and said : " How can we ever accomplish anything worth doing if for the honour of God we do not first abolish these sacrifices made to idols ?" and he told us

---

[1] Tianguiz or Tianguiztli.

to be all ready to fight should the Indians try to prevent us ; but even if it cost us our lives the idols must come to the ground that very day. We were all armed ready for a fight as it was ever our custom to be so, and Cortés told the caciques that the idols must be overthrown. When they saw that we were in earnest, the fat cacique and his captains told all the warriors to get ready to defend their idols, and when they saw that we intended to ascend a lofty *cue*—which was their temple—which stood high and was approached by many steps,—I cannot remember how many (steps there were)—the fat cacique and the other chieftains were beside themselves with fury and called out to Cortés to know why he wanted to destroy their idols, for if we dishonoured them and overthrew them, that they would all perish and we along with them. Cortés answered them in an angry tone, that he had already told them that they should offer no more sacrifices to those evil images ; that our reason for removing them was that they should no longer be deluded, and that either they, themselves, must remove the idols at once, or we should throw them out and roll them down the steps, and he added that we were no longer their friends but their mortal enemies, for he had given them good advice which they would not believe ; besides he had seen their companies come armed for battle and he was angry with them and would make them pay for it by taking their lives.

When the Indians saw Cortés uttering these threats, and our interpreter Doña Marina knew well how to make them understood, and even threatened them with the power of Montezuma which might fall on them any day, out of fear of all this they replied that they were not worthy to approach their gods, and that if we wished to overthrow them it was not with their consent, but that we could overthrow them and do what we chose.

The words were hardly out of their mouths before more

than fifty of us soldiers had clambered up [to the temple] and had thrown down their idols which came rolling down the steps shattered to pieces. The idols looked like fearsome dragons, as big as calves, and there were other figures half men and half great dogs of hideous appearance. When they saw their idols broken to pieces the caciques and priests who were with them wept and covered their eyes, and in the Totonac tongue they prayed their gods to pardon them, saying that the matter was no longer in their hands and they were not to blame, but these Teules who had overthrown them, and that they did not attack us on account of the fear of the Mexicans.

When this was over the captains of the Indian warriors who, as I have said, had come ready to attack us, began to prepare to shoot arrows at us, and when we saw this, we laid our hands on the fat cacique and the six priests and some other chiefs, and Cortés cried out that on the least sign of hostility they would all be killed. Then the fat cacique commanded his men to retire from our front and not attempt to fight, and when Cortés saw them calmed, he made them a speech which I will record later on, and thus they were all pacified.

This affair of Cingapacinga was the first expedition made by Cortés in New Spain, and it was very successful, and we did not, as the historian Gómara says, kill and capture and destroy thousands of men in this affair at Cingapacinga, and he who reads this can see how far one story differs from the other, and however good the style of his history may be, nothing is set down as it really happened.

CHAPTER LII.

How Cortés had an altar made and set up an image of Our Lady and a Cross, and how mass was said and the eight Indian damsels were baptized.

WHEN the Caciques, priests and chieftains were silenced, Cortés ordered all the idols which we had overthrown and broken to pieces to be taken out of sight and burned. Then eight priests who had charge of the idols came out of a chamber and carried them back to the house whence they had come, and burned them. These priests wore black cloaks like cassocks and long gowns reaching to their feet, and some had hoods like those worn by canons, and others had smaller hoods like those worn by Dominicans, and they wore their hair very long, down to the waist, with some even reaching down to the feet, covered with blood and so matted together that it could not be separated, and their ears were cut to pieces by way of sacrifice, and they stank like sulphur, and they had another bad smell like carrion, and as they said, and we learnt that it was true, these priests were the sons of chiefs and they abstained from women, but they indulged in the cursed practice of sodomy, and they fasted on certain days, and what I saw them eat was the pith or seeds of cotton when the cotton was being cleaned, but they may have eaten other things which I did not see.

Let us leave the priests and go back to Cortés who made them a good speech through our interpreters, Doña Marina and Jerónimo de Aguilar, and told them that now we would treat them as brothers and would help them all we could against Montezuma and his Mexicans, and we had already sent to tell him not to make war on them or levy tribute, and that as now they were not to have any more idols in their lofty temples he wished to leave with them a great lady who was the Mother of our Lord Jesus Christ whom we believe in and worship, and that they too should hold her for Lady and intercessor, and about this matter and others which were mentioned he made them an excellent discourse, so concisely reasoned, considering the time at his disposal, that there was nothing left to be said. He told them many things about our holy religion as well stated as only a priest could do it nowadays, so that it was listened to with good will. Then he ordered all the Indian masons in the town to bring plenty of lime so as to clean the place and he told them to clear away the blood which encrusted the cues and to clean them thoroughly. The next day when they were whitewashed, an altar was set up with very good altar cloths and he told the Indians to bring many of the roses which grew in the country and are very sweet-scented, and branches of flowers, and told the people to adorn the altar with garlands and always keep the place swept and clean. He then ordered four of the priests to have their hair shorn, for, as I have already said, they wore it long, and to change their garments and clothe themselves in white, and always keep themselves clean, and he placed them in charge of the altar and of that sacred image of our Lady, with orders to keep the place swept clean and decked with flowers. So that it should be well looked after, he left there as hermit one of our soldiers named Juan de Torres de Córdoba, who was old and lame. He ordered our carpenters, whose names I have already given, to make a cross and place it on a stone support which we had already built and plastered over.

The next morning, mass was celebrated at the altar by Padre Fray Bartolomé de Olmedo, and then an order was given to fumigate the holy image of Our Lady and the sacred cross with the incense of the country, and we showed them how to make candles of the native wax and ordered these candles always to be kept burning on the altar, for up to that time they did not know how to use the wax. The most important chieftains of that town and of others who had come together, were present at the Mass.

At the same time the eight Indian damsels were brought to be made Christians, for they were still in the charge of their parents and uncles and they were given to understand that they must not offer more sacrifices, nor worship idols, but believe in our Lord God. And they were admonished about many things touching our holy religion and were then baptized. The niece of the fat Cacique was named Doña Catalina, and she was very ugly; she was led by the hand and given to Cortés who received her and tried to look pleased. The daughter of the great Cacique, Cuesco, was named Doña Francisca, she was very beautiful for an Indian, and Cortés gave her to Alonzo Hernández Puertocarrero. I cannot now recall to mind the names of the other six, but I know that Cortés gave them to different soldiers. When this had been done, we took leave of all the Caciques and chieftains who from that time forward always showed us good will, especially when they saw that Cortés received their daughters and that we took them away with us, and after Cortés had repeated his promises of assistance [against their enemies] we set out for our town of Villa Rica.

What happened there I will speak of later on. This, however, is the true account of what took place in the town of Cempoala, and differs from the stories told by Gómara and the other historians which are all stuff and nonsense.

CHAPTER LIII.

How we returned to Villa Rica de la Vera Cruz and what happened
there.

AFTER we had finished our expedition and the people
of Cempoala and Cingapacinga had been reconciled to one
another, and the other neighbouring towns had given their
fealty to His Majesty, and the idols had been overturned
and the image of Our Lady and the Holy Cross set up in
their place, and the old soldier placed in charge as hermit,
and all the other things that I have told about had
happened, we returned to our settlement and took with us
certain chieftains from Cempoala. On the day of our
arrival there came into port a ship from the Island of
Cuba, under the command of Francisco de Saucedo, whom
we called *El Pulido*.[1] We called him this from his excessive
pride in his good looks and elegance. They say that he
was a native of Medina Rio Seco, and had been *Maestresala*[2] to the Admiral of Castille.

At the same time there arrived Luis Marin (a man
of great merit who was afterwards a captain in the expedition against Mexico) and ten soldiers. Saucedo brought a
horse, and Luis Marin a mare ; and they brought from
Cuba the news that the decree had reached Diego Velásquez from Spain giving him authority to trade and found
settlements, at which his friends were greatly rejoiced, all
the more when they learned that he had received his commission appointing him Adelantado of Cuba.

Being in that town without any plans beyond finishing
the fort, for we were still at work on it, most of us soldiers
suggested to Cortés to let the fort stand as it was, for a

---

[1] The elegant.

[2] *Maestresala*, the chief waiter at a nobleman's table.

memorial, (it was just ready to be roofed), for we had already been over three months in the country and it seemed to us better to go and see what this great Montezuma might be like and to earn an honest living and make our fortune ; but that before we started on our journey we should send our salutations to His Majesty, the Emperor, and give him an account of all that had happened since we left the Island of Cuba. It also began to be debated whether we should send to His Majesty all the gold that we had received, both what we had got from barter, as well as the presents that Montezuma had sent us. Cortés replied that it was a very wise decision and that he had already talked to some of the gentlemen about it, and that as perchance in this matter of the gold there might be some soldiers who wished to keep their shares, and if it were divided up there would be very little to send, that for this reason he had appointed Diego de Ordás and Francisco. de Montejo who were good men of business, to go from soldier to soldier among those whom it was suspected would demand their share of the gold, and say these words : " Sirs, you already know that we wish to send His Majesty a present of the gold which we have obtained here, and as it is the first [treasure] that we are sending from this land it ought to be much greater ; it seems to us that we should all place at his service the portions that fall to our share. We gentlemen and soldiers who have here written our names have signed as not wishing to take anything, but to give it all voluntarily to His Majesty, so that he may bestow favours on us. If anyone wishes for his share it will not be refused him, but whoever renounces it let him do as we have all done, and sign here."

In this way they all signed to a man. When this was settled, Alonzo Hernández Puertocarrero and Francisco de Montejo were chosen as proctors to go to Spain, for Cortés had already given them over two thousand dollars to keep

o

them in his interest. The best ship in the fleet was got ready, and two pilots were appointed, one of them being Anton de Alaminos, who knew the passage through the Bahama Channel, for he was the first man to sail through it, and fifteen sailors were told off, and a full supply of ship's stores given to them. When everything was ready, we agreed to write to tell His Majesty all that had happened. Cortés wrote on his own account, so he told us, an accurate narrative of the events, but we did not see his letter.

The Cabildo[1] wrote a letter jointly with ten of the soldiers from among those who wished to settle in the land and had appointed Cortés as their general, and the letter was drawn up with great accuracy so that nothing was omitted, and I put my signature to it ; and besides these letters and narratives, all the captains and soldiers together wrote another letter and narrative, and what was contained in the letter which we wrote is as follows :

CHAPTER LIV.

The narrative and letter which we sent to His Majesty by our proctors, Alonzo Hernández Puertocarrero and Francisco de Montejo, which letter was signed by a number of the Captains and soldiers.

AFTER beginning with the expressions of well deserved respect which were due from us to the great Majesty of the Emperor our Lord, for such his Catholic Christian Royal Majesty was, and after adding other matters which it was appropriate to state in a narrative and account of our doings and voyage, each chapter by itself, there followed this, which I will here briefly recapitulate. How we sailed from

---

[1] Cabildo—Municipality, the alguaciles, etc., already mentioned.

the Island of Cuba with Hernando Cortés ; and the proclamations which were made ; how we intended coming to
settle, but that Diego Velásquez was secretly minded to
trade and not to settle. How Cortés wished to return with
certain gold gained by barter in accordance with the
instructions that he brought from Diego Velásquez which
we have submitted to His Majesty. How we insisted on
Cortés forming a settlement, and chose him as Captain
General and Chief Justice, until His Majesty might please
to order otherwise. How we promised him [Cortés] the fifth
of what should be obtained, after the Royal fifth had been
deducted. How we arrived at Cozumel and by what chance
Jerónimo de Aguilar happened to be at Cape Catoche,
and about the way he said that he got there, he and a
certain Gonzalo Guerrero, who remained with the Indians
because he was married and had children and had already
become like an Indian. How we arrived at Tabasco, and
of the war they waged against us, and the battle we fought
with them, and how we brought them to peace. How that
wherever we went excellent discourses were addressed to
them [the Indians] to induce them to abandon their Idols,
and matters concerning our Holy faith were explained to
them. How they gave their fealty to His Royal Majesty,
and became the first vassals that he has in these parts.
How they [the Indians] brought a present of women, and
among them a Cacica, for an Indian a woman of great
importance, who knew the Mexican language, which is the
language used throughout the country and that with her
and Aguilar we possessed reliable interpreters. How we
landed at San Juan de Ulúa, and about the speeches of the
Ambassadors of the Great Montezuma, and who the Great
Montezuma was and what was said about his greatness,
and about the present that they brought. How we went
to Cempoala, which is a large town, and thence to another
town named Quiahuitztlan, which is fortified, and how in

O 2

in what manner they happened, in the form of a letter
intended for our King and not in the style that is here set
down in my story, we captains and soldiers who were on
the side of Cortés, all of us signed it. Two copies were
made of the letter, and Cortés begged us to show them
to him, and when he saw such a true narrative, and the
great praise which we gave to him, he was very pleased
and said that he would remember it to our credit and made
us great promises, but he did not wish us to mention or
allude to the fifth of the gold that we had promised him,
nor to say who were the first discoverers, because, as we
understood, he gave no account in his letter of Francisco
Hernández de Córdova nor of Grijalva, but attributed the
discovery, and the honour and glory of it all, to himself
alone, and he said that now at this time it would be better
to write thus, and not to report it to His Majesty.   There
were not wanting those who said to him that to our King
and Lord nothing that had happened should be left untold.
When these letters had been written and given to our
proctors, we impressed on them strongly, that on no
account should they enter Havana or go to a farm which
one of them, Francisco de Montejo, owned there, which
was called *El Marien* and was a harbour for ships, lest
Diego Velásquez should get to know what was happening.
They did not do as they were told as I shall show later on.
When everything was ready for them to embark, the Padre
de la Merced said Mass, commending them to the guidance
of the Holy Spirit.

On the 26th July 1519 they left San Juan de Ulúa and
with good weather, arrived at Havana, and Francisco de
Montejo with the greatest importunity allured and induced
the pilot Alaminos to steer to his farm, saying that he was
going to obtain supplies of pigs and cassava, until he got
him to do what he wanted which was to drop anchor at his
farm, for Puertocarrero was very ill and he (Montejo) paid

no attention to him, and on the very night they arrived
they despatched a sailor from the ship by land with letters
and information for Diego Velásquez, and we know that
Montejo sent the man who went with the letters, and this
sailor went post haste through the Island of Cuba, from
town to town making known all that I have here told,
until Diego Velásquez himself knew it, and what he did
about it I will tell later on.

CHAPTER LV.

How Diego Velásquez, the Governor of Cuba, learned for certain from
   letters, that we were sending proctors with an embassy and
   presents to our King and Lord, and what he did about it.

As Diego Velásquez the Governor of Cuba learnt the news
both from the letters which were secretly sent him, (rumour
said by Montejo) as well as from the sailor, who had been
present during all that I have related in the last chapter,
and who swam ashore to carry the letters to him, and when
he understood about the great present of gold that we were
sending to His Majesty, and knew who were the Ambassadors and proctors, he was taken with cold sweats as of
death and uttered most lamentable words and curses
against Cortés, and against his own secretary Duero, and
the accountant Amador de Lares who had advised him to
make Cortés a general, and he promptly ordered two ships
of small burden which were fast sailors, to be armed with
all the artillery and soldiers that could be provided and
two captains, one named Gabriel de Rojas, and the other
so and so de Guzman, to go in them and he ordered them
to go as far as the Havana, and thence to the Bahama
Channel and in any case to capture and bring the ship
in which our proctors were sailing and all the gold that
they were carrying. With all haste, in compliance with his
commands, they arrived after some days of sailing at the

Bahama Channel, and asked of some of the vessels which
were crossing the sea with cargo if they had seen a ship of
large size go by and all gave news of her and said that she
would already have passed out of the Bahama Channel, for
they had had continuous good weather. So after beating
about with those two ships between the Bahama Channel and
the Havana and finding no news of what they came to seek
they returned to Santiago de Cuba, and if Diego Velásquez
was upset before he despatched the vessels, he was far
more afflicted when he saw them return in this way, and
his friends promptly advised him to send to Spain and
complain to the Bishop of Burgos who was President
of the Council of the Indies, and was doing much for
him. He also sent his complaints to the Island of
Santo Domingo to the Royal *Audiencia* which resided
there and to the Jeronimite friars who were governors
of the Island, named Fray Luis de Figuerea and Fray
Alonzo de Santo Domingo and Fray Bernadino de
Manzanedo, and these ecclesiastics were wont to stay and
reside in the Mejorada Monastery two miles distant from
Medina del Campo, and he sent a ship post haste to
them to make many complaints against Cortés and all of
us. When they came to know about our great services,
the answer that the Jeronimite fathers gave him was that
no blame could be laid on Cortés and those who went with
him, for on all matters we turned to our King and Master,
and we had sent him so great a present, such as had not
been seen for a long time past in our Spain, and they said
this because at that time and season no Peru existed nor
any thought of it. They also sent to tell him that on the
contrary we were worthy to receive the greatest favours
from His Majesty; at the same time they sent to Cuba a
Licentiate named Zuazo to take the *residencia*[1] of Diego

---

[1] Residencia—that is the examination and formal account demanded
of a person holding public office.

Velásquez, or at least he arrived at the Island a few months later, and this same Licentiate made his report to the Jeronimite Friars. When that reply was brought to Diego Velásquez he was more dismayed than ever, and whereas before he was very stout he at this time became thin. With the greatest energy he at once ordered all the ships that could be found in the Island of Cuba to be searched out and soldiers and Captains to be got ready, and he took steps to send a powerful fleet to take Cortés and all of us prisoners, and he showed such personal energy, going from town to town and from one estate to the other, writing to all parts of the Island where he was not able to go himself, and entreating his friends to go on that expedition, that within eleven months or a year he got together eighteen sail, great and small, and over thirteen hundred soldiers including captains and seamen, for as they saw that he was so zealous and prompt, all the principal inhabitants of Cuba, his relations as well as those who possessed Indians, got ready to serve him. He sent as Captain General of the Fleet a gentleman named Pánfilo de Narvaez, a man tall of stature and robust, whose voice sounded hollow as if from a vault ; he was a native of Valladolid and married in the Island of Cuba a lady who was already a widow, named Maria de Valenzuela and he owned good towns of Indians and was very rich.

Here I will now leave him, forming and preparing his fleet, and will go back to our proctors and their good voyage, and as three or four things happened at the same time I must leave the story and subject which I was discussing, so as to be able to speak of that which is more material, and for this reason they must not blame me because I set out and depart from the regular course of events in order to speak of what happened later on.

Reporter of His Majesty's Royal Council and a near relation of Cortés, who worked on his behalf, decided to send a
messenger to Flanders with other letters, the same as those
they had given to the Bishop, for duplicates had been sent
by our Proctors, and they wrote to His Majesty an account
of all that was happening, and a memorandum of the
golden jewels of the present, and made complaint of the
Bishop and disclosed his business connection with Diego
Velásquez. There were even other gentlemen who favoured
them, those who did not stand well with Don Juan Rodríguez de Fonseca, for it was rumoured that he was generally
disliked on account of the great injustice and arrogance he
displayed in the high offices that he held. As our great
services were for God our Lord and for His Majesty, and
we always put our full strength into them, it pleased God
that His Majesty arrived at a clear knowledge of the
affair and when he saw and understood it he and the
Duke, Marquises, Counts and other gentlemen who were
at his royal Court, showed such great satisfaction that they
talked of nothing else but of Cortés and all of us who were
helping him in the conquests for several days, and of the
riches we were sending him from these lands. As for the
letters of comment which the Bishop of Burgos had written
to him about the matter, when His Majesty saw that it
was all contrary to the truth, from then onwards he took a
particular dislike to the Bishop, especially because he had
not sent all the articles of gold but had kept back a great
number of them. The Bishop got to know all this when it
was written to him from Flanders, and he was very angry
about it, and if the Bishop had spoken much that was evil
of Cortés and all of us before our letters had come before
His Majesty, from that time forward he openly called
us traitors, but it pleased God that he lost his fury and
vigour, and within two years he was defied and even
shamed and dishonoured and we were reputed as very

loyal subjects, as I shall relate further on when occasion arises. His Majesty wrote to say that he was soon coming to Castille and would take notice of the matters concerning us, and would grant us favours. As I shall later on narrate more fully, how and in what manner this happened, I will leave the matter here, with our Proctors awaiting the arrival of His Majesty.

Before I go on any further I wish to speak with regard to what certain gentlemen who are curious in the matter have asked me, and they have a right to know about it, how it is that I am able to write down in this narrative things that I did not see, as at the time when our Proctors delivered the letters, messages, and presents of gold which they were carrying for His Majesty and had these disputes with the Bishop of Burgos, I was engaged in the conquest of New Spain. I say this, that our Proctors wrote to us the true *conquistadores*, word for word in Chapters, all that was happening, both about the Bishop of Burgos, as well as what His Majesty was pleased to promise in our favour, and how it all happened ; and Cortés sent us to the towns where we were living at the time, other letters that he had received from our Proctors that we might see how well they negotiated with His Majesty and how hostile the Bishop was to us. This I give as an answer to what I have been asked. Let us leave this subject and tell in another chapter what happened in our camp.

so that orders could be there issued for our journey to Mexico. So Pedro de Alvarado was not present when, as I have described, justice was executed.

The orders which were issued when we came together in Cempoala, I will relate fully further on.

CHAPTER LVIII.

How we settled to go to Mexico and to destroy all the ships before starting, and what else happened, and how the plan of destroying the ships was done by advice and decision of all of us who were friends with Cortés.

BEING in Cempoala, as I have stated, and discussing with Cortés questions of warfare, and our advance into the country, and going on from one thing to another, we, who were his friends, counselled him, although others opposed it, not to leave a single ship in the port, but to destroy them all at once, so as to leave no source of trouble behind, lest, when we were inland, others of our people should rebel like the last ; besides, we should gain much additional strength from the masters, pilots and sailors who numbered nearly one hundred men, and they would be better employed helping us to watch and fight than remaining in port.

As far as I can make out, this matter of destroying the ships which we suggested to Cortés during our conversation, had already been decided on by him, but he wished it to appear as though it came from us, so that if any one should ask him to pay for the ships, he could say that he had acted on our advice and we would all be concerned in their payment. Then he sent Juan de Escalante (who was chief alguacil and a person of distinguished bravery and a great friend of Cortés, and an enemy of Diego Velásquez, because he had not given him good Indians in the Island of Cuba) to Villa Rica with orders to bring on shore all the anchors, cables, sails, and everything else on board which might prove useful, and then to destroy the ships and preserve nothing but the boats, and that the pilots, sailing masters and sailors, who were old and no use for war, should stay at the town, and with the two nets they possessed should undertake the fishing, for there was always fish in that harbour, although they were not very plentiful. Juan de Escalante did all that he was told to do, and soon after arrived at Cempoala with a company of sailors, whom he had brought from the ships, and some of them turned out to be very good soldiers.

When this was done, Cortés sent to summon all the Caciques of the hill towns who were allied to us and in rebellion against Montezuma, and told them how they must give their service to the Spaniards who remained in Villa Rica, to finish building the church, fortress and houses, and Cortés took Juan de Escalante by the hand before them all, and said to them : " This is my brother," and told them to do whatever he should order them, and that should they need protection or assistance against the Mexicans, they should go to him and he would come in person to their assistance.

All the Caciques willingly promised to do what might be asked of them, and I remember that they at once fumigated Juan de Escalante with incense, although he did not wish it done. I have already said that he was a man well qualified for any post and a great friend of Cortés, so he could place him in command of the town and harbour with confidence, so that if Diego Velásquez should send an expedition there, it would meet with resistance. I must leave him here and go on with my story.

It is here that the historian Gomara says that when Cortés ordered the ships to be scuttled that he did not dare to let the soldiers know that he wished to go to Mexico in search of the great Montezuma. It was not as

P

he states, for what sort of Spaniards should we be not to wish to go ahead, but to linger in places where there was neither profit nor fighting? This same Gomara also says that Pedro de Ircio remained as captain in Vera Cruz ; he was misinformed. I repeat that it was Juan de Escalante who remained there as Captain and chief Alguacil of New Spain, and that so far, Pedro de Ircio had not been given any position whatever—not even charge of a company.

CHAPTER LIX.

About a discourse which Cortés made to us after the ships had been destroyed, and how we hastened our departure for Mexico.

WHEN the ships had been destroyed, with our full know-ledge, and not [secretly] as is said by the historian Gomara, one morning after we had heard mass, when all the captains and soldiers were assembled and were talking to Cortés about military matters, he begged us to listen to him, and argued with us as follows :—

" We all understood what was the work that lay before us, and that with the help of our Lord Jesus Christ we must conquer in all battles and encounters [that fell to our lot], and must be as ready for them as was befitting, for if we were anywhere defeated, which pray God would not happen, we could not raise our heads again, as we were so few in numbers, and we could look for no help or assistance, but that which came from God, for we no longer possessed ships in which to return to Cuba, but must rely on our own good swords and stout hearts,"—and he went on to draw many comparisons and relate the heroic deeds of the Romans. One and all we answered him that we would obey his orders, that the die was cast for good fortune, as Cæsar said when he crossed the Rubicon, and that we

were all of us ready to serve God and the King. After
this excellent speech, which was delivered with more
honied words and greater eloquence than I can express
here, he [Cortés] at once sent for the fat Cacique and
reminded him that he should treat the church and cross
with great reverence and keep them clean ; and he also
told him that he meant to depart at once for Mexico to
order Montezuma not to rob or offer human sacrifices, and
that he now had need of two hundred Indian carriers to
transport his artillery, for as I have already said these
Indians can carry two arrobas[1] on their backs and march
five leagues with it.   He also asked fifty of the leading
warriors to go with us.   Just as we were ready to set out,
a soldier, whom Cortés had sent to Villa Rica with orders
for some of the men remaining there to join him, returned
from the town bearing a letter from Juan de Escalante,
saying that there was a ship sailing along the coast, and
that he had made smoke signals and others, and had raised
some white cloths as banners, and had galloped along
on horseback waving a scarlet cape so that those on ship-
board might see it, and he believed that they had seen
his signals, banners, horse and cape, but that they did
not wish to come into the harbour, and that he had sent
some Spaniards to watch to what place the ships should
go, and they had reported that the ship had dropped
anchor near the mouth of a river distant about three leagues,
and that he wished to know what he should do.

When Cortés had read the letter he at once ordered
Pedro de Alvarado to take charge of all his army at
Cempoala and with him Gonzalo de Sandoval who was
already giving proofs of being a very valorous man, as he
always remained.   This was the first time that Sandoval
was given a command, and because he was appointed

---

[1] Two arrobas = 50 lbs.

snowcapped volcano of Orizaba (17,365 ft.) to the tableland of Tlaxcala.

There is a considerable rise between Cempoala and Jalapa, which stands at an elevation of 4608 ft.

I am unable to ascertain the height of the pass between Perote and Orizaba, but it probably exceeds 10,000 ft., followed by a descent of about 3000 ft. to the plains of Tlaxcala and Puebla, which are 7000 ft. to 8000 ft. above sea level.

According to Bernal Díaz, the most difficult pass (Puerto de Nombre de Dios) was crossed before reaching the main divide.

After the passage between the mountains the Spaniards came to the salt lakes, marshes, and inhospitable stretches of sand and volcanic ash which extend along the western slope of the Cofre de Perote.

It is impossible to locate the exact route between the mountain pass and Zocotlan, as no names are given and part of the country is uninhabitable. Zocotlan itself was in all probability the Zautla of the modern map, but we are not on secure ground until the Spaniards reach Ixtacmaxtitlan, near the Tlaxcalan frontier. This frontier is still marked by the ruins of the wall built by the Tlaxcalans as a defence against their enemies, but the ruins are not marked on the Government map. However, the natural line of travel would be up stream from Ixtacmaxtitlan, and this would bring us to a place marked on the map Altlatlaya (no doubt *Atalaya*, which means *a watch tower*), and I have taken this to be the spot where the Spaniards passed the wall, and have so marked it on the map which accompanies this volume.

The march from Jalapa to Zocotlan must have been a most arduous one, and all the more difficult from the fact that it was undertaken in the middle of the rainy season. There is a much easier, although somewhat longer, route passing round the north of Cofre de Perote, but this was probably avoided by the Cempoalans as passing through too much of the enemies' country.

Appended is an Itinerary, with dates compiled from the writings of Bernal Díaz[1], Cortés,[2] Gomara[3], and Andrés de Tápia,[4] with the modern spelling of some of the names taken from Padre Agustin Rivera.[5]

August

16. Leave Cempoala.

17.

18. Jalapa.

19. Xico (modern map), Cocochima (B. D.), Sienchimalen (C.), Sienchimatl (G.), Xicochimilco (R.)

---

[1] (B. D.)   [2] (C.)   [3] (G.)   [4] (T.)   [5] (R.)

20. A high pass and Tejutla (B. D.), Puerto de Nombre de Dios and Ceyconacan (C.), Theuhixuacan (G.), Ceycoccnacan, now Ishuacan de los Reyes (note to Cortés' letter in Rivadeneyra Edition), Ixuacan, modern map.

21. Finish ascent of Mountain (B. D.), Despoblado—uninhabited country.

22. Despoblado. Lakes of salt water and Salitrales (T.), Salitrales (G.)

23. Despoblado. Puerto de la Leña.   March 2 leagues to

24. Çocotlan (B. D.), Zaclotan (G.), Xocotla (R.), valley called Caltanmi (C.), Zacatami (G.). Spaniards called it Castil Blanco. Probably the Zautla of modern maps.

25. Xocotlan.

26. Xocotlan.

27. Xocotlan.   March 2 leagues up the valley to

28. Iztacmastitan (C.), Iztacmixtlitan (G.), Ixtamaxtitlan (R.), Ixtacamastitlan (modern map).

     Xalacingo of Bernal Díaz (evidently an error.)

29. Ixtacmaxtitlan.

30. Ixtacmaxtitlan.

31. Cross the frontier into Tlaxcala at the great wall. March 4 leagues, skirmish with force of Tlaxcalans and Otomies.

September.

2. First battle with the Tlaxcalan army under Xicotenga.

5. Second battle.

23. Spaniards enter the city of Tlaxcala.

CHAPTER LXI.

How we settled to go to the City of Mexico and on the advice of the Cacique we went by way of Tlaxcala, and what happened to us in our warlike engagements and other matters.

WHEN our departure for Mexico had received full consideration, we sought advice as to the road we should take, and the chieftains of Cempoala were agreed that the best and most convenient road for us to take was through the province of Tlaxcala, for they [the Tlaxcalans] were their allies and mortal enemies of the Mexicans.

Forty chieftains, all warriors, were already prepared to accompany us and were of great assistance to us on that journey; and they provided us as well with two

give to their gods or idols and such like evil things. Our
Indian friends replied : "So at last you have found it out !
Take care not to do anything to annoy them, for they will
know it at once ; they even know one's thoughts. These
Teules are those who captured the tax gatherers of your
great Montezuma and decreed that no more tribute should be
paid throughout the sierras nor in our town of Cempoala ;
and they are the same who turned our Teules out of their
temples and replaced them with their own gods and who
have conquered the people of Tabasco and Chanpoton, and
they are so good that they have made friendship between
us and the people of Cingapacinga. In addition to this
you have seen how the great Montezuma, notwithstanding
all his power, has sent them gold and cloth, and now they
have come to your town and we see that you have given
them nothing ;—run at once and bring them a present ! "

It seems that we had brought good advocates with us,
for the townspeople soon brought us four pendants, and
three necklaces, and some lizards, all made of gold, but
all the gold was of poor quality ; and they brought us four
Indian women who were good for grinding maize for
bread, and one load of cloth.   Cortés received these things
with a cheerful good will and with many expressions of
thanks.

I remember that in the plaza where some of their
oratories stood, there were piles of human skulls so regularly
arranged that one could count them, and I estimated them
at more than a hundred thousand. I repeat again that
there were more than one hundred thousand of them. And
in another part of the plaza there were so many piles of
dead men's thigh bones that one could not count them ;
there was also a large number of skulls strung between
beams of wood, and three priests who had charge of these
bones and skulls were guarding them. We had occasion
to see many such things later on as we penetrated into the

country for the same custom was observed in all the towns, including those of Tlaxcala.

After all that I have related had happened, we determined to set out on the road to Tlaxcala which our friends told us was very near, and that the boundary was close by where some boundary stones were placed to mark it. So we asked the Cacique Olintecle, which was the best and most level road to Mexico, and he replied the road which passed by the large town named Cholula, and the Cempoalans said to Cortés :—" Sir, do not go by Cholula for the people there are treacherous, and Montezuma always keeps a large garrison of warriors in that town ; "—and they advised us to go by way of Tlaxcala where the people were their friends and enemies of the Mexicans. So we agreed to take the advice of the Cempoalans, trusting that God would direct us.

Cortés demanded of Olintecle twenty warrior chiefs to go with us, and he gave them at once. The next morning we set out for Tlaxcala and arrived at a little town belonging to the people of Xalacingo. From this place we sent two of the Cempoala chieftains as messengers, choosing two who had said much in praise of the Tlax-calans and had declared that they were their friends, and by them we sent a letter to the Tlaxcalans, although we knew that they could not read it ; and also a red fluffy Flemish hat, such as was then worn.

What happened I will relate further on.

Introductory Note.

BETWEEN the 31st August when the Spaniards crossed the Tlaxcalan frontier and fought a skirmish with some Otomi-Tlaxcalan troops, and the 23rd September when they entered the Capital of Tlaxcala, only two dates are mentioned by Bernal Díaz. He gives the 2nd September (Gomara says the 1st September) as the date of the first great battle against the Tlaxcalan army under Xicotenca (Xicotencatl), and the name of the battlefield as Tehuacingo or Tehuacacingo, which cannot now be identified.

After the battle the Spaniards took shelter in a village with a temple on a hill; this hill is still pointed out by the natives as the site of Cortés' camp. Here the Spaniards formed a fortified camp, which continued to be their headquarters until the war was over, and they marched to the Capital of Tlaxcala.

Bernal Díaz tells us that this camp was near Cunpanzingo, probably the Tzompantzingo of the modern maps.

Bernal Díaz gives the 5th September as the date of the second great battle, which was fought close by the camp.

Although the accounts of the war in Tlaxcala given by Bernal Díaz and Cortés agree in the main points, they do not always give the events in the same order. It seems probable that Bernal Díaz places the night attack too early, and that it took place after Xicotenga had sent the spies to the Spanish camp.

The boundaries of the so-called Republic of Tlaxcala appear to have been almost identical with those of the modern state of the same name.

It has become a commonplace to describe the Tlaxcalans as hardy mountaineers and their form of Government as Republican, but such discrimination is misleading. Their country was no more mountainous than that of the Mexicans, and their form of Government was much the same as that of other Nahuá communities; but as they had achieved no foreign conquests, they were compelled to be self-supporting, and in that differed from the Mexicans, who were becoming a military caste, supported to a great extent by tribute from conquered tribes. Their country was fertile, and there must have been a large agricultural population, and all the men were inured to hardship and continual border warfare.

According to Andrés de Tápia, the existence of the Tlaxcalans as an independent nation was owing to the forbearance of the Mexicans themselves, for when he asked why they had not been conquered, Montezuma himself answered: "We could easily do so, but then there would be nowhere for the young men to exercise themselves without going a long way off, and besides we always like to have people to sacrifice to our Gods."

BOOK IV.

THE WAR IN TLAXCALA.

CHAPTER LXII.

How we decided to go by way of Tlaxcala, and how we sent messengers to induce the Tlaxcalans to agree to our passage through their country, how the messengers were taken prisoners, and what else happened.

 O we set out from Castilblanco and began our march with the scouts in advance, constantly on the alert, and the musketeers and crossbowmen in good order, as was necessary, and the horsemen in even closer order, and we all carrying our arms, as was always our custom. I will say nothing more about this, for it is no use wasting words over it, for we were always so much on the alert both by day and night that if an alarm had been given ten times over we should have been found ready every time.

In such order we arrived at a little town of Xalacingo, where they gave us a golden necklace and some cloth and two Indian women, and from that town we sent two Cempoalan chieftains as messengers to Tlaxcala, with a letter, and a fluffy red Flemish hat, such as was then worn. We well knew that the Tlaxcalans could not read

Q

it. It will be said to-day—what was the use of all this preparation when there were no hostile warriors in sight to attack us ?   I answer this by repeating the words of Cortés :—" Gentlemen and comrades, seeing how few of us there are, it behoves us to be always as well prepared and as much on the alert as though we saw the enemy approaching to attack us, and not only saw them approaching, but we should behave as though we were already fighting them ; and, as it often happens that they seize the lances with their hands, we have to be prepared for such an emergency as well as for anything else that may happen to a soldier.   I have fully understood that, when fighting, there should be no need of directions, for I know, and am very willing to acknowledge it, that you behave much more courageously [without them]."

In this way we marched about two leagues, when we came upon a fortress strongly built of stone and lime and some other cement, so strong that with iron pickaxes it was difficult to demolish it and it was constructed in such a way both for offence and defence, that it would be very difficult to capture.   We halted to examine it, and Cortés asked the Indians from Zocotlan for what purpose the fortress had been built in such a way.   They replied that, as war was always going on between the people of Tlaxcala and their lord, Montezuma, the Tlaxcalans had built this fort so strong the better to defend their towns, for we were already in their territory.   We rested awhile and this, our entry into the land of Tlaxcala and the fortress, gave us plenty to think about.   Cortés said : " Sirs, let us follow our banner which bears the sign of the holy cross, and through it we shall conquer ! "   Then one and all we answered him : " May good fortune attend our advance, for in God lies the true strength."   So we began our march again in the order I have already noted.

We had not gone far when our scouts observed about

thirty Indians who were spying. These carried two-handed swords, shields, lances and plumes of feathers. The swords are made with stones which cut worse than knives, so cleverly arranged, that one can neither break nor pull out the blades; they are as long as broadswords; and as I have already said, these spies wore devices and feather head-dresses, and when our scouts observed them they came back to give us notice. Cortés then ordered the same scouts to follow the spies, and to try and capture one of them without hurting them; and then he sent five more mounted men as a support, in case there should be an ambush. Then all our army hastened on in good order and with quick step, for our Indian friends who were with us said that there was sure to be a large body of warriors waiting in ambush.

When the thirty Indian spies saw the horsemen coming towards them, and beckoning to them with their hands, they would not wait for them to come up and capture one of them; furthermore, they defended them-selves so well, that with their swords and lances they wounded some of the horses.

When our men saw how fiercely the Indians fought and that their horses were wounded, they were obliged to kill five of the Indians. As soon as this happened, a squadron of Tlaxcalans,[1] more than three thousand strong, which was lying in ambush, fell on them all of a sudden, with great fury and began to shower arrows on our horse-men who were now all together; and they made a good fight with their arrows and fire-hardened darts, and did wonders with their two-handed swords. At this moment we came up with our artillery, muskets and crossbows, and

---

[1] Probably Otomís from the Otomí town of Tecoac. Cortés says the chiefs of Tlaxcala sent messengers to say that the attack was made by communities (of Otomís?) without their knowledge.

wounded and ran great danger. As the battle went on
they surrounded us on all sides and we could do little
or nothing. We dared not charge them, unless we charged
all together, lest they should break up our formation ; and
if we did charge them, as I have said, there were twenty
squadrons ready to resist us, and our lives were in great
danger for they were so numerous they could have blinded
us with handfuls of earth, if God in his great mercy had
not succoured us.

While we found ourselves in this conflict among these
great warriors and their fearful broad swords, we noticed
that many of the strongest among them crowded together
to lay hands on a horse. They set to work with a furious
attack, laying hands on a good mare known to be very
handy either for sport or for charging. The rider, Pedro
de Moron, was a very good horseman, and as he charged
with three other horsemen into the ranks of the enemy
(they were ordered thus to charge together, so as to help
one another) the Indians seized hold of his lance and he
was not able to drag it away, and others gave him cuts
with their broadswords and wounded him badly, and then
they slashed at the mare, and cut her head off at the neck
so that it hung by the skin, and she fell dead. If his
mounted companions had not come at once to his rescue
they would also have finished killing Pedro de Moron.
We might possibly have helped him with our whole
battalion, but I repeat again that we hardly dared to move
from one place to another for fear that they would finally
rout us, and we could not move one way or another ; it
was all we could do to hold our own and prevent ourselves
from being defeated. However, we rushed to the conflict
around the mare and managed to save Moron from the
hands of the enemy who were already dragging him off
half dead and we cut the mare's girths so as not to leave
the saddle behind. In that act of rescue, ten of our men

were wounded and I remember that at the same time we killed four of the (Indian) captains, for we were advancing in close order and we did great execution with our swords. When this had happened, the enemy began to retire, carrying the mare with them, and they cut her in pieces to exhibit in all the towns of Tlaxcala, and we learnt afterwards that they made an offering to their idols of the horseshoes, of the Flemish felt hat, and the two letters which we had sent them offering peace.

The mare that was killed belonged to Juan Sedeño and it was because Sedeño had received three wounds the day before that he had given her to Moron who was a good horseman. I did not see Moron again for he died of his wounds two days later.

To return to our battle : we were a full hour fighting in the fray, and our shots must have done the enemy much damage for they were so numerous and in such close formation, that each shot must have hit many of them. Horsemen, musketeers, crossbowmen, swordsmen, and those who used lance and shield, one and all, we fought like men to save our lives and to do our duty, for we were certainly in the greatest danger in which we had ever found ourselves. Later on they told us that we killed many Indians in this battle, and among them eight of their leading captains, sons of the old Caciques who lived in their principal town, and for this reason they drew off in good order. We did not attempt to follow them, and we were not sorry for it as we were so tired out we could hardly stand, and we stayed where we were in that little town. All the country round was thickly peopled, and they even have some houses underground like caves in which many of the Indians live.

The place where this battle took place is called Tehua-cingo or Tehuacacingo and it was fought on the 2nd day of the month of September in the year 1519. When we saw that victory was ours we gave thanks to God who had delivered us from such great danger.

From the field of battle we withdrew the whole force to some Cues which were strong and lofty like a fortress. We dressed the wounded men, who numbered fifteen, with the fat of the Indian I mentioned before. One man died of his wounds. We also doctored four or five horses which had received wounds, and we rested and supped very well that night, for we found a good supply of poultry and little dogs in the houses. And taking every precaution by posting spies, patrols and scouts, we rested until the next morning.

In that battle we captured fifteen Indians, two of them chieftains. There was one peculiarity that the Tlaxcalans showed in this and all the other battles—that was to carry off any Indian as soon as he was wounded so that we should not be able to see their dead.

CHAPTER LXIV.

How we pitched our camp in some towns and hamlets called Teoaçingo or Tevaçingo and what we did there.

As we felt weary after the battles we had fought, and many of the soldiers and horses were wounded and some died there, and it was necessary to repair the crossbows and replenish our stock of darts, we passed one day without doing anything worthy of mention. The following morning Cortés said that it would be as well for all the horsemen who were fit for work to scour the country, so that the Tlaxcalans should not think that we had given up fighting on account of the last battle, and that they should see that we meant to follow them up ; for on the previous day we had halted without sallying forth to look for them, and it was better for us to go out and attack them than for them

to come and attack us and thus find out our weakness.
As the country was level and thickly populated, we set out
with seven horsemen and a few musketeers and crossbowmen and about two hundred soldiers and our Indian allies,
leaving the camp as well guarded as was possible. In the
houses and towns through which we passed, we captured
about twenty Indian men and women without doing them
any hurt, but our allies, who are a cruel people, burnt many
of the houses and carried off much poultry and many dogs
for food. When we returned to the camp which was not
far off, Cortés set the prisoners free, after giving them
something to eat, and Doña Marina and Aguilar spoke
kindly to them and gave them beads and told them not to
be so mad any longer, but to make peace with us, as
we wished to help them and treat them as brothers. Then
we also released the two prisoners who were chieftains and
they were given another letter, and were to tell the high
Caciques who lived in the town—which was the capital of
all the towns of the province—that we had not come to do
them any harm or to annoy them, but to pass through
their country on our way to Mexico to speak to Montezuma.
The two messengers went to Xicotenga's camp which was
distant about two leagues among some towns and houses
which I think they called Cuadçinpacingo, and when they
gave him the letter and our message the reply that their
captain Xicotenga gave them was, that we might go to his
town where his father was living ; that there peace would
be made by satiating themselves on our flesh, and honour
paid to his gods with our hearts and blood, and that we
should see his answer the very next day.

When Cortés and all of us heard that haughty message,
as we were already tired out with the battles and encounters
we had passed through, we certainly did not think that
things looked well. So Cortés flattered the messengers
with soft words for it seemed that they had lost all fear,

and ordered them to be given some strings of beads, as he wished to send them back as messengers of peace.

Cortés then learned from them more fully all about the Captain Xicotenga, and what forces he had with him. They told him that Xicotenga had many more men with him now than he had when he attacked us before for he had five captains with him and each captain had brought ten thousand warriors. This was the way in which the count was made : Of the followers of Xicotenga who was blind from age—the father of the captain of the same name—ten thousand ; of the followers of another great chief named Mase Escasi,[1] another ten thousand ; of the followers of another great chief named Chichimeca-tecle,[2] the same number ; of another great Cacique, lord of Topeyanco, named Tecapacaneca, another ten thousand ; and of another great chief named Guaxoban, another ten thousand ; so that there were in all fifty thousand. That their banner and standard had been brought out, which was a white bird with the appearance of an ostrich, with wings outstretched, as though it wished to fly, and that each company had its device and uniform, for each Cacique had a different one, as do our dukes and counts in our own Castile.

All that I have here said we accepted as perfectly true, for certain Indians among those whom we had captured and who were released that day, related it very clearly, although they were not then believed. When we knew this, as we were but human and feared death, many of us, indeed the majority of us, confessed to the Padre de la Merced and to the priest, Juan Díaz, who were occupied all night in hearing our repentance and commending us to God and praying that He would pardon us and save us

---

[1] Maxixcatzin.

[2] Chichimecatecuhtli.

from defeat. In this way the time passed until the next day, and the attack which they made on us I will now describe.

CHAPTER LXV.

Concerning the great battle which we fought against the forces of Tlaxcala, in which it pleased our Lord God to give us the victory, and what else happened.

THE next morning, the 5th of September, 1519, we mustered the horses. There was not one of the wounded men who did not come forward to join the ranks and give as much help as he could. The crossbowmen were warned to use the store of darts very cautiously, some of them loading while the others were shooting, and the musketeers were to act in the same way, and the men with sword and shield were instructed to aim their cuts and thrusts at the bowels [of their enemies] so that they would not dare to come as close to us as they did before. The artillery was all ready for action, and the horsemen had already been instructed to aid one another and to hold their lances short, and not to stop to spear anyone except in the face and eyes—charging and returning at a hand gallop and no soldier was on any account to break away from the ranks. With our banner unfurled, and four of our comrades guarding the standard-bearer, Corral, we set out from our camp. We had not marched half a quarter of a league before we began to see the fields crowded with warriors with great feather crests and distinguishing devices, and to hear the blare of horns and trumpets.

Here would be a great opportunity to write down in proper order what happened to us in this most perilous and doubtful battle, for so many warriors surrounded us on all sides that [the situation] might be compared to a

soldiers, and all the soldiers who were wounded did the same ; for if the wounds were not very dangerous, we had to fight and keep guard, wounded as we were, for few of us remained unwounded.

Then we returned to our camp, well contented, and giving thanks to God. We buried the dead in one of those houses which the Indians had built underground, so that the enemy should not see that we were mortals, but should believe that, as they said, we were Teules. We threw much earth over the top of the house, so that they should not smell the bodies, then we doctored all the wounded with the fat of the Indian, as I have related before. It was cold comfort to be even without salt or oil with which to cure the wounded. There was another want from which we suffered, and it was a severe one—and that was clothes with which to cover ourselves, for such a cold wind came from the snow mountains, that it made us shiver, for our lances and muskets and crossbows made a poor covering. That night we slept with more tranquillity than on the night before, when we had so much duty to do, with scouting, spies, watchmen and patrols.

I will leave off here and relate what we did on the next day. In this battle we captured three Indian chieftains.

CHAPTER LXVI.

How next day we sent messengers to the Caciques of Tlaxcala, begging them to make peace, and what they did about it.

AFTER the battle which I have described was over, in which we had captured three Indian chieftains, our Captain Cortés sent them at once in company with the two others who were in our camp and who had already been sent as messengers, and ordered them to go to the Caciques of Tlaxcala and tell them that we begged them to make peace

and to grant us a passage through their country on our
way to Mexico, as we had already sent to request them,
and to say that if they did not now come to terms, we
would slay all their people, but that as we were well
disposed towards them and wished to treat them as
brothers, we had no desire to annoy them, unless they
gave us reason to do so; and he said many flattering
things to them so as to make friends of them, and the
messengers then set out eagerly for the capital of Tlaxcala
and gave their message to all the Caciques already mentioned by me, whom they found gathered in council with
many other elders and priests.   They were very sorrowful
both over the want of success in the war and at the
death of those captains, their sons and relations, who had
fallen in battle.   As they were not very willing to listen to
the message, they decided to summon all the soothsayers,
priests, and those others called *Tacal naguas* (who are
like wizards and foretell fortunes), and they told them to
find out from their witchcraft, charms, and lots what people
we were, and if by giving us battle day and night without
ceasing we could be conquered, and to say if we were
Teules, (which, as I have already said many times, are evil
beings, like devils,) as the people of Cempoala asserted,
and to tell them what things we ate, and ordered them to
look into all these matters with the greatest care.

When the soothsayers and wizards and many priests
had got together and made their prophecies and forecasts,
and performed all the other rites according to their use,
it seems that they said that by their divinations they
had found out we were men of flesh and blood and ate
poultry and dogs and bread and fruit when we had
them, and that we did not eat the flesh nor the hearts of
the Indians whom we killed.   It seems that our Indian
friends whom we had brought from Cempoala had made
them believe that we were Teules, and that we ate the

R

hearts of Indians, and that the cannon shot forth lightning, such as falls from heaven, and that the Lurcher, which was a sort of lion or tiger, and the horses, were used to catch Indians when we wanted to kill them, and much more nonsense of the same sort.

The worst of all that the priests and wizards told the Caciques was, that it was not during the day, but only at night that we could be defeated, for as night fell, all our strength left us. Furthermore, their wizards told them that by day we were very valiant, and all this strength lasted throughout the day up to sunset, but that as soon as night came on we had no strength whatever. When the Caciques heard this, and they were quite convinced of it, they sent to tell their captain general Xicotenga that as soon as it was possible he should come and attack us in great force by night. On receiving this order Xicotenga assembled ten thousand of the bravest of his Indians and came to our camp, and from three sides they began alternately to shoot arrows and throw single pointed javelins from their spear throwers, and from the fourth side the swordsmen and those armed with macanas and broadswords approached so suddenly, that they felt sure that they would carry some of us off to be sacrificed. Our Lord God provided otherwise, for secretly as they approached, they found us well on the alert, and as soon as our outposts and spies perceived the great noise of their movement, they ran at breakneck speed to give the alarm, and as we were all accustomed to sleep ready shod, with our arms on us and our horses bitted and saddled, and with all our arms ready for use, we defended ourselves with guns, crossbows and sword play so that they soon turned their backs. As the ground was level and there was a moon the horsemen followed them a little way, and in the morning we found lying on the plain about twenty of them dead and wounded. So they went back with great loss and sorely repenting this night expedition, and I have heard it said, that as what the priests and wizards had advised did not turn out well they sacrificed two of them.

That night, one of our Indian friends from Cempoala was killed and two of our soldiers were wounded and one horse, and we captured four of the enemy. When we found that we had escaped from that impetuous attack we gave thanks to God, and we buried our Cempoala friend and tended the wounded and the horse, and slept the rest of the night after taking every precaution to protect the camp as was our custom.

When we awoke and saw how all of us were wounded, even with two or three wounds, and how weary we were and how others were sick and clothed in rags, and knew that Xicotenga was always after us, and already over forty-five of our soldiers had been killed in battle, or succumbed to disease and chills, and another dozen of them were ill, and our Captain Cortés himself was suffering from fever as well as the Padre de la Merced, and what with our labours and the weight of our arms which we always carried on our backs, and other hardships from chills and the want of salt, for we could never find any to eat, we began to wonder what would be the outcome of all this fighting, and what we should do and where we should go when it was finished. To march into Mexico we thought too arduous an undertaking because of its great armies, and we said to one another that if those Tlaxcalans, which our Cempoalan friends had led us to believe were peacefully disposed, could reduce us to these straits, what would happen when we found ourselves at war with the great forces of Montezuma? In addition to this we had heard nothing from the Spaniards whom we had left settled in Villa Rica, nor they of us. As there were among us very excellent gentlemen and soldiers, steady and valiant men of good counsel, Cortés never said or did anything [important] without first asking

with us; and they sent at once to summon all the other
Caciques and captains who were in their towns, and those
of a neighbouring province called Huexotzingo who were
their friends and allies, and when all had come together
to the town where they were, which was their capital, Mase
Escasi and Xicotenga the elder, who were very wise men,
made them a speech, as we afterwards learned, to the
following effect, if not exactly in these words :

"Brothers and friends, you have already seen how many
times these Teules who are in this country expecting to be
attacked, have sent us messengers asking us to make peace,
saying that they come to assist us and adopt us as
brothers ; and you have also seen how many times they
have taken prisoners numbers of our vassals to whom they
do no harm, and whom they quickly set free. You well
know how we have three times attacked them with all our
forces, both by day and by night, and have failed to
conquer them, and that they have killed during the attacks
we made on them, many of our people, and of our sons,
relations and captains. Now, again, they have sent to ask
us to make peace and the people of Cempoala whom they
are bringing in their company say that they are the
enemies of Montezuma and his Mexicans, and have ordered
the towns of the Totonac sierra and those of Cempoala
no longer to pay tribute to Montezuma. You will remember
well enough that the Mexicans make war on us every year,
and have done so for more than a hundred years, and you
can readily see that we are hemmed in in our own lands, so
that we do not dare to go outside even to seek for salt,
so that we have none to eat, and we have no cotton, and
bring in very little cotton cloth, and if some of our people
go out or have gone out to seek for it, few of them return
alive, for those traitorous Mexicans and their allies kill
them or make slaves of them. Our wizards[1] and sooth-

---

[1] Tacal naguas.

sayers and priests have told us what they think about the persons of these Teules, and that they are very valiant. It seems to me that we should seek to be friends with them, and in either case, whether they be men or Teules, that we should make them welcome, and that four of our chieftains should set out at once and take them plenty to eat, and should offer them friendship and peace, so that they should assist us and defend us against our enemies, and let us bring them here to us, and give them women, so that we may have relationship with their offspring, for the ambassadors whom they have sent to treat for peace, tell us that they have some women with them."

When they had listened to this discourse, all the Caciques and chiefs approved of it and said that it was a wise decision and that peace should be made at once, and that notice should be sent to the Captain Xicotenga and the other captains who were with him to return at once and not to attack again, and that they should be told that peace was already made, and messengers were immediately sent off to announce it. However, the Captain Xicotenga the younger would not listen to the four chiefs, and got very angry and used abusive language against them, and said he was not for peace, for he had already killed many of the Teules and a mare, and that he wished to attack us again by night and completely conquer us and slay us.

When his father, Xicotenga the elder, and Mase Escasi and the other Caciques heard this reply they were very angry, and sent orders at once to the captains and to all the army that they should not join Xicotenga in attacking us again, and should not obey him in anything that he ordered unless it was in making peace. And even so he would not obey, and when they [the Caciques] saw the disobedience of their captain, they at once sent the same four chieftains whom they had sent before, to bring food to our camp and treat for peace in the name of all and he [Cortés] sent those [same] priests [as messengers], for, by the other messengers whom we had sent we had so far received no reply whatever.   Concerning the circumstance I have mentioned of the Caciques of Tlaxcala sending four chieftains to treat for peace, up to that time these had not arrived.

These priests of the town quickly searched for more than forty cocks and hens and two women to grind tortillas, and brought them to us, and Cortés thanked them for it, and ordered them at once to send twenty Indians to our camp, and they came with the food without any fear whatever and stayed in the camp until the afternoon, and they were given little beads with which they returned well contented to their homes, and in all the small hamlets in our neighbourhood they spread word that we were good because we caused them no annoyance, and the priests and elders sent notice to the captain Xicotenga and told him how they had given us the food and the women, and he rated them severely, and they went at once to the capital to make it known to the old Caciques.   As soon as they heard that we had not done the people any harm, although we might have killed many of them that night, and that we were sending them to treat for peace, they were greatly pleased, and ordered that we should be supplied every day with all that we needed ; and they again ordered the four Caciques, whom they had before charged with the mission of peace, to depart instantly for our camp, and carry with them all the food that had been prepared.   We then returned to our camp with our supplies of food and the Indian women, all of us well contented.

I must leave off here and relate what passed in the camp while we were gone away to that town.

CHAPTER LXIX.

How when we returned with Cortés from Tzumpantzingo[1] with
supplies, we found certain discussions being carried on in our
camp, and what Cortés replied to them.

WHEN we returned from Tzumpantzingo,[2] as the town is
called, with our supplies of food, very contented at leaving
the place pacified, we found that in camp there had been
meetings and discussions about the very great danger we
were running day by day during this war, and on our arrival
the discussion grew most lively. Those who talked most
and were most persistent, were those who had left houses
and assignments of Indians behind them in Cuba, and as
many as seven of these men (whose names I will not
mention so as to save their honour) met together and went
to the hut where Cortés was lodging, and one of them who
spoke for all, for he was very fluent of speech and knew
very well what they had come to propose, said, as though
he were giving advice to Cortés, that he should take heed
of the condition we were in, wounded and thin and half-
hearted, and the great hardships that we endured by
night as sentinels and spies, or patrols and scouts, and
both by day and night in fighting. According to the
accounts he had made up, since leaving Cuba we had lost
over fifty-five of our comrades, and knew nothing about
those whom we had left as settlers at Villa Rica; and
although God had given us victory in the battles and
skirmishes since we came from Cuba to this province and
by His great pity had sustained us, we ought not to tempt
Him so many times, and might it not turn out worse than
Pedro Carbonero[3]; that he [Cortés] had got us into an

---

[1] Çinpançingo in the original.   [2] Çunpanzingo in the original.
[3] Spoken proverbially of Pedro Carbonero, who penetrated into the
land of the Moors, but failed to return, and perished there with all his
followers.

unexpected situation, and that some day or other we should be sacrificed to the idols, which please God would not happen ; but that it would be a good thing to return to our town and the fortress which we had built, and stay among the towns of our friends the Totonacs until we could build a ship which should be dispatched to Diego Velásquez and to other parts and islands to ask them to send us help and assistance ; and that now the ships which we sunk would have been useful to us, and we might have left at least two of them in case of necessity arising, but without consulting them about this, or about anything else, by the advice of those who did not know how to provide for changes of fortune, he [Cortés] had ordered them all to be sunk, and please God that he and those who had given him such advice would not repent of it ; that we were no longer able to support the burden much less the many overburdens [which we were carrying] and that we were going along worse than beasts of burden ; for when a beast has done its day's work its packsaddle is taken off and it is given food and rest ; but we went booted and loaded down with our arms both by day and night ; and they told Cortés besides that he could see in any history that neither the Romans nor Alexander, nor any other of the most famous captains whom the world had known, had dared to destroy their ships and with such a small force throw themselves against such a great population with so many warriors as he had done, and that it would be the cause of his own death and that of all his followers ; that he should wish to preserve his life and the lives of us all, and that we should at once return to Villa Rica as the country there was at peace ; that they had not said all this before, as there had been no time to do so on account of the many warriors who were opposed to us every day, both in front and on our flanks ; and although they had not returned to the attack they believed that they would do so, and since Xicotenga with his great power had not been to look for us during the last three days, that he must be collecting his forces and we ought not to await another battle like the last; and they said more to the same effect.

Cortés noticing that they spoke somewhat haughtily, considering that their words took the form of unasked advice, answered them very gently and said that he was aware of many of the things that they had mentioned, and that from what he had seen and believed, there was not in the whole world another [company of] Spaniards who were hardier, or who had fought with greater courage, or had endured such excessive hardships as we had, and that if we had not marched with arms continually on our backs, and kept watch, and gone on patrol, and suffered cold, and if we had not done all this we should already have perished, and that it was to save our lives that we had to endure those hardships and even greater ones, and he said: "Why, sirs, should we talk about deeds of valour when in truth our Lord is pleased to help us? When I remember seeing us surrounded by so many companies of the enemy and watching the play of their broadswords so close to us, it even now terrifies me, especially when they killed the mare with a single sword cut; we indeed seemed to be defeated and lost, and then I appreciated your great courage more than ever. As God then freed us from such great danger, so I have trust in Him that He will do the same in the future; and I will say more—that in all such dangers you will find no slackness on my part when I share them with you." He had good reason to say so for in all the battles he was to be found in the front. "I wish you, sirs, to bear in mind, that as our Lord has been pleased to help us, we have hope that so it may be in the future, for ever since we have penetrated into this country, in all the towns we have passed through, we have preached

your duty—as good soldiers; for after God, who is your
aid and support, we must rely on our own strong arms."

When Cortés had given this reply, those soldiers renewed
their argument. They admitted that all that Cortés had
told them had been well said, but that when we left the
town where we had made a settlement, our intention was,
and now still is, to go to Mexico, which has such a great
reputation on account of the strength of the city and its
great number of warriors. The people of Cempoala said
that the Tlaxcalans were a peaceful people, and they had
no such reputation as those of Mexico, yet we had been in
great danger of losing our lives, and if they should attack
us next day in another battle such as those we had gone
through, we were too exhausted to hold our own. If they
did not attack us again, still the journey to Mexico seemed
to them a very terrible thing, and that he should reconsider
what he was saying and commanding.

Cortés answered half angrily that " It was better to die
in a good cause, as the Psalms said, than to live dishonoured ! " And in addition to this which Cortés told
them, the greater number of the soldiers, those who had
elected Cortés captain, and had given him counsel about
destroying the ships, cried out loudly that he should not
trouble himself about gossip or listen to such tales, for
with the help of God, by acting well together, we should
be ready to do the right thing, and so all the talk ended.

It is true enough that they grumbled at Cortés and
cursed him, and even at us who had advised him, and at
the Cempoalans who had brought us here, and said other
unworthy things, but in such times they were overlooked.
Finally all were fairly obedient, and I will leave off talking
about this, and will relate how the aged Caciques again
sent messengers from the capital of Tlaxcala to their
captain general Xicotenga to say that without fail he
should immediately visit us in peace and bring us food,

for so it was decreed by all the caciques and chieftains of their land and of Huexotzingo. They also sent to order the captains who were in Xicotenga's company, to refuse him all obedience if he did not go and make peace. This they sent to say three times, for they knew for certain that Xicotenga did not wish to obey them, but was determined once again to attack our camp by night, and for this purpose had assembled twenty thousand men, and being haughty and very stubborn, that now, as at other times, he would not obey.

What he did in the matter I will tell further on.

CHAPTER LXX.

How the Captain Xicotenga had got ready twenty thousand picked warriors to attack our camp and what was done about it.

WHEN Mase Escasi and Xicotenga the elder, and the greater number of the Caciques of the capital of Tlaxcala sent four times to tell their captain not to attack us but to go and treat for peace, he was very close to our camp, and they sent to the other captains who were with him and told them not to follow him unless it was to accompany him when he went to see us peacefully.

As Xicotenga was bad tempered and obstinate and proud, he decided to send forty Indians with food, poultry, bread and fruit and four miserable looking old Indian women, and much copal and many parrots' feathers. From their appearance we thought that the Indians who brought this present came with peaceful intentions, and when they reached our camp they fumigated Cortés with incense without doing him reverence, as was usually their custom. They said : "The Captain Xicotenga sends you all this so that you can eat. If you are savage Teules, as the Cempoalans say you are, and if you wish for a sacrifice,

S

take these four women and sacrifice them and you can eat
their flesh and hearts, but as we do not know your manner
of doing it, we have not sacrificed them now before you ;
but if you are men, eat the poultry and the bread and
fruit, and if you are tame Teules we have brought you
copal (which I have already said is a sort of incense) and
parrots' feathers ; make your sacrifice with that."

Cortés answered through our interpreters that he had
already sent to them to say that he desired peace and had
not come to make war, but had come to entreat them and
make clear to them on behalf of our Lord Jesus Christ,
whom we believe in and worship, and of the Emperor Don
Carlos, whose vassals we are, that they should not kill or
sacrifice anyone as was their custom to do. That we were
all men of bone and flesh just as they were, and not Teules
but Christians, and that it was not our custom to kill anyone ; that had we wished to kill people, many opportunities
of perpetrating cruelties had occurred during the frequent
attacks they had made on us, both by day and night.
That for the food they had brought he gave them thanks,
and that they were not to be as foolish as they had been,
but should now make peace.

It seems that these Indians whom Xicotenga had sent
with the food were spies sent to examine our huts and
ranchos, and horses and artillery and [to report] how many
of us there were in each hut, our comings and goings, and
everything else that could be seen in the camp. They remained there that day and the following night, and some of
them went with messages to Xicotenga and others arrived.
Our friends whom we had brought with us from Cempoala
looked on and bethought them that it was not a customary
thing for our enemies to stay in the camp day and night
without any purpose, and it was clear to them that they
were spies, and they were the more suspicious of them in
that when we went on the expedition to the little town of

Tzumpantzingo, two old men of that town had told the Cempoalans that Xicotenga was all ready with a large number of warriors to attack our camp by night, in such a way that their approach would not be detected, and the Cempoalans at that time took it for a joke or bravado, and not believing it they had said nothing to Cortés; but Doña Marina heard of it at once and she repeated it to Cortés.

So as to learn the truth, Cortés had two of the most honest looking of the Tlaxcalans taken apart from the others, and they confessed that they were spies; then two others were taken and they also confessed that they were spies from Xicotenga and the reason why they had come. Cortés ordered them to be released, and we took two more of them and they confessed that they were neither more nor less than spies, but added that their Captain Xicotenga was awaiting their report to attack us that night with all his companies. When Cortés heard this he let it be known throughout the camp that we were to keep on the alert, believing that they would attack as had been arranged. Then he had seventeen of those spies captured and cut off the hands of some and the thumbs of others and sent them to the Captain Xicotenga to tell him that he had had them thus punished for daring to come in such a way, and to tell him that he might come when he chose by day or by night, for we should await him here two days, and that if he did not come within those two days that we would go and look for him in his camp, and that we would already have gone to attack them and kill them, were it not for the liking we had for them, and that now they should quit their foolishness and make peace.

They say that it was at the very moment that those Indians set out with their hands and thumbs cut off, that Xicotenga wished to set out from his camp with all his forces to attack us by night as had been arranged; but when he saw his spies returning in this manner he wondered

greatly and asked the reason of it, and they told him all
that had happened, and from this time forward he lost his
courage and pride, and in addition to this one of his
commanders with whom he had wrangles and disagree-
ments during the battles which had been fought, had left
the camp with all his men.

Let us get on with our story.

CHAPTER LXXI.

How the four chieftains who had been sent to treat for peace arrived
in our camp and the speech they made, and what else happened.

WHILE we were in camp not knowing that they would
come in peace, as we had so greatly desired, and were busy
polishing our arms and making arrows, each one of us
doing what was necessary to prepare for battle, at that
moment one of our scouts came hurrying in to say that
many Indian men and women with loads were coming
along the high road from Tlaxcala, and without leaving the
road were making for our camp, and that the other scout, his
companion, who was on horseback, was watching to see
which way they went; meanwhile the other scout, his
companion, who was on horseback, arrived and said that
the people were close by and coming straight in our
direction, and every now and then were making short
stops. Cortés and all of us were delighted at this news, for
we believed that it meant peace, as in fact it did, and
Cortés ordered us to make no display of alarm and not to
show any concern, but to stay hidden in our huts. Then,
from out of all those people who came bearing loads, the
four chieftains advanced who were charged to treat for
peace, according to the instructions given by the old
caciques. Making signs of peace by bowing the head, they
came straight to the hut where Cortés was lodging and

placed one hand on the ground and kissed the earth and
three times made obeisance and burnt copal, and said that
all the Caciques of Tlaxcala and their allies and vassals,
friends and confederates, were come to place themselves
under the friendship and peace of Cortés and of his brethren
the Teules who accompanied him. They asked his pardon
for not having met us peacefully, and for the war which
they had waged on us, for they had believed and held for
certain that we were friends of Montezuma and his
Mexicans, who have been their mortal enemies from times
long past, for they saw that many of his vassals who paid
him tribute had come in our company, and they believed
that they were endeavouring to gain an entry into their
country by guile and treachery, as was their custom to do,
so as to rob them of their women and children; and this
was the reason why they did not believe the messengers
whom we had sent to them. In addition to this they said
that the Indians who had first gone forth to make war on
us as we entered their country had done it without their
orders or advice, but by that of the Chuntales[1] Estomies,
who were wild people and very stupid, and that when they
saw that we were so few in number, they thought to
capture us and carry us off as prisoners to their lords
and gain thanks for so doing; that now they came to
beg pardon for their audacity, and had brought us food,
and that every day they would bring more and trusted
that we would receive it with the friendly feeling with
which it was sent; that within two days the captain
Xicotenga would come with other Caciques and give a

---

[1] " Chontal in the Mexican language means barbarous," *Relaciones
de Yucatan*, vol. ii, p. 342 ; it here means the barbarous Otomís. The
Otomis, according to Aztec tradition, were the earliest owners of the
soil in Central Mexico ; their headquarters were in what are now
known as the States of Queretaro and Guanajuato, but there were
Otomí communities living among other tribes in many parts of
Central Mexico.

CHAPTER LXXII.

How ambassadors from Montezuma, the great lord of Mexico, came
to our camp, and of the present which they brought.

As our Lord God, through his great loving kindness, was
pleased to give us victory in those battles in Tlaxcala, our
fame spread throughout the surrounding country, and
reached the ears of the great Montezuma in the great City
of Mexico ; and if hitherto they took us for Teules, which
is the same as their idols, from now on they held us in
even greater respect as valiant warriors, and terror fell on
the whole country at learning how, being so few in number
and the Tlaxcalans in such great force, we had conquered
them and that they had sued us for peace. So that now
Montezuma, the great Prince of Mexico, powerful as he
was, was in fear of our going to his city, and sent five
chieftains, men of much importance, to our camp at
Tlaxcala to bid us welcome, and say that he was rejoiced
at our great victory against so many squadrons of warriors,
and he sent a present, a matter of a thousand dollars worth
of gold, in very rich jewelled ornaments, worked in various
shapes, and twenty loads of fine cotton cloth, and he sent
word that he wished to become the vassal of our great
Emperor, and that he was pleased that we were already
near his city, on account of the good will that he bore
Cortés and all his brothers, the Teules, who were with
him (for so they called us) and that he [Cortés] should
decide how much tribute he wished for every year for our
great Emperor, and that he [Montezuma] would give it in
gold and silver, cloth and chalchihuites, provided we would
not come to Mexico. This was not because he would not
receive us with the greatest willingness, but because the
land was rough and sterile, and he would regret to see us
undergo such hardships which perchance he might not

be able to alleviate as well as he could wish. Cortés answered by saying that he highly appreciated the good will shown us, and the present which had been sent, and the offer to pay tribute to his Majesty, and he begged the messengers not to depart until he went to the capital of Tlaxcala, as he would despatch them from that place, for they could then see how that war ended, and he did not wish to give them his reply at once, because he had purged himself the day before with some camomiles such as are found in the Island of Cuba, and are very good for one who knows how to take them. I will leave this subject and tell what else happened in our camp.

CHAPTER LXXIII.

How Xicotenga, the Captain General of Tlaxcala, came to treat for peace, and what he said and what he settled with us.

CORTÉS was talking to the ambassadors of Montezuma, as I have already said, and wanted to take some rest, for he was ill with fever and had purged himself the day before, when they came to tell him that the Captain Xicotenga was arriving with many other Caciques and Captains, all clothed in white and red cloaks, half of the cloak was white and the other half red, for this was the device and livery of Xicotenga, [who was approaching] in a very peaceful manner, and was bringing with him in his company about fifty chieftains.

When Xicotenga reached Cortés's quarters he paid him the greatest respect by his obeisance, and ordered much copal to be burned. Cortés, with the greatest show of affection, seated him by his side and Xicotenga said that he came on behalf of his father and of Mase Escasi and all the Caciques, and Commonwealth of Tlaxcala to pray Cortés to admit them to our friendship, and that he came to render obedience to our King and Lord, and to ask pardon for having taken up arms and made war upon us. That this had been done because they did not know who we were, and they had taken it for certain that we had come on behalf of their enemy Montezuma, and as it frequently happened that craft and cunning was used to gain entrance to their country so as to rob and pillage it, they had believed that this was now the case, and for that reason had endeavoured to defend themselves and their country, and were obliged to show fight. He said that they were a very poor people who possessed neither gold, nor silver, nor precious stones, nor cotton cloth, nor even salt to eat, because Montezuma gave them no opportunity to go out and search for it, and that although their ancestors possessed some gold and precious stones, they had been given to Montezuma on former occasions when, to save themselves from destruction, they had made peace or a truce, and this had been in times long past; so that if they had nothing to give now, we must pardon them for it, for poverty and not the want of good will was the cause of it. He made many complaints of Montezuma and his allies who were all hostile to them and made war on them, but they had defended themselves very well. Now they had thought to do the same against us, but they could not do it although they had gathered against us three times with all their warriors, and we must be invincible, and when they found this out about our persons they wished to become friends with us and the vassals of the great prince the Emperor Don Carlos, for they felt sure that in our company they and their women and children would be guarded and protected, and would not live in dread of the Mexican traitors, and he said many other words placing themselves and their city at our disposal.

Xicotenga was tall, broad shouldered and well made;

his face was long, pockmarked and coarse, he was about
thirty-five years old and of a dignified deportment.

Cortés thanked him very courteously, in a most flattering
manner, and said that he would accept them as vassals of
our King and Lord, and as our own friends.   Then Xicotenga begged us to come to his city, for all the Caciques,
elders and priests were waiting to receive us with great
rejoicing.   Cortés replied that he would go there promptly,
and would start at once, were it not for some negotiations
which he was carrying on with the great Montezuma, and
that he would come after he had despatched the messengers.   Then Cortés spoke somewhat more sharply and
severely about the attacks they had made on us both by
day and night, adding that as it could not now be mended
he would pardon it.   Let them see to it that the peace we
now were granting them was an enduring one, without any
change, for otherwise he would kill them and destroy their
city and that he [Xicotenga] should not expect further
talk about peace, but only of war.

When Xicotenga and all the chieftains who had come
with him heard these words they answered one and all,
that the peace would be firm and true, and that to prove
it they would all remain with us as hostages.

There was further conversation between Cortés and
Xicotenga and most of his chiefs, and they were given blue
and green beads for Xicotenga's father, for himself, and for
the other Caciques, and were told to report that Cortés
would soon set out for their city.

The Mexican Ambassadors were present during all these
discussions and heard all the promises that were made, and
the conclusion of peace weighed on them heavily, for they
fully understood that it boded them no good.   And when
Xicotenga had taken his leave these Ambassadors of
Montezuma half laughingly asked Cortés whether he believed any of those promises which were made on behalf

of all Tlaxcala, [alleging] that it was all a trick which deserved no credence, and the words were those of traitors and
deceivers; that their object was to attack and kill us as soon
as they had us within their city in a place where they could
do so in safety ; that we should bear in mind how often
they had put forth all their strength to destroy us and had
failed to do so, and had lost many killed and wounded, and
that now they offered a sham peace so as to avenge
themselves. Cortés answered them, with a brave face, that
their alleged belief that such was the case did not trouble
him, for even if it were true he would be glad of it so as to
punish them [the Tlaxcalans] by taking their lives, that it
did not matter to him whether they attacked him by day
or by night, in the city or in the open, he did not mind one
way or the other, and it was for the purpose of seeing
whether they were telling the truth that he was determined
to go to their city.

The Ambassadors seeing that he had made up his mind
begged him to wait six days in our camp as they wished
to send two of their companions with a message to their
Lord Montezuma, and said that they would return with a
reply within six days. To this Cortés agreed, on the one
hand because, as I have said he was suffering from fever,
and on the other because, although when the Ambassadors
had made these statements he had appeared to attach no
importance to them, he thought that there was a chance
of their being true, and that until there was greater
certainty of peace, they were of a nature requiring much
consideration.

As at the time that this peace was made the towns all
along the road that we had traversed from our Villa Rica
de Vera Cruz were allied to us and friendly, Cortés wrote
to Juan de Escalante who, as I have said, remained in the
town to finish building the fort, and had under his command
the sixty old or sick soldiers who had been left behind.

In these letters he told them of the great mercies which our Lord Jesus Christ had vouchsafed to us in the victories which we had gained in our battles and encounters since we had entered the province of Tlaxcala, which had now sued for peace with us, and asked that all of them would give thanks to God for it. He also told them to see to it that they always kept on good terms with our friends in the towns of the Totonacs, and he told him to send at once two jars of wine which had been left behind, buried in a certain marked place in his lodgings, and some sacred wafers for the Mass, which had been brought from the Island of Cuba, for those which we had brought on this expedition were already finished.

These letters were most welcome, and Escalante wrote in reply to say what had happened in the town, and all that was asked for arrived very quickly.

About this time we set up a tall and sumptuous cross in our camp, and Cortés ordered the Indians of Tzumpantzingo and those who dwelt in the houses near our camp to whitewash it, and it was beautifully finished.

I must cease writing about this and return to our new friends the Caciques of Tlaxcala, who when they saw that we did not go to their city, came themselves to our camp and brought poultry and tunas,[1] which were then in season, each one brought some of the food which he had in his house and gave it to us with the greatest good will without asking anything in return, and they always begged Cortés to come with them soon to their city. As we had promised to wait six days for the return of the Mexicans, Cortés put off the Tlaxcalans with fair speeches. When the time expired, according to their word, six chieftains, men of great importance, arrived from Mexico, and brought a rich present from the great Montezuma consisting of valuable

---

[1] Tuna=the prickly pear, the fruit of the Nopal Cactus (Opuntia).

gold jewels wrought in various shapes worth three thousand pesos in gold, and two hundred pieces of cloth, richly worked with feathers and other patterns. When they offered this present the Chieftains said to Cortés that their Lord Montezuma was delighted to hear of our success, but that he prayed him most earnestly on no account to go with the people of Tlaxcala to their town, nor to place any confidence in them, that they wished to get him there to rob him of his gold and cloth, for they were very poor, and did not possess a decent cotton cloak among them, and that the knowledge that Montezuma looked on us as friends, and was sending us gold and jewels and cloth, would still more induce the Tlaxcalans to rob us.

Cortés received the present with delight, and said that he thanked them for it and would repay their Lord Montezuma with good works, and if he should perceive that the Tlaxcalans had that in mind against which Montezuma had sent them to warn him, they would pay for it by having all their lives taken, but he felt sure they would be guilty of no such villainy, and he still meant to go and see what they would do.

While this discussion was proceeding, many other messengers from Tlaxcala came to tell Cortés that all the old Caciques from the Capital and from the whole province had arrived at our ranchos and huts, in order to see Cortés and all of us, and to take us to their city. When Cortés heard this he begged the Mexican Ambassadors to wait for three days for the reply to their prince, as he had at present to deliberate and decide about the past hostilities and the peace which was now offered, and the Ambassadors said that they would wait.

What the old Caciques said to Cortés I will now go on to relate.

CHAPTER LXXIV.

How the old Caciques of Tlaxcala came to our Camp to beg Cortés
and all of us to go with them at once to their city, and what
happened about it.

WHEN the old Caciques from all Tlaxcala saw that we did
not come to their city, they decided to come to us, some in
litters, others in hammocks or carried on men's backs, and
others on foot. These were the Caciques already mentioned by me, named Mase Escasi, Xicotenga the elder,
Guaxolocingo, Chichimecatecle, and Tecapaneca of Topeyanco.[1] They arrived at our camp with a great company of
chieftains, and with every sign of respect made three
obeisances to Cortés and to all of us, and they burnt copal
and touched the ground with their hands and kissed it,
and Xicotenga the elder began to address Cortés in the
following words :—

" Malinche, Malinche,[2] we have sent many times to im-
plore you to pardon us for having attacked you and to
state our excuse, that we did it to defend ourselves from
the hostility of Montezuma and his powerful forces, for we
believed that you belonged to his party and were allied
to him. If we had known what we now know, we should
not only have gone out to receive you on the roads with
supplies of food, but would even have had them swept for
you, and we would even have gone to you to the sea where
you keep your *acales* (which are the ships). Now that you
have pardoned us, what I and all these Caciques have come
to request is, that you will come at once with us to our
City, where we will give you of all that we possess and
will serve you with our persons and property. Look to it

---

[1] Padre Rivera gives the names of the four Caciques of Tlaxcala as
Maxixcatzin, Xicotencatl, Tlehuexolotzin, and Citlalpopocatzin. (*Anales
Mexicanos*, p. 98.)

[2] Sometimes spelt Malinchi, sometimes Malinche.

for peace or a truce, to prevent their making war on us, so do not consider the small value of the gift, but accept it with a good grace as the gift of friends and servants which we will be to you." Then they brought, separately, a large supply of food.

Cortés accepted it most cheerfully, and said to them that he valued it more as coming from their hands with the good will with which it was offered, than he would a house full of grains of gold brought by others, and it was in this spirit that he accepted it, and he displayed much affection towards them.

It appears that it had been arranged among all the Caciques to give us from among their daughters and nieces the most beautiful of the maidens who were ready for marriage, and Xicotenga the elder said "Malinche, so that you may know more clearly our good will towards you and our desire to content you in everything, we wish to give you our daughters, to be your wives, so that you may have children by them, for we wish to consider you as brothers as you are so good and valiant. I have a very beautiful daughter who has not been married, and I wish to give her to you," so also Mase Escasi and all the other Caciques said that they would bring their daughters, and that we should accept them as wives, and they made many other speeches and promises. Throughout the day Mase Escasi and Xicotenga the elder never left Cortés' immediate neighbourhood. As Xicotenga the elder was blind from old age, he felt Cortés all over his head and face and beard and over all his body.

Cortés replied to them that, as to the gift of the women, he and all of us were very grateful and would repay them with good deeds as time went on. The Padre de la Merced was present and Cortés said to him "Señor Padre, it seems to me that this would be a good time to make an attempt to induce these Caciques to give up their

Idols and their sacrifices, for they will do anything we tell them to do on account of the great fear they have of the Mexicans." The friar replied, "Sir, that is true, but let us leave the matter until they bring their daughters and then there will be material to work upon, and your honour can say that you do not wish to accept them until they give up sacrifices—if that succeeds, good, if not we shall do our duty."

So thus the matter rested until next day, and what was done I will go on to relate.

CHAPTER LXXVII.

How they brought their daughters to present to Cortés and to all of us, and what was done about it.

THE next day the same old Caciques came and brought with them five beautiful Indian maidens, and for Indians they were very good looking and well adorned, and each of the Indian maidens brought another Indian girl as her servant, and all were the daughters of Caciques, and Xicotenga said to Cortés, "Malinche, this is my daughter who has never been married and is a maiden, take her for your own," and he gave her to him by the hand, "and let the others be given to the captains." Cortés expressed his thanks, and with every appearance of gratification said that he accepted them and took them as our own, but that for the present they should remain in the care of their parents. The Chiefs asked him why he would not take them now, and Cortés replied that he wished first to do the will of God our Lord, whom we believed in and worshipped, and that for which our Lord the King had sent us, which was to induce them to do away with their Idols, and no longer to kill and sacrifice human beings, and the other infamies they were wont to practise, and to lead them to

their forces and with the help of the people of Huexotzingo
they defended themselves and made counter attacks.   That
as all the provinces which had been raided by Montezuma
and placed under his rule were ill disposed towards the
Mexicans, and that as their inhabitants were carried off by
force to the wars, they did not fight with good will ; indeed,
it was from these very men that they received warnings,
and for this reason they had defended their country to the
best of their ability.

The place from which the most continuous trouble came
to them was a very great city a day's march distant, which
is called Cholula, whose inhabitants are most treacherous.
It was there that Montezuma secretly mustered his companies and, as it was near by, they made their raids by
night.   Moreover, Mase Escasi said that Montezuma kept
garrisons of many warriors stationed in all the provinces
in addition to the great force he could bring from the city,
and that all the provinces paid tribute of gold and silver,
feathers, stones, cloth and cotton, and Indian men and
women for sacrifice and others for servants, that he
[Montezuma] was such a great prince that he possessed
everything he could desire, that the houses where he dwelt
were full of riches and [precious] stones and chalchihuites
which he had robbed and taken by force from those who
would not give them willingly, and that all the wealth of
the country was in his hands.

Then they told us about the great staff of servants in
his house, and the story would never cease were I to
attempt to describe it all here, and of the many women
he possessed, and how he married off some of them ; in
fact they gave us an account of everything.

Then they spoke of the great fortifications of the city,
and what the lake was like, and the depth of water, and
about the causeways that gave access to the city, and the
wooden bridges in each causeway, and how one can go in

and out [by water] through the opening that there is in
each bridge, and how when the bridges are raised one can
be cut off between bridge and bridge and not be able to
reach the city.   How the greater part of the city was built
in the lake, and that one could not pass from house to
house except by draw-bridges and canoes which they had
ready.   That all the houses were flat-roofed and all the
roofs were provided with parapets so that they could fight
from them.

They also told us about the way the city was provided
with fresh water from a spring called Chapultepec distant
about half a league from the city, and how the water enters
by an aqueduct and reaches a place whence they can carry
it in canoes to sell it in the streets.   Then they told us
about the arms that were used, such as two pronged
javelins which they hurl with throwing sticks,[1] and will
go through any sort of armour, and that there are many
good archers, and others with lances with flint edges which
have a fathom of cutting edge, so cleverly made that they
cut better than knives, and they have shields, and cotton
armour, and there are many slingers who sling rounded
stones, and others with very good and long lances and
stone edged two handed swords.

They brought us pictures of the battles they had fought
with the Mexicans painted on large henequen cloths,
showing their manner of fighting.

As our captain and all of us had already heard about all
that these Caciques were telling us, we changed the subject,
and started them on another more profound, which was,
how was it that they came to inhabit that land, and from
what direction had they come? and how was it that they
differed so much from and were so hostile to the Mexicans,
seeing that their countries were so close to one another.

---

[1] Atlatls, or spear throwers.

mountain range where the volcano stands was shaken, and
that they stopped still without taking a step in advance for
more than an hour, when they thought that the outburst
had passed and not so much smoke and ashes were being
thrown out ; then they climbed up to the mouth which was
very wide and round, and opened to the width of a quarter
of a league. From this summit could be seen the great
city of Mexico, and the whole of the lake, and all the
towns which were built in it. This volcano is distant
twelve or thirteen leagues from Mexico.

Ordás was delighted and astonished at the sight of
Mexico and its cities and after having had a good look at
the view he returned to Tlaxcala with his companions, and
the Indians of Huexotzingo and of Tlaxcala looked on
it as a deed of great daring. When he told his story to
Captain Cortés and all of us, we were greatly astonished
at it, for at that time we had not seen nor heard of such
things as we have to-day, when we know all about it, and
many Spaniards and even some Franciscan friars have
made the ascent to the crater.

When Diego de Ordás went to Castille he asked the
King for it [the mountain] as his [coat of] arms and his
nephew who lives at Puebla, now bears them.

Since we have been settled in this land we have never
known the volcano to throw out so much fire or make such
a noise as it did when we first arrived, and it has even
remained some years without throwing out any fire, up to
the year 1539 when it threw up great flames and stones
and ashes.

Let us cease telling about the volcano, for now that we
know what sort of a thing it is, and have seen other
volcanoes such as those of Nicaragua and Guatemala, one
might have been silent about those of Huexotzingo, and
left them out of the story.

I must tell how in this town of Tlaxcala we found

wooden houses furnished with gratings, full of Indian men and women imprisoned in them, being fed up until they were fat enough to be sacrificed and eaten. These prisons we broke open and destroyed, and set free the prisoners who were in them, and these poor Indians did not dare to go in any direction, only to stay there with us and thus escape with their lives. From now on, in all the towns that we entered, the first thing our Captain ordered us to do was to break open these prisons and set free the prisoners.

These prisons are common throughout the land and when Cortés and all of us saw such great cruelty, he showed that he was very angry with the Caciques of Tlaxcala, and quarrelled with them very angrily about it, and they promised that from that time forth they would not kill and eat any more Indians in that way. I said [to myself] of what benefit were all those promises, for as soon as we turned our heads they would commit the same cruelties. Let us leave this subject, and I will relate how we arranged to go to Mexico.

CHAPTER LXXIX.

How our Captain Hernando Cortés decided that all of us Captains and soldiers should go to Mexico, and what happened about it.

WHEN our Captain remembered that we had already been resting in Tlaxcala for seventeen days, and that we had heard so much said about the great wealth of Montezuma and his flourishing city, he arranged to take counsel with all those among our captains and soldiers whom he could depend on as wishing to advance, and it was decided that our departure should take place without delay, but there was a good deal of dissent expressed in camp about this

U

tall cues, and situated on a beautiful plain—and indeed at
that time it looked from a distance like our city of Valladolid in Old Castile,—and on the other hand, because it
was almost surrounded by other considerable towns and
could provide ample supplies, and our friends of Tlaxcala
were near at hand. We intended to stay there until we
could decide how to get to Mexico without having to fight
for it, for the great power of the Mexicans was a thing to be
feared, and unless God our Lord, by His Divine mercy
which always helped us and gave us strength, should first
of all so provide, we could not enter Mexico in any
other manner.

After much discussion it was settled that we should take
the road by Cholula, and Cortés at once sent messengers
to ask the people of Cholula how it happened that being
so near to us they had not come to visit us, and pay that
respect which was due to us as the messengers of so great
a prince as the King who had sent us to the country to tell
them of their salvation. He then requested all the Caciques
and priests of that city to come and see us and give their
fealty to our Lord and King, and if they did not come he
would look upon them as ill disposed towards us. While
he was giving this message and saying other things about
which it seemed right that they should be informed, someone came to tell Cortés that the great Montezuma had sent
four Ambassadors with presents of gold, (for so far as we
have seen they never send a message without a present of
gold and cloth, as it is looked on as an affront to send a
message without sending a present with it,) and what these
messengers said I will go on to relate.

CHAPTER LXXX.

How the great Montezuma sent four Chieftains of great importance with a present of gold and cloth, and what they said to our Captain.

WHILE Cortés was talking to us all and to the Caciques of Tlaxcala about our departure and about warfare, they came to tell him that four Ambassadors, all four chieftains who were bringing presents, had arrived in the town.

Cortés ordered them to be called, and when they came before him they paid the greatest reverence to him and to all of us soldiers who were there with him, and presented their gift of rich jewels of gold of many sorts of workmanship, well worth two thousand dollars, and ten loads of cloth beautifully embroidered with feathers.

Cortés received them most graciously, and the Ambassadors said, on behalf of their Lord Montezuma, that he greatly wondered that we should stay so many days among a people who were so poor and so ill bred, who were so wicked, and such traitors and thieves that they were not fit even to be slaves, and that when either by day or by night we were most off our guard they would kill us in order to rob us. That he begged us to come at once to his city, and he would give us of all that he possessed, although it would not be as much as we deserved or he would like to give, and that although all the supplies had to be carried into the city, he would provide for us as well as he was able.

Montezuma did this so as to get us out of Tlaxcala, for he knew of the friendship we had made, which I have recorded in the chapter which treats of that subject, and how, to perfect it, they [the Tlaxcalans] had given their daughters to Malinche, and the Mexicans fully understood that our confederation could bring no good to them.   It was for this reason that they primed us with gold and presents, so as to induce us to go to their country or at least to get us out of Tlaxcala.

I must add regarding the ambassadors, that the people of Tlaxcala knew them well, and told our Captain that all of them were lords over towns and vassals, and men whom Montezuma employed to conduct affairs of the greatest importance.

Cortés thanked the messengers with many caressing expressions and signs of affection, and gave as his answer that he would go very soon to see their Lord Montezuma, and he begged them to remain a few days with us.

At that time Cortés decided that two of our Captains, men especially chosen, should go and see and speak to the great Montezuma, and see the great city of Mexico and its great armies and fortresses, and Pedro de Alvarado and Bernaldino Vásquez de Tápia had already set out on the journey, accompanied by some of the ambassadors of the great Montezuma who were used to being with us, and the four ambassadors who had brought the present remained with us as hostages.   As at that time Cortés had sent those gentlemen trusting to good luck, we dissuaded him from it, saying that as he was sending them to Mexico merely to see the city[1] and its strength, we did not think it well advised, and that he should send and tell them not to proceed any further, so he wrote to them telling them to return at once.   Besides this Bernaldino Vásquez de Tápia had already fallen ill of fever on the road, and as soon as they saw the letters they returned.

The ambassadors with whom they were travelling gave an account of their doings to Montezuma, and he asked them what sort of faces and general appearance had these two Teules who were coming to Mexico, and whether they

---

[1] See note at end of chapter.

were Captains, and it seems that they replied that Pedro
de Alvarado was of very perfect grace both in face and
person, that he looked like the Sun, and that he was a
Captain, and in addition to this they brought with them a
picture of him with his face very naturally portrayed, and
from that time forth they gave him the name of Tonatio,
which means the Sun or the child of the Sun, and so they
called him ever after. Of Bernaldino Vásquez de Tápia,
they said that he was a robust man, and of a very pleasant
disposition, and that he also was a captain, and Montezuma
was much disappointed that they had turned back again.
Those ambassadors had reason for the description given
to the Lord Montezuma both as to features and general
appearance, for Pedro de Alvarado was very well made
and active, and of good features and bearing, and both in
appearance and in speech and in everything else he was so
pleasing that he seemed always to be smiling. Bernaldino
Vásquez de Tápia was somewhat sturdy, but he had a
good presence ; when they returned to our camp, we joked
with them and told them that it was not a very successful
mission that Cortés had sent them on. Let us leave this
subject, for it does not bear much on our story, and I will tell
about the messengers whom Cortés sent to Cholula and
the reply that they brought.

NOTE.—In the original MS. the following passage is scratched out :
"To see the great city of Mexico and its great army and fortresses,
and it seems to me that they were Pedro de Alvarado and Bernaldino
Vásquez de Tápia, and four of the ambassadors who brought the
present remained as hostages, and the others went with them. As at
that time I was very badly wounded and was fully occupied in trying
to get well I did not know everything that was going on. I have
already written to Mexico to three of my friends who were present
throughout the conquest to send me an account [of what took place],
so that the matter should not be in doubt. If I do not repeat here all
that they say on the subject, I submit myself to the conquerors for
correction, but I know without any doubt that Bernaldino Vásquez de
Tápia, when on the road had a bad fever and remained at a town

called * * * * , and that Pedro de Alvarado went towards Mexico and turned back on the road, and that it was then that those four chieftains whom he took with him gave him the name of Tonatio, which in the Mexican language means Sun, and so they called him from that time on. They gave him that name because he was of fine presence and active and of good features and bearing, so that both in face and in speech and in everything else he was so pleasing, that he appeared always to be smiling. I also know what I have stated that these said Captains never arrived at Mexico, for when they set out from our camp all the soldiers were distressed at their going, and we said to our Captain, 'why send two such excellent men when there is a chance that they may be killed'; so Cortés wrote to them at once to return. I am not quite sure about it, I leave it to the judgment of those who were present. Others of the Conquistadores have told me that as Bernaldino Vásquez de Tápia was ill in one of the towns, that the messengers informed Montezuma of the fact, and he sent to say that neither he nor Pedro de Alvarado should proceed any further, for if they should go to Mexico there would not be a thing that would not be clearly known to all the soldiers."

CHAPTER LXXXI.

How the people of Cholula sent four Indians of little consequence to make their excuses for not having come to Tlaxcala, and what happened about it.

I HAVE already said in the last chapter how our Captain sent messengers to Cholula to tell the Caciques of that City to come and see us at Tlaxcala. When the Caciques understood what Cortés ordered them to do, they thought that it would be sufficient to send four unimportant Indians to make their excuses, and to say that because they were ill they had not come, and they brought neither food nor anything else, but merely stated that curt reply. The Caciques of Tlaxcala were present when these messengers arrived, and they said to our Captain, that the people of Cholula had sent those Indians to make a mock of him and of all of us, for they were only commoners of no standing; so Cortés at once sent them back with four other Cempoala Indians to tell the people of Cholula that they must send some chieftains, and as the distance was only five leagues that they must arrive within three days, otherwise he should look on them as rebels; that when they came he wished to tell them some things necessary for the salvation of their souls and for the cleanliness of their well being, and to receive them as friends and brothers as he had received their neighbours the people of Tlaxcala, and that if they decided otherwise and did not wish for our friendship that we should take measures which would displease them and anger them.

When the Caciques of Cholula had listened to that embassy they answered that they were not coming to Tlaxcala, for the Tlaxcalans were their enemies, and they knew that they [the Tlaxcalans] had said many evil things about them and about their Lord Montezuma; that it was for us to come to their city and to leave the confines of Tlaxcala, and that then if they did not do what they ought to do we could treat them as such as we had sent to say they were.

When our Captain saw that the excuse that they made was a just one we resolved to go to Cholula, and as soon as the Caciques of Tlaxcala perceived that we were determined to go there, they said to Cortés, "So you wish to trust to the Mexicans and not to us who are your friends, we have already told you many times that you must beware of the people of Cholula and of the power of Mexico, and so that you can receive all the support possible from us, we have got ready ten thousand warriors to accompany you." Cortés thanked them very heartily for this, but after consultation with all of us it was agreed that it would not be advisable to take so many warriors to a country in which we were seeking friends, and that it

would be better to take only one thousand, and this number we asked of the Tlaxcalans and said that the rest
should remain in their houses.   Let us leave this discussion
and I will tell about our march.

MASK OF QUETZALCOATL.

From the original in the British Museum.

Reproduced and printed for the Hakluyt Society by Donald Macbeth, 1908.

Plate 13.

To face page 299.

APPENDIX.

MONTEZUMA'S GIFTS TO CORTES.

PADRE SAHAGUN, in his history of the Conquest, states that the first presents sent by Montezuma to Cortés were the ornaments of the Temple of Quetzalcoatl. Montezuma is reported to have said to his messengers : " Our Lord Quetzalcoatl has arrived, go and receive him and listen to what he says with great attention, see to it that you do not forget anything that he may say, you see that these jewels that you are presenting to him on my behalf, are all the priestly ornaments that belong to him." Then follows a detailed description of the ornaments of the deity beginning with "A mask worked in a mosaic of turquoise ; this mask has a double and twisted snake worked in the same stones whose fold was (on) the projection of the nose, then the tail was parted from the head and the head with part of the body went above one of the eyes so that it formed an eyebrow, and the tail with a part of the body went over the other eye to form the other eyebrow. This mask was decked with a great and lofty crown, full of rich feathers, very long and beautiful, so that on placing the crown on the head, the mask was placed over the face," etc. The messengers also carried for presentation to Cortés " The ornaments or finery with which Tezcatlipoca was decorated," and "the ornaments and finery of the God called Tlalocantecutli " (Tlaloc). Also other ornaments of the same Quetzalcoatl, a mitre of tiger skins, etc.

It is interesting to know that the masks belonging to these four costumes and adornments of the Gods are still in existence, and that three of them can be seen in the room devoted to American Antiquities in the British Museum.

The mask of Quetzalcoatl with the folds of the snake's body forming the eyebrows is easily·identified, and the mask with the eyes of pyrites and the bands across the face is probably the mask of the God Tezcatlipoca.

The presents sent by Cortés to Charles V were conveyed to Spain in the charge of Alonzo Hernández Puertocarrero and Francisco de Montejo, who sailed from Villa Rica in July, 1519, and reached Valladolid probably in October of the same year, where they awaited the arrival of the Emperor. Bernal Díaz says that Charles V was in Flanders when the presents arrived in Spain, but this is not correct; the Emperor was in Catalonia and did not return to Valladolid until some time in 1520, when he was on his way to Coruña, whence he sailed for Flanders in May, 1520.

It is, however, remarkable that these masks and ornaments of the Gods do not appear in the list of the presents, signed by Puertocarrero and Montejo, which accompanied the letter from the Municipality of Vera Cruz, dated 10th July, 1519, nor in the *Manual del Tesorero de la Casa de Contratacion de Sevilla*, both of which documents were published in the *Documentos Ineditos para la historia de España*, Madrid, 1842. A note to the former document states that the gifts and the letter from the Municipality were received by the King, Don Carlos, in Valladolid during Holy Week, in the beginning of April, 1520.

As, however, this note mentions the letter from the Municipality only (*con la carta y relacion de suso dicha que el concejo de la Vera Cruz envió*), and makes no mention of the first letter sent to the Emperor by Cortés himself, which letter has never yet been found, it is possible that the masks and ornaments of the Gods were sent separately with Cortés's first letter, and were therefore not included

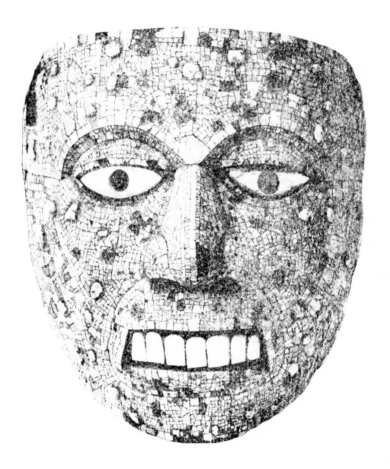

MASK OF QUETZALCOATL.

From the original in the British Museum.

Reproduced and printed for the Hakluyt Society by Donald Macbeth, 1908.

Plate 14.   *To face page 300.*

in the list of gifts sent by Cortés in conjunction with the Municipality.

Las Casas (*Hist. de las Indias*, Cap. CXXI), writing about these presents, which included two great discs, one of gold and the other of silver, says :—"These wheels were certainly wonderful things to behold. I saw them and all the rest (of the presents) in the year 1520 at Valladolid, on the day that the emperor saw them, for they arrived there then sent by Cortés."

There is a tradition that Charles V presented these gifts to the Pope (a Medici) for the family Museum, which is well known to have existed, and of which the present Museum of Natural History at Florence is an outcome. If these gifts were sent to Rome, as is probable, soon after their arrival in Spain, they must have been sent to Leo X (Giovanni de Medici), who died in 1521. If they were not sent before the death of Leo X, it is not likely that they were sent to Italy during the troublous years that followed, but they may have been taken to Spain by Cortés himself when he returned in 1528 and have been given to Clement VII (Giulio de Medici) when Charles V was crowned by him as King of the Romans at Bologna in 1529-30.

However that may be, I have the authority of Professor H. Giglioli, the Director of the Museum of Natural History in Florence, for stating that nearly all the known group of objects—namely, mosaic masks, mosaic decorated knife-handles, gold-plated and figured atlatls (spear throwers), etc.—were at one time in Florence. At the end of the sixteenth century, when Aldrovandi, who was a friend of the the Medici, founded his celebrated Museum at Bologna, he was given some of these articles from the Medici Collection at Florence ; and these, with the exception of the turquoise mosaic mask mentioned below, were discovered by Professor L. Pigorini in the attics of the Bologna University and transferred to the Ethnographic Museum in Rome, which he was then forming and which now contains perhaps the finest collection of these relics. However, the greater number of them up to the years 1819-21 were registered in the Florentine Museum under the title of *Maschere e strumenti de popoli barbari,* and were partly sent thence to the *Officina delle pietre dure* in that city to be broken up and used for mosaic work, being *Maschere di cattivi turchesi!*

The last turquoise mosaic mask (now in Rome) was found a few years ago by Professor Luigi Pigorini in the store-room of the *pietre dure* laboratory, labelled with an inventory value of two francs and a half! As this mask shows the remains of tusk-like teeth, it is probably the Mask of Tlaloc.

Five years ago two magnificent plated atlatls[1] were found in the garret of a nobleman's palace in Florence, and sold by a dealer to the Ethnographical Museum in that city, for 500 *lire*, as " Indian Sceptres"; they were in a leathern case, stamped with the Medici arms. One of them is double-grooved, for throwing two darts at a time.

The whole number of known examples of this class of Mexican work did not exceed twenty in 1893, and of these eight are now in the British Museum. Many of them were bought by Mr. Christy and Sir Augustus Franks in Northern Italy, where they had been scattered after the dispersal of the Medicean Collection.

A full account of these interesting objects, by Mr. C. H. Read, is given, with illustrations, in *Archæologia*, vol. liv, 1895. Professor Pigorini published, in 1885, a full account, with coloured plates, of the collection in the Ethnographical Museum at Rome, in the *Memorie* of the R. Accademia dei Lincei at Rome. Another interesting paper on the subject was published by Dr. W. Lehmann in *Globus* (Band 91, No. 21), 6th June, 1907.

---

[1] Described and figured in the *American Anthropologist* (N.S.), vol. vii, No. 2, April-June, 1905.

MASK OF TEZCATLIPOCA.

From the original in the British Museum.

Reproduced and printed for the Hakluyt Society by Donald Macbeth, 1908.

Plate 15.

To face page 302.

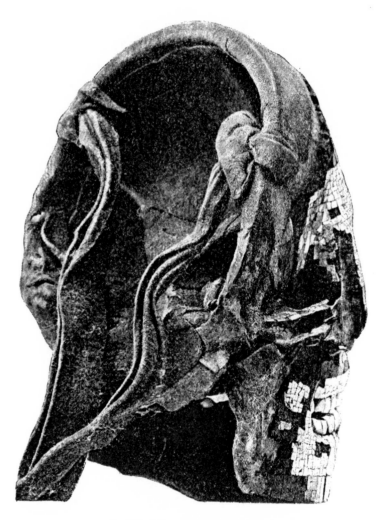

MASK OF TEZCATLIPOCA.
Back view, showing how it was worn.
From the original in the British Museum.

Reproduced and printed for the Hakluyt Society by Donald Macbeth, 1908.

Plate 16.

To face page 302.

sacado de la librania del Maches de Ciche en Madrid. januar. 8 A.º 1690.
por. f. Gsparwrn fili.

CARTAS YNSTRVCIO
NES YŒDVLAS. DESV
MAGESTAD. I FORTIFICA
CIONES. ECHAS PORELIN
GENERO BAVTISTA. AN.

TONELI. Ansi enespaña como enlas Yn_
dias ocidentales. conlas plantas Y discrepciones
delos puertos y costas. Yoffensa y defensa dellas
y anssi mismo dealgunas plaças deafrica como
eneste discurso sebera. Año de. 1608

*5. 26 _ M. IL_*

Facsimile of Title-page of

BAUTISTA ANTONELI : CARTAS, &c., 1608.

*Reproduced, through the courtesy of Mr. Bernard Quaritch,
by Donald Macbeth for the Hakluyt Society, 1908.*

Plate 6.

El Rey

Bautista Antonil Vimos Vra carta de Veinte y nuebe del pasado
y esta bien que amistais a las obras y fortificaciones de peniscula y
y en lo de los beinte y cinco Ducados de sueldo al mes que decis os se
ñalo Vespasiano Gonçaga colona vro lugar Theniente y capitan
General de ese Reino y que don luis fferrer procuro que se os quita
sen y emos escripto al dho Don luis fferrer que os les aga Continuar
san lorenço el Real a beinte y tres de Junio Mil y quinientos setenta
y ocho Años.

yo El Rey

Por mandado de su Magd.

A Bautista Antonil   Juan delgado.

La villa de peniscula en el Reyno de Valençia esta quareinta
y dos grados de lebaçion del polo sera lugar de tres cientas cassas esta
situado sobre Vnapeña demas de ochenta pies de alto esta casse

Facsimile of Prefatory leaf

BAUTISTA ANTONELI: CARTAS, &c., 1608.

Reproduced, through the courtesy of Mr. Bernard Quaritch,
by Donald Macbeth for the Hakluyt Society. 1908.

Plate 7.   To face page 303.

GLOSSARY OF MEXICAN, SPANISH,

AND

OTHER FOREIGN WORDS.

Acales (Mex.), ships, from a = water and calli = a house.

Adelantado, governor-in-chief.

Alacranes, the name of a dangerous reef, from alacran, a scorpion.

Alala, an Indian exclamation.

Alcalde, chief magistrate or mayor.

Alférer, ensign or standard-bearer.

Alguacil, a constable.

Alguacil Mayor, chief constable.

Alguacil del Real, constable or storekeeper.

Amales, amal (Mex.), paper, letters.

Atalaya, a watch-tower.

Arriero, a muleteer, carrier.

Arroba, a Spanish weight of 25 lbs.

Atlatl (Mex.), a spear-thrower or throwing-stick (tiradera, Span.).

Audiencia, a court of judicature, the law officers appointed to hold a judicial inquiry.

Barranca, a ravine.

Cacao, Cacahuatl (Mex.), the fruit of Theobroma Cacao. Chocolate, made from the cacao fruit, takes its name from the Mexican word chocolatl.

Cacique, a Cuban word meaning chieftain.

Cacica, the female form of the title Cacique.

Calachoni, Calachone, Calachione, Calacheoni or Calachuni, the title of chieftain among the Mayas.

Camarero, chamberlain.

Cedula (real), Royal letters patent.

Ceiba, Bombax ceiba, the silk-cotton tree.

Cenote, Tznóte, deep natural wells or caverns in the limestone rock whence the natives of Yucatan obtain water.

Chalchihuite, Chalchivies or Chalchihuys (B.D.), Chalchihuitl (Mex.), Jadeite, highly valued by the Indians as a precious stone.

Compadre, godfather, friend.

Copal, a resinous substance burnt for incense, the gum of the *Rhus copallinum*.

Cue, a shrine, temple, a word picked up by the Spaniards in the Antilles.

Despoblado, uninhabited country.

Enaguas, petticoats, or the upper skirt of a woman's dress.

Encomienda. The Indians, at first slaves, were next subjected to the system of *repartimientos*, that is, divided among masters, who had a property in their labour, not in their persons ; and, lastly, they were distributed in *encomiendas*, paying to the *encomendero*, or owner of the district, a tribute or produce-rent, in return for protection (Herman Merivale—Lectures on Colonisation).

Escopeteros, musketeers.

Fraile de la Merced, a friar of the Order of Mercy.

Hennequen, or sisal hemp ; enequen (B. D.), a species of aloe (Agave Ixtli) ; the fibre is now largely used for cordage.

Hidalgo a gentleman by birth.

Huajolotes (Mex.), turkeys.

Jiquipil (Maya), a body of warriors eight thousand strong.

Lienzo, a painting on linen or cotton cloth.

Lope luzio (Totonac), prince or great lord. Used by the Spaniards as a nickname for the Totonac Indians.

Macana or Maquihuitl (Mex.), a wooden sword edged with sharp pieces of flint or obsidian.

Maestresala, the chief waiter in a nobleman's household.

Mamei, the fruit of the Mamie Zapote tree.

Mastel, a loin cloth.

Monte, in Spanish meaning a mountain, a hill is used in Spanish America in the way *bush* is used in Australia or *veldt* in South Africa.

Nahuatatos (Mex.), interpreters.

Pelota, a Basque and Spanish ball game.

Penacho, a tuft of feathers, a plume.

Petaca, a trunk or leather-covered hamper.

Petate, a plaited mat ; Petlatl (Mex.).

Piragua, a large canoe.

Plaza, a square, market-place.

Pueblo, a town or village, used especially to designate a township or community of American Indians.

Regidor, magistrate, prefect.

Repartimiento. See Encomienda.

Residencia, the examination and formal account demanded of a person holding public office.

Rubrica, the flourish which forms part of the signature of a Spaniard.

Salitrales, salt marshes.

Tacal Naguas (Mex.), wizards, soothsayers.

Tamenes (Mex.), porters, carriers.

Tapias, mud walls, walls made of earth stamped into a mould.

Tatuan (B. D.), Tlatoan (Mex.), a chieftain.

Teleçiguata, a great lady.

Teocalli (Mex.), a temple, usually raised on a pyramidal foundation.

Tepuzques (B. D.), the Mexican word for cannon, from *Tepusque*, iron.

Tianguez or Tianguiz (Mex.), a market or market-place.

Tiradera, an Atlatl (Mex.) or spear-thrower, throwing-stick.

Tonatio (B. D.), Tonatiuh (Mex.), the sun, or child of the sun; the name given by the Mexicans to Pedro de Alvarado.

Tortilla, a little cake; the thin cake made from maize, the staple food of the Mexicans.

Tuna, the prickly pear, fruit of the Nopal Cactus (*Opuntia*).

Vecino, a neighbour, a citizen.

Veedor (obsolete), overseer, official in charge of stores.

Xexenes, a small kind of mosquito.

Yuca, Yuca de Casave, *Jatropha Manihot*, or *Manihot utilissima*. Cassava bread is made from the root of *Jatropha Manihot*.

PLACE - NAMES.

Acalá, a province situated about 18° Lat. N., 91° 30′ Long. W. Gueacala or Hueyacala, Great Acalá.

Altlatlaya (B. D.), (Atalaya) from Atalaya, a watch tower.

Axaruco or Ajaruco. On the north coast of Cuba.

Ayagualulco (B. D.), Ahualolco (O. y B.).

Cempoala, Çenpoal (B. D.).

Chanpoton (Potonchan). See note on pages 21-22.

Chichimecatecle (B. D.), Chichimecatecuhtli (O. y B.).

Cholula, Cholulan.

Coatzacoalcos, Guaçacalco or Guacagualco (B. D.).

Cotaxtla, or Cuetlaxtla, Cotastan or Cotustan (B. D.)

Cuauhtémoc, Guatemuz (B. D.) ; Guatemucin (C.) ; Guatemoc, successor to Montezuma and Cuitlahuac as ruler of Mexico.

Culua, Culoa or Ulua. The land of the Mexicans.

Estomies (B. D.) or Otomis : this tribe is reputed to be the earliest settled in Central Mexico.

Huexotzingo, Huexoçingo, Guaxoçingo or Guaxalçingo (B. D.), a district and town allied to Tlaxcala ; Guaxoloçingo (B. D.), a chieftain of Tlaxcala (?).

Huichilobos (B. D.), Huitzipochtli, the Mexican God of War.

Kukulcan or Cukulcan, the Maya Culture God, the same as the Mexican God Quetzalcoatl.

Malinchi or Malinche, the name given to Cortés by the Mexicans, see p. 273.

Montezuma (B. D.), Motecuhzoma (O. y B.), Motecutzoma.

Papaloapan, Papaloaba (B. D.).

Pitalpitoque (B. D.), Cuitlalpitoc (O. y B.). A Mexican chieftain called by the Spaniards Ovandillo.

Potonchan (Chanpotan). See note on pp. 21-22.

Quetzalcoatl, from the bird Quetzal (*Trogon resplendens*), and Coatl, a serpent. The Serpent-bird God, the Culture God of the Mexicans. The same as the Maya God Kukulcan.

Quiahuitztlan, Quiahuyztlan (B. D.).

Tehuacingo, Teoacingo, Tehuacaçingo or Tevacingo (B. D.), Tehuatzinco.

Tendile (B. D). Teuhtlilli, Governor of Cuetaxtla.

Tenochtitlan, the City of Mexico ; Tenuztitlan (B. D.), Temixtitan (C.).

Tezcatepuca (B. D.), Tezcatlipoca or Tetzcatlipoca, the Mexican God of Hell.

Tlaltelolco or Tlatelulco. The northern division of the City of Mexico.

Tzumpantzingo, Çunpanzingo (B. D), Çinpançingo (B. D.), Teocadçunpançingo (B. D.), possibly Teoll (God) or Teocalli (Temple). Tzumpantzingo, the part of the town or district where the temples stood.

Ulua, see Culua.

Xicotenga (B. D.), Xicoténcatl.

> B. D. = Bernal Díaz.
> O. y. B. = Orozco y Berra.
> C. = Hernando Cortés.

BIBLIOGRAPHY OF MEXICO.

———

ALPHABETICALLY ARRANGED.

With the British Museum Press-Marks.

"A PAINFULL WORK IT IS I'LL ASSURE YOU, AND MORE THAN DIFFICULT; WHEREIN WHAT TOYLE HATH BEEN TAKEN, AS NO MAN THINKETH, SO NO MAN BELIEVETH, BUT HE THAT HATH MADE THE TRIALL."

ANTHONY À WOOD —*History of Oxford*

BIBLIOGRAPHY.

NOTE.—This Bibliography does not pretend to be exhaustive. A more complete List will be issued with the final Volume of this Translation. A Bibliography of the Maps of Mexico will be issued with Volume II.

1. **Abelin**, Johann Philipp.—Neue Welt und Amerikanische Historien. Alles aus verschiedenen Historien-Schreibern . . . getragen . . . durch J. L. Gottfriedt [*i.e.* Johann Philipp Abelin].
   J. T. de Bry: Frankfurt a/M., 1631. fol.
   [G. 6635. From the Library of the Right Hon. Thomas Grenville.
   —1655. 566. k. 12.]

2. **Aglio**, Augustine.—Antiquities of Mexico. Comprising Fac-similes of ancient Mexican Paintings and Hieroglyphics, preserved in the Royal Libraries of Paris, Berlin, and Dresden, in the Imperial Library of Vienna, in the Vatican Library, in the Borgian Museum at Rome, in the Library of the Institute at Bologna, and in the Bodleian Library at Oxford. Together with The Monuments of New Spain, by M. Dupaix. With their respective scales of measurement and accompanying descriptions. The whole illustrated by many valuable inedited Manuscripts. By Augustine Aglio [and Edward King, Viscount Kingsborough.] In seven [or rather 9] volumes. [With pp. 1-60 of vol. 10.]
   Published by A. Aglio, 36, Newman Street; to be had also of Whittaker, Treacher, and Co., Ave-Maria Lane: [Henry G. Bohn:]
   London, MDCCCXXX-XLVIII. fol.
   [564. h. 1-9.]

2 a. Vol. 1.—Copy of the Collection of Mendoza, preserved in the Bodleian Library at Oxford. 73 Pages. Marked Arch. Seld. A. I. Cat. MSS. Angl. 3134.
   Copy of the Codex Telleriano-Remensis, preserved in the Royal Library at Paris. 93 Pages. Marked 14 Reg. 1616. [A copy by Pedro de los Rios, a Dominican Monk, of a Mexican Calendar.]
   Fac-simile of an Original Mexican Hieroglyphic Painting, from the Collection of Boturini. 23 Pages.
   Fac-simile of an Original Mexican Painting, preserved in the Collection of Sir Thomas Bodley, in the Bodleian Library at Oxford. 40 Pages. Marked Arch. Bodl. A. 75. Cat. MSS. Angl. 2858.
   Fac-simile of an Original Mexican Painting, preserved in the Selden Collection of MSS. in the Bodleian Library at Oxford. 20 Pages. Marked Arch. Seld. A. 2. Cat. MSS. Angl. 3135.
   Fac-simile of an Original Mexican Hieroglyphic Painting, preserved amongst the Selden Collection in the Bodleian Library at Oxford. A Roll, marked Arch. Seld. A. Rot. 3. Cat. MSS. Angl. 3207.
   1830. fol.
   [564. h. 1.]

2 b. Vol. 2. Copy of a Mexican MS. preserved in the Library of the Vatican. 149 Pages. Marked No. 3738.

Fac-simile of an Original Mexican Painting given to the University of Oxford by Archbishop Laud, and preserved in the Bodleian Library. 46 Pages. Marked Laud B. 65. nunc 678 Cat. MSS. Angl. 546.

Fac-simile of an Original Mexican Painting preserved in the Library of the Institute at Bologna. 24 Pages.

Fac-simile of an Original Mexican Painting preserved in the Imperial Library at Vienna. 66 Pages.

Fac-similes of Original Mexican Paintings deposited in the Royal Library at Berlin by the Baron de Humboldt, and of a Mexican Bas-Relief preserved in the Royal Cabinet of Antiques.

1830. fol.

[564. h. 2.]

2 c. Vol. 3. Fac-simile of an Original Mexican Painting preserved in the Borgian Museum, at the College of Propaganda in Rome. 76 Pages.

Fac-simile of an Original Mexican Painting preserved in the Royal Library at Dresden. 74 Pages.

Fac-simile of an Original Mexican Painting in the possession of M. de Fejérváry, at Pess in Hungary. 44 Pages.

Fac-simile of an Original Mexican Painting preserved in the Library of the Vatican. 96 Pages.

1830. fol.

[564. h. 3.]

2 d. Vol. 4. Monuments of New Spain, by M. Dupaix, from the original drawings executed by order of the King of Spain. In three parts.

Specimens of Mexican Sculpture, in the possession of M. Latour Allard, in Paris.

Specimens of Mexican Sculpture preserved in the British Museum.

Plates copied from the Giro del Mondo of Gemelli Careri. With an engraving of a Mexican Cycle, from a Painting formerly in the possession of Boturini.

Specimen of Peruvian Quipus, with Plates representing a carved Peruvian Box containing a collection of supposed Peruvian Quipus.

1830. fol.

[564. h. 4.]

2 e. Vol. 5. Extrait de l'Ouvrage de M. de Humboldt sur les Monumens de l'Amérique. pp. 1-36

Explicacion de la Coleccion de Mendoza. pp. 37-126.

Explicacion del Codex Telleriano-Remensis, pp. 127-158

Codice Mexicano, che si conserva nella Biblioteca Vaticana, al No. 3738. MS. pp. 159-206.

Viages de Guillelmo Dupaix sobre las Antigüedades Mejicanas. pp. 207-343.

Libro Sexto de la Retorica y Filosofia, Moral y Teologia de la Gente Mexicana, donde hay cosas muy curiosas tocantes a los primores de su lengua, y cosas muy delicadas tocante a las virtudes morales. Por el M. R. P. Frayle Bernardino de Sahagun, de la Orden de los Frayles Menores de la Observancia. (Indice.) pp. 345-493.

1830. fol.

[564. h. 5.]

2 f. Vol. 6. The Interpretation of the Hieroglyphical Paintings of the Collection of Mendoza. pp. 3-94.

The Explanation of the Hieroglyphical Paintings of the Codex Telleriano-Remensis. [An Original Mexican Calendar, painted on paper of the Agave, resembling this Codex, is preserved in the Library of the Chamber of Deputies, at Paris.] pp. 95-153.

The Translation of the Explanation of the Mexican Paintings of the Codex Vaticanus. No. 3738. pp. 155-420.

The Monuments of New Spain, by M. Dupaix. [English Translation.] pp. 421-540.

1830. fol.

[564. h. 6.]

2 g. Vol. 7. Historia Universal de las Cosas de Nueva España. Por el M. R. P. Fr. Bernardino de Sahagun, de la Orden de los Frayles Menores de la Observancia. pp. vii. 1-464.

1830. fol.

[564. h. 7.]

2 h. Vol. 8. Supplementary Notes to the Antiquities of Mexico. [Continuation of Notes at end of vol 6.] pp. 1-268.

Supplementary Extracts from Spanish Authors. De la Monarquia Indiana de Torquemada, Acosta, Historia Natural, García, sobre el Origen de los Indios. pp. 1-89.

Sermam do Auto da Fé. Que se celebrou na Praça do Rocio desta Cidade de Lisboa, junto dos passos da Inquisiçam, em 6 de Setembro de 1705, em presença de suas Altezas. Pregado pelo Illustrissimo e Reverendissimo Senhor Dom Diogo da Annunciaçam Justiniano, do Conselho de Sua Magestade, que Deos guarde, e Arcebispo que foy de Cranganor. *Lisboa : Na officina de Antonio Pedro Ozogalrão.* 6 Setembro, 1705. pp. 91-115.

Respuesta al Sermon predicado por el Arçobispo de Cranganor en el Auto da Fe, celebrado en Lisboa, en 6 Septiembre, Año de 1705. Por el Author de las Noticias Reconditas de la Inquizicion, Obra Posthuma. *Impresso en Villa-Franca, por Carlos Vero, à la Insignia de la Verdad.* pp. 117-157.

Historia del Origen de las Gentes que poblaron la America Septentrional, que llaman la Nueva-España. Con noticia de los primeros que establecieron la Monarquia que en ella floreció de la nacion Tolteca, y noticias que alcanzaron de la Creacion del Mundo. Su autor el Licenciado Don Mariano Fernandez de Echevarria y Veitia, Caballero Profeso del Orden Militar de Santiago. pp. 159-217.

Tercera (Cuarta) Noticia de la Segunda Parte de las Noticias Historiales de las Conquistas de Tierra Firme en el Nuevo Reyno de Granada, por Fr. Pedro Simon, ofrecida à Nuestro Invictisimo Cesar Filipo IV. en el Real Consejo de Indias, Año 1624. [Published for the first time, and copied from the MS. of the Author.] pp. 219-271.

History of the North American Indians, their Customs, &c. By James Adair. [1775.] pp. 273-400.

[Cinco] Cartas Ineditas de Hernando Cortés. Escritas à S. M. desde 15 de Mayo de 1522 hasta 10 de Octubre de 1530 . . . Y al fin un Memorial que presentó á S. M. en Valladolid á 3 de Febrero de 1544, &c. pp. 401-424.

1848. fol.

[564. h. 8.]

2 i. Vol. 9. Cronica Mexicana de Fernando de Alvarado Tezozomoc (Advertencia del Padre Francisco García Figueroa.) pp. 1-196. Historia Chichimeca. Por Don Fernando de Alva Ixtlilxochitl. pp. 197-468.
1848. fol.
[564. h. 9.]

2 j. Vol. 10. Ritos Antiguos, Sacrificios é Idolatrias de los Indios de la Nueva España y de su conversion á la Fée y quienes fueron los que primero la predicaron. (Epistola Proemial de un Frayle Menor al Ilustrisimo Señor Don Antonio Pimentel, sexto Conde de Benavente.) pp. 1-60.
[On page 60 of vol. 10 : " End of vol. IX., which concludes the work."]
1848. fol.
[564. h. 9.]

3. **Alcedo,** Antonio de.—Diccionario geográfico-histórico de las Indias Occidentales ó America: es á saber ; de los Reynos del Peru, Nueva España, Tierra-Firme, Chile, y Nuevo Reyno de Granada . . . Escrito por el Coronel D. Antonio de Alcedo, *etc.* 3 vols.
Benito Cano: Madrid, 1786-88. 8°.
[978. i. 19-21. From the Library of Sir Joseph Banks.—K. 279. i. 15-19. From the Library of King George III.—G. 2975-9. From the Library of the Right Hon. Thomas Grenville.]

4. ———.—The Geographical and Historical Dictionary of America and the West Indies. Containing an entire Translation of the Spanish Work of Colonel Don Antonio de Alcedo, Captain of the Royal Spanish Guards, and Member of the Royal Academy of History. With large Additions and Compilations from Modern Voyages and Travels, and from original and authentic information. By G. A. Thompson, Esq. In Five Volumes.
Printed for James Carpenter, Old Bond-Street; Longman, Hurst, Rees, Orme, and Brown, Paternoster-Row ; White, Cochrane and Co., and Murray, Fleet-Street, London ; Parker, Oxford; and Deighton, Cambridge, 1812-1815. 4°.
[797. i. 30.—K. 146. d. 15-19. From the Library of King George III.]

4a. ———.—Atlas to Thompson's Alcedo, or Dictionary of America and West Indies. Collated with all the most recent authorities, and composed chiefly from scarce and original documents for that work, by A. Arrowsmith, Hydrographer to His Royal Highness the Prince Regent. 5 Maps.
Printed by George Smeeton: London, 1819. fol.
[Maps 92. f. 19.—K. 12. TAB. 45. From the Library of King George III.—G. 2980-82. Without Title. From the Library of the Right Hon. Thomas Grenville.]

5. **Aldrovandi,** Ulisse.—Ulyssis Aldrovandi, Patricii Bononiensis, Musaeum Metallicum in Libros IIII. distributum Bartholomæus Ambrosinus Labore et Studio composuit cum Indice copiosissimo. Marcus Antonius Bernia propriis impensis in lucem edidit. Ad Serenissimum Rantium II Farnesium Parmæ Placentiæ, *etc.* Ducem VI. (Vol. xii. Opera Aldrovandi.) pp. 979.
Typis Io. Baptistæ Ferronij: Bononiæ, 1648. fol.
[K. 38. g. 12. From the Library of King George III.—459. b. 7. From the Library of Sir Joseph Banks, with his Book-plate.]

1579.

6. **Alfaro de Santa Cruz,** Melchior.—Relación de Melchor de Alfaro Sant Cruz, 1579. (Relaciones Histórico-Geográficas de las Provincias de Yucatán. Tabasco-Relaciones de Yucatán. [Edited by José María Asensio y Toledo.] Tom. I. pp. 318-341.—In "Colección de Documentos Inéditos relativos al Descubrimiento, Conquista y Organización de las Antiguas Posesiones Españolas de Ultramar. Segunda Serie, publicada por la Real Academia de la Historia. Tomo núm. II.")

Establecimiento Tipográfico, Sucesores de Rivadeneyra: Madrid, 1898. 8°.

[9551. g.]

7. **Alva Ixtlilxochitl,** Fernando d'.—Cruautés Horribles des Conquérants du Mexique, et des Indiens qui les aidèrent à soumettre cet Empire à la couronne d'Espayne. Mémoire de Don Fernando d'Alva Ixtlilxochitl. Supplémen tà *l'Histoire* du Père Sahagun. Publié et dédié au gouvernement suprême de la confédération mexicaine, por Charles - Marie de Bustamante. *México: de l'Imprimerie du citoyen Alexandre Valdès.* [Translated by Henri Ternaux-Compans.] (In "Voyages, Relations et Mémoires Originaux pour servir à l'Histoire de la Découverte de l'Amérique. Publiés pour la première fois en français par H. Ternaux-Compans." tom. 8. pp. 312.)

Arthus Bertrand: Paris, MDCCCXXXVIII. 8°.

[G. 15810. From the Library of the Right Hon. Thomas Grenville. —1196. i. 6.]

8. ———.—Histoire des Chichimèques, ou des anciens Rois de Tezcuco. Par Don Fernando d'Alva Ixtlilxochitl. Traduite sur le manuscrit espagnol . . . Inédite. 2 pts. (In "Voyages, Relations, et Mémoires Originaux pour servir à l'Histoire de la Découverte de l'Amérique, publiés par la première fois en Français, par H. Ternaux-Compans." Tom. 12, 13.)

Arthus Bertrand: Paris, MDCCCXL. 8°.

[G. 15814-5. From the Library of the Right Hon. Thomas Grenville. —1196. i. 7, 8.]

9. ———.—Orribili Crudelta dei Conquistatori del Messico e degl' Indiani che gli Aiutarono a sottomettere questo Impero alla Corona di Spagna. Memoria di Don Fernando d'Alva Cortes Ixtlilxochitl. Publicata e dedicata al Governo Supremo della Confederazione Messicana da Carlo Maria de Bustamante. Versione di Felice Scifoni. (In "Raccolta di Viaggi dalla Scoperta del Nuovo Continente fino à di nostri. Compilata da F. C. Marmocchi." tom. II. pp. 275-436.)

Fratelli Giachetti: Prato, 1843. 8°.

[1424. i. 5.]

10. **Alvarado,** Pedro de.—Di Pietro d'Alvarado a Fernando Cortese. Lettere di Pietro d'Alvarado, nelle quali racconta le guerre & battaglie fatte nell' acquisto di Ciapotulan, Checialtenego & Vilatan, & de pericoli ne quale incorse come fece abbruciar li Signori di Vilatan, & parimente essa città & constitui Signori i lor figliuoli: di due montagne, una d'allumi, l'altra di zolfo. *Di Vilatan a gli undici d'Aprile.* (In "Terzo Volume

delle Navigationi et Viaggi Raccolto gia da M. Gio. Battista Ramusio."
fol. 296-298.)

In Venetia: nella Stamperia de' Giunti, l'Anno MDLXV. fol.

[G. 6820.—From the Library of the Right Hon. Thomas Grenville.—
679. h. 10. From the Library of the Rev. Clayton Mordaunt
Cracherode. With the arms and cyphers of Jacques Auguste de
Thou, and his first wife, Marie Barbançon.]

11. ———.—Altra Relation fatta per Pietro d'Alvarado a Fernando Cortese·
Nella quale si contiene l'acquisto di molte città & provincie, le guerre,
scaramuccie, & battaglie, tradimenti & ribellioni che vi sono seguite,
com' egli edificò una città, di due montagne, una che getta fuoco, l'altra
che eshala fumo, d'un fiume che arde tutto, & d'un altro freddo & come
l'Alvarado d'una saetta rimase storpiato. *Di questa città di Sant' Iago
a ventiotto di Luglio,* 1524. (In "Terzo Volume delle Navigationi et
Viaggi. Raccolto gia da M. Gio Battista Ramusio." fol. 298-300.)

In Venetia: nella Stamperia de' Giunti, l'Anno MDLXV. fol.

[G. 6820. From the Library of the Right Hon. Thomas Grenville.—
679. h. 10. From the Library of the Rev. Clayton Mordaunt
Cracherode. With the arms and cyphers of Jacques Auguste de
Thou, and his first wife, Marie Barbançon.]

12. ———.—Atra Relacion hecha por Pedro de Alvarado a Hernando Cortés,
en que se refiere la Conquista de muchas Ciudades, las Guerras, Batallas,
Traiciones, i Rebeliones, que sucedieron, i la Poblacion que hiço de una
Ciudad. De dos Volcanes: uno, que exalaba Fuego, i otro Humo,
de un Rio hirviendo, i otro frio, i como quedó Alvarado herido de un
Flechaço. (In "Historiadores Primitivos de las Indias Occidentales,
que juntó, traduxo en parte, y sacó á luz, ilustrados con erudítas Notas,
y copiosos Indices, el Ilustrisimo Señor D. Andres Gonzalez Barcia, del
Consejo, y Camara de S. M. Divididos en tres Tomos, cuyo contenido
se verá en el folio siguiente." Tom. 1. Part 2. pp. 161-166.)

Madrid, año MDCCXLIX. fol.

[K. 145. f. 9. From the Library of King George III.]

13. ———.—Lettres de Pédro de Alvarado à Fernand Cortés. (Seconde
Lettre. Santiago, le 28 de juillet, 1524. In "Voyages, Relations et
Mémoires Originaux pour servir à l'Histoire de la Découverte de
l'Amérique. Publiés pour la première fois en Français par H. Ternaux-
Compans.—Tom. X. Recueil de Pièces relatives à la Conquête du
Mexique. Inédit. pp. 107-150.)

Arthus Bertrand: Paris, MDCCCXXXVIII. 8°.

[G. 15812. From the Library of the Right Hon. Thomas Grenville.
—1196. i. 7.]

14. **Alvarado Tezozomoc,** Fernando de.—Histoire du Mexique. Par Don
Alvaro Tezozomoc. Traduite sur un manuscrit inédit par H. Ternaux-
Compans. 2 tom.

Chez P. Jannet: Paris, 1853. 8°.

[9771. d. 21.]

15. ———.—Cronica Mexicana. Escrita por D. Hernando Alvarado Tezozo-
moc, hácia el año de MDXCVIII, anotada por el Sr. Lic. D. Manuel
Orozco y Berra, y precedida del Codice Ramirez, Manuscrito del siglo
XVI intitulado: Relacion del origen de los Indios que habitan esta
Nueva España segun sus historias, y de un examen de ambas obras, al
cual va anexo un estudio de Cronologia Mexicana por el mismo Sr.

Orozco y Berra. Jose M. Vigil, Editor. [With a preface by José F. Ramirez, and 11 Plates of drawings of Indians.] (Biblioteca Mexicana.) pp. viii. 712.

Imprenta y Litografia de Ireneo Paz : México, 1878-81. 8°.

[9771. g. 3.]

16. **Alzate y Ramirez,** Joseph Antonio de.—Observaciones Meteorologicas de los ultimos nueve meses de el año de mil setecientos sesenta y nueve. Hechas en esta Ciudad de Mexico. Por D. Joseph Antonio de Alzate y Ramirez. pp. 14.

Impressas con las licencias necessarias en México : en la Imprenta del Lic. D. Joseph de Jauregui, en la Calle de S. Bernardo, Año de 1770. 4°.

[8755. bbb. 36.]

17. **Amandus,** *of Zieriksee.*—Chronica Compendiosissima ab exordio mundi usq' ad annum Domini millesimum, quingentesimũ, trigesimũ quartum : per venerandum patrem, F. Amandum Zierixeensem, ordinis Fratrum Minorũ, regularis observantiæ, virum en Divinis & humanis rebus peritissimum . . . Adjectæ sunt . . . Aliæ quoq' tres epistolæ, ex nova maris Oceani Hispania ad nos transmissæ, de fructu mirabili illic surgentis novæ Ecclesiæ, ex quibus animus Christianus merito debeat lætari.

Antverpiæ : apud Simonem Cocum, Anno Domini, MCCCCCXXXIV, *Mense Maio.* 12°.

[9006. a. 24. Letters from Martinus de Valentia, and Petrus de Gante, alias de Mura.]

18. **Anghiera,** Pietro Martin d'.—The History of Travayle in the West and East Indies, and other countreys lying eyther way, towardes the fruitfull and ryche Moluccaes. As Moscouia, Persia, Arabia, Syria, Ægypte, Ethiopia, Guinea, China in Cathayo, and Giapan. With a discourse of the Northwest passage. Gathered in parte, and done into Englyshe [from Pietro Martire d'Anghiera, and others] by Richarde Eden. Newly set in order, augmented, and finished by Richard Willes. (An Abridgement of P. Martyr his 5, 6, 7 and 8 Decades, and particulerly of Ferd. Cortesius conquest of Mexico. By R. W. [*i.e.,* Richard Willes.]) [Dedicated to the Lady Brigit, Countesse of Bedforde.] ff. 466.

Imprinted at London by Richarde Iugge, 1577. 4°.

[K. 304. d. 10. From the Library of King George III.—G. 7305. From the Library of the Right Hon. Thomas Grenville. —979. c. 28. From the Library of Sir Joseph Banks. Wants Title-page, and 8 pages of preliminary matter.]

19. **Anonymous Conqueror.**—Relacion Anonyma de la Conquista de la Nueva España.—In "Colección de Documentos para la Historia de México. Publicada por Joaquin García Icazbalceta. Tom. 1.

J. M. Andrade : México, 1858. 8°.

[9771. f. 15.]

20. **Armin,** Theodor.—Das alte Mexico und die Eroberung Neuspaniens durch Ferdinand Cortez. Nach W. Prescott und Bernal Díaz, sowie unter Benutzung der Schriften von Alexander von Humboldt, des Abbé Brasseur, des Abt Fr. X. Clavigero u. A. Bearbeitet von Th. Arnim. Mit über 120 in den Text gedruckten Abbildungen, sechs Tonbildern, einem Frontispice, sowie einer Karte von Anahuac. pp. xiv. 376.

Verlag von Otto Spamer : Leipzig, 1865. 8°.

[9771. eee. 2.]

21. **Athanasius,** *Inca, of Cusco.*—West-Indische Spieghel. Waer inne men sien kan alle de Eylanden, Provintien, Lantschappen, het Machtige Ryck van Mexico, en 't Gout en Silver-rycke Landt van Peru. 'Tsampt de Coursen, Havenen, Klippen, Koopmanschappen, *etc.*, soo wel inde Noort als in de Zuyt-zee. Als mede hoe die vande Spanjaerden eerst ge invadeert syn. Door Athanasium Inga, Peruaen., van Cusco. pp. 435.

> *'t Amstelredam : By Broer Jansz. ende Jacob Pietersz, Wachter, Boeckvercooper op den Dam in de Wachter, Anno* 1624. 4°.

[G. 7158. From the Library of the Right Hon. Thomas Grenville. With a fine engraved Title-page, giving a portrait of Motenchuma, *etc.*, and 3 Maps, and 6 Illustrations.—10408. d. 11.—Another copy is in the John Carter Brown Library.]

22. **Bandelier,** Adolph Francis Alphonse.—Notes on the Bibliography of Yucatan and Central America. Comprising Yucatan, Chiapas, Guatemala (the Ruins of Palenque, Ocosingo, and Copan), and Oaxaca (Ruins of Mitla). A List of some of the writers on this subject from the Sixteenth Century to the present time. By Ad. F. Bandelier. From Proceedings of the American Antiquarian Society, October 21, 1880. (New Series. Vol. I. pp. 82-118.)

> *Press of Chas. Hamilton : Worcester, [Mass.]* 1881. 8°.

[Ac. 5798/2.]

23. ———.—Report of an Archæological Tour in Mexico in 1881. By A. F Bandelier. (Papers of the Archæological Institute of America. American Series. II). Second edition. pp. x. 326.

> *Published for the Institute by Cupples, Upham and Co. : Boston,*
> *[Mass.]; N. Trübner and Co.: London,* 1885. 8°.

[Ac. 5790/8.]

24. **Batres,** Leopoldo.—Arqueologia Mexicana. Civilizacion de algunas de las diferentes tirbus que habitarion el territorio hoy Mexicano en la antiguedad. pp. 100. 5 Chromos. 26 Plates.

> *Mexico,* 1888. 8°.

[Not in the British Museum.]

25. ———.—Clasificacion del tipo etnico de las tribus zapoteca del estado de Oaxaca y Acolhua del Valle de México. pp. 8. 2 Plates.

> *México,* 1890. 8°.

[Not in the British Museum.]

26. **Beaufoy,** Mark.—Mexican Illustrations, founded upon facts, indicative of the present condition of Society, Manners, Religion, and Morals among the Spanish and Native Inhabitants of Mexico. With observations upon the Government and resources of the Republic of Mexico, as they appeared during part of the years 1825, 1826, and 1827. Interspersed with occasional remarks upon the climate, produce, and antiquities of the country, mode of working the mines, &c. By Mark Beaufoy, late of the Coldstream Guards. Illustrated. pp. xii. 312.

> *Carpenter and Son : London,* 1828. 8°.

[792. e. 16.—10410. d. 26. (2.)]

27. **Berendt,** Carl Hermann, *M.D.*—Report of Explorations in Central America. By Dr. C. H. Berendt. [Dated : New York, December 24, 1867.] (In the 22nd *Annual Report of the Board of Regents of the Smithsonian Institution.* 1867. pp. 420-426.]
Government Printing Office : Washington, 1868. 8°.
[R. Ac. 1875/3.]

28. ———.—Analytical Alphabet for the Mexican & Central American Languages. By C. Hermann Berendt, M.D. Published by the American Ethnological Society. [With a Biographical Note on Dr. C. H. Berendt, and on his Maya Dictionary.] pp. iv. 8.
Reproduced in Fac-simile by the American Photo-Lithographic Company (Osborne's Process) : New York, 1869. 8°.
[12907. dd. 5.]

29. ———.—A Dictionary of the Maya Language. With a comparative review of all the Indian Languages spoken between the Isthmuses of Tehuantepec and Honduras, embracing more than 600 words in each, which comprises all the Languages belonging to the Maya Family. 2500 quarto pages. MS. 1869. 4°.
[Described in his " Analytical Alphabet." 1869. p. iv.

30. ———.—Los Escritos de D. Joaquin García Icazbalceta. (*Revista de Mérida.* Tom. II.)
Mérida de Yacatan, 1870.
[Not in the British Museum.]

31. ———.—Cartilla en Lengua Maya para la enseñanza de los niños indigenes.
Mérida, 1871. 8°
[Not in the British Museum.]

32. ———.—El Ramie. Tratado sobre el cultivo y algunas noticias de esta planta. (*Revista de Mérida.*)
Mérida de Yucatan, 1871.
[Not in the British Museum.]

33. ———.—Mexico. [Dr. C. H. Berendt compiled the article : Mexico, in :] Deutsch-amerikanisches Conversations-Lexicon . . . Bearbeited von Prof. Alexander J. Schem. Band 7. pp. 261-288.
E. S. Aeiger : New York, 1872. 8°.
[735. c. 7.]

34. ———.—Die Indianer des Isthmus von Tehuantepec. (*Zeitschrift für Ethnologie.* Band 5.)
Berlin, 1873. 8°.
[P. P. 3863. b.]

35. ———.—Zur Ethnologie von Nicaragua. (In *Correspondenz-Blatt der deutschen Gesellschaft für Anthropologie, Ethnologie, und Urgeschichte.* Redigirt von Dr. A. v. Frantzius in Heidelberg. No. 9. September, 1874. pp. 70-72.)
Friedrich Vieweg und Sohn : Braunschweig, 1875. 4°.
[P. P. 3947. d.]

36. ————.—Remarks on the Centres of Ancient Civilization in Central America, and their Geographical Distribution. Address read before the American Geographical Society. July 10, 1876. With a Map.
New York, 1876. 8°.
[Not in the British Museum.]

37. ————.—Remarks on the Centres of Ancient Civilisation in Central America, &c. By C. H. Berendt, M.D. (In *Petermann's Mittheilungen*, 1877. p. 82.)
Justus Perthes: Gotha, 1877. 4°.
[R. P. P. 3946.]

38. ————.—Collections of Historical Documents in Guatemala. By Dr. C. H. Berendt. (In the 31st *Annual Report of the Board of Regents of the Smithsonian Institution*. 1876. pp. 421-423.)
Government Printing Office: Washington, 1877. 8°.
[R. Ac. 1875/3.]

39. **Beristain de Souza Fernandez de Lara,** José Mariano.—Biblioteca Hispana Americana Septentrional . . . La escribia . . . J. M. Beristain de Souza. [Tom. 2 & 3 edited by José Rafael Enriquez Trespalacios Beristain.] 3 tom.
México, 1816-19. 8°.
[10880. g. 32.—1883. 11904. a. 22.]

40. **Bibliotheca Mejicana.** — Bibliotheca Mejicana. A Catalogue of an extraordinary Collection of Books and Manuscripts, almost wholly relating to the History and Literature of North and South America, particularly Mexico. pp. ii. 312.
London, 1869. 8°.
[Not in the British Museum.]

41. **Bienvenida,** Lorenzo de.—Lettre du Chapelain Frère Lorenzo de Bienvenida à Philippe II., alors Prince Héréditaire. [Report on Yucatan.] *De Yucaan*, le 10 de février, 1548. *Simancas.*—In " Voyages, Relations, et Mémoires Originaux pour servir à l'Histoire de la Découverte de l'Amérique. Publiés pour la première fois en Français par H. Ternaux-Compans."—Tom. x. Recueil de Pièces relatives à la Conquête du Mexique. Inédit. pp. 307-343.)
Arthus Bertrand: Paris, MDCCCXXXVIII. 8°.
[G. 15812. From the Library of the Right Hon. Thomas Grenville. —1196. i. 7.]

42. **Bird,** Robert Montgomery.—The Infidel, or, The Fall of Mexico. A Romance. By the Author of " Calavar" [Robert Montgomery Bird]. Second Edition. 2 vols.
Carey, Lea & Blanchard: Philadelphia, 1835. 8°.
[12703. e. 20.]

43. ————.—Cortes, or, The Fall of Mexico. By Dr. Bird, Author of " Calavar". 3 vols.
Richard Bentley: London, 1835. 8°.
[N. 1170.—Another edition of *The Infidel.*]

44. **Brasseur de Bourbourg,** Étienne Charles.—Collection de Documents dans les Langues Indigènes, pour servir à l'étude de l'histoire et de la philologie de l'Amérique Ancienne. [Edited by the Abbé Étienne Charles Brasseur de Bourbourg.] 4 tom.

Aug. Durand: Paris, 1861-68. 8°.

[7703. aa. 2-5.]

44 a. ———.—Tom. 1. Popol Vuh. Le Livre Sacré et les Mythes de l'antiquité Américaine, avec les Livres héroïques et historiques des Quichés. Ouvrage original des Indigènes de Guatémala. Texte Quiché et traduction française en regard, accompagnée de notes philologiques et d'un commentaire sur la mythologie et les migrations des peuples anciens de l'Amérique, *etc.*, composé sur des documents originaux et inédits. Par l'Abbé Brasseur de Bourbourg. pp. cclxxix. 368.

1861. 8°.

[7703. aa. 2.]

44 b. ———.—Tom. 2. Gramatica de la Lengua Quiché. Grammaire de la langue Quichée, espagnole-française, mise en parallèle avec ses deux dialectes, Cakchiquel et Tzutuhil. Tirée des manuscrits des meilleurs auteurs, guatémaliens. Ouvrage accompagné de notes philologiques, avec un vocabulaire comprenant les sources principales du Quiché comparées aux langues germaniques, et suivi d'un essai sur la poésie, la musique, la danse et l'art dramatique chez les Mexicains et les Guatémaltèques avant la Conquête. Servant d'introduction au Rabinal-Achi, drame indigène (transcrite pour la première fois par Bartolo Zig), avec sa musique originale, texte Quiché et traduction française en regard. Recueilli par l'Abbé Brasseur de Bourbourg, *etc.* 2 pts.

1862. 8°.

[7703. aa. 3.]

44 c. ———.—Tom. 3. Relation des Choses de Yucatan de Diego de Landa. [1573-1579.] Texte espagnol et traduction française en regard, comprenant les signes du calendrier et de l'alphabet hiéroglyphique de la langue Maya, accompagné de documents divers historiques et chronologiques, avec une grammaire et un vocabulaire abrégés Français-Maya. Précédés d'un essai sur les sources de l'histoire primitive du Mexique et de l'Amérique Centrale, *etc.*, d'après les monuments égyptiens et de l'histoire primitive de l'Égypte d'après les monuments américains. Par l'Abbé Brasseur de Bourbourg, *etc.* pp. cxii. 516.

1864. 8°.

[7703. aa. 4.]

44 d. ———.—Tom. 4. Quatre Lettres sur le Mexique. Exposition absolue du système hiéroglyphique mexicain, la fin de l'age de pierre, époque glaciaire temporaire, commencement de l'age de bronze, origines de la civilisation et des religions de l'antiquité d'après le Teo-Amoxtli et autres documents mexicains, *etc.* Par M. Brasseur de Bourbourg, *etc.* pp. xx. 463.

1868. 8°.

[7703. aa. 5.]

Y

(In "Colección de Documentos Inéditos para la Historia de España. Por el Marqués de la Fuensanta del Valle y D. José Sancho Rayon." Tom. 62-66.)

Imprenta de Miguel Genesta : Madrid, 1875-76.   8°.

[9197. ff.]

56. ———.—An Account of the First Voyages and Discoveries made by the Spaniards in America. Containing the most Exact Relation hitherto publish'd, of their unparallel'd Cruelties on the Indians, in the destruction of above Forty Millions of People. With the Propositions offer'd to the King of Spain, to prevent the further Ruin of the West-Indies. By Don Bartholomew de las Casas, Bishop of Chiapa, who was an Eyewitness of their Cruelties. Illustrated with Cuts. To which is added, The Art of Travelling, shewing how a Man may dispose his Travels to the best advantage. [With 2 Plates of 22 Scenes.] pp. 248. 4o.

London : Printed by J. Darby for D. Brown at the Black Swan and Bible without Temple-Bar, J. Harris at the Harrow in Little Britain, and Andr. Bell at the Cross-keys and Bible in Cornhil, MDCXCIX. 8°.

[G. 15933. From the Library of the Right Hon. Thomas Grenville.]

57. ———.—Lettere di Bartolommeo di las Casas a Filippo II., Re di Spagna. (In " Raccolta di Viaggi dalla Scoperta del Nuovo Continente fino a' di nostri. Compilata da F. C. Marmocchi." tom. 11. pp. 461-546.)

Fratelli Giachetti : Prato, 1843.   8°.

[1424. i. 5.]

58. **Catherwood,** Frederick.— Views of Ancient Monuments in Central America, Chiapas and Yucatan. By F. Catherwood, Archt. Owen Jones Chromolith. pp. 24. Outline Map, with Sites. 25 Plates.

F. Catherwood: London, 1844. fol.

[1263. i. 19.]

59. **Cepeda,** Fernando de, and **Carrillo,** Fernando Alfonso.—Relacion Universal Legitima y Verdadera del Sitio en que esta fundada la muy noble, insigne, y muy leal Ciudad de México, cabeça de las Provincias de toda la Nueva España. Lagunas, Rios, y Montes que la ciñen y rodean. Calçadas que las dibiden. Y Azequias que la atraviesan. Ynundaciones que à padecido desde su Gentilidad. Remedios aplicados. Desagues propuestos, y emprendidos. Origen y fabrica del de Gueguetocar y estado en que oy se halla. Ymposiciones, derramas, y gastos que se an hecho. Forma con que se á auctuado desde el año de 1553 hasta el presente de 1637. De Orden y mandato del Excellētissimo Señor D. Lope Diez de Armēdariz, Marques de Cadereita, del Consejo de Guerra de su Majestad, su Mayordomo, Virrey, Governador y Capitā General de la Nueva España, y Presidente de la Real Audiēcia que en esta Ciudad reside. Dispuesta y ordenada por el Licenciado Don Fernando de Cepeda, Relator della. Y Don Fernando Alfonso Carillo, Escrivano Mayor del Cavildo. Corregida, ajustada, y concertada con el Licenciado Don Juan de Albares Serrano, del Consejo de su Magestad Oydor mas antiguo de la dicha Real Audiencia. 3 parts.

En México : en la Imprenta de Francisco Salbago, Ministro del S. Officio, Año de 1637. fol.

59 a. ———.—Impressa, y Publicada esta Relacion en 7 de Abril deste Año se presentò contra ella por parte de Don Antonio Urrutia de Vergara ante el señor Virrey una peticiõ de addiciones, pretendiendo no averse hecho con el ajustamiento que se devia, *etc.*
México, à 22 de Julio de 1637. fol.
[K. 145. e. 15.—From the Library of King George III.]

60. **Cervántes de Salazar,** Francisco.—México en 1554. Tres Diálogos Latinos que Francisco Cervántes Salazar escribió é imprimió en México en dicho Año. Los reimprime, con Traduccion Castellana y Notas, Joaquin García Icazbalceta, *etc.* [Dedicated to Señor Don José María Andrade.] pp. L. 344.
Antigua Libreria de Andrade y Morales, Portal de Agustinos núm. 3: *México*, 1875. 8°.
[10480. ee. 3.—180 copies only printed.]

61. **Chappe d' Auteroche,** Jean.—Voyage en Californie pour l'Observation du Passage de Vénus sur le Disque du Soleil, le 3 Juin 1769. Contenant les observations de ce phénomène, & la description historique de la route de l'Auteur à travers le Mexique. Par feu M. Chappe d'Auteroche, de l'Académie Royale des Sciences. Rédigé & publié [with "Histoire Abrégée de la Parallaxe du Soleil",] par M. de Cassini fils, de la même Académie, Directeur en survivance de l'Observatoire Royal de Paris, &c. [At Page 32 : Plan de la Ville de Mexico. De la Gardette sculp. This finely engraved Plan measures 20½ × 15 Inches, and has been reproduced in fac-simile by Mr. Donald Macbeth for the Second Volume of the present work.] pp. 172.
À Paris: Chez Charles-Antoine Jombert, Libraire du Roi pour l'Artillerie & le Génie, rue Dauphine, à l'Image Notre-Dame ; (de l'Imprimerie de Fr. Ambroise Didot, rue Pavée), M.DCC.LXXII. 4°.
[K. 145. d. 7. From the Library of King George III.—983. d. 23. From the Library of Sir Joseph Banks.]

62. ———.—A Voyage to California, to observe the Transit of Venus. By Mons. Chappe d'Auteroche. With an Historical Description of the Author's Route through Mexico, and the Natural History of that Province. Also, A Voyage to Newfoundland and Sallee, to make experiments on Mr. Le Roy's Time Keepers. By Monsieur de Cassini. pp. 215. [With a reduction of the Plan of the City of Mexico, engraved by M. de La Gardette, 10 × 7½ Inches.]
Printed for Edward and Charles Dilly, in the Poultry : London, MDCCLXXVIII. 8°.
[792. g. 31. (2.) From the Library of King George III., though not placed with the Royal Collection. At page 104 is the following note : "We are farther obliged to Don Alzate for a very accurate map of Mexico, which he has delineated from the best accounts of such travellers as he is within reach of consulting in that country. He has also sent us a map, drawn up in Cortèse's life time, by which it is evident that in those early times they already knew California to be a peninsula, and the extent of it was as well ascertained as it has since been by later discoveries. Had this map been published in his time, it would have saved many disputes about California. The readiness of Don [Joseph Antonio de] Alzate y Ramirez to communicate to us whatever might be interesting in a country so near to us, together with his talents and personal qualities, have deserved the encomiums, and excited the gratitude of the members of the Academy [Académie Royale des Sciences], who have testified their sense of his merit, by admitting him to be one of their correspondents."]

326 BIBLIOGRAPHY.

63. **Charnay,** Désiré.—Le Mexique. Souvenirs et Impressions de Voyage. 1858-1861. pp. 439.
>   *E. Dentu : Paris,* 1863. 8°.
>   [10480. bb. 29.]

64. ———.—Les Anciennes Villes du Nouveau Monde. Voyages d'explorations au Mexique et dans l'Amérique Centrale. Par Désiré Charnay. 1857-1882. Ouvrage contenant 214 gravures et 19 cartes ou plans. pp. xii. 469.
>   *Hachette et Cie.: Paris,* 1885. fol.
>   [1789. d. 10.]

65. **Clavigero,** Francesco Saverio.—Storia Antica del Messico. Cavata da' migliori storici Spagnuoli, e da' Manoscritti, e dalle pitture antiche degl' Indiani. Divisa in dieci libri, e corredata di carte geografiche, e di varie figure: e Dissertazioni sulla Terra, sugli Animali, e sugli abitatori del Messico. Opera dell' Abate D. Francesco Saverio Clavigero. 2 tom. 21 Plates. 2 Maps.
>   *Per Gregorio Biasini all' Insegna di Pallade: in Cesena,* MDCCLXXX-I. 4°.
>   [K. 145. c. 7-10. From the Library of King George III.—983. d. 21, 22. From the Library of Sir Joseph Banks.]

66. ———.—The History of Mexico. Collected from Spanish and Mexican Historians, from Manuscripts, and Ancient Paintings of the Indians. Illustrated by Charts, and other Copper Plates. To which are added, Critical Dissertations on the Land, the Animals, and Inhabitants of Mexico. By Abbé D. Francesco Saverio Clavigero. Translated from the original Italian by Charles Cullen, Esq. In Two Volumes.
>   *Printed for G. G. J. and J. Robinson, No.* 25, *Pater-noster Row, London,* MDCCLXXXVII. 4°.
>   [K. 147. d. 13, 14. From the Library of King George III.—984. f. 19, 20. From the Library of Sir Joseph Banks.]

66 a. ———.—The Second Edition. In Two Volumes.
>   *Printed for J. Johnson, St. Paul's Churchyard, by Joyce Gold, Shoe Lane: London,* 1807. 4°.
>   [9771. f. 17.]

67. ———.—Historia Antigua de Megico. Sacada de los mejóres Historiadores españoles, y de los manuscritos, y de las pinturas antiguas de los Indios. Dividida en diez libros. Adornada con mapas y estampas, e ilustrada con Disertaciones sobre la tierra, los animales, y los habitantes de Megico. Escrita por D. Francisco Saverio Clavigero, y traducida del Italiano por José Joaquin de Mora. 2 tom.
>   *Londres: lo publica R. Ackermann, Strand, y en su establecimiento en Megico: asimismo en Colombia, en Buenos Ayres, Chile, Peru, y Guatemala,* 1826. 8°.
>   [1061. k. 17, 18.]

68. **Codex Ramirez.**
>   *See* Ramirez, José Fernando. 1903.

69. **Codex Troano-Americano.** —La Conquista de México efectuada por Hernán Cortés. Segun el Codice Jeroglifico Troano-Americano. Edición especial, que con preliminares de la clave jeroglifica, dedica al Señor Presidente de la Republica Mexicana, General Don Porfirio Diaz el Presbítero Dámaso Sotomayor, Miembro no residente de la Asociacion Americanista de Francia. [Illustrated.] pp. 40.
Tipografía de la Oficina Impresora del Timbre : México, 1897. fol.
[7705. h. 36.]

Cortés, Hernando, *Marqués del Valle de Guajaca.*

[FIVE LETTERS.]

70. ———.—Cartas de Relacion [I-V] de Fernando Cortés sobre el Descubri ⁻ miento y Conquista de la Nueva España. [1519-1526.] (In " Biblioteca de Autores Españoles, desde la formacion del lenguaje hasta nuestro dias. Historiadores Primitivos de Indias. [Tom. I.] Coleccion dirigida é ilustrada por Don Enrique de Vedía." Tom. XXII. pp. xv-xvii. I-153.)
Imprenta y Estereotipía de M. Rivadeneyra : Madrid, 1852. 8°.
[2044. a.]

71. ———.—Cartas y Relaciones de Hernan Cortés al Emperador Carlos V. [1519-1544.] Colegidas é ilustradas por Don Pascual de Gayángos, *etc.* pp. li. 575.
Imprenta Central de los Ferro-Carriles, A. Chaix y Cª.: Paris, 1866. 8°.
[9771. f. 16.]

72. ———.—Lettres de Fernand Cortes à Charles-Quint sur la Découverte et la Conquête du Mexique. Traduites par Désiré Charnay. Avec Préface du docteur E. T. Hamy, membre de l'Institut. pp. x. 387.]
Hachette et Cie.: Paris, 1896. 8°.
[9551. dd. 6.]

73. ———.—Letters of Cortés. The Five Letters of Relation from Fernando Cortés to the Emperor Charles V. Translated, and Edited, with a Biographical Introduction and Notes compiled from Original Sources, by Francis Augustus MacNutt. 2 vols.
G. P. Putnam's Sons : New York and London, 1908. 8°.
[9551. g. 3.]

[LETTERS TWO TO FIVE.]

74. ———.—The Despatches of Hernando Cortés, the Conqueror of Mexico addressed to the Emperor Charles V., written during the Conquest, and containing a narrative of its events. [Letters 2 to 5.] Now first translated into English from the Original Spanish, with an Introduction and Notes, by George Folsom, one of the Secretaries of the New York Historical Society, &c., &c. pp. xii. 431.
Wiley and Putnam : New York & London, 1843. 8°.
[1446. k. 1.]

[LETTERS TWO TO FOUR.]

75. ———.—Carta de Relacion, embiada a su Sacra Magestad del Emperador Nuestro Señor por el Capitan General de la Nueva España, llamado D. Fernando Cortés, *etc.* [Printed by Jacobo Cromberger, Sevilla, Nov. 8, 1522.] (Carta Tercera, *etc.*—Carta o Quarta Relacion, *etc.*—In

87. ———.—Carta de Relacion. In "Biblioteca de Autores Españoles desde la formacion del lenguaje hasta nuestros dias. Historiadores Primitivos de Indias. [Tom. I.] Colección dirigida é ilustrada por Don Enrlque de Vedía." Tom. XXII.)

M. Rivadeneyra : Madrid, 1852. 8°.

[2044. a.]

[SECOND LETTER.]

October 30, 1520.

88. ———.—Carta de relaciõ ẽbiada a su S. majestad del ẽpador nr̃o señor por el capitã general de la nueva spaña : llamado fernãdo cortes. En la q̃l haze relaciõ dlas tierras y provicias sin cuẽto q̃ hã descubierto nuevamẽte enel yucatã del año de xix a esta pte : y ha sometido a la corona real de su S. M. En especial haze relaciõ de una grãdissima provicia muy rica llamada Culua : ẽla q̃l ay muy grãdes ciudades y de maravillosos edificios : y de grãdes tratos y riq̃zas. Entre las q̃les ay una mas maravillosa y rica q̃ todas llamada Timixtitã : q̃ esta por maravillosa arte edificada sobre una grãde laguna. dela q̃l ciudad y provicia es rey un grãdissimo señor llamado Muteeçuma : dõde le acaecierõ al capitã y a los españoles espãtosas cosas de oyr. Cuenta largamẽte del grãdissimo señorio del dicho Muteeçuma y de sus ritos y cerimonias. y de como se sirve. [G. L. 28 leaves. sig. a-d. 47 to 49 lines in a full page. On the Title a woodcut, representing the Emperor Charles V. seated on a Throne.]

La presente carta de relacion fue impressa en la muy noble & muy leal ciudad de Sevilla : por Jacobo crõberger aleman. A. viii dias de Noviembre. Año de M. d. & xxii. [November 8, 1522.] fol.

[C. 20. e. 26. (1.)—G. 6815. (1.) From the Library of the Right Hon. Thomas Grenville.]

88 a. ———.—[Another edition.] Carta de relacion embiada a su S. majestad del Emperador nuestro señor por el Capitan general de la nueva España : llamado Fernando cortes, *etc.* [G. L. 28 leaves. sig. a-d. 48 lines to a full page. On the Title is a woodcut, representing the Emperor Charles V., with a suite of eight persons, receiving the letter from a messenger with five companions. Above the dedication, folio I, *verso*, is a woodcut of Cortés, and two of his vessels.]

La presente carta de relacion fue impressa èn la muy noble & muy leal ciudad de Caragoça : por George Coci, Aleman. A. v. dias de Enero. Año de M. d. & xxiii. fol.

[G. 6815. (2.) From the Library of the Right Hon. Thomas Grenville.]

89. ———.—La preclara Narratione di Ferdinando Cortese della Nuova Hispagna del Mare Oceano, al Sacratissimo & Invictissimo Carlo di Romani Imperatore sempre Augusto Re Dhispagna, & cio che siegue, nell año del Signore M.D.XX. trasinessa : Nella quale si cõtẽgono molte cose degne di scienza, & ammiratione, circa le cittadi egregie di quelle Provincie costumi dhabitatori, sacrifici di Fanciulli, & Religiose persone, Et massimamente della celebre citta Temixtitan, & varie cose maravigliose di quella, e quali diletteranno mirabilmẽte il lettore per il Dottore Pietro Savorgnano Forojuliense Del Riverendo Messer Giovañi de Revelles Vescovo di Vienna Secretario dal iddioma Hispagniuolo in lingua latina. Conversa Nel Anno M.D.XXIIII. di Primo Marzo : Hora nellestesso Millesimo di xvii. Agosto. Voi Candidissimi lettori leggerete con dilettatione & piacere grandissimo la prefata Narratione di

BIBLIOGRAPHY. 333

Ferdinando Corte se dalla Facŏdia latina al splēdore della lingua volgare p' Messer Nicolo Liburnio cŏ fidelta & diligēza tradotta al
cŏmodo, & sodiffatione de glhonesti & virtuosi ingegni.
*Stampata in Venetia per Bernardino de Viano de Lexona Vercellese.
Ad instantia de Baptista de Pederzani Briziani. Anno domini*
M.D.XXIIII. *Adi* XX. *Agosto.* [August 20, 1524.] 4°.
[9771. b. 11. With the rare wood-cut Plan of the City of Mexico,
and a large Printer's Device, an elephant carrying a castle, on a
single leaf, following the Colophon.—G. 6763. Wants the Plan.
From the Library of the Right Hon. Thomas Grenville.—1446.
h. 12. With the Book-plate of Augustus Frederick, Duke of
Sussex. Wants the Plan, & also the Printer's Device.]

90. ———.—Di Fernando Cortese la Seconda Relatione della Nuova Spagna.
Perche la Prima da lui fatta, benche da noi diligentemente ricercata
non habbiamo potuto infino a hoggi rètrovare. Al Sereniss, et
Invitiss. Imperatore Carlo V. *Della Città della Securezza de confini
della Nuova Spagna del Mare Oceano, alli* 30 *d' Ottobre,* 1520. (In
" Terzo Volume delle Navigationi et Viaggi. Raccolto gia da M.
Gio. Battista Ramusio." fol. 225-254.)
In Venetia: nella Stamperia de' Guinti, l'Anno MDLXV. fol.
[G. 6820.—From the Library of the Right Hon. Thomas Grenville.—
679. h. 10. From the Library of the Rev. Clayton Mordaunt
Cracherode. With the arms and cyphers of Jaques Auguste de
Thou, and his first wife, Marie Barbançon.]

91. ———.—Lettere di Ferdinando Cortes al Serenissimo ed Invittisimo
Imperatore Carlo V. Intorno ai fatti della Nuova Spagna o Messico.
Dalla Città della Sicurezza dei Confini della Nuova Spagna del Mare
Oceano ; addi 30 ottobre 1520. (In " Raccolta di Viaggi dalla Scoperta
del Nuovo Continente fino a' dì nostri. Compilata da F. C. Mar-
mocchi." tom. II. pp. 69-275.)
Fratelli Giachetti : Prato, 1843. 8°.
[1424. i. 5.]

92. ———.—Fernand Cortez, Voyageur espagnol, 1519-1547. [With a
French translation of the Second Letter, October 30, 1520.] Biblio-
graphie. (In " Voyageurs Anciens et Modernes, ou Choix des Relations de Voyages les plus intéressantes et les plus instructives depuis le
cinquième siécle jusqu' au dix-neuvième siècle avec
Biographies, Notes et Indications Iconographiques par M. Edouard
Charton, Redacteur en Chef du *Magasin Pittoresque*." Tom. 3.
pp. 357-424.)
Aux Bureaux du " Magasin Pittoresque" : Paris, 1869. 8°.
[2060. b.—10027. g. 2.]

[THIRD LETTER.]
May 15, 1522.

93. ———.—Carta tercera de relaciō : embiada por Fernādo cortes capitan
& justicia mayor del yucatan llamado la nueva espāna del mar oceano :
al muy alto y potentissimo cesar & ivictissimo señor dō Carlos emperador semper augusto y rey de españa nuestro señor : de las cosas
sucedidas & muy dignas de admiracion en la conquista y recuperacion
de la muy grande & maravillosa ciudad de Temixtitan : y de las otras
provincias a ella subjetas que se rebelaron. En la qual ciudad & dichas
provincias el dicho capitan y españoles configuieron grandes y señaladas
victorias dignas de perpetua memoria. Assi mesmo haze relacion como

hã descubierto el mar del Sur : y otras muchas & grãdes provincias muy ricas de minas de oro: y perlas: y piedras preciosas : & aun tienen noticia que ay especeria. [G. L. 30 leaves. sig. a-d. 48 lines in a full page. With a woodcut of Charles V., as in the Second Letter. 1522.]

La p̃sente carta d' relacio fue impressa ẽ la muy noble & muy leal ciudad d' sevilla por Jacobo cröberger alemã : acabo se a. xxx. dias de março : año d' mill & quiniẽtõs & xxiii. [March 30, 1523.] fol.

[C. 20. e. 26. (2.)—G. 6815. (3.) From the Library of the Right Hon. Thomas Grenville.]

94. ———.—Di Fernando Cortese la Terza Relatione della Nuova Spagna. *Della Città di Cuioacan di questa sua nuova Spagna del mare Oceano, Alli quindici di Maggio, L'anno del Signore 1522.* (In " Terzo Volume delle Navigationi et Viaggi. Raccolto gia da M. Gio Battista Ramusio." fol. 254-284.)

In Venetia : nella Stamperia de' Giunti, l'Anno MDLXV. fol.

[G. 6820.—679. h. 10.]

[FOURTH LETTER.]
October 15, 1524.

95. ———.—La quarta relacion q̃ Fernãdo cortes governador y capitan general por su majestad en la nueva España d'el mar oceano embio al muy alto & muy potentissimo invictissimo señor don Carlos emperador semper augusto y rey de España nuestro señor : en la qual estan otras cartas & relaciones que los capitanes Pedro de alvarado & Diego godoy embiaron al dicho capitan Fernardo cortes. [G. L. 22 leaves, the last blank. sig. a-c. 50 lines in a full page. On the Title page is a woodcut ornamental border, and above the Title a double-headed eagle, with the Royal Arms of Spain, and the Pillars of Hercules.]

Fue impressa la presente carta de relacion en la ymperial ciudad de Toledo por Gaspar de avila. Acabo se a veynte dias del mes de Octubre. Año del nascimiento de nuestro salvador Jesu Christo de mil & quinientos & veynte y cinco años. [October 20, 1525.] fol.

[C. 20. e. 26. (3.)—G. 6815. (4.) From the Library of the Right Hon. Thomas Grenville.]

96. ———.—Di Fernando Cortese la Quarta Relatione della Nuova Spagna. *Dalla gran città di Temistitan di questa nuova Spagna il quindici d'Ottobre del 1524.* (In " Terzo Volume delle Navigationi et Viaggi. Raccolto gia da M. Gio. Battista Ramusio." fol. 284-296.)

In Venetia : nella Stamperia de' Giunti, l'Anno MDLXV. fol.

[G. 6820.—679. h. 10.]

[FIFTH LETTER.]
September 3, 1526.

97. ———.—The Fifth Letter of Hernan Cortés to the Emperor Charles V., Containing an Account of his Expedition to Honduras in 1525-26. Translated from the Original Spanish by Don Pascual de Gayángos. pp. xvi. 156. Hakluyt Society Publications. First Series. Vol. 40.

Hakluyt Society: London, 1868. 8°.

[R. Ac. 6172/35.]

[MONTEZUMA'S PRESENTS.]

98. ———.—Inventory of Presents of Montezuma. (In "Colección de Documentos Inéditos para la Historia de España." Tom. I. p. 461.) *Madrid,* 1842. 8°.

99. ———.—Inventory of Presents of Montezuma. (In " Historia Antigua de Megico . . . Escrita por D. Francisco Saverio Clavigero, y traducida del Italiano por José Joaquin de Mora. *México,* 1844. 8°.

[This Inventory was collated in 1754 by Juan Batista Muñoz with the copy in the Manual del Tésorero in the Casa de la Contratacion at Sevilla.]

[APPENDIX.]

100. ———.—The Conquest of Mexico by Hernando Cortes. [With ten Engravings.] pp. viii. 252. (In "The World Displayed, or, A' Curious Collection of Voyages and Travels, selected from the Writers of all Nations. [With an Introduction by Samuel Johnson.] . . . The Fourth Edition. Vol. II.)

Printed for T. Carnan, and F. Newbery, Jun., at 65 in St. Paul's Church-Yard: London, MDCCLXXVII. 12°.

[1424. b. 2.—With the Book-plate of Mr. Calverley.]

101. ———.—The Voyage and Expedition of H. Cortés, and Conquest of Mexico. [With a Plate, W. G. del. I. Ray sc.] pp. 60.

London : Printed by T. Maiden, Sherbourn-Lane, for Ann Lemoine, White Rose Court, Coleman-Street, and J. Roe, No. 90, *Houndsditch,* [1806.] 12°.

[9771. aa. 6.]

102. ———.—Conquête du Pérou [or rather, Mexico]. Par Fernand Cortez. (In *Nouvelle Bibliothèque des Voyages Anciens et Modernes.* [Edited by Auguste Duponchel.] Tom. 12. pp. 78-130.)

P. Duménil: Paris, [1842.] 8°.

[1424. e. 6.]

103. ———.—Sumario de la Residencia tomada à D. Fernando Cortés, Gobernador y Capitan General de la N. E., y á otros gobernadores y oficiales de la misma. [1528-1537.] Paleografiado del original por el Lic. Ignacio Lopez Rayon. (In " Archivo Mexicano.") 2 tom.

Tipografia de Vicente García Torres: México, 1852-53. 8°.

[9771. c. 31.]

104. ———.—*Bibliography.*
　　See Charton, Édouard. 1869.

105. ———.—*Biography.*
　　See Trueba y Cosío, Joaquin Telesfors de. 1829.

106. ——— *See* Prescott, William Hickling. 1843.
　　　　　　　　　　　　　　　　　　　1844.
　　　　　　　　　　　　　　　　　　　1875.
　　　　　　　　　　　　　　　　　　　1906.

107. ——— *See* Charton, Édouard. 1869.

108. ——— *See* Helps, *Sir* Arthur, *K.C.B.* 1871.

109. ——— *See* Haebler, Konrad. 1887.

110. ——.—*Conquest of Mexico.*
     See López de Gómara, Francisco. 1552.

111. ——   *See* Anghiera, Pietro Martire d'. 1577.

112. ——   *See* Campbell, John. 1748.
                                    1764.

113. ——   *See* Dilworth, W. H., *A. M.* 1759.

114. ——   *See* Curths, Carl. 1828.

115. ——   *See* Cubitt, George, *Wesleyan Minister.* 1848.
                                                         1878.

116. ——   *See* D., H. P. [*i.e.* Henry Peter Dunster.] 1860.

117. ——   *See* Dalton, William, *Miscellaneous Writer.* 1862.
                                                            1872.

118. ——   *See* Codex Troano-Americano. 1897.

119. ——.—*Elogios.*
     See Lasso de la Vega, Gabriel. 1601.

120. ——.—*Eroismo.*
     See Caballero, Ramon Diosdado. 1806.

121. ——.—*Hechos.*
     See Lasso de la Vega, Gabriel. 1588.

122. ——.—*Naves.*
     See Fernández Duro, Cesáreo. 1882.

123. ——.—*Report of Alvarado.*
     See Alvarado, Pedro de. 1565.
                                1749.
                                1838.

124. ——.—*Report of Godoy.*
     See Godoy, Diego. 1565.
                          1749.
                          1838.

125. ——.—*Romances in which Cortés appears.*
     See Bird, Robert Montgomery. 1835.

126. ——.—*Viaje.*
     See Soto Hall, Máximo. 1900.

127. ——.—*Voyages & Discoveries.*
     See Britton, John. 1799.

128. **Cubitt**, George, *Wesleyan Minister.*—Cortes, or, The Discovery and
     Conquest of Mexico. By George Cubitt. (Memorable Men and
     Memorable Events.) pp. 160.
     John Mason: London, 1848. 12°.
     [1156. a. 18.]

129. ———.—Cortés, or, The Discovery and Conquest of Mexico. By George Cubitt. [With an Illustration of the Colossal Head at Izamal.] pp. 142.

Wesleyan Conference Office: London, [1878.] 8°.

[9772. aa. 5.]

130. **Curths,** Carl.—Die Eroberung Mexico's durch Hernandez Cortez. Historisches Gemälde für die Jugend. Von Carl Curths, Verfasser der Fortsetzung der von Schiller begonnenen Geschichte des Abfalls der vereinigten Niederlande. Zweite Ausgabe. [With a preface by August Rücker.] pp. xxx. 277.

August Rücker: Berlin, [1828.] 8°.

[1446. h. 3. A new issue of the first edition of 1818, with a new Title-page.]

131. **D.,** H. P. [*i.e.*, HENRY PETER DUNSTER.] Conquest of Mexico and Peru, by Hernando Cortés and Francis Pizarro. Illustrated. [By H. P. D., *i.e.* Henry Peter Dunster.] pp. 295.

James Blackwood: London, [1860.] 8°.

[9772. a. 12.]

132. **Dalton,** William, *Miscellaneous Writer.*—Cortés and Pizarro. The Stories of the Conquests of Mexico and Peru. With a sketch of the early adventures of the Spaniards in the New World. Re-told for youth by William Dalton . . . With Illustrations by John Gilbert. pp. x. 499.

Griffin, Bohn, and Co.: London, 1862 [1861]. 8°.

[9781. a. 15.]

132a. ———.—[Another edition.] Stories of the Conquests of Mexico and Peru . . . By William Dalton . . . With Illustrations by Godwin. pp. viii. 499.

James Blackwood & Co.: London, [1872.] 8°.

[9772. aaa. 40.]

133. **Díaz,** Juan, *Clerigo.*—Qui comincia lo Itinerario de Lisola de Iuchathan novamente ritrovata per il Signor Ioan de Grisalue Capitan Generale de Larmata del Re de Spagna & per il suo Capellano composta.

(In " Itinerario de Ludovico de Varthema Bolognese ne lo Egypto ne la Suria ne la Arabia deserta & Felice ne la Persia ne la India ne la Ethiopia. La sede el vivere & costüi de la p'fate, puicie. Et al p'sente agiötovi alcüe isole novamëte ritrovate.")

Impresso in Vinetia per Zorzi di Rusconi Milanese, nell' anno della Incarnatione del nostro Signore Jesu Christo, M.D.XX. *adi* III. *de Marzo. Regnando lo inclito Principe Duca de Venetia.* 12°.

[C. 32. a. 36.—Purchased June 11, 1868.—Registro. A—N. Tutti sono Quaderni.]

134. ———.—Qui comincia lo Itinerario de Lisola de Iuchatan novamente ritrovata per il Signor Ioan de Grisalue Capitan Generale de Larmata del Re de spagna & p' il suo Capellano cöposta. (In " Itinerario de Ludovico de Varthema Bolognese," *etc.*)

Impresso in Venetia Nell' anno della Incarnatione del nostro Signore Jesu Christo Del M.D.XXVI. *Adi* XVI. *Aprile. Regnando Lo Inclito Principe Andrea Griti.* 12°.

[10027. aa. 4 Purchased July 6, 1876.—With the Book-plate of I. Lee, of Doctors' Commons.]

Z

135. ———.—Qui comincia lo Itinerario de Lisola de Iuchatan novamente ritrovata per il Signor Ioan de Grisalve Capitan Generale de Larmata del Re de Spagna & p' il suo Capellano cōposta. (In " Itinerario de Ludovico de Varthema Bolognese," etc. fol. 89-100.)

Stampato in Vinegia per Francesco di Alessandro Bindone, &° Mapheo Pasini compani, a santo Moyse al segno de Langelo Raphael, nel M.D.XXXV. *del mese d'Aprile.* 12°.

[G. 7062. From the Library of the Right Hon. Thomas Grenville. On the last leaf is the Printer's Device, the Archangel Raphael & Tobias.—790 a. 12. Damaged, and imperfect.]

136. ———.—Itinéraire du Voyage de la Flotte du Roi Catholique à l'Île de Yucatan dans l'Inde. Fait en l'an 1518, sous les ordres du capitaine général, Juan de Grijalva. Rédigé et dédié à S. A. [Don Diégo Colomb] par le chapelain en chef [Juan Díaz] de ladite flotte. (In " Voyages, Relations et Mémoires Originaux pour servir à l'Histoire de la Découverte de l'Amérique. Publiés pour la première fois en Français par H. Ternaux-Compans.—Tom. x. Recueil de Pièces relatives à la Conquête du Mexique. Inédit." pp. 1-47.)

Arthur Bertrand : Paris, MDCCCXXXVIII. 8°.

[G. 15812. From the Library of the Right Hon. Thomas Grenville. —1196. i. 7.]

137. ———.—Itinerario del Viaggio che la Flotta del Re Cattolico fece nel 1518 nell' Yucatan sotto gli ordini del Capitano Generale Giovanni di Grijalva. Compilato e dedicato a S. A. Don Diego Colombo Ammiraglio e Vicere delle Indie da Giovanni Díaz, Primo Cappellano della Flotta Medesima. (In " Raccolta di Viaggi dalla Scoperta del Nuovo Continente fino a' dì nostri. Compilata da F. C. Marmocchi." Tom. II. pp. 43-67.)

Fratelli Giachetti : Prato, 1843. 8°.

[1424. i. 5.]

138. ———.—Itinerario de la Armada del Rey Católico á la Isla de Yucatan, en la India, el año 1518, en la que fué por Comandante y Capitan General Juan de Grijalva. Escrito para Su Alteza por el Capellan Mayor de la dicha Armada.—Itinerario de larmata del Re Catholico, *etc.* (Texto italiano y traduccion.—In "Coleccion de Documentos para la Historia de Mexico. Publicada por Joaquin García Icazbalceta." Tom. I. pp. 281-308.)

Libreria de J. M. Andrade : México, 1858. 8°.

[9771. f. 15.]

139. **Díaz del Castillo,** Bernal.—Carta de Bernal Díaz del Castillo al Emperador D. Carlos dando cuenta de los abusos que se cometian en la gobernacion de las provincias del Nuevo Mundo.—*Santiago de Guatimala,* 22 de febrero de 1552. (In *Cartas de Indias.* pp. 38-44.)

Imprenta de Manuel G. Hernandez : Madrid, 1877. fol.

[1857. b. 5.—Maps 36. e. 1.]

140. ———.—Carta de Bernal Díaz del Castillo al Rey D. Felipe II., en la que denuncia algunos abusos cometidos con los indios, y pide se le nombre fiel-ejecutor de Guatimala, en atencion á los servicios que expone. *Guatimala,* 20 de febrero de 1558. [Facsimile E.] (In *Cartas de Indias.* pp. 45-47, & Facsimile E, 6 pages.)

Imprenta de Manuel G. Hernandez : Madrid, 1877. fol.

[1857. b. 5.—Maps 36. e. 1.]

141. ———.—Historia Verdadera de la Conquista de la Nueva-España. Escrita por el Capitan Bernal Díaz del Castillo, uno de sus Conquistadores. Sacada á luz por el P. M. Fr. Alonso Remon, Predicador, y Coronista General del Orden de Nuestra Señora de la Merced Redempcion de Cautivos. Á la Catholica Magestad del Mayor Monarca Don Felipe Quarto, Rey de las Españas y Nuevo Mundo, N. Señor. ff. 254.

En Madrid: en la Imprenta del Reyno, Año de 1632. fol.

[G. 6417. From the Library of the Right Hon. Thomas Grenville.— K. 145 e. 18. From the Library of King George III.—674. k. 16. From the Library of the Rev. Clayton Mordaunt Cracherode.]

142. ———.—Historia Verdadera de la Conquista de la Nueva España. Escrita por el Capitan Bernal Díaz del Castillo, uno de sus Conquistadores. Sacada á luz por el P. M. Fr. Alonso Remon, Predicador y Coronista General del Orden de N. S. de la Merced, Redencion de Cautivos. Á la Catholica Magestad del Mayor Monarca D. Filipe IV., Rey de las Españas y Nuevo Mundo, N. S. ff. 256.

En Madrid: en la Emprenta del Reyno, [1632.] fol.

[601. l. 10. With an engraved pictorial Title-Page by J. de Courbes.—601. l. 24. Wants the Title-Page and preliminary leaves.—fol. 255, 256 contain a new chapter : " Este capitulo, que es el ultimo del original, por parecer escusado, se dexo de imprimir ; y oy a peticion de un Curioso se añade.]

143. ———.—Historia Verdadera de la Conquista de la Nueva España. Escrita por el Capitan Bernal Díaz del Castillo, uno de sus Conquistadores. 4 tom.

En Madrid: en la Imprenta de Don Benito Cano, Año de 1795, 1796. 8°.

[1197. b. 11, 12.]

144. ———.—The True History of the Conquest of Mexico. By Captain Bernal Díaz del Castillo, one of the Conquerors. Written in the year 1568 . . . Translated from the original Spanish by Maurice Keatinge, Esq. [With a plan of the City and Lake of Mexico.] pp. viii. 515.

London: Printed for J. Wright, Piccadilly, by John Dean, High Street: Congleton, 1800. 4°.

[G. 4293. From the Library of the Right Hon. Thomas Grenville. K. 145. d. 1.]

145. ———.—The True History of the Conquest of Mexico. By Captain Bernal Díaz del Castillo, one of the Conquerors. Written in the year 1568 . . . Translated from the original Spanish by Maurice Keatinge, Esq. Second Edition. 2 tom.

Cushing & Appleton : Salem, 1803. 8°.

[Not in the British Museum.]

146. ———.—History of the Discovery and Conquest of Mexico. Written in the year 1568, by Captain Bernal Díaz del Castillo, one of the Conquerors. [Based on the translation by Maurice Keatinge, 1800.] In " A General

Z 2

160. ———.—Történelmi Konyotár. Franklin. társulat. Cortez Hernando, Mexico meghóditoja. Diaz Bernal után elmeséli Gaal Mozes. (No. 86 of the Collection.) pp. 124.

    Franklin társulat: Budapest, 1899. 12°.

    [Not in the British Museum.]

161. ———.—Historia Verdadera de la Conquista de la Nueva España. Por Bernal Díaz del Castillo, uno de sus Conquistadores. Unica edición hecha según el Códice Autógrafo. La publica Genaro García. (Bibliografia.) [With a Portrait, and coat of arms, of Bernal Díaz del Castillo.] 2 tom.

    Oficina Tipográfica de la Secretaría de Fomento: México, 1904. 8°.

    [2398. g. 5.]

162. **Díaz de la Calle,** Juan.—Memorial Informatorio al Rey Nuestro Señor, en su Real y Supremo Conseio de las Indias, Camara, y Junta de Guerra. En Manos del Señor Juan Baptista Saenz Navarrete, Cavallero de la Orden de Alcantara, de su Consejo, su Secretario en èl, y el de la Camara, y Junta. Contiene lo que su Magestad provee en su Cösejo, y Junta, y por las dos Secretarias de la Nueva España, y Pirù, Ecclesiastico, Secular, Salarios, Estipendios, y Presidios, su Gente, y Costa, y de que Cajas, y Hazienda Real se paga ; valor de las Encomiendas de Indios, y otras cosas curiosas, y necessarias. Por Juan Diez de la Calle. ff. 32.

    [*Madrid,*] Año de MDCXXXXV. 4°.

    [K. 279. h. 25. (1.) From the Library of King George III.]

163. ———.—Memorial y Noticias Sacras, y Reales del Imperio de las Indias Occidentales. Al Muy Catolico, Piadoso, y Poderoso Señor Rey de las Españas, y Nuevo Mundo, D. Felipe IV., N. S. en su Real y Supremo Conseio de las Indias, Camara, y Iunta de Guerra en manos de Juã Baptista Saenz Navarrete, Cavallero de la Ordẽ Militar de Alcantara, de su Consejo, y su Secretario en el, y en el de la Camara, y Iunta : Confirmador de los privilegios Reales de Castilla. Comprehende lo Eclesiastico, Secular, Politico, y Militar, que por su Secretaria de la Nueva-España se provee : Presidios, gente, y costas, valor de las Encomiendas de Indios, y otras cosas curiosas, necesrias [*sic*], y dignas de saberse. Escriviale por el año de 1646 Juan Diaz de la Calle, Oficial Segundo de la misma Secretaria. ff. 183. 5. 8.

    [*Madrid,* 1646.] 4°.

    [K. 279. h. 25. (2.)—798. f. 3.]

164. **Dilworth,** W. H., *A.M.*—The History of the Conquest of Mexico. By the celebrated Hernan Cortés. Containing a Faithful and Entertaining Detail of all his Amazing Victories, in that vast Empire, its Laws, Customs, Religions, &c. A Work abounding with Strokes of Generalship, and the most refined Maxims of Civil Policy. To which is added, The Voyage of Vasca de Gama, extracted from Osorio, Bishop of Sylves. Published for the Improvement and Entertainment of the British Youth of both Sexes. By W. H. Dilworth, A.M. pp. 1-127.

    Printed for William Anderson, at the Oxford-Theatre, Pater-noster-Row: London, MDCCLIX. 12°.

    [9772. aa. 13. Wants all after page 127.]

165. **Dunster,** Henry Peter.—Conquest of Mexico and Peru, by Hernando
Cortés and Francis Pizarro. Illustrated. [By H. P. D., *i.e.* Henry
Peter Dunster.] pp. 295.
James Blackwood: London, [1860.] 8°.
[9772. a. 12.]

166. **Dupaix,** Guillelmo.—The Monuments of New Spain. By M. Dupaix.
With their respective scales of measurement and accompanying descriptions. (In Aglio, Augustine : *Antiquities of Mexico.* vols. 4, 6.)
A. Aglio: London, 1830. fol.
[564. h. 4, 6.]

167. **Duran,** Diego.—Historia de las Indias de Nueva-España y Islas de
Tierra Firme. Por el Padre Fray Diego Duran, Religioso de la Orden de
Predicadores, Escritor del siglo XVI. La publica con un atlas de
[66 coloured] estampas, notas é ilustraciones José F. Ramirez, Individuo
de varias Sociedades Literarias Nacionales y extranjeras. [Tom. 2.
edited by Gumesindo Mendoza, Director del Museo Nacional, Mexico.]
2 tom.
Imprenta de J. M. Andrade y F. Escalante ; Ignacio Escalante: Mexico,
1867-80. 4°.
[9771. g. 8.]

168. **Encyclopedias.** — Diccionario Enciclopedico Hispano - Americano de
Literatura, Ciencias y Artes. Edicion profusamente ilustrada. 25 tom.
Montaner y Simón: Barcelona, 1887-99. 4°.
[2103. c, d.]

169. **Fernandez de Echeverría y Veytia,** Mariano.—Historia Antigua de
Méjico. Escrita por el Lic. D. Mariano Veytia. La publica con
varias notas y un apendice el C. F. Ortega. [With a portrait of the
Author.] 3 tom.
Imprenta a Cargo de Juan Ojeda: Méjico, 1836. 8°.
[9771. a. 11.]

170. **Fernández de Oviedo y Valdés,** Gonzalo.—Oviedo de la natural
hystoria de las Indias. G. L. Pt. I. ff. 52.
Por industria de maestre Remõ de Petras: en la cibdad de Toledo,
MDXXVI. fol.
[G. 6268.—From the Library of the Right Hon. Thomas Grenville.—
With a large plate of the arms of Charles V. on the title-page.—
795. l. 17. (1.)—982. i. 9. From the Library of Sir Joseph
Banks.]

171. ———.—La historia general de las Indias. (Escripta por el capitan
gonçalo hernandez de Oviedo y Valdes.) ff. 193.
En la emprẽta de Juan Cromberger: Sevilla, 1535. fol.
[C. 20. d. 4.—From the Library of Sir Joseph Banks.—With a finely
engraved title-page, with the arms of Charles V., and the Pillars of
Hercules, surrounded by an ornamental border. On fol. cxciii is
the autograph signature of the author, and on the *verso* is a large
plate of the author's coat of arms.]

172. ———.—Coronica de las Indias. La hystoria general de las Indias agora
nuevamente impresa corregida y emendada. (Libros de los infortunios
y naufragios de casos acaecidos en las mares de las Indias, yslas y tierra
firme del mar oceano, con el qual se da fin a la primera parte de la
general & natural hystoria de las Indias.—Libro xx. De la segunda
parte de la general historia de las Indias . . . que trata del estrecho de
Magallans.) Y con la conquista del Peru [por Francisco de Xéres].
G. L.   Pts. 1, 2.

Juan de Junta: Salamanca, 1547 ; Francisco Fernandez de Córdova:
Valladolid, 1557.   fol.

C. 33. m. 3. (1.)—This work was arranged for publication in three
parts, forming together 50 *Libros,* numbered consecutively. The
Libro de los infortunios y naufragios, of which chapters i-xi only
are here printed with Part i, was to form Libro l. No more was
published after Book i of Part 2 which forms " Libro xx" of the
entire work. The *Conquista del Perú* was bound up with this
edition.—K. 146. e. 10. From the Library of King George III.
Another copy of Part i.—G. 6269. From the Library of the Right
Hon. Thomas Grenville. Another copy of Part ii.—On the Title-
page of Part i is a large plate of the arms of Charles V., with the
Pillars of Hercules.]

173. **Fernández Duro,** Cesáreo.—Las Joyas de Isabel la Católica, las Naves
de Cortés, y el Salto de Alvarado. Epístola dirigida al Ilmo Señor
Don Juan de Dios de la Rada y Delgado por Cesáreo Fernández Duro.
pp. 53.

Imprenta de Manuel G. Hernandez : Madrid, 1882.   8°.

[9180. ff. 6.]

174. **Fernández Leal,** Manuel, *Ministro de Fomento.*—Códice Fernández
Leal. Publicado por el Dr. Antonio Peñafiel. pp. 8.   14 Plates, 12 in
colour.

Oficina Tipografica de la Secretaria de Fomento : México, 1895.   fol.

[1701. c. 7.]

175. **Francesco,** *de Bologna, Monk.*—Lettre du Révérend Père Francesco de
Bologne, écrite de la ville de Mexico dans l'Inde, ou la Nouvelle-
Espagne, au Révérend Père Clément de Monélia, Provincial de
Bologne, et à tous les révérends pères de cette province.   Traduite en
langue vulgaire par un frère dudit ordre de l'Observance.   *Venise: de*
l'Imprimerie de Paulo Danza. (In " Voyages, Relations, et Mémoires
Originaux pour servir à l'Histoire de la Découverte de l'Amérique.
Publiés pour la première fois en Français par H. Ternaux-Compans.—
Tom. x.   Recueil de Pièces relatives à la Conquête du Mexique.
Inédit."   pp. 205-221.)

Arthus Bertrand : Paris, MDCCCXXXVIII.   8°.

[G. 15812. From the Library of the Right Hon. Thomas Grenville.—1196. 1. 7.]

176. ———.—Lettera del Reverendo Padre Francesco da Bologna, scritta
dalla Città di Messico nell' India o Nuova Spagna al Reverendo Padre
Clemente da Monelia, Provinciale di Bologna, ed a tutti i reverendi
Padri di quella provincia tradotta in lingua volgare da un Frate dello
stesso Ordine dell' Osservanza. (In " Raccolta di Viaggi dalla Scoperta
del Nuovo Continente fino á di nostri.   Compilata da F. C. Marmocchi."   tom. 11.   pp. 547-558.)

Fratelli Giachetti : Prato, 1843.   8°.

[1424. i. 5.]

177. **García**, Genaro.—Carácter de la Conquista Española en América y en México. Según los Textos de los Historiadores Primitivos. Por Genaro García. pp. 456.
Oficina Tipográfica de la Secretaría de Fomento : México, 1901. 8°.
[9770. h. 12.]

178. ———.—El Plan de Independencia de la Nueva España en 1808. Por Genaro García. [With a Bibliography.] pp. 72.
Imprenta del Museo Nacional : México, 1903. fol.
[9770. i. 13.—No. 114 of 150 copies.]

179. **García**, Genaro, and Pereyra, Carlos.—Documentos Inéditos ó muy Raros para la Historia de México. Publicados por Genaro García y Carlos Pereyra. Tom. 1-16, *etc.*
Librería de la Vda. de Ch. Bouret : México, 1905-1908, *etc.* 8°.
[9772. cc.]

180. **García**, Gregorio, *Dominican.*—Historia Ecclesiastica y Seglar de la Yndia Oriental y Occidental, y Predicacion del Sancto Evãgelio en ella por los Apostoles. Averiguad por el P. Presentado Fr. Gregorio Garcia, de la Orden de Predicadores. En que hallara el lector cursado en letras, discursos que deleyten su entendimiento, y el curioso Romancista, cosas de mucho gusto, piedad y devocion : particularmente desde el segundo libro de este Tratado. A la Sacratissima y siempre Virgen Maria del Rosario. (Tabla.) ff. 250.
Impresso en Baeça : por Pedro de la Cuesta, Año de 1626. 12°.
[K. 296. g. 32.]

181. ———.—Origen de los Indios de el Nuevo Mundo, e Indias Occidentales. Averiguado con discurso de opiniones por el Padre Presentado Fray Gregorio García, de la Orden de Predicadores. Tratanse en este Libro varias cosas, y puntos curiosos, tocantes á diversas ciencias y facultades, con que se haze varia historia, de mucho gusto para el ingenio y entendimiento de hombres agudos y curiosos. Dirigido al Angelico Dotor Santo Thomas de Aquino. (Tabla.) pp. 535.
En Valencia : en casa de Pedro Patricio Mey, junto a San Martin, MDCVII. 12°.
[1061. b. 11.]

182. ———.—Origen de los Indios de el Nuevo Mundo e Indias Occidentales. Averiguado con discurso de opiniones por el Padre Presentado Fr. Gregorio García, de la Orden de Predicadores. Tratanse en este Libro varias cosas, y puntos curiosos, tocantes á diversas Ciencias, i Facultades, con que se hace varia Historia, de mucho gusto para el Ingenio, i Intendimiento de Hombres agudos i curiosos. Segunda Impresion. Enmendada y añadida de algunas opiniones, ò cosas notables en maior prueba de lo que contiene, con Tres Tablas mui puntuales de los Capitulos, de las Materias, y Autores, que las tratan. Dirigido al Angelico Doct. Sto. Tomas de Aquino. (Tabla.) pp. 336.
En Madrid : En la Imprenta de Francisco Martinez Abad, Año de 1729. fol.
[G. 7225. L.P. From the Library of the Right Hon. Thomas Grenville.—K. 146. e. 4. From the Library of King George III. Cropped.]

346 BIBLIOGRAPHY.

183. **García de Palacio,** Diego.—Carta dirijida al Rey de España. Por el
Licenciado Dr. Don Diego García de Palacio, Oydor de la Real
Audiencia de Guatemala. Año 1576. Being a Description of the
Ancient Provinces of Guazacapan, Izalco, Cuscatlan, and Chiquimula,
in the Audiencia of Guatemala. With an account of the Languages,
Customs and Religion of their Aboriginal Inhabitants, and a Description
of the Ruins of Copan. pp. 131. (In "Collection of Rare and Original
Documents and Relations concerning the Discovery and Conquest of
America, chiefly from the Spanish Archives. Published in the Original,
with Translations, illustrative Notes, Maps, and Biographical Sketches.
By E. G. Squier, M.A., F.S.A." No. 1.)
Charles B. Norton : New York, MDCCCLX. 4°.
[9551. c. 18.]

184. **García Icazbalceta,** Joaquin.—Apuntes para un Catálogo de Escritores
en Lenguas Indígenas de América. Por Joaquin García Icazbalceta.
pp. xiii. 157.
*Se han impreso 60 ejemplares en la imprenta particular del autor
México,* 1866. 12°.
[11901. aa. 30.—No. 51 of 60 copies printed.]

185. ———.—Bibliografía Mexicana del Siglo XVI. Primera Parte. Catálogo
razonado de Libros impresos en México de 1539 á 1600. Con Biografías
de autores y otras ilustraciones. Precedido de una noticia acerca de la
introducción de la imprenta en México. Por Joaquin García Icazbalceta . . . Obra adornada con facsímiles fotolitográficos y fototipo-
gráficos. pp. xxix. 423.
Librería de Andrade y Morales, Sucesores: México, 1886. 8°.
[11901. k. 26.—11905, f. 30.]

186. ———.—Colección de Documentos para la Historia de México. Publicada por Joaquin García Icazbalceta. 2 tom.
Librería de J. M. Andrade ; Antigua Librería: México, 1858-66. 8°.
[9771. f. 15.]

187. ———.—Nueva Colección de Documentos para la Historia de México.
Publicada por Joaquin García Icazbalceta. 5 tom.
*Antigua Librería de Andrade y Morales, Sucesores : Francisco Diaz
de Leon : México,* 1886-92. 8°.
[9771. bbb. 2.]

187 a. ———.—Tom. 1.—Cartas de Religiosos de Nueva España. 1539-
1594.
1886. 8°.

187 b. ———.—Tom. 2.—Códice Franciscano. Siglo XVI. Informe de la
Provincia del Santo Evangelio al Visitador Lic. Juan de Ovando.
Informe de la Provincia de Guadalajara al Mismo. Cartas de Religiosos. 1533-1569.
1889. 8°.

187 c.———.—Tom. 3.—Pomar y Zurita. Pomar. Relación de Tezcoco.
Zurita. Breve Relación de los Señores de la Nueva España. Varias
Relaciones Antiguas. Siglo XVI.
1891. 8°.

187 d, e.————.—Tom. 4, 5.—Códice Mendieta. Documentos Franciscanos. Siglos XVI y XVII. [Part 1. 1557-1583. Part 2. 1585-1622.] (Codice de Tlatelolco.—Anales de Tecamachalco.)

1892. 8°.

188. ————.—Obras de D. J. García Icazbalceta. [With a Portrait.] 10 tom. (Biblioteca de Autores Mexicanos. Historiadores. Tom. 1-3, 6, 9, 12, 14, 18, 20, 23.)

Imp. de V. Agüeros: México, 1896-99. 8°.

[12231. c. 11.]

189. **García Peláez,** Francisco de Paula, *Bishop of* ⌊*Guatemala.*—Memoria para la Historia del Antiguo Reyno de Guatemala. 2 tom.

Guatemala, 1851-52. 8°.

[Not in the British Museum.]

190. **Giovio,** Paulo, *Bishop of Nocera, the Elder.*—Pauli Iovii Novocomensis, episcopi Nucerini, Historiarum sui temporis Tomus Primus (Secundus). [With a Prefatory Letter by Andreas Alciatus.] 2 tom.

Florentiæ: in officina Laurentii Torrentini Ducalis Typographi, MDL, MDLII. fol.

[K. 212. g. 1. From the Library of King George III.]

191. **Godoy,** Diego.—Relation fatta per Diego Godoi a Fernando Cortese. Lettere di Diego, nelle quali tratta del scoprimento & acquisto di diverse città & provincie : delle guerre & battaglie che per tal cosa fueron fatte, la maniera dell' arme da combattere et da coprirsi che usano quelli, della provincia di Chamula, di alcune strade molto difficili & pericolose, de portamenti del reggente, & della divisione de beni che gia furono divisi in quelle bande. (In "Terzo Volume delle Navigationi et Viaggi. Raccolto gia da M. Gio. Battista Ramusio." fol. 300-304.)

In Venetia: nella Stamperia de' Giunti, l'Anno. MDLXV. fol.

[G. 6820.—From the Library of the Right Hon. Thomas Grenville.— 679. h. 10. From the Library of the Rev. C. M. Cracherode. With the arms and cyphers of Jacques Auguste de Thou, and his first wife, Marie Barbançon.]

192. ————.—Relacion hecha por Diego Godoy, a Hernando Cortés, en que trata del Descubrimiento de diversas Ciudades, i Provincias, i Guerra, que tuvo con los Indios, i su modo de pelear : De la Provincia de Chamula, de los Caminos dificiles, i peligrosos ; i repartimiento que hiço de los Pueblos. (In "Historiadores Primitivos de las Indias Occidentales, que juntó, traduxo en parte, y sacó á luz, ilustrados con erudítas Notas, y copiosos Indices, el Ilustrisimo Señor D. Andres Gonzalez Barcia, del Consejo, y Camara de S. M. Divididos en tres Tomos, cuyo contenido se verá en el folio siguiente." Tom. 1. Part 2. pp. 166-173.)

Madrid, Año MDCCXLIX. fol.

[K. 145. f. 9. From the Library of King George III.]

193. ———.—Relation de Diégo de Godoi, adressée à Fernand Cortés. (In "Voyages, Relations, et Mémoires Originaux pour servir à l'Histoire de la Découverte de l'Amérique. Publiés pour la première fois en Français par H. Ternaux-Compans.—Tom. x. Recueil de Pièces relatives à la Conquête du Mexique. Inédit." pp. 151-191.)

Arthus Bertrand: Paris, MDCCCXXXVIII. 8°.

[G. 15812. From the Library of the Right Hon. Thomas Grenville. —1196. i. 7.]

194. **González Obregón,** Luis.—El Capitan Bernal Díaz del Castillo, Conquistador y Cronista de Nueva España. Noticias biográficas y bibliográficas compiladas por Luis González Obregón. pp. 88. ii.

Oficina Tip. de la Secretaria de Fomento: México, 1894. 8°.

[10600. g. 21. (1.)]

195. **Gottfried,** Johann Ludwig, *pseud.* [*i.e.,* Johann Philipp Abelin].—Neue Welt und Amerikanische Historien. Alles aus verschiedenen Historien-Schreibern . . . getragen . . . durch J. L. Gottfriedt.

J. T. de Bry: Frankfurt a/M., 1631. fol.

[G. 6635. From the Library of the Right Hon. Thomas Grenville.— 1655. 566. k. 12.]

196. **Grijalva,** Juan de, *Augustinian.*—Cronica de la Orden de N. P. S. Augustin en las provincias de la nueva españa. En quatro ĕdades desde el año de 1533 hasta el de 1592. Por el P. M. F. Joan de Grijalva, prior del convento de N. P. S. Augustin de México. Dedicada a la provincia del Sᶜ S. nombre de Jesus de México. ff. 224.

México: En el Religiosissimo convento de S. Augustin, y imprenta de Joan Ruyz, Año de 1624. fol.

[4785. g. 39.—With an engraved Title-page.]

197. **Gunckel,** Lewis Winters.—The Direction in which Mayan Inscriptions should be read. By Lewis W. Gunckel. From the *American Anthropologist* for May, 1897. Vol. x. pp. 146-162.

Judd & Detweiler: Washington, D.C., 1897. 8°.

[Ac. 6239/2.—07703. g. 10. (8.)]

198. **Haebler,** Konrad.—Aus dem Leben des ersten Vicekönigs von Mejiko. Von Dr. Konrad Häbler in Dresden. (In "Historisches Taschenbuch. Begründet von Friedrich von Raumer. Herausgegeben von Wilhelm Maurenbrecher." Folge 6. Jahrgang 6. pp. 123-137.)

F. A. Brockhaus: Leipzig, 1887. 8°.

[P. P. 3625.]

199. **Heger,** Franz.—Altmexicanische Reliquien aus dem Schlosse Ambras in Tirol. Von Franz Heger. Mit fünf Tafeln in Lichtdruck, davon eine in Farbendruck. (In "Annalen des K. K. Naturhistorischen Hofmuseums. Redigirt von Dr. Franz Ritter von Hauer." Band VII. 1892. pp. 379-400.)

Alfred Holder: Wien, 1892. 8°.

[Ac. 2911.]

200. **Helps,** *Sir* Arthur, *K.C.B.*—The Life of Hernando Cortes. By Arthur Helps, Author of "The Spanish Conquest in America." [Dedicated to Thomas Carlyle.] 2 vols.

Bell and Daldy: London, 1871. 8°.

[2402. b. 15.]

201. **Heredia,** José Maria de.—Les Trophées. Par José-Maria de Heredia. [Poems.] Sixième édition. pp. iv. 218.

Alphonse Lemerre: Paris, MDCCCXCIII. 8°.

[11483. d. 21.—1895. 11483. aa. 40.—1905. 011843. eee. 67. The First Edition is not in the British Museum.]

202. **Herrera Tordesillas,** Antonio de.—Historia General de los Hechos de los Castellanos en las Islas i Tierra Firme del Mar Oceano. Escrita por Antonio de Herrera, Coronista Mayor de su M^d.: de las Indias y su Coronista de Castilla. En quatro [or rather, nine] Decadas desde el Ano de 1492 hasta el de 1531. Al Rey Nu^{ro}. Señor. 3 vols.

En Ma^d.: en la Emplenta Rea[l]; por Juan Flamenco; por Juan de la Cuesta, Ano M.DCI, M.DCXVI, M.DCI. fol.

G. 7206-8. From the Library of the Right Hon. Thomas Grenville. —601. k. 12-15.—601. k. 8-11. The Ninth Decade is entitled: *Descripcion de las Indias Ocidentales,* 1601. The Decades have finely engraved Title-pages, with medallion portraits, battle-scenes, &c. Four are reproduced in this volume. *See* pages 36, 58, 62, 287.]

203. ———.—Descripcion de las Indias Ocidentales de Antonio de Herrera, Coronista Mayor de su Mag^d. de las Indias, y su Coronista de Castilla. Al Rey N^{ro}. Señor. [Edited by Andrès Gonzalez de Barcia Carballido y Zuñiga.] 4 tom.

En Madrid: En la Oficina Real de Nicolas Rodriguez Franco, Año de 1730. fol.

[K. 145. f. 5-8. From the Library of King George III.—The Colophon of Tom. 4 reads: *En la Imprenta de Francisco Martinez Abad, Año de* MDCCXXVIII.]

204. **Hochstetter,** Ferdinand von.—Ueber Mexicanische Reliquien aus der Zeit Montezuma's in der K. K. Ambraser Sammlung. Von Ferdinand von Hochstetter, wirklichem Mitgliede der Kaiserlichen Akademie der Wissenschaften. Mit fünff Tafeln [in Colour] und einer Abbildung im Texte. Vorgelegt in der Sitzung am 5 December, 1883. (In "Denkschriften der Kaiserlichen Akademie der Wissenschaften." Philosophisch-Historische Classe." Band 35. pp. 83-104.)

In Commission bei Carl Gerold's Sohn: Wien, 1885. 4°.

[Ac. 810/12.]

205. **Ibarra,** Francisco de.—Mémoire des services rendus par le Gouverneur Don Francisco de Ibarra pendant la conqûete et la colonisation qu'il a faites dans les provinces de Copala, de la Nouvelle-Biscaye, de Chiametla, et en découvrant des mines. Extrait des enquêtes instruites d'office à la requête dudit gouverneur, et présentees au conseil en 1574. Copala, Nouvelle-Biscaye et Chiametla, année 1554, et suivantes. *Simancas.* (In "Voyages, Relations, et Mémoires Originaux pour

servir à l'Histoire de la Découverte de l'Amérique. Publiés pour la première fois en Français par H. Ternaux-Compans.—Tom. x. Recueil de Pièces relatives à la Conquête du Mexique. Inédit." pp. 367-399.)

Arthus Bertrand : Paris, MDCCCXXXVIII. 8°.

G. 15812. From the Library of the Right Hon. Thomas Grenville. —1196. i. 7.]

206. **Indias.**—Cartas de Indias. Publícales por primera vez el Ministerio de Fomento. [Dedicated to King Alfonso XII. by the Conde de Toreno. Letters of Columbus, Vespucci, Bartolomé de Las Casas, Bernal Díaz del Castillo, & others, on matters relating to the Spanish Indies. Together with Notes, a Geographical Vocabulary, Biographical Notes, a Glossary, Facsimiles of MSS., of signatures of Conquistadores, &c., and of 3 Maps.—No. VI. Carta de Bernal Díaz del Castillo al Emperador D. Carlos dando cuenta de los abusos que se cometian en la gobernacion de las provincias del Nuevo Mundo. SANTIAGO DE GUATIMALA, 22 de febrero de 1552. No. VII. Carta de Bernal Díaz del Castillo al Rey D. Felipe II., en la que denuncia algunos abusos cometidos con los indios, y pide se le nombre fiel-ejecutor de Guatimala, en atencion á los servicios que expone. GUATIMALA, 20 de febrero de 1558. *See* Facsimile E.] pp. xvi. 877.

Imprenta de Manuel G. Hernandez : Madrid, 1877. fol.

[1857. b. 5.—Maps 36. e. 1.]

207. ———.—Isagoge Historico Apologetico general de todas las Indias y especial de la Provincia de Sⁿ. Vicente Ferrer de Chiapa y Goathemala de el Orden de Predicadores. Libro inédito. [Edited by José Maria Reina Barrios.] pp. 445.

Tipografia de Tomas Minuesa de los Rios : Madrid, 1892. 8°.

[Not in the British Museum.—A copy in the Library of Alfred P. Maudslay.]

208. **John Carter Brown Library.** Bibliotheca Americana. A Catalogue of Books relating to North and South America, in the Library of John Carter Brown, of Providence, R. I. Part I. 1493 to 1600. (Part II. 1601 to 1700.) With Notes by John Russell Bartlett. 2 vol.

Providence [Rhode Island], 1865, 66. 8°.

[11901. d. 10.]

208 a. ———.—[Another edition.] Part I. 1482-1601. (Part II. 1600-1700. Second Edition.—Part III. Vol. 1, 2. 1701-1800.) With Notes by John Russell Bartlett. 4 vol.

Providence [Rhode Island], 1875, 82, 70, 71. 8°.

[11901. d. 11.]

209. **Jourdanet,** Denis.—Influence de la pression de l'Air sur la vie de l'Homme. Climats d'altitude et climats de montagne. Par D. Jourdanet, Docteur en Médecine, Chevalier de la Legion d'Honneur. Gravures par Boetzel, cartes en couleurs dessinées et gravées chez Erhard. 2 tom.

G. Masson : Paris, 1875. 8°.

[7686. g. 2.]

210. ———.—Le Mexique et l'Amérique Tropicale. Climats, Hygiène et Maladies. Par D. Jourdanet, Docteur en Médecine des Facultés de Paris et de Mexico. Avec une carte de Mexique. pp. 459.

J. B. Baillière et Fils : Paris, 1864. 8°.

[7687. aa. 32.]

211. **Juarros**, Domingo.—A Statistical and Commercial History of the Kingdom of Guatemala in Spanish America. Containing important particulars relative to its productions, manufactures, customs, &c. &c. &c. With an account of its Conquest by the Spaniards, and a narrative of the principal events down to the present time. From original Records in the archives, actual observation, and other authentic sources. By Don Domingo Juarros, a native of New Guatemala. Translated by J. Baily, Lieutenant R.M. Embellished with two Maps. pp. viii. 520.

Printed for John Hearne, 81 Strand, by J. F. Dove, St. John's Square : London, 1823. 8°.

[G. 15997.—From the Library of the Right Hon. Thomas Grenville. —798. f. 2.]

212. **Lasso de la Vega,** Gabriel.—Primera Parte de Cortés valeroso, y Mexicana, de Gabriel Lasso de la Vega, criado del Rey nuestro señor, natural de Madrid. Dirigida a Don Fernando Cortés, nieto de don Fernando Cortés, Marques del Valle, descubridor y conquistador del Nuevo Mundo. [With an oval portrait : Ferdinandus Cortesius, Dux invictisimus aetatis 63. Below are the arms of Cortes.] ff. 193.

En Madrid : En casa de Pedro Madrigal, Año M.D.LXXXVIII. 4°.

[1071. m. 7. (2.)]

213. ———.—Elogios en Loor de los Tres Famosos Varones Don Iayme, Rey de Aragon, Don Fernando Cortes, Marques del Valle, y Don Álvaro de Baçan, Marques de Santacruz. Côpuestos por Gabriel Lasso de la Vega, Côtino del R.N.S. Dirigidos a Don Gaspar Galçaran de Castro y Pinos, Côde de Guimaran, Vizcôde de Ebol, &c. [fol. 34-95 relate to Cortés. With the Portrait and Arms of Cortés, as in " Primera Parte de Cortés Valoroso." 1588.] ff. 144.

En Çaragoça por Alonso Rodriguez, Año 1601. 8°.

[614. b. 19.—1450. a. 12.]

214. **Leon Pinelo,** Antonio de.—Epitome de la Biblioteca Oriental i Occidental, Nautica i Geografica. Al Excelentiss. Señor D. Ramiro Nuñez Perez Felipe de Guzman, . . . Duque de Medina de las Torres . . . Por el Licenciado Antonio de Leon, Relator del Supremo i Real Consejo de las Indias. (Apendice.) pp. 186. xii.

En Madrid : Por Juan Gonzalez, Año de MDCXXIX. 4°.

[G.647. From the Library of the Right Hon. Thomas Grenville.—619. d. 27. On the back of the binding of the copy is the monogram Φ Φ, intertwined, to be found on all books purchased for the Jesuits' College at Paris, from the legacy bequeathed to them by Nicolas Fouquet, 1615-1680, Finance Minister of Louis XIV.]

215. ———.—Epitome de la Bibliotheca oriental y occidental, nautica y geografica de Don Antonio de Leon Pinelo, del Consejo de su Mag. en la Casa de la Contratacion de Sevilla, y Coronista Major de las Indias. Añadido y enmendado nuevamente, en que se contienen los Escritores de las Indias Orientales y Occidentales y Reinos convecinos . . . Al Rey Nuestro Señor. Por Mano del Marques de Torre-Nueva, su Secretario del Despacho Universal de Hacienda, Indias y Marina. [Edited by Andrès Gonzalez de Barcia Carballido y Zuñiga.]

En la Oficina de Francisco Martinez Abad : en Madrid, Año de MDCCXXXVII-VIII. fol.

[G. 489. From the Library of the Right Hon. Thomas Grenville.— K. 125. g. 14. From the Library of King George III.—620. i. 5.]

216. **Lopez Cogolludo,** Diego.—Historia de Yucathan. Compuesta por el
M. R. P. Fr. Diego Lopez Cogolludo, lector jubilado, y padre per-
petuo de dicha provincia. Consagrada, y dedicada Al Excelentissimo
Señor Don Fernando Joachin Faxardo de Requesens y Zuñiga, Marquès
de los Velez, Molina y Martorel, Señor de las Varonias de Castelvi, de
Rosanes, Molins de Rey, y otras en el Principado de Cataluña, Señor
de las Villas de Mula, Alhama y Librilla, y de las siete del Rio de
Almanzora las Cueuas, y Portilla, Alcayde perpetuo de los Reales
Alcaçares, de las Ciudades de Murcia, y Lorca, Adelantado, y Capitan
Mayor del Reyno de Murcia, Marquesado de Villena, Arcedianto de
Alcaraz, Campo de Montiel, Sierra de Segura, y sus Partidos, Comen-
dador de la Encomienda de los Bastimentos de Castilla, del Orden de
Santiago, Gentilhombre de Camara de su Magestad de sus Consejos de
Estado, y Guerra, Presidente en el de Indias, y Superintendente General
de la Real Hazienda, &c. Sacala a luz el M. R. P. Fr. Francisco de
Ayeta, Predicador, Ex-Custodio del Nueuo Mexico, Comissario General
del Santo Oficio, Custodio actual de la Prouincia del Santo Euangelio
en el Reyno de la Nueua España, y Procurador General en esta Corte
de todas las Prouincias de la Religion Serafica del dicho Reyno.
pp. 26. 760. 31.
  En Madrid : Por Juan Garcia Infanzon, Año 1688.   fol.
  [K. 147. d. 1.   From the Library of King George III.]

217. ————.—Historia de Yucatan.   Escrita en el Siglo XVII.   Por el
R. P. Fr. Diego López Cogolludo.   Provincial que fue de la Orden
franciscana. [Two volumes in one.] pp. vi. 615, 663. Tercera Edicion.
  Merida : Imprenta de Manuel Aldana Rivas. 1867, 68.   4°.
  [9771. d. 13.]

218. ————.—Los Tres Siglos de la Dominacion Española en Yucatan, o Sea
Historia de Esta Provincia, desde la Conquista Hasta la Independencia.
Escribióla el R. P. Fr. Diego López Cogolludo, provincial que fué de la
órden franciscana ; y la continúa un yucateco. Tomo 1°. pp. ix. 481.
  Campeche : Impreso por José María Peralta. 1842.   8°.
  [9771. c. 17.]

219. **López de Gómara,** Franciso.—La istoria de las Indias y conquista de
Mexico. [Por Francisco Lopez de Gómara.] ff. 139.
  Fue Impressa en casa de Agustin Millan : Çaragoça, 1552.   fol.
  [983. g. 17.   From the Library of Sir Joseph Banks.—On the title-
  page is a large woodcut of the arms of Charles V., with the Pillars
  of Hercules, 7 × 9¼ inches.]

220.————.—Historia de Mexico.   Con el Descubrimiento de la nueva
España, conquistada por el muy illustre y valeroso Principe don Fernando Cortes, Marques del Valle.   Escrita por Francisco Lopez de
Gomara, clerigo.   Añadiose de la nuevo descripcion y traça de todas
las Indias, con una Tabla alphabetica de las materias, y hazañas
memorables enella contenidas.   [At folio 8 is a Facsimile of the Map :
Brevis exactq' Totius Novi Orbis ejusq' Insularum Descriptio Recens
a Joan. Bellero edita. By Jaˢ. A. Burt. Purchased 11 August, 1871.]
ff. 349.
  *En Anvers : En casa de Juan Steelsio ; Impresso en Anvers por Juan
    Lacio,* 1554.   8°.
  [G. 6309. From the Library of the Right Hon. Thomas Grenville.—
  1061. b. 7. From the Library of Queen Mary I. With the original
  Map.—This work is another edition of Part II. of *La Istoria de las
  Indias,* 1552.]

221. ———.—Historia del Illustriss. et Valorosiss. Capitano don Ferdinando Cortes, Marchese della Valle, et quando discoperse, et acquisto la Nuova Hispagna. Scritta per Francesco Lopes de Gomara in lingua Spagnuola, & hora tradotta nella Italiana per Augustino de Cravaliz. ff. 240.

Impressa in Roma per Valerio & Luigi Dorici fratelli nel MDLVI. 8°.

[G. 6760. From the Library of the Right Hon. Thomas Grenville.
—The Colophon reads: *In Roma per Valerio Dorico, & Luigi fratello Bresciani, nel* MDLVI.—There is also a second Title-page: Historia di Mexico, &c. *In Roma: Appresso Valerio & Luigi Dorici fratelli,* MDLV.]

222. ———.—Historia di Don Ferdinando Cortés, Marchese della Valle, Capitano Valorissimo. Con le sue maravigliose prodezze, nel tempo che discoprì, & acquistò la nuova Spagna. (In "Historia delle Nuove Indie Occidentali. Con tutti i Discoprimenti & cose notabile, avvenute dopo l'acquisto di esse. Parté seconda. Composta da Francesco Lopez di Gomara in lingua Spagnuola. Tradotta nella Italiana da Agostino di Cravaliz.") [Dedicated "Al Signor Cosmo de Medici, Prencipe della Republica Fiorentina."] ff. 348.

In Venetia: Per Francesco Lorenzini da Turino, MDLX. 8°.

[1061. b. 26.]

222 a.———.—[Another edition, wanting the Title-page. Dedicated to Ridolfo Pio, Prince of Carpi, Cardinal.] ff. 355.

In Venetia per Giovanni Bonadio, MDLXIIII. 8°.

[1061. b. 27.]

223.———.—Historia di Don Ferdinando Cortes, Marchese della Valle, Capitano Valorissimo. Con le sue maravigliose prodezze, nel tempo che discoprì, & acquistò la nuova Spagna. Parte Terza [of *Historia delle Nuove Indie Occidentali.* Edited by Agostino di Cravaliz.] Composta da Francesco Lopez di Gomara in lingua Spagnuola. Tradotta nella Italiana per Agostino di Craualiz. pp. 343.

In Venetia: Appresso Camillo Franceschini, 1576. 12°.

[G. 14934. From the Library of the Right Hon. Thomas Grenville.
—K. 278. a. 33. From the Library of King George III. With the arms of King William III. on the covers.]

224. ———.—The Pleasant Historie of the Conquest of the Weast India, now called new Spayne, achieved by the worthy Prince Hernando Cortés, Marques of the valley of Huaxacac, most delectable to Reade. Translated out of the Spanishe tongue [from Francisco Lopez de Gomara] by T. N. [Thomas Nicholas.] Anno 1578. B. L. pp. 412.

Imprinted at London by Henry Bynneman, [1578.] 4°.

[G. 7091. From the Library of the Right Hon. Thomas Grenville.
—1196. b. 28. Wants 2 leaves at end.]

225. ———.—Voyages et Conquestes du Capitaine Ferdinand Courtois, és Indes Occidentales. Histoire traduite de langue Espagnole, par Guillaume le Breton, Nivernois. ff. 416.

À Paris: Chez Abel L'Angelier, au premier pilier de la grand' Sale du Palais, M.D.LXXXVIII. 8°.

[1061. a. 25.—Wants the last leaf.]

A A

226. ———.—The Pleasant Historie of the Conquest of the West India, now called new Spaine. Atchieved by the most woorthie Prince Hernando Cortés, Marques of the Valley of Huaxacac, most delectable to reade. Translated out of the Spanish tongue [from Francisco Lopez de Gomara], by T. N. [Thomas Nicholas], Anno 1578. pp. 412.

London: Printed by Thomas Creede, 1596. 4°.

[G. 2473. From the Library of the Right Hon. Thomas Grenville. With the book-plate of Lord Shelburne.—K. 278. a. 1.—1196. b. 30. With the Book-plates of Sir Peter Thompson, F.R.S., and James Bindley, F.S.A.

227. ———.—Historia de las Conquistas de Hernando Cortés. Escrita en Español por Francisco Lopez de Gomára. Traducida [from Part II. of *La Itoria de las Indias*] al Mexicano y aprobado por verdadera por D. Juan Bautista de San Anton Muñon Chimalpain Quauhtlehuanitzin, Indio Mexicano. Publícala para instruccion de la juventud nacional, con varias notas y adiciones, Carlos Maria de Bustamante. (Suplemento . . . ó sea : Memoria sobre la guerra del Mixtón en el Estado de Xalisco, cuya capital es Guadalaxara. pp. 39. *México.* 1827. *Imprenta de Galvan á cargo de Mariano Arévalo.*) 2 tom.

Imprenta de la testamentaría de Antiveros: México, Año de 1826 [-27]. 4°.

[9771. b. 6. (1, 2.)]

228. ———.—Cenni sulla Scoperta della Penisola di Yucatan, fatta de Francesco Hernandez di Cordova, l'anno 1517. Estratti dalla Storia Generale delle Indie di Francesco Lopes di Gomara. (In "Raccolta di Viaggi dalla Scoperta del Nuovo Continente fino a' di nostri. Compilata da F. C. Marmocchi." tom. II. pp. 35-41.)

Fratelli Giachetti: Prato, 1843. 8°.

[1424. i. 5.]

229. **Maudslay,** Alfred Percival.—Explorations in Guatemala, and examination of the newly discovered Indian Ruins of Quiriguá, Tikal, and the Usumacinta. By A. P. Maudslay. Read . . . December 11th, 1882. With Map and Plans. (In *Proceedings of the Royal Geographical Society,* April, 1883. pp. 185-204.)

Edward Stanford: London, 1883. 8°.

[R. Ac. 6170/2.]

230. ———.—Explorations of the Ruins and Site of Copan, Central America. By A. P. Maudslay. Read . . . June 28th, 1886. With Map, Plan, & Plate. (In *Proceedings of the Royal Geographical Society,* Sept. 1886. pp. 568-595.)

Edward Stanford: London, 1886. 8°.

[R. Ac. 6170/2.]

231. **Maudslay,** Anne Cary, and Alfred Percival.—A Glimpse at Guatemala, and some Notes on the Ancient Monuments of Central America. By Anne Cary Maudslay and Alfred Percival Maudslay. With Maps, Plans, Photographs, and other Illustrations. pp. xvii. 289.

John Murray: London, 1899. 4°.

[TAB. 443. c. 1.]

232. **Mendieta,** Gerónimo de.—Historia Eclesiástica Indiana. Obra escrita a fines del Siglo XVI. Por Fray Gerónimo de Mendieta, de la Orden de San Francisco. La publica por primera vez Joaquin García Icazbalceta. (Con algunas advertencias del P. Fray Joan de Domayquia, Predicador y Guardian de S. Francisco de la dicha Ciudad de Vitoria . . . Dirigida á Nuestro P. Fr. Antonia de Trejo, Lector Jubilado, y Comisario General de todas las Indias.) pp. xlv. 790.

Antigua Librería, Portal de Agustinos, No. 3: *México,* MDCCCLXX. 8°.
[4765. f. 13.]

233. **Mendoza,** Antonio de, *Conde de Tendilla, Viceroy of Mexico.*—Avis du Vice-roi Don Antonio de Mendoza sur les Prestations personelles et les Tamemes. 1550. *Simancas.* (In "Voyages, Relations, et Mémoires Originaux pour servir à l'Histoire de la Découverte de l'Amérique. Publiés pour la première fois en Français par H. Ternaux-Compans.— Tom. x. Recueil de Pièces relatives a la Conqûete du Mexique. Inédit." pp. 345-365.)

Arthus Bertrand: Paris, MDCCCXXXVIII. 8°.
[G. 15812. From the Library of the Right Hon. Thomas Grenville. —1196. i. 7.]

234. **Mexico.**—Relatione d'alcune cose della Nuova Spagna, & della gran città di Temistitan Messicò. Fatta per un gentil' huomo del Signor Fernando Cortese. [With a View of a Mexican Temple, and of the City of Temistitan.]

("In Terzo Volume delle Navigationi et Viaggi. Raccolto gia da M. Gio. Battista Ramusio." fol. 304-310.)

In Venetia : nella Stamperia de' Giunti, l'Anno MDLXV. fol.
[G. 6820. From the Library of the Right Hon. Thomas Grenville.— 679. h. 10. With the arms and cyphers of Jacques Auguste de Thou, and his first wife, Marie Barbançon.]

235. ———.—Ritos Antiguos, Sacrificios é Idolatrías de los Indios de la Nueva España y de su conversion á la Fe, y quienes fueron las que primero la predicaron. Va dividido el libro en tres tratados. Copiada del códice X. 11-21 de la Biblioteca del Escorial. [c. 1560.] (In "Coleccion de Documentos Inéditos para la Historia de España. Por los Señores Marques de Miraflores y D. Miguel Salva, Individuos de la Academia de la Historia." tom. 53. pp. 295-575.)

Imprenta de la Viuda de Calero : Madrid, 1869. 8°.
[9197. ff.]

236. Archivo Mexicano. Documentos para la Historia de Mexico. 2 tom.
Tipografía de Vicente García Torres: México, 1852-53. 8°.
[9771. c. 31.]

237. ———.—Documentos para la Historia de Méjico. (Diario de Mexico, 1548-1798.) Prima Serie. 7 tom.
Imprenta de Juan R. Navarro: Méjico, 1853-54. 8°.
[9771. bbb. 22.]

237 a.———.—Segunda Serie. 4 tom.
Imprenta de F. Escalante y Comp. : México, 1854-55. 8°.
[9771. bbb. 23.]

237 b. ———.—Tercera Serie. Tom. I. (Supplement.) [With Notes by Francisco García Figueroa.]

Imprenta de Vicente García Torres. México, 1856. fol.

[9771. h. 9.]

237 c. ———.—Cuarta Serie. [Documents relating to Sonora, Sinaloa, Nueva Vizcaya, & Nueva California. With Notes by Francisco García Figueroa.]

Imprenta de Vicente García Torres: México, 1856-57. 8°.

[9771. bbb. 24.]

238. ———.—Documentos Historicos de Méjico. [Edited by Luis García Pimentel.]

En casa del Editor: Méjico; A. Donnamette: Paris; Gabriel Sánchez: Madrid, 1903, 1904, *etc.* 8°.

[9770. h.]

238 a. ———.—Tom. I. Memoriales de Fray Toribio de Motolinia. [c. 1540.] Manuscrito de la Coleccion del Señor Don Joaquin García Icazbalceta. Publicalo por primera vez su hijo Luis García Pimentel. Con una lámina. pp. x. 364.

1903. 8°.

238 b. ———.—Tom. 2. Relacion de los Obispados de Tlaxcala, Michoacan, Oaxaca y otros lugares en el siglo XVI. Manuscrito de la Coleccion del Señor Don Joaquin García Icazbalceta. Publicalo por primera vez su hijo Luis García Pimentel. pp. 190.

1904. 8°.

239. Michoacan, *Mexico.*—Relacion de las ceremonias y ritos, problacion y gobierno de los Indios de la provincia de Mechuacan, hecha al Ilmo. Sr. D. Antonio de Mendoza, Virey y Gobernador de Nueva España. Sacada del codice original c. IV. 5, existente en la Biblioteca del Escorial, por Don Florencio Janer [c. 1545.] (In "Colección de Documentos Inéditos para la Historia de España, por los Señores Marques de Miraflores y D. Miguel Salva, Individuos de la Academia de la Historia." tom. 53. pp. 5-293.)

Imprenta de la Viuda de Calero: Madrid, 1869. 8°.

[9197. ff.]

240. Milla, José.—Historia de la América, Central, desde el descubrimiento del país por los españoles (1502) hasta su independencia de la España (1821). Precedida de una Noticia Histórica relativa á las naciones que habitaban la América Central á la llegada de los españoles. [Tom. 1, 2.] Por D. José Milla, Sócio Correspondiente de la Real Academia Española, &c. [Tom. 3-5, *etc.* Obra continuada bajo la administracion del Señor General Don José María Reyna Barrios y en virtud de Encargo Oficial por Agustín Gómez Carrillo, Individuo de la Facultad de Derecho de Guatemala, &c.]

Establecimiento Tipográfico de "El Progreso"; Tipografía Nacional: Guatemala, 1879-1905, *etc.* 8°.

[9772. pp.]

241. **Montúfar**, Alonso, *Archbishop of Mexico.*—Descripcion del Arzobispado de México hecha en 1570 [by Alonso Montúfar], y otros documentos. [Edited by Luis García Pimentel.] pp. iv. 464.
>*Jose Joaquin Terrazas e Hijas Imps.: México,* 1897. 8°.
>[4745. dd. 13.]

242. **Nepean**, Evan, *Captain.*—An Account of certain Antiquities in the Island of Sacrificios. Communicated to the Society of Antiquaries by Captain Nepean, in a Letter addressed to . . . the Earl of Aberdeen, K.T., President. Followed by a Report upon the examination of them, by Samuel Birch, Esq. (From the *Archæologia.* Vol. xxx. pp. 138-143.) pp. 8.
>*Printed by J. B. Nichols and Son: London,* 1843. 4°.
>[2111. e.—7703. a. 20.]

243. **Nuttall**, Zelia.—Preliminary Note of an Analysis of the Mexican Codices and Graven Inscriptions. By Zelia Nuttall, Peabody Museum, Cambridge, Mass. From the *Proceedings of the American Association for the Advancement of Science.* Vol. xxxv. Buffalo Meeting, August 1886. pp. 325-7.
>*Washington,* 1886. 8°.
>[R. Ac. 3065.]

244. ———.—The Terracotta Heads of Teotihuacan. By Zelia Nuttall. [With Two Plates.] pp. 37.
>*American Journal of Archæology: Baltimore,* 1886. 8°.
>[P. P. 1925. m.]

245. ———.—Das Prachtstück altmexicanischer Federarbeit aus der Zeit Montezuma's im Wiener Museum. Von Zelia Nuttall, am Peabody Museum für Amerikanische Archaeologie u. Ethnologie, Cambridge, Mass. Mit zwei colorirten Tafeln. pp. 29. (In " Abhandlungen und Berichte des Königl. Zoologischen und Anthropologisch-Ethnographischen Museums zu Dresden. 1886/7. Herausgegeben . . . von Dr. A. B. Meyer, K. S. Hofrath und Director des Museums." No. 7. pp. 29.)
>*Verlag von R. Friedländer & Sohn: Berlin,* 1887. 4°.
>[Ac. 3562.]

246. ———.—Standard or Head-Dress? An Historical Essay on a Relic of Ancient Mexico. By Zelia Nuttall, Special Assistant of the Peabody Museum. With Three Coloured Plates. (*Archæological and Ethnological Papers of the Peabody Museum, Harvard University.* Vol 1, no. 1. pp. 52.
>*Peabody Museum of American Archæology and Ethnology: Cambridge, Mass.,* 1888. 8°.
>[R. Ac. 2692. a.]

247. ———.—The Atlatl or Spear-Thrower of the Ancient Mexicans. By Zelia Nuttall, Special Assistant of the Peabody Museum. With Three Plates. (*Archæological and Ethnological Papers of the Peabody Museum, Harvard University.* Vol. i. no. 3.) pp. 30.
>*Peabody Museum of American Archæology and Ethnology: Cambridge, Mass.,* 1891. 8°.
>[R. Ac. 2692. a.]

260. **Prescott,** William Hickling.—History of the Conquest of Mexico. With a preliminary view of the ancient Mexican civilization, and the Life of the Conqueror, Hernando Cortés. By William H. Prescott, Author of "The History of Ferdinand and Isabella." In Three Volumes. [Illustrated.]

> *Richard Bentley: London,* MDCCCXLIII. 8°.

> [G. 14873-75. From the Library of the Right Hon. Thomas Gren⁻ ville.—9771. eee. 8.]

261. ———.—Historia de la Conquista de Mejico. Con un bosquejo pre- liminar de la civilizacion de los antiguos Mejicanos, y la Vida del Conquistador Hernando Cortes, escrita en Ingles por Guillermo H. Prescott, Autor de la "Historia de Fernando e Isabel," traducida al Castellano por D. Jose Maria Gonzalez de la Vega, y anotada por D. Lucas Alaman. 2 Tom.

> *Imprenta de V. G. Torres, Calle del Espiritu Santo Num. 2: México,* 1844. 8°.

> [9771. e. 9. With the Book-plates of the Emperor Maximilian of Mexico, and of J. M. Andrade.]

262. ———.—History of the Conquest of Mexico. By William H. Prescott. Edited by John Foster Kirk. Illustrations on steel. (Edition de Luxe. Vols. 4-6.) 3 vols.

> *J. B. Lippincott & Co.: Philadelphia,* [1875.] 8°.

> 12297. a. 1. With the Book-plate of H. S. Ashbee.]

263. ———.—History of the Conquest of Mexico. By William H. Prescott. Edited by Wilfred Harold Munro, Professor of European History in Brown University, and comprising the Notes of the Edition by John Foster Kirk. [1875.] (Montezuma Edition. Vols. 1-4.) Illustrated.

> *J. B. Lippincott Company: London,* [1906.] 8°.

> [12296. gg. 1.]

264. **Quad,** Matthias.—Enchiridion Cosmographicum : dass ist, Ein Handt- büchlin der gantzen Welt gelegenheit also kurtz und nach Notturfft volkommentlich begreiffende wie solches andere berhümbte Cosmo- graphi als Munsterus, Artelius, Wagener, Boterus, &c. vor dieser Zeit der Lenge nach beschrieben . . . Dem gemeinen einfeltigen und frommen Teutschen Leser zu gefallen mit compendioser und richtiger Ordnung in alsolches Format gestellet durch Mattheis Quaden Kup- fferstecher. [Mexico. Book 4. pp. 244-251.]

> *Gedruckt zu Cölln am Rhein: bey Wilhelm Lützenkirchen im jahr* 1599. 8°.

> [10002. bbb. 10. Purchased April 21, 1876.]

265. **Ramirez,** José Fernando.—Manuscrit Ramirez. Histoire de l'Origine des Indiens, qui habitent la Novelle Espagne selon leurs Traditions. Publié par D. Charnay (Lettre Préface de M. le Sénateur Alfredo Chavero à M. Désiré Charnay sur Don José Fernando Ramirez. Tom. XIX. Recueil de Voyages et de Documents pour servir á l'Histoire de la Géographie depuis le XIIIᵉ jusqu'à la fin du XVIᵉ Siècle. Publié sous la direction de MM. Charles Schefer, membre de l'Institut et Henri Cordier.) pp. xix. 246.

> *Ernest Leroux: Paris,* 1903. 8°.

> [10024. i.]

266. **Read,** Charles Hercules, *President of the Society of Antiquaries.*—On an Ancient Mexican Head-piece, coated with Mosaic. By Charles Hercules Read, Esq., Secretary. Read December 14th, 1893.—Note on Mexican Turquoise. By F. W. Rudler, Esq., F.G.S. With 1 coloured Plate & 6 Illustrations in the Text. In *Archæologia.* Vol. LIV. pp. 383-398.

Printed by Nichols and Sons: London, 1895. 4°.

[2111. f.]

267. **Remesal,** Antonio de.—Historia General de las Indias Ocidentales, y particular de la Governacion de Chiapa, y Guatemala. Escrivese juntamente los principios de la Religion de Nuestro Glorioso Padre Santo Domingo, y de las demas Religiones. Al Conde de la Gomera del Consejo del Rey Nuestro Señor, su Presidente, y Capitan General. Por el Presentado Fray Antonio de Remesal, de la Orden de Predicadores de la Provincia de España. pp. 784.

En Madrid: Por Francisco de Abarca, Año MDCXX. fol.

[G. 6415. From the Library of the Right Hon. Thomas Grenville. —K. 146. e. 18. From the Library of King George III.—601. k. 6. —601. k. 7.]

268. **Rivera,** Agustin.—Anales Mexicanos ó sea Cuadro Cronologico de los Hechos mas notables pertenecientes a la Historia de Mexico, desde el siglo VI hasta este año de 1889. Escritos por Agustin Rivera.

Tipografia de Vicente Veloz; á cargo, de Ausencio Lopez Arce: Lagos [Mexico], 1889. *etc.* 8°.

[Not in the British Museum.]

269. **Robertson,** William, *D.D., the Historian.*—The History of America. By William Robertson, D.D., Principal of the University of Edinburgh, and Historiographer to His Majesty for Scotland. 2 vols. [With 4 Maps.]

London: Printed for W. Strahan; T. Cadell, in the Strand; and J. Balfour, at Edinburgh, MDCCLXXVII. 4°.

[K. 147. d. 18, 19. From the Library of King George III.—601. k. 1, 2. Wants the maps.]

270. ———.—The History of America. By William Robertson, D.D. . . . Member of the Royal Academy of History at Madrid. The Thirteenth Edition, in which is included the Posthumous Volume, containing the History of Virginia, to the year 1668, and of New England, to the year 1652. In Four Volumes. [Illustrated.]

Printed for Cadell and Davies; F. C. and J. Rivington; G. Wilkie [and 21 others]*: London,* 1817. 8°.

[1061. f. 25.]

271. **Rovirosa,** José N.—Nombres Geográficos del Estado de Tabasco. Estudio etimológico por el Sr. José N. Rovirosa. Se publica por acuerdo del Señor General Carlos Pacheco, Secretario de Fomento bajo el Cuidado de la Direccion General de Estadística. pp. 36.

Oficina Tip. de la Secretaría de Fomento: México, 1888. fol.

[12903. i. 10. (3.)]

272. **Sahagun**, Bernardino de.—Historia General de las Cosas de Nueva España, que en doce libros y dos volumenes escribió el R. P. Fr. Bernardino de Sahagun, de la Observancia de San Francisco, y uno de los primeros Predicadores del Santo Evangelio en aquellas regiones. Dala a luz con notas y suplementos Carlos Maria de Bustamente, Diputado por el Estado de Oaxaca en el Congreso General de la Federacion Mexicana, y la dedica a Nuestro Santisimo Padre Pio VIII. 3 tom.

Imprenta del Ciudadano Alejandro Valdés: México, 1829-30.   8°.

[9771. b. 5.]

273. ——.—Historia de la Conquista de México. [Book XII. of the *Historia de las Cosas de Nueva España.*] Escrita por el R. P. Fr. Bernardino Sahagun, del Orden de S. Francisco, y uno de los primeros enviados a la Nueva España para propagar el Evangelio. Publicala por separado de sus demas obras Carlos Maria de Bustamente, Diputado de la cámara de representantes del congreso general de la federacion por el estado libre de Oaxaca, quien lo dedica á los beneméritos generales Nicolás Bravo y Miguel Barragan, y á sus dignos compañeros en la confinacion que hoy sufren.   pp viii. 69.

Imprenta de Galvan á cargo de Mariano Arévalo, calle de Cadena núm. 2 : México, 1829.   8°.

[9771. b. 12.]

274. ——.—La Aparicion de N^tra. Señora de Guadalupe de México, comprobaba con la refutacion del argumento negativo que presenta D. Juan Bautista Muñoz, fundandose en el testimonio del P. Fr. Bernardino Sahagun : ó sea : Historia Original de este Escritor, que altera la publicada en 1829 en el equivocado concepto de ser la unica y original de dicho autor. (Relacion de la Conquista de esta Nueva-España, como la contaron los soldados indios, que se hallaron presentes. Convertióse en lengua española, llana é inteligible, y bien enmendada en este año de 1585.) Publícala, precediendo una disertacion sobre la Aparicion Guadalupana, y con notas sobre la conquista de México, Cárlos Ma. de Bustamente, Individuo del Supremo Poder Conservador.   pp. xxii 247. [With a Portrait of N. S. de Guadalupe de Mexico, la mas semejante à sù Original.

Impreso por Ignacio Gumplido : México, 1840.   8°.

[9771. b. 10.—Nota. La continuacion de esta historia está en la Memoria de D. Fernando de Alva Ixtilxochitl, publicada por el editor de esta obra en 118 fojas, el año de 1829, intitulada :]

274 a. **Alva Ixtilxochitl**, Fernando de.—Horribles Crueldades de los Conquistadores de México, y de los Indios que los auxiliaron para subyugarlo a la corona de Castilla. O sea Memoria escrita por D. Fernando de Alva Ixtilxochitl. Publicala por supplemento a la *Historia del Padre Sahagun* Cárlos María de Bustamente, y la dedica al Supremo Gobierno General de la Federacion Mexicana. (Décima tercia Relacion de la Venida de los Españoles y Principio de la Ley Evangélica. Escrita por D. Fernando Alva Ixtilxóchitl.)   pp. xii. 118.

Imprenta del ciudadano Alejandro Valdés: Mexico, Año de 1829.   8°.

[9771. b. 10.]

275. ——.—Histoire Générale des Choses de la Nouvelle-Espagne. Par le R. P. Fray Bernardino de Sahagun.   Traduite et annotée par D. Jourdanet, auteur de divers ouvrages sur la Climatologie du Mexique, et traducteur de la Chronique de Bernal Díaz del Castillo, et par Rémi

Simeon, éditeur, avec commentaires, de la Grammaire Nahuatl, du R. P. Fray Andrès de Olmos. pp. lxxix. 898.

G. Masson: Paris, 1880. 8°.

[9771. f. 6.—On p. xvii. are two facsimiles of the signature of Bernal Díaz del Castillo.]

276. **Santa Cruz,** Alonso de.—Die Karten von Amerika in dem Islario General des Alonso de Santa Cruz, Cosmógrafo Mayor des Kaisers Karl V. [1542.] Mit dem spanischen Originaltexte und einer kritischen Einleitung herausgegeben von Franz R. v. Wieser. Festgabe des K. u. K. Oberstkämmer-Amtes für den XVI. Internat. Amerikanisten-Kongress. pp. xx. 59. 15 Plates. [The original MS. is in the Vienna K. K. Hof-Bibliothek.]

Verlag der Wagnerschen Universitäts - Buchhandlung: Innsbruck, 1908. fol.

[Map Department, British Museum.—Plate 6. Cuba. Plate 10. Yucatan.—Plate 11. Temixtitan.]

277. **Santo María de la Victoria.**—Relación de la Villa de Santa María de la Victoria. 1579. (Relaciones Histórico-Geográficas de las Provincias de Yucatán, Tabasco.—Relaciones de Yucátan. [Edited by José María Asensio.] Tom. 1. pp. 341-374.—In "Colección de Documentos Inéditos relativos al Descubrimiento, Conquista y Organización de las Antiguas Posesiones Españolas de Ultramar. Segunda Serie, publicada por la Real Academia de la Historia. Tomo núm. 11.")

Establecimiento Tipográfico, Sucesores de Rivadeneyra: Madrid, 1898, 1900. 8°.

[9551. g.]

278. **Solis y Ribadeneyra,** Antonio de.—Historia de la Conquista de Mexico, Poblacion, y Progressos de la America Septentrional, conocida por el nombre de Nueva España. Escriviala Don Antonio de Solis, Secretario de su Magestad, y su Chronista mayor de las Indias. Y la pone a los pies del Rey Nuestro Señor por mano del Excelentissimo Señor Conde de Oropesa. pp. 548.

En Madrid: En la Imprenta de Bernardo de Villa-Diego, Impressor de su Magestad, Año M.DC.LXXXIV. fol.

[9771. f. 13. With a second engraved pictorial Title-page : Theod. Ardeman inv. I. F. Leonardo sculp.—With the Crest and Initials of Henri Ternaux-Compans stamped in gold on the covers.]

278 a.———.—[Another edition.] Dedicase al Illustrissimo Señor Don Guillen de Rocafull y Rocaberti, por la Gracia de Dios Vizconde de Rocaberti, Conde de Peralada, y de Albatera, &c. pp. 548.

Barcelona: En la Imprenta de Joseph Llopis, Impressor de Libros ; y a su Costa. Vendese en su Casa, en la calle de Santo Domingo, Año 1691. fol.

[601. l. 12.]

279. ———.—The History of the Conquest of Mexico by the Spaniards. Done into English from the original Spanish of Don Antonio de Solis, Secretary and Historiographer to His Catholick Majesty. By Thomas Townsend, Esq.

With 9 Illustrations.

1. Hernan Cortès. Ex pictura Titiani in Œdibus præhon^blis. Domini D. Pauli Methuen. Geo. Vertue sculpsit 1724. Frontispiece.

2. Meeting of Cortes and Montezuma in the City of Mexico. I. Schijnooet invent. et fec. p. 1.

3. Map of Mexico or New Spain. J. Clark sc. Book I. p. 31.

4. [Map of] The Lake of Mexico and Parts adjacent. Book I. p. 50.

5. [View of] The Great Temple of Mexico. Book II. p. 72.

6. View of the City of Mexico from Tezcuco. J. Clark sc. 1724. Book III. p. 69.

7. [View of] The City of Mexico. J. Clark sc. 1723. Book III. p. 70.

8. [View of] The Engagem$^{nt.}$ between y^e Spanish Brigantines and the Canoes of the Mexicans. J. Clark sc. 1723. Book V. p. 124.

9. Guatimozin taken in his Retreat by Holguin. J. Clark sc. 1724. Book V. p. 146.] Dedicated to James, Duke of Chandos. 3 parts.

> *London : Printed for T. Woodward at the Half-Moon, and J. Hooke at the Flower-de-Luce, both against St. Dunstan's Church, in Fleet Street ; and J. Peele at Locke's Head in Pater-Noster-Row,* M.DCC.XXIV. fol.

[601. m. 14.]

280. ———.—The History of the Conquest of Mexico by the Spaniards. Translated into English . . . by Thomas Townsend, Esq., late Lieutenant-Colonel in Brig.-Gen. Newton's Regiment. The whole Translation Revised and Corrected by Nathaniel Hooke Esq., Translator of *The Travels of Cyrus,* and *The Life of the Archbishop of Cambray.* [With the 9 Plates of the 1724 edition.] 2 vols.

> *London : Printed for T. Woodward, at the Half-Moon between the Two Temple Gates ; and H. Lintot, at the Cross-Keys against St. Dunstan's Church, in Fleet-street,* MDCCXXXVIII. 8°.

[9771. de. 6.—Purchased November 5, 1895.]

——— The Third edition.

> *London : Printed for H. Lintot ; J. Whiston and B. White, at Mr. Boyle's Head, and L. Davis, at Lord Bacon's Head, both in Fleet-street ; and D. Wilson, at Plato's Head, in the Strand,* MDCCLIII. 8°.

[9771. b. 16.—Purchased June 27, 1850.]

281. **Soto Hall,** Máximo.—De México á Honduras. El Viage de Hernán Cortés. pp. 103.

> *Tipografía Nacional : San José,* 1900. 8°.

[010480. e. 26.]

282. **Spencer,** Herbert.—Herbert Spencer. El Antiguo Yucatán. Traducción [of Sections of Div. II. Part I. B. of "Descriptive Sociology," 1873-81.] hecha por Daniel y Genaro García. (Bibliografia.) pp. 153. 1 Table.

> *Oficina Tipográfica de la Secretaría de Fomento : México,* 1898. 8°.

[9770. cc. 3.]

283. ———.—Herbert Spencer. Los Antiguos Mexicanos. Traducción [of Sections of Div. II. Part I. B. of "Descriptive Sociology,' 1873-81.] por Daniel y Genaro Garcia. (Bibliografia.) pp. 229. vi. 3 Tables.

> *Oficina Tipográfica de la Secretaría de Fomento : México,* 1896. 8°.

[9770. dd. 4.]

284. **Stephens,** John Lloyd.—Incidents of Travel in Central America, Chiapas and Yucatan. By John L. Stephens, Author of "Incidents of Travel in Egypt, Arabia Petræa, and the Holy Land," *etc.* Illustrated by numerous Engravings [by F. Catherwood]. 2 vols.

John Murray: London, MDCCCXLI. 8°.

[G. 15779-80. From the Library of the Right Hon. Thomas Grenville.—1431. h. 15.—1854. 791. k. 26.]

284 a. ————.—New Edition. 2 vols.

John Murray: London, MDCCCXLII. 8°.

[2374. d. 14. The covers bear the name of *Harper & Bros.: New York.*]

285. **Tápia,** Andrés de.—Relacion hecha por el Señor Andrés de Tápia sobre la Conquista de México. [16th cent. MS. In Real Academia de la Historia, Madrid. Tom. 115. Papeles varios de Jesuitas. Est. 15. gr. 5a.] (In "Coleccion de Documentos para la Historia de México. Publicada por Joaquin García Icazbalceta." Tom. 2. pp. 554-594.)

Antigua Librería, Portal de Agustinos N. 3: México, 1866. 8°.

[9771. f. 15.]

286. **Torquemada,** Juan de, *a Franciscan.*—Primera (—Tercera) Parte de los Veinte i un Libros Rituales i Monarchia Indiana. Con el origen y guerras de los Indios Occidentales, de sus Poblaciones, Descubrimiento, Conquista, Conversion y otras cosas maravillosas de la mesma tierra distribuydos en tres tomos. Compuesto por P. Juan de Torquemada, Ministro Provincial de la Orden de Nuestro Serafico Padre San Francisco en la Provincia del Santo Evangelio de México en la Nueva España. [Edited by Andrés Gonzalez de Barcia Carbillado y Zuñiga.] 3 tom.

En Madrid: en la oficina y á costa de Nicolas Rodriguez franco, 1723. fol.

[K. 146. e. 11-13.—With an engraved pictorial title-page.—From the Library of King George III.]

287. **Trueba y Cosío,** Joaquin Telesforo de.—Life of Hernan Cortes. By Don Telesforo de Trueba y Cosio, Author of "Gomez Arias," "The Castilians," &c. [With an engraved frontispiece: Montezuma shows Cortes his Idols. Drawn by D. O. Hill. Engraved by J. West.] pp. 2. ii. 344. (In "Constable's Miscellany of Original and Selected Publications in the various Departments of Literature, Science, & the Arts." Vol. 49.)

Printed for Constable and Co.: Edinburgh; and Hurst, Chance and Co.: London, 1829. 12°.

[1157. d. 3.]

288. **Valentini,** Philipp J. J. Mexican Paper. By Ph. J. J. Valentini, Ph.D. (In *Proceedings of the American Antiquarian Society.* New Series. Vol. I. pp. 58-81.)

Published by the Society: Worcester [*Mass.*], 1882. 8°.

289. **Vera Cruz.**—Liste Générale des Flottes et Azoques qui sont entrés dans le port de la Vera-Cruz depuis la conquête jusqu'à l'année 1760. [1581-1760.—Copied from a list in the possession of Don Antonio d'Enriquez, Judge in the Maritime Tribunal of Cadiz.] (In "Voyages, Relations,

et Mémoires Originaux pour servir à l'Histoire de la Découverte de
l'Amérique. Publiés pour la première fois en Français par H. Ternaux-
Compans.—Tom. x. Recueil de Pièces relatives á la Conquête du
Mexique. Inédit. pp. 455-470.)

Arthus Bertrand: Paris, MDCCCXXXVIII. 8°.

[G. 15812. From the Library of the Right Hon. Thomas Grenville.
—1196. i. 7.]

290. **Vetancurt,** Augustin de. Teatro Mexicano. Descripcion Breve de los
Sucessos Exemplares, Historicos, Politicos, Militares, y Religiosos del
nuevo mundo Occidental de las Indias. Dedicado al Esposo de la que
es del mismo Dios Esposa, Padre putativo del Hijo, que es Hijo del
mismo Dios Christo, Dios, y hombre verdadero. Al que con el sudor de
su rostro sustentó al que todo lo sustenta : Al que fue Angel de Guarda
de la Ciudad de Dios milagro de su Omnipotencia, y abismo de la
gracia. Maria Señora Nuestra. Al Glorioso Patriarca de la Casa de
Dios Señor S. Joseph. Dispuesto por el R. P. Fr. Augustin de Vetancurt, Mexicano, hijo de la misma Provincia, Difinidor actual, Ex-Lector
de Theologia, Predicador Jubilado General, y su Chronista Apostolico,
Vicario, y Cura Ministro, por su Magestad, de la Iglesia Parrochial de
S. Joseph de los Naturales de Mexico. 4 parts. Sucessos Naturales,
etc. pp. 170. Tratado de la Ciudad de Mexico, y las grandezas que
la ilustran despues que la fundaron Españoles. Tratado de la Ciudad
de la Puebla de los Angelos, y grandezas que la ilustran. pp. 56.
Chronica de la Provincia del Santo Evangelio de Mexico. Quarta
parte del Teatro Mexicano, *etc.* pp. 138.

*En Mexico, por Doña Maria de Benavides, Viuda de Juan de Ribera,
Año de* 1697. fol.

Menologio Franciscano de los Varones Mas Señalados, que con sus
vidas exemplares, perfeccion Religiosa, ciencia, predicacion Evangelica,
en su vida, y muerte ilustraron la Provincia de el Santo Evangelio de
México. Recopiladas por el Padre Fray Augustin de Vetancurt, *etc.*
pp. 156.

*En México por Doña Maria de Benavides, Viuda de Juan de Ribera,
Año de* 1698. fol.

[9771. f. 14.—Purchased June 7, 1862.]

291. **Villa - Senor y Sanchez,** José Antonio de. — Theatro Americano.
Descripcion General de los Reynos, y Provincias y de la Nueva-España,
y sus Jurisdicciones. Dedicala al Rey Nuestro Señor el Señor
D. Phelipe Quinto, Monarcha de las Españas. Su Author D. Joseph
Antonio de Villa-Señor, y Sanchez, Contador General de la Real Con-
taduria de Azoguez, y Cosmographo de esto Reyno. Quien la escribió
de Orden del Excelentissimo Señor Conde de Fuen-Clara, Virrey Gobernador, y Capitan General de esta Nueva-España, y Presidente de su
Real Audiencia, &c. 2 pts.

*Con Licencia en México: En la Imprenta de la Viuda de Joseph
Bernardo de Hogal, Impressora del Real, y Apostolico Tribunal de
la Santa Cruzada en todo esta Reyno, Calle del as Capuchinas,
Año de* 1746-48. fol.

[K. 146. e. 5. From the Library of King George III.]

292. **Viollet le Duc,** Eugène Emmanuel.—Cités et Ruines Américaines. Mitla,
Palenqué, Izamal Chichen-itza, Uxmal. Recueillies et Photographiées
par Désiré Charnay, avec un Texte Par M. Viollet-le-Duc, Architecte
du Gouvernement. Suivi du Voyage et des Documents de l'Auteur.

Ouvrage dédié à S. M. l'Empereur Napoléon III. et publié sous la patronage de Sa Majesté. pp. ix. 543.

Paris : Gide, Editeur, 5, rue Bonaparte. A. Morel et C⁰·, 18, rue Vivienne. 1863. 8°.

[10481. g. 12.—Atlas. 14000. k. 4.]

293. **Vivien de Saint-Martin,** Louis.—Nouveau Dictionnaire de Géographie Universelle . . . Ouvrage commencé par M. Vivien de Saint-Martin . . . et continué par Louis Rousselet. (Tom. 3. Mexico, Mexique. pp. 824-851. With a valuable Bibliography of Books and Maps.)

Hachette et Cie. : Paris, 1887. fol.

[2060. e.]

294. **Ximenez,** Francisco, *Missionary.*—Las Historias del Origen de los Indios de esta Provincia de Guatemala. Traducidas de la Lengua Quiché al Castellano para mas comodidad de los Ministros del S. Evangelio. Por el R. P. F. Francisco Ximenez, Cura Doctrinero por el Real Patronato del Pueblo de S. Thomas Chuila. Exactamente segun el texto español del Manuscrito Original que se halla en la Biblioteca de la Universidad de Guatemala, publicado por la primera vez, y aumentado con una introduccion y anotaciones por el Dr. C. Scherzer. A expensas de la Imperial Academia de las Ciencias. pp. xvi. 216.

En casa de Carlos Gerold é Hijo, Libreros de la Academia Imperial de las Ciencias : Vienna, 1857. 8°.

[9771. d. 14.]

295. **Yucatán.**—Relaciones de Yucatán. Tom. I. II. [Edited by José María Asensio.] (Colección de Documentos Inéditos relativos al Descubrimiento, Conquista y Organización de las Antiguas Posesiones Españolas de Ultramar. Segunda Serie, publicada por la Real Academia de la Historia. Tomo núm. 11, 13.)

Establecimiento Tipográfico, Sucesores de Rivadeneyra : Madrid, 1898, 1900. 8°.

[9551. g.—There seems to be no entry under *Yucatan* for these volumes in the British Museum Catalogue.]

296. **Zarate,** Juan de, *Bishop of Antequera.*—Lettre de Don Juan de Zarate, Evêque d'Antequera, à Philippe II. [Report on the Diocese of Guaxaca, or Oaxaca.] *Simancas.* (In "Voyages, Relations, et Mémoires Originaux pour servir à l'Histoire de la Découverte de l'Amérique. Publiés pour la première fois en Français par H. Ternaux-Compans.—Tom. x. Recueil de Pièces relatives à la Conquête du Mexique. Inédit." pp. 287-306.)

Arthus Bertrand : Paris, MDCCCXXXVIII. 8°.

[G. 15812. From the Library of the Right Hon. Thomas Grenville. —1196. i. 7.]

297. **Zurita,** Alonso de.—Rapport sur les différentes classes de chefs de la Nouvelle-Espagne, sur les lois, les mœurs des habitants, sur les impôts établis avant et depuis la conquête, *etc., etc.* Par Alonzo de Zurita, ex-Auditeur à l'Audience Royale de Mexico. Inédit. [From the copy made by Boturini from the original MS. in the Library of the Colelge of Saint Peter and Saint Paul Mexico, case 48. no. 19.] pp. xvi. 418.

(In " Voyages, Relations et Memoires Originaux, pour servir à l'Histoire de la Découverte de l'Amérique, publiés pour la première fois en français par H. Ternaux-Compans." Tom. XI.)

Arthus Bertrand: Paris, MDCCCXL. 8°.

[G. 15813. From the Library of the Right Hon. Thomas Grenville. —1196. i. 7.]

ADDENDA.

González Obregón, Luis.—Época Colonial. México Viejo. Noticias Históricas, Tradiciones, Leyendas y Costumbres por Luis Gonzáles Obregón. Nueva Edición aumentada y 'corregida. Con profusión de illustraciones: dibujos originales, retratos, vistas, planos, sacados de antiguos cuadros al óleo, láminas y litografias; y fotografias, tomadas directamente de monumentos, monedas y medallas. pp. xiii. 742.

Libreria de la V^{da} de C. Bouret. Paris, 23 *Rue Visconti*, 23. *México*, 14, *Cinco de Mayo*, 14. 1900. 8°.

[9770. f. 12.]

———.—Los Precursores de la Independencia Mexicana en el Siglo XVI. pp. 388.

Librería de la V^{da} de C. Bouret. Paris, 23 *rue Visconti*, 23. *México, Calle del* 5 *de Mayo*, 14. 1906. 8°.

[9772. df. 11.]

INDEX.

INDEX.

ib. ; his mare, *ib.* ; sets out with Bernal Díaz del Castillo to fight natives of Chiapas, 1523, xxiii

Marina, Doña, of Tabasco, 1519, 126 ; a Cacica, biography of, 132, etc. ; mistress of Alonzo Hernández Puertocarrero, 129 ; of Hernan Cortés, *ib.* ; mother of Martin Cortés, *ib.* ; marries Juan Jaramillo at Orizaba, 1523, 133 ; interpreter to Cortés, 1519, 134, etc. ; 218, 219, 244, 273 ; Marina's Captain, 273

Marta, mother of Doña Marina, 133

Martin, Benito. *See* Martínez, Benito

Martín de Valencia, Fray, with his twelve Franciscan companions, entertained by Cortés at Mexico, June 18, 1524, xxv

Martínez, Benito, Chaplain to Diego Velásquez, 65 ; his mission to Spain, 1518, *ib.*, 74 ; 1519, 203

Martínez del Freginal, ——, two brothers, join Cortés at Havana, 84

Martires, Los, lxiii, 30

Maschere di cattivi turchesi, 302

Maschere e strumenti de popoli barbari, 302

Mase Escasi (Maxixcatzin), 236 245, 265, 271, 275

Masks, Mosaic, 301

Masonry Houses, Yucatan, 1518 37, 41

Masteles, 15

Matanzas, lxiii ; etymology of, 38 ; port, Grijalva sails from, April 8, 1518, xii, 38

Matlatan, town of, xxii

Maudslay, Alfred Percival, *A Glimpse at Guatemala,* London, 1899, liv

Maudslay, Anne Cary, *A Glimpse at Guatemala, and some Notes on the Ancient Monuments of Central America,* by Anne Cary and Alfred Percival Maudslay, London, 1899, cited, liv

Maxixcatzin (Mase Escasi), a Cacique of Tlascala, 1519, 236, 245 ; declares for peace, 246, 257, 265 ; visits Cortés, 271 ; welcomes Cortés to Tlascala, 275 ; opposes proposal of Cortés to attack Montezuma, 290

Maya Language, xv

Maya race, its high culture, l

Maya script, at Monte Alban, state of Oaxaca, li ; no inscriptions as yet found in Central Mexico, li

Maya sculptures, absence of bows and arrows, lvii

Maya Quiché race, probably descendants of Mayas and their Nahua conquerors, lii ; occupied the Highlands of Guatemala, 1519, *ib.*

Mayas. *See* also Tzendals

Mayas, described by Bernal Díaz del Castillo, liv ; not subdued by the Spaniards till 1547, lv

Mayordomo, 74

Mazapa, river, Cortés ascends the, xxvii

Mazariegos, Diego de, robs Bernal Díaz del Castillo of three *encomiendas,* 1527, xxxii

Mazatecas, country of the, Cortés in the, 1525, xxviii

Medellin, Estramadura, Hernan Cortés, a native of, 69, 71

Medellin, a woman of, carried off to the Indies, 203 ; Count of, 78, 129, 203

Medici, Giovanni de, Pope, as Leo X., d. 1521, 301

Medici, Giulio de, Pope, as Clement VII., 301

Medici Arms, stamped on leathern case of the two atlatls in the Florentine Museum, 1903, 302

Medici Collection, Dispersal of the, 302

Medici Museum, Florence, 301

Medina, Antonio de, welcomes Bernal Díaz to Trinidad, 34

Medina del Campo, Bernal Díaz del Castillo born at, 1492, ix, 5 ; Santo Domingo, 200

Medina Rio Seco, Francisco de Saucedo, a native of, 192

Mejía, Gonzalo. *See* Mexía, Gonzalo

Méjico, Colua, 49

Melchior, a cross-eyed Indian, of Yucatan, 17 ; taken to Cuba, 1518, 31, 40 ; interpreter with the Grijalva expedition, 46 ; accompanies Cortés, 1519, 91, 94, 97 ; deserts Cortés, 113, 127 ; his murder, 128

Melchorejo. *See* Melchior

Memoirs of the Conquistador, Bernal Díaz del Castillo, 1844. *See* Díaz del Castillo, Bernal

Memorie della R. Accademia dei Lincei, Rome, 1885, cited, 302

Mendoza, Don Antonio de, First Viceroy of Mexico, 1535-1540 ; arrives in Mexico, 1535, xxxiv

Merced, Fraile de la, lxii

LONDON:

PRINTED AT THE BEDFORD PRESS, 20 AND 21, BEDFORDBURY, W.C.